GLOBAL IM-POSSIBILITIES

JUST SUSTAINABILITIES

Just Sustainabilities contributes to understanding, theorizing and ultimately developing strategies toward the development of more just and sustainable communities in both the global North and South. Through a collection of solutions-orientated books, the series looks at policy and planning themes that improve people's quality of life and well-being, both now and into the future; that are carried out with an intentional focus on just and equitable processes, outputs and outcomes in terms of people's access to environmental, social, political and economic space(s); and that aim to achieve a high quality of life and well-being within environmental limits.

SERIES EDITOR
Julian Agyeman

TITLES ALREADY PUBLISHED

Julian Agyeman, *Introducing Just Sustainabilities: Policy, Planning, and Practice*
Karen Bickerstaff, Gordon Walker, Harriet Bulkeley, *Energy Justice in a Changing Climate: Social Equity and Low-carbon Energy*
Peter Utting, *Social and Solidarity Economy: Beyond the Fringe*
Jenny Pickerill, *Eco-Homes: People, Place and Politics*
Dean Saitta, *Intercultural Urbanism: City Planning from the Ancient World to the Modern Day*

GLOBAL IM-POSSIBILITIES

Exploring the Paradoxes of Just Sustainabilities

Edited by
Phoebe Godfrey and Mary Buchanan

BLOOMSBURY ACADEMIC
LONDON · NEW YORK · OXFORD · NEW DELHI · SYDNEY

BLOOMSBURY ACADEMIC
Bloomsbury Publishing Plc
50 Bedford Square, London, WC1B 3DP, UK
1385 Broadway, New York, NY 10018, USA
29 Earlsfort Terrace, Dublin 2, Ireland

BLOOMSBURY, BLOOMSBURY ACADEMIC and the Diana logo
are trademarks of Bloomsbury Publishing Plc

First published in Great Britain 2021
This paperback edition published 2023

Copyright © Phoebe Godfrey and Mary Buchanan, 2021

Phoebe Godfrey and Mary Buchanan have asserted their right under the Copyright,
Designs and Patents Act, 1988, to be identified as Authors of this work.

All rights reserved. No part of this publication may be reproduced or
transmitted in any form or by any means, electronic or mechanical,
including photocopying, recording, or any information storage or retrieval
system, without prior permission in writing from the publishers.

Bloomsbury Publishing Plc does not have any control over, or responsibility for,
any third-party websites referred to or in this book. All internet addresses given
in this book were correct at the time of going to press. The author and publisher
regret any inconvenience caused if addresses have changed or sites have
ceased to exist, but can accept no responsibility for any such changes.

A catalogue record for this book is available from the British Library.

A catalogue record for this book is available from the Library of Congress.

ISBN: HB: 978-1-7869-9954-2
PB: 978-1-7869-9955-9
ePDF: 978-1-7869-9953-5
eBook: 978-1-7869-9951-1

Series: Just Sustainabilities

Typeset by Integra Software Services Pvt. Ltd.

To find out more about our authors and books visit
www.bloomsbury.com and sign up for our newsletters.

Coeditors:
We would like to dedicate this book to the contributors, whose patience, diligence, and commitment to the project made it possible, tipping our quandary on the [im]possibilities for just sustainabilities in the direction of the possible.

Phoebe:
I would also like to offer my deep gratitude and appreciation to my coeditor, who, at a moment's notice, took up this role and has exceeded all expectations. I could not have done it without you!
I would also like to thank my wife Tina for her ongoing support.

Mary:
Many, many thanks to my coeditor for spear-heading this project and keeping morale high with cheery good humor the whole way through! Thanks to Carol Atkinson-Palombo for early support.

CONTENTS

List of Figures	ix
Contributors	x
INTRODUCTION – PHOEBE GODFREY, MARY BUCHANAN	1

Part I
PROMISES AND DELIVERIES

1 DESTROY AND REBUILD: CONSIDERING HARM, COMMUNITY BENEFITS, AND ENVIRONMENTAL ORNAMENTATION IN COMMUNITY DEVELOPMENT IN ATLANTA – DR. LEMIR TERON, MS. T'SHARI WHITE, MS. FARAH NIBBS AND MS. FARZANEH KHAYAT ... 7

2 THE SOVEREIGNTY PARADOX: NEGOTIATING VALUES AMID TRIBAL ADAPTATION TO SHALE OIL EXTRACTION – JACQLINE WOLF TICE, DAVID CASAGRANDE ... 25

3 ACTIVISM OR EXTRACTIVISM: INDIGENOUS LAND STRUGGLES IN EASTERN BOLIVIA – EVAN SHENKIN ... 47

Part II
WHOSE CITIES?

4 THE BIPOLAR WATERFRONT: PARADOXES OF SHORELINE PLACE-MAKING IN CONTEMPORARY ACCRA AND COLOMBO – RAPTI SIRIWARDANE-DE ZOYSA, EPIFANIA A. AMOO-ADARE ... 69

5 NEGOTIATIONS AND CONTESTATIONS OF JUST MOBILITY: RICKSHAWS IN DHAKA, BANGLADESH – MD MUSLEH UDDIN HASAN ... 89

6 PARADOXES OF JUST SUSTAINABILITIES IN URBAN WATER SOCIOTECHNICAL SYSTEMS: LESSONS FROM ATHENS, GREECE – MARCIA ROSALIE HALE ... 107

Part III
SCALES OF DECISION-MAKING AND ACTION

7 RESISTANCE TO RESTRICTING? THE POLITICS OF CARS IN COPENHAGEN – KEVIN T. SMILEY ... 129

8 POPULAR CONSULTATIONS AND EXTRACTIVISM IN COLOMBIA: FROM LOCAL TO GLOBAL ACTIONS AGAINST MINING AND CLIMATE CHANGE – ARACELY BURGOS-AYALA, EMERSON HARVEY CEPEDA-RODRÍGUEZ ... 147

9   RESCALING ENERGY GOVERNANCE AND THE DEMOCRATIZING POTENTIAL
    OF "COMMUNITY CHOICE" – SEAN KENNEDY   169

Part IV
REIMAGINING THE POSSIBLE

10 ORGANIC (DIS)ORGANIZATION AND TRANSFORMATION: STORIES OF
    RESISTANCE AND RETURN AT CERES COMMUNITY ENVIRONMENT PARK –
    NATALIE OSBORNE, DEANNA GRANT-SMITH   191
11 JUST SUSTAINABILITIES ON THE RANGE: EMPOWERING DECISIONS AT THE
    SOIL SURFACE – ANDREA MALMBERG, TONY MALMBERG   207
12 WELCOME TO TUBMAN HOUSE – ANTHONY BAYANI RODRIGUEZ   221

CONCLUSION: GLOBAL [IM]-POSSIBILITIES FOR JUST SUSTAINABILITIES? –
PHOEBE GODFREY, MARY BUCHANAN   235

Index   236

LIST OF FIGURES

1.1 Neighborhood Planning Unit L and Mercedes Benz Stadium, Image courtesy of the author — 16

1.2 Neighborhood Planning Units in Atlanta and the city's Black population. Mercedes Benz Stadium and the Georgia World Congress Center are a de facto boundary as the Black population rises to the south and west of the site. Data source: Atlanta Regional Commission 2010. Image courtesy of the author — 17

2.1 The location of Fort Berthold Reservation within the oil-rich Bakken Shale creates a paradox of using oil development to promote sovereignty without sacrificing the traditional land ethic of the Mandan, Hidatsa, and Arikara who live there. Our survey and interviews were conducted with tribal members from New Town, Mandaree and Parshall. Image courtesy of the author — 33

8.1 Municipalities, cities, and departments in Colombia where popular consultations and institutional actions were made against extractivism from 2013 to 2018, Image courtesy of the author — 157

9.1 California CCAs, Source: Kennedy, Sean F., and Bailey Rosen. "The rise of community choice aggregation and its implications for California's energy transition: A preliminary assessment." Energy & Environment (2020): 0958305X20927381 — 170

9.2 CCA Case studies, Image courtesy of the author — 175

9.3 Bundled vs. unbundled renewable energy certificates (RECs), Image courtesy of the author — 177

CONTRIBUTORS

Phoebe Godfrey is Associate Professor-in-Residence in Sociology at the University of Connecticut and coeditor of *Systemic Crises of Global Climate Change* and *Emergent Possibilities for Global Sustainability*. **Mary Buchanan** is a geography doctoral candidate at the University of Connecticut.

1. **Lemir Teron** is an assistant professor at SUNY ESF, researching environmental justice, cities, and climate change. **T'Shari White, Farah Nibbs, and Farzaneh Khayat** are doctoral students.
2. **Jacqline Wolf Tice**, MLS, specializes in Indigenous Peoples Law, researching sovereignty, environment, and culture. **David Casagrande** is a professor of anthropology at Lehigh University who studies human relationships with nature.
3. **Evan Shenkin** is a sociology professor at Western Oregon University. He has forthcoming articles on postdevelopment, prison abolition, and renewable energy in The Encyclopedia of the UN Sustainable Development Goals.
4. **Rapti Siriwardane-de Zoysa** is a senior scientist at the Leibniz Centre for Tropical Marine Research, Germany. **Epifania Akosua Amoo-Adare** is an independent scholar and founder of Biraa Creative Initiative (BCI) Ltd.
5. **Md. Musleh Uddin Hasan** is a professor at BUET in the Department of Urban & Regional Planning. His research interests include active transport, "mo(accessi)bility," and planning for health and just sustainabilities.
6. **Marcia Rosalie Hale** is an assistant professor of peace and conflict studies at UNCG. She takes a justice approach to her research at the intersection of social and environmental conflict.
7. **Kevin T. Smiley** is an assistant professor in the Department of Sociology at Louisiana State University and coauthor of *Market Cities, People Cities: The Shape of Our Urban Future*.
8. **Aracely Burgos-Ayala** is an ecology PhD student with research interests in biodiversity conservation. **Emerson Cepeda-Rodríguez** is a human rights PhD student with research interests in social movements.
9. **Sean Kennedy** is an assistant professor at the University of Illinois at Urbana-Champaign in the Department of Urban & Regional Planning. His research examines the political ecologies of energy transitions.
10. **Natalie Osborne** is a lecturer with the School of Environment & Science, Griffith University. **Deanna Grant-Smith** is an associate professor and a deputy-director of Centre for Decent Work & Industry, QUT Business School.

11. **Andrea and Tony Malmberg** are recognized leaders in holistic management, influencing people throughout the world to run enjoyable, profitable, regenerative agricultural enterprises. They make their home ranching and restoring land and rivers in northeastern Oregon.
12. **Anthony Bayani Rodriguez** is an assistant professor at St. John's University in the Department of Sociology & Anthropology, and former scholar-in-residence at the Schomburg Center for Research in Black Culture.

INTRODUCTION

Phoebe Godfrey
Mary Buchanan

*The pessimist complains about the wind;
the optimist expects it to change; the realist adjusts the sails.*
William Arthur Ward

As we write, we are reminded of the famous opening lines of Charles Dickens' *The Tale of Two Cities*:

> *It was the best of times, it was the worst of times, it was the age of wisdom, it was the age of foolishness, it was the epoch of belief, it was the epoch of incredulity, it was the season of Light, it was the season of Darkness, it was the spring of hope, it was the winter of despair, we had everything before us, we had nothing before us…*
> (Dickens 1998: 1)

Such a depiction of extremes could not be more apt for our current national and global zeitgeist. Increasing polarization, be it cultural, political, and/or economic (recognizing the obvious overlaps among these spheres), appears to be the defining trajectory of our moment. It is in such a context that we seek to explore what new challenges and opportunities this increasing polarization offers for the theoretical lens of just sustainabilities (Agyeman 2013). Just sustainabilities builds on the more general term "sustainability," which came to global attention with a 1987 World Commission on Environment and Development report and has henceforth been used to characterize a myriad of activities aimed, at least nominally, at environmental protection; we too seek to continue this project of "building upon." The just sustainabilities framework—"The need to ensure a better quality of life for all, now and into the future, in a just and equitable manner, whilst living within the limits of supporting ecosystems" (Agyeman, Bullard, & Evans 2003: 2)—was developed to explicitly include *justice* in the conception of sustainability and refers to plural sustainabilities in order to acknowledge "the relative, culturally, and place-bound nature of the concept" (Agyeman 2013: 5). In other words, sustainability will look different depending on context and case; in this edited volume we seek to explore whether or not just sustainabilities "will look" possible or impossible, or perhaps more precisely [*im*]possible, reflecting a "both/ and" type of truth as opposed to "either/or." This emphasis on "both/and" comes from the work of Kimberlé Crenshaw (1989) and her theory of intersectionality, which emerged from her recognition of the need to theorize African American women's "intersectional experience... [as] greater than the sum of racism and sexism," thereby urging that "the entire framework that has been used as a basis for translating 'women's experience' or 'the Black experience' into concrete policy... be rethought and recast" (Crenshaw 1989: 140). Likewise, we attempt here to continue rethinking and recasting the policies, practices, and plans in relation to sustainability writ large, and just sustainabilities in particular, turning them over and over, thereby revealing the intersecting layers of who/who for, what/what for, how/how long, and where in relation to place and scale. This volume presents twelve original case studies from around the globe that bring together *both* the lens of just sustainabilities *and* that of intersectionality. Our theoretical goal here is to offer these case studies to demonstrate and unpack the complexities involved in attempting to achieve and analyze just sustainabilities, while also incorporating intersectional lenses to further unpack the micro details of each case.

We argue that it is in critically analyzing such details that we can best gain increasing insights into *both* the possibilities *and* the impossibilities for achieving Agyeman's call for improvement in individual and social well-being, measured not *only* by economic metrics but more importantly by holistic metrics such as life satisfaction, health, education, equality in resource distribution, and availability of public goods (Agyeman 2013). Actionable improvement, not perfection, is the goal. Yet in order to evaluate such potential improvements (and for whom, under what conditions, where, and for how long) the addition of an intersectional lens is invaluable, for in a world of increasing levels of contradictions and crises, the paths toward this space of "actionable improvement" are murky and maze-like in their complexity. As this book will show, attempts to achieve just sustainabilities through policies, plans, and practices are often riddled with contradictions and other unforeseen outcomes, many of which manifest unevenly depending on who looks at them, as well as from where, when, and how. This collection of case studies from across the globe provides intersectional analyses related to achieving just sustainabilities, while weaving together the incremental stages along the trajectory of policies, plans, and practices. We return repeatedly to areas of paradox, contradiction, and tension, where good intentions clash with eventual outcomes, underlying assumptions create ripple effects, and seemingly sound reasoning may lead to unwanted and/or unforeseen outcomes. In the details of each chapter we can see the both/and nature of the contestations in question, as the layered dimensions of time, people, places, and actions continually intersect.

This book is organized into four parts, each of which considers this overall theme through a specific angle—(1) *Promises and Deliveries*; (2) *Whose Cities?* (3) *Scales of Decision-Making and Action*; and (4) *Reimagining the Possible*. This order is not the only way to read this book; the layers highlighted in each part can also be found threading through the other sections as well, as all of the cases are multifaceted and resist oversimplification. Nevertheless, we have collected the chapters thusly in order to offer the reader a guided path to understanding the thorny challenges faced by those seeking to enact just sustainabilities (or culturally appropriate parallel ideas) and the ongoing outcomes of their efforts, in which both success and failure often overlap and at times become indistinguishable. In the aggregate, these cases serve to inspire a more realistic and comprehensive analysis of both what is currently being done around the world to enact just sustainabilities and the extent of what remains to be achieved. Our final hope is thereby that these case studies help to prepare readers to "adjust the sails" (Ward) rather than give into either idealism or despair, even now.

References

Agyeman, J. (2013), *Introducing Just Sustainabilities: Policy, Planning, & Practice*, London: Zed Books.
Agyeman, J., R.D. Bullard, & B. Evans (2003), "Joined-up thinking: Bringing together sustainability, environmental justice, and equity," in J. Agyeman, R.D. Bullard, & B. Evans (eds.), *Just Sustainabilities: Development in an Unequal World*, 1–16, Cambridge: MIT Press.
Crenshaw, K. (1989), "Demarginalizing the intersection of race and sex: A black feminist critique of antidiscrimination doctrine, feminist theory and antiracist politics," *University of Chicago Legal Forum*, 1(8): 139–67.
Dickens, C. (1998), *A Tale of Two Cities*, London: Penguin Classics.
Ward, A.W. https://www.goodreads.com/author/quotes/416931.William_Arthur_Ward

Part I

PROMISES AND DELIVERIES

A promise and/or a plan—whether articulated by people, through treaties, through marketing, in a collectively shared vision for the future, or through a myriad of other forms—is inherently temporal. A potential changed state of being is foreseen and communicated, and some degree of action is pledged to make it happen in the future. This temporal path from intention to impact is, however, far from straightforward, with the hoped-for outcomes muddled both by seemingly insincere actors and by genuine actors whose sincerity is nevertheless not enough to surmount ideological and logistical hurdles. The past, too, shapes this process, as historical contexts surround every site of potential action, and decisions made by long-ago actors still reverberate in meaningful and structural ways. The case studies in this section are heavily steeped in history, folded within legacies of colonization, discrimination, and structural marginalization. Other temporal measurements become critical as well—shortened life spans of both people and buildings, the geologic age of fuels with the moniker "fossil," the sharp pivot points of presidential elections and presidential removals, and more.

Chapter 1 examines claims of economic growth and sustainability surrounding new sports stadiums in Atlanta, fast-tracked on the path to development with promises of economic gain and environmental ornamentation, overlaid on neighborhoods shaped by decades of structural racism. Chapters 2 and 3 explore case studies emerging from the centuries-long continent-spanning effects of genocide, colonialism, and land loss, examining communities in North Dakota and Bolivia who wrestle with the threats posed by extractivism and their simultaneously urgent need for economic security. In Chapter 2, time and place are inseparable for the Mandan Hidatsa Arikara (MHA) Nation, whose land is both the keeper of ancestral spirits and also a rich source of oil and gas resources. In Chapter 3, the historic nature of Evo Morales' role as the first indigenous president in the 500 years since colonization nevertheless failed to mitigate the ongoing threats to indigenous territory and sovereignty, or the lasting power dynamics left over from colonial supply lines. In all of these cases, the clear concern for the possible *futures* is also a key temporal element, as of course, none of these stories are finished.

1

Destroy and Rebuild: Considering Harm, Community Benefits, and Environmental Ornamentation in Community Development in Atlanta

Dr. Lemir Teron
Ms. T'Shari White
Ms. Farah Nibbs
Ms. Farzaneh Khayat

Planning and Marginalization

The brutality of racial discrimination propelled by the state, through practices such as redlining, restrictive covenants, and iterations of urban renewal, has driven racial segregation in cities throughout America's history. The effects of this segregation have been chronicled at various points for over a century (see DuBois in the seminal *The Philadelphia Negro* and Woodson's *The Mis-Education of the Negro*), and the contemporary consequences range from inadequate schooling, to food insecurity, to substandard housing. Along with other environmental factors, and in concert with economic and psychosocial considerations, these factors have severe public health consequences for Black Americans, who consequently suffer from shortened life expectancies across all age ranges, compared to white counterparts (Cunningham et al. 2017). Central to propelling racial inequality has been public policy, which in various incarnations has placed a premium on racial exclusion and isolation (Coates 2014). Whether it be through cities' use of red-lining to perpetuate segregation, racist transportation policies that isolate and underserve low-income communities (Stone 1989), or urban renewal leading to increasingly marginalized and disenfranchised urbanites (Wilson 1987), dedicated forces used to push disadvantaged groups to the socioeconomic margins have continually isolated African Americans and other marginalized populations, producing harmful intergenerational consequences. It is vital that attempts to ameliorate socioeconomic, health, and environmental inequality in cities recognize the racial components at the root of many dilemmas; thus, environmental sustainability initiatives are a critical player in this equation.

This chapter explores the challenges and contradictions facing cities as they simultaneously purport to advance pro-environmental and community agendas, while engaging in economic development strategies that propel corporate interests. While many distressed communities are in or adjacent to areas targeted for redevelopment, the plights of residents are often not central to strategies, thus further driving marginalization. This research features a case study evaluating the Mercedes-Benz Stadium in Atlanta, Georgia, completed in 2017, exploring possible threats to the potential for just sustainabilities (Agyeman 2013) in urban practice when prerequisite attention and deference is not given to deep understandings of environmental and racial justice that affect procedural concerns. As a result, marginalized communities' interests are placed in direct conflict with the politics and practices of urban economic development. Agyeman notes that cities, subject to the colonizing force of Western capitalism, face threats from "the increasing privatization of public spaces" (2013: 99). In order to evaluate the potential for just sustainabilities, it is necessary to evaluate planning dynamics to gauge the potential for equitable sustainability planning. Hence, we evaluate the Mercedes Benz Stadium project, which has been propelled by hundreds of millions of public dollars, and explores the potential contradictions pertaining to environmentally sustainability as it embodies the hyper-replacement model, all while boosting sustainability credentials (including LEED Platinum certification, solar PV and electric vehicle charging, and rainwater capture capacity) as it replaces a facility whose useful life, structurally, was far from exhaustion.

City on the Ascent and Underlying Conditions

Since the 1980s, Atlanta, Georgia, has emerged as the South's epicenter of commerce, a global tourist destination, and home to a number of the nation's most prominent corporations (including several Fortune 100 companies). With an exploding regional population that added on average over 77,000 residents annually between 1990 and 2010 (Atlanta Regional Commission 2014), the consequences of uneven development and consequential sprawl have become synonymous with the region.

As a bustling hub for jobs and home to a swelling population, largely autocentric development has created a host of issues for the region, ranging from environmental threats (including air quality issues and deforestation), to housing and residential segregation, to educational disparities (Bullard, Johnson, & Torres 2000). Much of the region's working (and playing) population is bound by automobile to get from suburban areas into job and entertainment districts, mostly located within city limits or elsewhere inside the perimeter of the I-285 corridor, the interstate that encircles the city and surrounding urbanized suburbs. Of the over 4.2 million people that live in the 10-county metropolitan area, less than 40 percent inhabit Fulton and DeKalb Counties (the two counties in which Atlanta is contained) and only 10 percent of all metropolitan residents reside in Atlanta (Atlanta Regional Commission 2014). As the region's population has grown, racialized housing patterns have persisted from earlier decades. For example, between 2000 and 2010, counties adding African American populations mostly lost white population, as the inner-core suburban counties became more African American, while whites congregated to the region's outer-counties (Pooley 2015). This contemporary urban/suburban and racial dichotomy has also been characteristic of historic divides that have played out in a number of contexts, including politics around mass transit siting (Stone 1989), which saw several counties rejecting interconnectivity over the decades. This would ultimately factor into one of the most significant, yet unsung, toxic air crises in US history, as Atlanta holds the distinction of being the first city in the nation's history to lose federal highway funding because of air toxicity (Shrouds 2000). The city only recently reached compliance with the 1997 ozone standards of 84 ppb, by coming in at 80 ppb some sixteen years later. Due to federal cuts, numerous highway projects were sacked, with the loss of hundreds of millions of dollars in federal funds. Nearly two decades later, asthma-involved emergency room visits for children in metro Atlanta are among the highest in the state, with Black boys under the age of five as the state's most vulnerable population (Annor et al. 2015). The lack of foresight in planning over decades and a strong legacy of pro-growth policies all scaffolded by racial politics have resulted in geographic racial disparities, which have limited the potential for just sustainabilities in the contemporary urban space (Agyeman 2013). Black Americans in urban America have been subject to a litany of racist activities, including redlining policies by the Home Owners Loan Corporation in the 1930s, racial covenants in home deeds restricting sales to African American buyers, and the Realtor Code of Ethics, which declared, "A Realtor should never be instrumental in introducing into a neighborhood a character of property or occupancy, members of any race or nationality, or any individuals whose presence will clearly be detrimental to property values in that neighborhood" (National Association of Real Estate Boards 1924). The legacies of the above all inform contemporary urban life in cities across the nation.

The toxic air conditions in metro Atlanta have significant public health consequences, particularly for populations with respiratory vulnerabilities. In 2010, just two of Atlanta's hospitals alone had over 500 ER visits related directly to smog (Henderson 2006; Williams 2013). Going back to 1996, the CDC identified that during the Olympic Games (with its reduced traffic volumes due to city regulations restricting traffic) daily ozone reductions decreased by nearly 28 percent (falling from 81.3 ppb to 58.6 ppb) corresponding with a 22.5 percent decrease in morning rush hour traffic. During this same window, asthma acute care events related hospitalizations dropped by over 41 percent (Friedman et al. 2001).[1] The racial implications of asthma-related visits during this era were profound. Black children accounted for over two-thirds of all asthma-related pediatric emergency room visits in Atlanta, but less than half of all emergency room hospitalizations (Tolbert et al. 2000). Perhaps the most alarming consequences of public health disparities are life expectancy gaps across adjacent neighborhoods, which in

Atlanta are as large as thirteen years between some inner-city communities (Minyard et al. 2016). This distressing gulf warrants attention from not only public health officials but also urbanists, planners, and developers, as these parties have all historically contributed to driving health, economic, and political disparities. The Georgia Regional Transportation Authority (GRTA), created to combat Atlanta's transportation and air quality issues, declares its mission is "to reduce congestion and improve mobility" while operating "high-quality, efficient regional commuter services" and creating "a lean responsive state transportation authority working to improve Georgia's world-class transportation network" (GRTA 2017). Conspicuously absent from this mission are public health concerns, which are ironically *not* essential to the agency's charge.

Stadium Development

As stadium financing is increasingly backed by public investment (Berkeley Economic Review 2019), it is imperative to explore the economic rationale that supporters champion. In addition, as Atlanta's stadium is touted for its environmental credentials, a critique of the facility from an environmental sustainability lens is appropriate, especially given the areas' high rates of pollution. While supporters have argued that the Atlanta facility has the capacity to spur economic development (Reed 2017), the shortening life span of facilities, generally, along with the potential for displacement and gentrification, presents challenges for municipalities to promote and deliver just and sustainable development. Furthermore, threats to procedural justice, in which projects are seemingly fast-tracked without ample public review, undermine democratic processes in urban planning, further reducing the potential for just sustainabilities.

While this work examines a twenty-first-century sports venue and its environmental, economic, and equity consequences, Atlanta's pursuit of sports facilities to create jobs and spur economic growth has a multigenerational history. Indeed, a major part of making Atlanta a "national city" was former mayor Ivan Allen's pursuit of major-league sports teams (Stone 1989). Just prior to his initial mayoral run in the early 1960s, Allen, then head of the City's Chamber of Commerce, developed a six-pronged program for redevelopment that embodied urban renewal: constructing expressways, constructing rapid-transit, acquiring professional baseball, setting up civic centers, and city advertising (Keating 2001). This required infrastructure and investment in the form of stadiums and arenas to accommodate sporting events. Atlanta has engaged in venue construction for multiple sports since the city lured the Atlanta Braves from Milwaukee in the 1950s. The impetus for a baseball facility was perhaps the capstone project of the earlier rounds of post–Second World War urban renewal.

The pursuit of public sporting events and facilities is not a uniquely Atlanta (or even American) venture (Zimbalist 2015)—and the social ills associated with high-profile venues are ubiquitous, ranging from bribery to secure Olympic games, to alleged slave labor used in the construction of World Cup facilities, along with relocation-driven extortion that is seemingly omnipresent in cities around the United States as team owners vie for publicly financed sports facilities which often pits municipalities against one another (Longman 2000; Waldron 2012; Pattisson 2013). This creates a paradox in which, though facilities are ostensibly public goods, the anti-democratic means involved in finance and construction highlight the internally flawed logic behind many of these ventures.

A key part in Atlanta's public development face has been the city's willingness to remove the (perceived) unsightly—including peoples, both poor and homeless—and a semiotics built on image (Whitelegg 2000). This erasure incapacitates *problem* residents from the experiences of urban dreams related to economic expansion. Further, it is indicative of the tensions involved in municipal planning that places urban growth and development in direct opposition to human security and dignity by means of erasure. Atlanta has also criminalized homelessness in other contexts, including (argued in the name of public safety) via anti-panhandling, loitering, and drunkenness ordinances acutely enforced in business and tourism districts (Stone 1989). Though often touted by members of the local growth machine (including municipal economic development agencies, businesses, and politicians) as vehicles to improve housing stock and create much-needed jobs, Whitelegg (2000) alternatively views the pursuit of public sporting venues as part of a deep-seated insecurity within metro Atlanta's leadership which seeks to position itself as an international city, on par with the likes of New York and Chicago.

Atlanta's pursuit of the 1996 Olympics was viewed as a panacea for multiple social ills; the space and construction needs of the project (along with subsequent ventures and attitudes) necessitated the dispersal of 1,000 homeless residents—and in the Olympics' case over seventy local businesses and four shelters (Whitelegg 2000). An instrumental feature in this ensemble was the notorious one-way bus tickets to leave town that many homeless Atlantans received around the time of the Olympic Games, accompanied by the requisite documents stating that they would not return. Also noteworthy is that even though Atlanta has continuously made efforts to support downtown tourism since the time of urban renewal's heyday, with projects including the long-troubled festive marketplace Underground Atlanta, it has consistently failed to become a mainstream attraction for commerce and retail. Holliman (2009) noted the city "had unilaterally emphasized white downtown business expansion even as white tourists and shoppers alike continued to abandon downtown" (370). Over the last decade, as Georgia State University has morphed from a largely commuter school in the 1990s to one of the largest universities in the nation, with a substantial imprint in Downtown, the characteristics of the neighborhood have changed to complement expansion. The dorm-based student population more than doubled between 2007 and 2017, ultimately accommodating 5,300 students. This is in addition to private development projects, which, while catering to students, have consequently changed the profile of Downtown Atlanta (Sinderman 2017).

The Battle of (New) Atlanta (Stadium)

In 2012 it was announced that the then-twenty-year-old Georgia Dome would be demolished by 2017 and replaced by an adjacent facility, now known as Mercedes-Benz Stadium (MBS). The project courted controversy, particularly among nearby residents who felt disenfranchised from the decision-making process and those who had serious questions about the financial soundness of building a new stadium. There have been broken promises from similar efforts in the past (including Turner Field across town and the Georgia Dome itself) and the dearth of transparency and community involvement involved in the process. The impetus for MBS originated largely from Arthur Blank, cofounder of Home Depot and owner of the Atlanta Falcons. Because of the push from Blank and other members of the growth machine, and a perceived rubber stamp from city government, the project was fast-tracked for development, to the consternation of local groups, thus prompting a lawsuit[2] in which local residents challenged the legality of $200+ million in public financing via hotel tax bonds. A county Superior Court judge rejected the lawsuit and the issue was appealed to the State's Supreme Court, which ultimately backed the city's bond financing scheme.

MBS can accommodate up to 75,000 spectators and is located on the southern tip of the Georgia World Congress Center (GWCC), adjacent to the Vine City and English Avenue neighborhoods, both of which are predominantly Black and have not excelled during Atlanta's economic boom over the last several decades. When the proposal for a new stadium was introduced, two sites in the stadium district were offered as tenable: one site on the north side of the GWCC, which would have bordered a largely white middle-class neighborhood, and the ultimately chosen south side location. The latter, located on the edge of a Black and economically distressed community, was considered optimal by developers partly because of its unobstructed view of the Downtown skyline. This site, which was chosen after a short but inflammatory process of protests and community pushback, set off a wave of community demonstrations, the aforementioned lawsuit, and press conferences to articulate the detachment from the planning process that many residents felt.

Souled Out

The buying of property from, and subsequent demolitions, of two historically African American churches is perhaps the most lingering concern associated with MBS. Friendship Baptist and Mount Vernon Baptist, both over 100 years old, with the former dating back to the mid-nineteenth century, became involved in separate negotiations with the city and the Georgia World Congress Center respectively, to sell the churches' properties, which were ultimately sold for a collective $34 million through a combination of funds from the state and the Atlanta Falcons (Leslie 2013; Stafford 2013). Then-Mayor Kasim Reed was a conspicuous champion for the new stadium's development and the city's broader growth agenda. The sacrifice of the churches and their ties to the city and residents and the looming potential for replacement sitting outside of city limits[3] is seemingly the antithesis of the city's aspirations of promoting strong neighborhoods. Similar to the churches, Morris Brown College, the local HBCU that has struggled financially and with accreditation for years, proactively sold thirty acres of its property for $14 million. This came following the objections of nearby Clark Atlanta University (CAU), arguing that Morris Brown did not have the right to sell the property (Saporta 2014), along with CAU's successful legal claims that allowed contested properties to be reverted back to CAU's ownership. A local environmental justice attorney questioned the overall schemes behind the development plans and challenged that a city that is willing to disrupt historic institutions for economic development purposes would potentially expose other Black institutions to similar ordeals (Rumley 2014). Indeed, the forces of gentrification, in Atlanta, and elsewhere, necessitate indifference to the historic and cultural relevance of Black institutions under the guise of economic expansion and development.

Had the disruption of community life stopped with the sale of private property, though public engagement opportunities would have been undermined, the capacity of the public's involvement may have been limited, notwithstanding the very public purposes of those institutions being sold. The ancillary processes also involved a controversial road closing and realigning of Martin Luther King Jr. Drive, a major artery giving local residents entrée into the city. This became contentious for numerous reasons, not the least of which was the fact that just a week before the closing, the city firmly stated that a closing was not imminent (Rumley 2014). Notwithstanding dubious information regarding the project, an even more embedded structural inequality concern relates to who has rights and access to the city and decision-making power and who is susceptible to disenfranchisement. Agyeman and Evans (2003) have noted the necessity for deep and critical attention to the overlap between sustainability and justice policies in cities in order for communities to be livable for *all* residents. The street closing has been perceived by activist and community members as a conscious effort to limit their access within a larger gentrification process. The closing represents not only the imposing of development values on communities but the lack of capacity that said communities have in their own self-determination.

Perhaps the most significant consideration regarding public planning concerns is the lack of public engagement and involvement throughout the development and maturation of the process, as the timetable including announcement, public input, and negotiations occurred in a time span of less than a year. Once again, if one holds that the community development plans and processes are to have meaning beyond being functions of bureaucracy, and in order for jargon on community participation in development to have any credibility, these processes require substantial publicly facing deliberation by governing and planning authorities, along with public oversight that has residents meaningfully involved in project development and outcomes. In contrast to the expedited timeline of the stadium project, the Atlanta BeltLine, a twenty-two-mile loop whose goal is to connect nearly four dozen in-town neighborhoods using trails, parks, and potentially mass transit, has involved a public process that has played out over years. Development for large scale projects should reflect this process if they are functions of democratic governance, especially given the desire of the growth machine for multi-billion dollar development projects, and particularly if public funds and transactions are significant drivers for the process. If a $1.2 billion project does not warrant extensive public review, and for all practical purposes excludes communities from the development process, questions abound regarding what magnitude of a project would warrant substantive engagement between city officials and the public. Furthermore, what confidence can evaluators have that non-high-profile, city-backed projects will give consideration to equity and justice concerns, as they may not capture significant media nor broad public attention? This is fundamental to the development paradox, which is unlikely to ameliorate the health, economic, and environmental gaps that a just sustainabilities entrenched urban planning would call for.

Functioning Within Environmental Boundaries

The most prominent feature of the stadium development's environmental impacts is its embodiment of fast consumption. MBS replaced a facility that was twenty-five years old at the time of demolition. The grounds for this, as with many sporting facilities across the nation, have been staked on the argument that the current configurations of older facilities do not allow for maximal capitalization (e.g., through the sale of luxury services to corporate partners, like skyboxes, along with other revenue drivers that have come into vogue over the last fifteen years). This has played out across cities nationally as team ownership uses the threat of relocation (both within and beyond metropolitan boundaries)—and recently executed by the formerly crosstown Atlanta Braves who fled the city and moved to the northwestern suburbs—if ransoms in the form of public financing or other capitulations are not paid. In spite of seemingly interminable stadium battles between proponents of publicly backed stadiums—which are often predicated on arguments concerning (temporary) job creation, ancillary spending in the local community, and tourism benefits—public financing for sports venues does not pay off for governments (from local to state scales). Most recreational spending is derived from local residents, and many of the high-salaried professionals associated with the venues (players, coaches, and executives) often reside far outside of the sports facilities districts (Legislative Reference Bureau 2013). In the case of Atlanta, and other publicly backed facilities across the nation, while the public pays, the corporations—in the form of sports teams—literally play.

Environmental Ornamentation

The MBS project claimed strong sustainability credentials from the design stage. This included the pursuit of LEED Certification, the use of recycled content for building materials, composting food waste, and related activity to make the facility meet zero-waste standards, the installation of solar panels, and the promotion of three nearby public transit stations (New Atlanta Stadium 2015).[4] This embodies what we refer to as *environmental ornamentation*, or the conscientious festooning of large-scale projects with green accoutrements (e.g., solar panels) in the absence of some overall sustainability strategy, and operates with underlying factors that run counter to a sustainable consumption paradigm. Zehner's (2012) proposition of the green illusion, that is the fetishization of renewable energy in the absence of anchoring to solutions for systemic environmental crises, is exemplified by the Atlanta example. In the case of the MBS, the irony is that it is being touted as a green project while the underlying conundrum of replacing a facility without a comprehensive life cycle analysis, particularly within the context of replacing a structurally sound and relatively young facility, remains. Life cycle assessments (Fortier et al. 2019) as part of evaluation are critical for any meaningful analyses of projects such as MBS.

Equity Implications

Regarding equity implications and the potential for the manifestation of a just sustainability, the conspicuous absence of equity/justice-based language in prominent planning material is suggestive of the city's weakness on related issues. The lack of attention to such concerns has been highlighted in the just sustainabilities scholarship (Agyeman 2013). The deficit in language that addresses environmental racism and racial equality in Atlanta's sustainability policy (the city's 2014 *Power to Change* sustainability plan contained one environmental justice mention, in contrast to economic concerns being mentioned several dozen times) evidences this (Teron 2015). By not acknowledging the structural conditions that undermine urban life, which informs public planning, it should not be surprising that the stadium-related planning has also been deficient in this area. The intra-generational implications of the MBS project and negotiated tradeoffs are significant. In order to ameliorate local resistance, $45 million earmarked for local community benefits pooled from a combination of state and local government, along with the Atlanta Falcons, have been designated to community improvement for nearby neighborhoods (Burns 2013). This is a significant investment for a community with catastrophic unemployment, half its families living below the federal poverty level, and with nearly 40 percent of homes unoccupied.

Historically (and into the contemporary) the surrounding community has been the site of concentrated Black poverty. Dr. Martin Luther King, in an effort to shame the city establishment into alleviating those conditions, said in regard to then-Mayor Allen, "I do not believe he knows such conditions exist in Atlanta" (JET 1966). The community benefits agreement rings eerily similar to promises made in the early 1990s, when progressive mayor Maynard Jackson pushed redevelopment to the same neighborhoods during the conception phase of the Georgia Dome. While an $8 million Georgia Dome Trust Fund was established for the purposes of developing single-family units and to encourage home ownership, along with improving the rental stock in the area, the area remained one of the most economically distressed communities within the city. Again, in 2004, the Vine City Civic Association, in collaboration with the city of Atlanta, developed a redevelopment plan for the neighborhood that involved future land use, a robust transportation plan, an overall action plan that included funding mechanisms, and a twenty-year strategic plan. NPU-L, the cluster of neighborhoods largely dominated by English Ave and Vine City (see Figures 1.1 and 1.2), would go on to lose over

Figure 1.1 Neighborhood Planning Unit L and Mercedes Benz Stadium.

City of Atlanta Neighborhood Planning Units

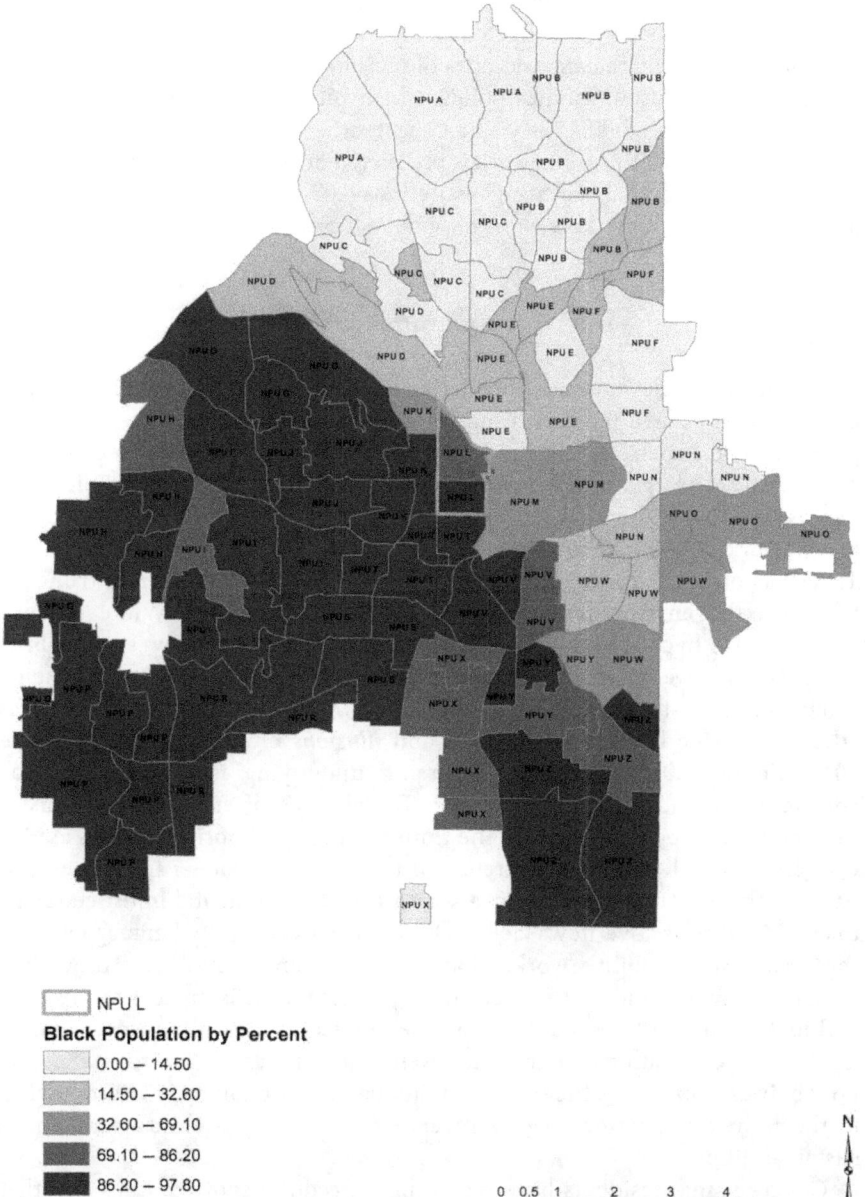

Figure 1.2 Neighborhood Planning Units in Atlanta and the city's Black population. Mercedes Benz Stadium and the Georgia World Congress Center are a de facto boundary as the Black population rises to the south and west of the site. Data source: Atlanta Regional Commission 2010.

1,000 residents between the 2000 and 2010 Censuses. And notwithstanding the $8 million Georgia Dome Trust Fund, which was set up in 1989 (Garey n.d.), the area gained little economic momentum over the years since the fund's creation. This decades-long history, composed of neglect, mismanagement, negligence, and misfortune, illuminates how targeted economic development strategies alone are not enough to counterbalance decades of racism, marginalization, and economic isolation. A just sustainabilities policy, which mandates intricate concerns and attention on policy inputs, as well as substantive action related to procedural justice, is necessary. This framework is predicated on activity that is measured, not by intentions but both by ensuring institutions have *capacity* to address inequality and considering achieved *outcomes* of policy actions.

Conclusions

The push for the development of Mercedes-Benz Stadium as a replacement to a facility that existed for only a quarter of a century, and the expendability of pillar African American churches with histories going back over a century, is emblematic of a larger trend endemic to major American sports. A further irony here is that this is done on the figurative backs of a largely African American player workforce.[5] With multiple NFL facilities either on track to open (see Table 1.1) or in the conceptualization phase, and a recent pattern of truncated lifespans, the environmental considerations are profound. While attempts to offset the hyper-replacement model may be obscured by sustainability credentialing, we view these projects as manifestations of environmental ornamentation—featuring strategies that are noncomprehensive and cynical attempts to ride both the *greenwave* and *illusions* of sustainability (Checker 2011; Zehner 2012), without addressing underlying issues of extraction, consumption, and material life spans. The absence of environmental justice protections and policies lends to the traumas that neighborhoods such as Vine City are exposed to. More concrete will lead to more water runoff issues, for one; Southwest Atlanta already deals with this environmental injustice related to combined sewer overflows (Jelks 2008). The lack of equity language guiding the urban sustainability work, along with the anti-democratic timetables, disables equitable and just process in city planning. It is critical to view this within Agyeman's (2013) guidance on the implications on urban space and the nexus with community security—as well as the potential for resistance and possibilities. Ultimately, the truncated life span of functioning stadiums, driven by the desire for operators to grow revenue streams, is a systemic assault on just sustainabilities.

Concerns that residents have regarding procedural shortcomings and their lack of faith in planning processes further perpetuate planning's paradox and present a challenge toward just sustainabilities in urban planning. More fundamentally, faith in institutions by residents may be irreparably ruptured when centuries-old institutions are readily replaced for entertainment establishments with life spans of, perhaps, only a few decades. If institutions that anchor communities are not beyond the reach of urban development and economic expansion, then questions abound regarding what the private sector will offer of commensurate value to fill the vacuum. The filling of voids left from discarded social institutions in inner-city urban areas, particularly those with understandings of local conditions, is often neglected by development proponents, although certainly issues cannot be healed solely by economic development-focused drivers. This embodies the paradox of urban planning and development, in which the expansion of capital makes nonprofitable institutions expendable. If the purchase, leveling, and displacement of parishioners to new locales, while upending generational and communal ties, do not constitute as antithetical to community continuity—which along with parallel collaboration and social connectedness had been advanced by the local sustainability regime— perhaps no project would meet that standard. These conditions mandate the need for urban policy and practice that are guided by just sustainabilities at the core of planning.

It is also critical to consider the potential for stadium development and other municipally backed activity to propel environmental ornamentation, that is, activity that is not supported by meaningful steps toward healing the environmental commons and does not propel involved actors toward a just sustainability. While sustainability initiatives associated with MBS such as solar panels and the repurposing of waste materials may offer environmental benefits, the project simultaneously amplifies existing environmental inequalities. These conditions will work to deepen the vulnerability of an economically and environmentally marginalized community.

Complicating resistance to the accelerated construction pace of sporting venues is the economic development features that these projects often champion. Certainly they bring temporary construction jobs and seasonal employment, although the verdict is mixed on any deeper economic gains that are brought to communities, especially when said communities are already economically marginalized. This makes the trade-offs (including increased traffic and noise, pollution, and potentially gentrification) all the more suspect and threatening. It is vital that cities address the contradictions that exist between the interests of economic development forces and those of environmental justice communities. Urban planning that is predicated on just sustainabilities and its attention to quality-of-life concerns, intragenerational justice demands, and procedural justice considerations, while functioning within environmental system boundaries, is part of ameliorating this paradox. Cities must resist the temptation to reflexively champion any economic development and undercut rival municipalities, and work substantively toward models built on the integration of community and regional development based on cooperation and authentic goals for achieving sustainability. Lacking such commitments, the accelerated consumption of stadiums (and other such projects) and the dispersal of hundreds of millions of dollars in public funding giveaways for projects that make only limited contributions to economic development, let alone sustainability, will further inequality in marginalized communities.

Table 1.1 NFL stadiums, locations, and age. Of the fourteen stadiums completed in the twenty-first century prior to the 2020 football season, the average age of the facility replaced was approximately thirty-five years. If recent trends persist, there will be massive stadium developments in many cities in the coming years, accompanied by battles over public finance and displacement.

Field/coliseum/stadium	Location	Year opened	Age of facility replaced (for stadiums built after 2000)
Allegiant	Las Vegas, NV	2020	
Arrowhead	Kansas City, MO	1972	
AT&T	Arlington, TX	2009	37
Bank of America	Charlotte, NC	1996	
Century Link	Seattle, WA	2002	33
Edward Jones Dome	St. Louis, MO	1995	
Everbank	Jacksonville, FL	1985	
Fawcett	Canton, OH	1924	
FedEx	Hyattsville, MD	1997	
First Energy	Cleveland, OH	1999	
Ford	Detroit, MI	2002	26
Gillette	Foxboro, MA	2002	31
Heinz	Pittsburgh, PA	2001	30
Lambeau	Green Bay, WI	1957	
Levi	Santa Clara, CA	2015	54
Lincoln	Philadelphia, PA	2003	32
Lucas	Indianapolis, IN	2008	23
M&T	Baltimore, MD	1998	
Mercedes-Benz	Atlanta, GA	2017	25
Met Life	East Rutherford, NJ	2010	33
Nissan	Nashville, TN	1999	
NRG	Houston, TX	2002	
Paul Brown	Cincinnati, OH	2000	29
Ralph Wilson	Orchard Park, NY	1973	
Raymond Jones	Tampa Bay, FL	1998	
SoFi	Inglewood, CA	2020	
Soldier	Chicago, IL	1924	
Sports Authority	Denver, CO	2001	52
Sun Life	Miami Garden, FL	1987	
Superdome	New Orleans, LA	1975	
TCF Bank	Minneapolis, MN	2009	41
University of Phoenix	Glendale, AZ	2006	48

Notes

1 Non-asthma medical hospitalizations did not drop during that time frame.
2 *Love et al. v. Fulton County Board of Tax Assessors*, 2017.
3 During this time, the Atlanta Braves, which played just south of Downtown Atlanta since 1997, fled to a suburb north of Atlanta after a failed negotiation on a stadium deal.
4 Atlanta has previously coupled sporting events with environmental progress using green marketing. The 2013 NCAA Final Four, for example, related each of Atlanta's Sustainability Impact Areas to the event; the education component featured a video informing attendees of the city's sustainability initiatives, while community health and vitality programming initiatives were achieved via a clothing drive for charity (Atlanta Local Organizing Committee 2013).
5 Notwithstanding the NFL's Rooney Rule, which mandates interviewing opportunities for candidates of Color for head coaching and managerial positions, Black Americans have been largely locked out of coaching and senior-level positions across the league notwithstanding their conspicuousness on the field (Bryant 2018).

References

Agyeman, J. (2013), *Introducing Just Sustainabilities: Policy, Planning and Practice*, London: Zed Books.

Agyeman, J. & T. Evans (2003), "Toward just sustainability in urban communities: Building equity rights with sustainable solutions," *Annals of the American Academy of Political & Social Science*, 590(1): 35–53.

Annor, F., A. Bayakly, M. Vajani, C. Drenzek, F. Lopez, & J. O'Connor (2015), *Georgia Asthma Burden Report*, Georgia Department of Public Health, Health Protection, Epidemiology, Chronic Disease, Healthy Behaviors & Injury Epidemiology Section. Available online: https://dph.georgia.gov/sites/dph.georgia.gov/files/Asthma%20 Burden%20Report_11.12.15.pdf (Accessed May 25, 2020).

Atlanta Local Organizing Committee (2013), *Sustainability Impact Report: The Road to Atlanta is Paved Green*, Atlanta: Atlanta Local Organizing Committee.

Atlanta Regional Commission (2014), "ARC's 2014 population estimates: Steady as she goes." Available online: http://documents.atlantaregional.com/research/pop_estimates_main2014.pdf (Accessed May 25, 2020).

Berkeley Economic Review (2019), "The economics of sports stadiums: Does public financing of sports stadiums create local economic growth, or just help billionaires improve their profit margin?" Available online: https://econreview.berkeley.edu/the-economics-of-sports-stadiums-does-public-financing-of-sports-stadiums-create-local-economic-growth-or-just-help-billionaires-improve-their-profit-margin/ (Accessed May 25, 2020).

Bryant, H. (2018), *The Heritage: Black Athletes, a Divided America, and the Politics of Patriotism*, Boston: Beacon Press.

Bullard, R.D., G.S. Johnson, & A.O. Torres (2000), *Sprawl City: Race, Politics, and Planning in Atlanta*, Washington, DC: Island Press.

Burns, R. (2013), "It's going to take more than $45 million* to help Vine City," *Atlanta Magazine*, March 13. Available online: http://www.atlantamagazine.com/civilrights/its-going-to-take-more-than-45-million-to-help-vine-city/ (Accessed May 25, 2020).

Checker, M. (2011), "Wiped out by the 'greenwave': Environmental gentrification and the paradoxical politics of urban sustainability," *City & Society*, 23(2): 210–29.
Coates, T.-N. (2014), "The case for reparations," *The Atlantic*. Available online: http://www.theatlantic.com/features/archive/2014/05/the-case-for-reparations/361631/ (Accessed May 25, 2020).
Cunningham, T.J., J.B. Croft, Y. Liu, H. Lu, P.I. Eke, & W.H. Giles (2017), "Vital signs: Racial disparities in age-specific mortality among blacks or African Americans—United States, 1999–2015," *MMWR: Morbidity & Mortality Weekly Report*, 66(17): 444.
DuBois, W. (1995), *The Philadelphia Negro: A Social Study*, Philadelphia: University of Pennsylvania Press.
Fortier, M.O.P., L. Teron, T.G. Reames, D.T. Munardy, & B.M. Sullivan (2019), "Introduction to evaluating energy justice across the life cycle: A social life cycle assessment approach," *Applied Energy*, 236: 211–9.
Friedman, M.S., K.E. Powell, L. Hutwagner, L.M. Graham, & W.G. Teague (2001), "Impact of changes in transportation and commuting behaviors during the 1996 summer Olympic Games in Atlanta on air quality and childhood asthma," *Journal of the American Medical Association*, 285(7): 897–905.
Garey, E. (n.d.), *Georgia Dome Community/Housing Development Trust Fund*, Atlanta: Invest Atlanta.
GRTA (2017), *Improving the Experience: Georgia Regional Transportation Authority Fiscal Year 2017 Annual Report*. Available online: https://www.srta.ga.gov/wp-content/uploads/2018/02/GRTA_AR17_FINAL.pdf (Accessed May 25, 2020).
Henderson, J. (2006), "Secessionist automobility: Racism, anti-urbanism, and the politics of automobility in Atlanta, Georgia," *International Journal of Urban & Regional Research*, 30(2): 293–307.
Holliman, I.V. (2009), "From crackertown to model city? Urban renewal and community building in Atlanta, 1963–1966," *Journal of Urban History*, 35(3): 369–86.
Jelks, N.O. (2008), "Sewage in our backyards: The politics of race, class, + water in Atlanta, Georgia," *Projections: MIT Journal of Planning*, 8: 172–89.
JET (1966), "Dr. King takes walk in slum area, calls it 'appalling'," *JET Magazine*, February 17: 45–6.
Keating, L. (2001), *Atlanta: Race, Class, and Urban Expansion*, Philadelphia: Temple University Press.
Legislative Reference Bureau (2013), *Review of Economic Impact of Selected Professional Sports Venues and Downtown Revitalization Efforts in Oklahoma City*, Milwaukee: Legislative Reference Bureau.
Leslie, K. (2013), "Mount Vernon Baptist Church accepts offer to sell for stadium," *Atlanta Journal Constitution*, September 19. Available online: https://www.ajc.com/news/mount-vernon-baptist-church-accepts-offer-sell-for-stadium/eyH98Lyq8UwAwlQc4sjkzK/ (Accessed May 25, 2020).
Longman, J. (2000), "Olympics: Leaders of Salt Lake Olympic Bid are indicted in bribery scandal," *New York Times*, July 21. Available online: http://www.nytimes.com/2000/07/21/sports/olympics-leaders-of-salt-lake-olympic-bid-are-indicted-in-bribery-scandal.html (Accessed May 25, 2020).
Minyard, K., K. Lawler, E. Fuller, M. Wilson, & E. Henry (2016), "Reducing health disparities in Atlanta," *Stanford Social Innovation Review*, Spring.
National Association of Real Estate Boards (1924), Code of Ethics, Article 34.
New Atlanta Stadium (2015), "Stadium." Available online: https://mercedesbenzstadium.com/the-stadium/ (Accessed May 25, 2020).

Pattisson, P. (2013), "Revealed: Qatar's World Cup 'slaves,'" *Guardian*, September 25. Available online: http://www.theguardian.com/world/2013/sep/25/revealed-qatars-world-cup-slaves (Accessed May 25, 2020).

Pooley, K. (2015), "Race, and the declining prospects for upward mobility," *Southern Spaces*. Available online: https://southernspaces.org/2015/segregations-new-geography-atlanta-metro-region-race-and-declining-prospects-upward-mobility (Accessed May 25, 2020).

Reed, K. (2017), "Impact of new stadium on the Atlanta economy," [Interview], August 25.

Rumley, M. (2014), [Interview], August 26.

Saporta, M. (2014), "Judge approves sale of Morris Brown property to city and friendship," *Atlanta Business Chronicle*, June 18. Available online: http://www.bizjournals.com/atlanta/news/2014/06/18/judge-approves-sale-of-morris-brown-property-to.html?page=all (Accessed May 26, 2020).

Shrouds, J.M. (2000), "Atlanta 'conforms' to clean air requirements," *Public Roads*, 64(2). Available online: https://www.fhwa.dot.gov/publications/publicroads/00septoct/atlanta.cfm (Accessed May 26, 2020).

Sinderman, M. (2017), "GSU impact on downtown all-encompassing," *Atlanta Business Chronicle*, March 10. Available online: https://www.bizjournals.com/atlanta/feature/gsu-impact-on-downtown-all-encompassing.html (Accessed May 26, 2020).

Stafford, L. (2013), "Friendship Baptist makes room for stadium," *Atlanta Journal Constitution*, September 22. Available online: https://www.ajc.com/news/friendship-baptist-makes-room-for-stadium/6fIDcWr4wuuF06rCUvy7RP/(Accessed May 26, 2020).

Stone, C.N. (1989), *Regime Politics: Governing Atlanta, 1946–1988*, Lawrence: University Press of Kansas.

Teron, L. (2015), "A language of (in) justice: Expanding the sustainability planning lexicon," *Environmental Justice*, 8(6): 221–6.

Tolbert, P.E., J.A. Mulholland, D.L. MacIntosh, F. Xu, D. Daniels, O. Devine, B.P. Carlin, M. Klein, J. Dorley, A. Butler, D.F. Nordenberg, H. Frumkin, P.B. Ryan, & M.C. White (2000), "Air quality and pediatric emergency room visits for asthma in Atlanta, Georgia," *American Journal of Epidemiology*, 151(8): 798–810.

Waldron, T. (2012), "Foul play: Five cities that want taxpayer money to finance pro sports stadium boondoggles," *ThinkProgress*, June 12. Available online: https://thinkprogress.org/foul-play-five-cities-that-want-taxpayer-money-to-finance-pro-sports-stadium-boondoggles-b1c56c9e51c5/ (Accessed May 26, 2020).

Whitelegg, D. (2000), "Going for gold: Atlanta's bid for fame," *International Journal of Urban & Regional Research*, 24(4): 801–17.

Williams, M. (2013), "Metro area reaches 1997 air quality standards—but not newer ones," *Atlanta Journal Constitution*, February 4. Available online: https://www.ajc.com/news/local/metro-area-reaches-1997-air-quality-standards-but-not-newer-ones/LozUgF0t6TY7YbGTtNtcUP/ (Accessed May 25, 2020).

Wilson, W.J. (1987), *The Truly Disadvantaged: The Inner City, the Underclass, and Public Policy*, Chicago: University of Chicago Press.

Woodson, C.G. (2000), *The Mis-Education of the Negro*, Chicago: Associated Publishers.

Zehner, O. (2012), *Green Illusions: The Dirty Secrets of Clean Energy and the Future of Environmentalism*, Lincoln: University of Nebraska Press.

Zimbalist, A. (2015), *Circus Maximus: The Economic Gamble behind Hosting the Olympics and the World Cup*, Washington, DC: Brookings Institution Press.

2

THE SOVEREIGNTY PARADOX: NEGOTIATING VALUES AMID TRIBAL ADAPTATION TO SHALE OIL EXTRACTION

Jacqline Wolf Tice
David Casagrande

Introduction

Since 2008, oil and gas extraction underneath Fort Berthold Indian Reservation in western North Dakota's Bakkan Formation has brought undeniable economic benefit to the Mandan Hidatsa Arikara (MHA) Nation, but not without equally undeniable externalized costs. These social, environmental, and cultural externalities, documented here through interviews and surveys, are drawn from a one-month field residency at Ft. Berthold to listen to tribal members and observe their experiences.[1] Expected fears of the future and frustration with extraction industry practices (EIP) are evident, but the predominant sentiments reported are arguably conflicted, even among those actively organizing against drilling. Rage and resignation at the environmental disruption is coupled with relief from the oppression of financial insecurity and promise of tribal sovereignty. These findings highlight a complex paradox within the *lived experience* of the MHA whereby the intersection of tribal societies and the dominant society on contractual economic terms demands a comingling of models in which the integrity of culture exists spatially regardless of environmental constraints and impacts. It also leads us to seriously consider the words of tribal elder, Elgin Crows Breast: "I think all this stuff was put here at some certain time for the People to use. But it's where you start abusing it is where we start getting it wrong."

This chapter examines historical and current sociopolitical contexts of the economic, environmental, and cultural issues facing the MHA Nation as they navigate their collective roles in an unprecedented oil boom. Our intent is to provide a lens whereby the effects of the extraction industry at Ft. Berthold (FB) can be seen on a continuum of values—from concrete/functional to conceptual/

This chapter is dedicated to the memory and life causes of Elgin (Fast Horse) Crows Breast and Barbara Young Bird—JWT.

ideal—and to articulate how that perception predicts ways the sustainability movement could impede sovereignty for fossil fuel-rich energy tribes. Our continuum attends to the enduring debate in cultural anthropology about the importance of ideational-versus-functional scales of motivation of cultural actors. People's beliefs about what an ideal world should be are often incongruent with what they actually do on a daily basis.

The existing discourse of sustainability rests on a continuum of values ranging from public-private partnerships in an "ecocorporatism" frame (Janicke 1996) to green activists boldly localizing initiatives in marginalized communities while, however unintentionally, disempowering the same vis-à-vis elitist, whitish, and, ultimately, unrepresentative frameworks (Blowers 2003). The objective presupposition of equity within "just sustainabilities" is to address the "multiscalar links between environmental quality and human equality" (Agyeman, Bullard, & Evans 2003: 324). However, who decides this in the context of sovereign Indigenous nations? Ideally, although environmental/cultural/economic/political integrity may align seeking justice, the paradox of sovereignty is that it challenges the framework that defines the coexistence of entitlement to equity while asserting sustainable means of *inherent* tribal sovereignty. As "distinct, independent, political communities retaining their original natural rights" (*see Worcester v. Georgia, 31 US 515, 1832; Cohen 1942*), we argue sovereignty is, implicitly, the lens through which justice and sustainability are understood by the MHA and, in general, Indigenous peoples. By responding to *that* position, we begin to contextualize the deeper landscape of values and meanings guiding tribal energy policies.

Our analysis is based on in-depth interviews with MHA tribal members and explores conflicting values and ethical dissonance as access to newfound prosperity intersects "entangled landscapes of power" internal to the tribe (Powell 2018). The dialectic within the sovereignty-by-extraction paradigm merits thoughtful consideration by energy tribes and environmentalists concerned with cultural integrity. Sovereignty describes a functional condition whereby a distinct population exercises economic, political, cultural, and territorial means for self-determination. As a concept, sovereignty relies on intrinsic philosophical values and assumptions formed and informed by localized (in this case, Indigenous) social conventions (Gillroy 2001). For the MHA, social forms and conventions, as well as tribal perceptions, appear to be shifting and emerging along with the oil boom.

From the expansive prairies and breathtaking Badlands south of Mandaree to Lake Sakakawea's ubiquitous presence at the heart of the reservation, oil development at FB imposes its sprawling mark on the environment vis-à-vis pumping jacks, drill rigs, injection wells, sand piles, gas flares, and storage tanks. Increased tribal revenue through oil development on the reservation has correlated with rising social tensions and crime, illicit drug use, sex trafficking, vehicular deaths, and uncertainty associated with the environmental, political, and economic changes at Ft. Berthold. Meanwhile, fossil fuel extraction presents to some tribal members, and the governing Tribal Business Council, a legitimate economic pursuit toward sovereignty amid its complicated politics and modification of cultural norms and values. Scholars and environmentalists have an obligation to challenge their romanticized stereotypes of Indian peoples' values as antithetical to economic development versus environmental preservation (Rosser 2010). Anything less does not admit the evolving capacity of energy tribes to emergent technological innovations, as well as culturally relevant and imaginative Indigenous policies in the twenty-first century.

Our analysis explores some conflicting values, presenting as *disruption* and measured as *dissonance*, in our scales and indices. The conundrum of assessment, through the lens of the socio-ecological *lived experience* of the MHA Nation at Ft. Berthold, is that observations and analyses are, necessarily, subjective and interpretive despite documentation. To square this bias, we include direct quotes throughout the chapter. The MHA's lived experience poses unexpected answers to questions about sustainability and justice, cultural ecology, and the political economic construction of space. Although Indian[2] people are culturally heterogeneous, extraction as a colonial enterprise does threaten fundamental Indigenous land ethics and cultural norms. Historical associations, therefore, should not be dismissed (Rosser 2010) and contextualize why, as a place-based culture, we contend oil development on the scale experienced at Fort Berthold introduces cognitive and ethical dissonance. How the MHA manages that dissonance is intrinsically bound to their functional and ideal exercise of sovereignty, defined on their own terms.

Living Relationship: Sovereignty and Trust as Indigenous Land Ethic

We began this work situating disruption and dissonance of the cultural ecology of the MHA within Aldo Leopold's (1949) "land ethic." Generally, values implied by the term "land ethic" are historically observed in localized economic and social dynamics of tribal entities (Murray et al. 2011). However, *land ethic* is a Western environmental construct, a non-Indigenous frame, and is, therefore, "limited in application" (Callicott 2013: 4). It does not consider *inherent sovereignty of tribes as the critical component* impacting governance, land use, jurisdiction, economy, sociocultural values, and decision-making. Tribes are set apart from other social subgroups by their distinct political identity, unbound from the race, class, and gender otherization addressed by distributive and environmental justice mechanisms found within the context of just sustainabilities (Agyeman 2013). For tribes, sovereignty *is* the implicit lens and paradigm through which the intersection of race, class, justice, and the *land ethic* is understood. It must, therefore, be the center pole of any discussion deliberating just sustainabilities in an Indigenous context.

Tribal elder Calvin Grinnell wrote, "Hills are sacred because there's spirits living in them… this water is really holy, it's sacred, and we live through the water… we still continue to communicate and beseech for help in the rains that come… for medicinal plants and for red paint [clay earth]" (Grinnell n.d.). The *living relationship* described by Grinnell between people, land, water, spirits—and their intrinsic purpose for being—demonstrates both functional and conceptual Indigenous intersectionality of principles found in justice frameworks. These principles are challenged by economic stratification of that *living relationship* vis-à-vis extraction industry practices (EIP). Economic value superseding relational value of kin (human and otherwise) challenges conventions embodied in MHA cultural memory and milieu. The social and historical infrastructure of the Three Affiliated Tribes is built on a communal economy and trust. Although all MHA tribal members receive general disbursements, including from the People's Fund,[3] as a result of oil and gas drilling, the asymmetrical force of wealth disparity taking place since the arrival of EIP directly upsets societal and familial balancing mechanisms previously secured by sociocultural norms and *idealized* shared values. Research shows greater relative inequality within communities portends poorer outcomes across health and social factors (Wilkinson & Pickett 2009). Increased social hierarchy also negatively impacts more subtle psychosocial dynamics, such as trust (Wilkinson & Pickett 2009), posing an existential risk to the MHA's cultural fabric. An elder recalls a time before another major colonial disruptor to the reservation—the 1953 construction of the Garrison Dam:

> Before that... everybody spoke Hidatsa there. When you went to visit... [they'd] take care of you and feed you. In those days too, it was really bad wintertime when we had the high snows. The doors were left open so if you lived in the country and you... couldn't make it home... you would stop at a house—even if they weren't home... you would go in there, start a fire, cook a meal, and sleep there a couple nights if you have to. But you clean everything up for them... and leave it the way you found it.... and maybe the next month, or in the Springtime, when you see them, you would tell them, "Oh, I was at your house, you know"... So, everybody trusted each other... that was the culture I knew at that time. (interview #NTAI-1, female elder)

Her narrative provides a lens into a historically embedded, culturally enduring value of the MHA Nation—*trust*. The Missouri River, home to the MHA, was a major trading route from the seventeenth through the early nineteenth centuries. Pemmican, corn, and hides offered by tribes were exchanged for cloth, metal implements, and glass beads from the Europeans. Intratribal trading focused on food and horses, and adoption ceremonies, which served as "diplomatic lubricant" (Fenn 2014: 231) against conflict. Bowers (1965) writes of the "reciprocal obligations and duties" (103) between relatives as well as villages "unifying... social[ly] integrating populations" (77). The Arikara formed "kinship ties with non-related individuals through ritual adoption" frequently "extended to traders and other whites" (Parks 1996: 93). These relationships were the basis for, according to Bowers (1950), "restricting warfare and promoting trade" (44). Reciprocity and trust are functional and conceptual signifiers of the MHA Nation. These signifiers not only bind people together but extend to *place*, which was traditionally managed based on kin ties and spiritual principles. Oil and gas extraction impacts *place* and disrupts historic *living relationship* values.

Unearthing the Sovereignty-by-Extraction Paradox

Socio-ecological approaches consider impacts on cultural systems within physical, societal, and interpersonal environments. According to Agyeman (2013), culture is a "complex, dynamic, and embodied set of realities in which people (re)create identities, meanings, and values" (136). Oil extraction is more than its impacts upon cultural systems though; it is a pervasive narrative (a norm or ethic) informing processes and relationships, shaping and challenging shared values, and monetizing constructs of "fetishism and consumption [that] specifically channel the way we inhabit and use our environment" (Oliver-Smith 2015; Jalbert et al. 2017). Land, and its conversion to revenue—an exploited *resource*—sits at a particularly critical locus for Indigenous cultures within the United States at this time. It is estimated that Indian reservations contain almost 30 percent of the coal reserves west of the Mississippi, 50 percent of potential uranium reserves, and 20 percent of known oil and gas reserves (U.S. Senate 2010; Anderson 2016). These facts require a more profound and nuanced study of the role of fossil fuel resources as an arbiter and potential liberator of tribal nations from centuries of economic dependency on settler governments and their constraining agendas. Any discussion of just sustainabilities as it relates to place-based communities must consider that some Native American tribes have been "allotted" a historical kismet by *claiming as home* some of the richest fossil fuel reserves in the United States. Evaluating just sustainabilities requires a longue durée perspective (Casagrande & Peters 2013) to avoid distortions inherent in short-term snapshots. In the culturally significant view of making decisions for the next seven generations, the irony of reservations as isolated and, at times, oppressive lands is not lost on Indian people.

Western civilization's historic imperialist conquests on Indian lands contradict inherent Indigenous *land ethics* (sovereignty) by indoctrinating expansion, development, and capitalistic pursuits vis-à-vis excessive mining of natural resources and promotion of export-driven, market-based globalized consumption. This *extraction ethic* challenges MHA cultural and conceptual perceptions of ancestral integrity while also introducing the functional impacts of oil as a *resource curse*. Auty and Gelb (2001) explain the negative relationship between oil-rich resource development and institutional stability (governance, infrastructures) as an outcome of rapid (rabid) production leading to corruption and the slow burn between a boom and a bust.

Jos Aguto, former policy advisor for the National Congress of American Indians on Climate Change, Clean Energy, Natural Resources, and the Environment, laments that the traditional relationship Native Americans have with the land has been tarnished by the influences of mainstream Western culture. Forced by poor economic and social systems to become part of a larger commerce stream rather than by resources on their own lands, "the resource curse visits the Indigenous people, and they're forced into the most profound conflict: do I extract coal, uranium, and oil and gas inconsistent with my values, yet knowing my people are unemployed? That's the cosmic choice that so many tribes have tragically had to encounter" (Halpert 2012).

Indigenous sovereignty requires cultural dynamism not be preordained by colonial mechanisms. Rachel Carson (1962) famously said, "The question is whether any civilization can wage relentless war on life without destroying itself, and without losing the right to be called civilized." As long as economic benefit contributing to tribal sovereignty is acquired and defined within the resource extraction ethic, a deep contestation is present for some Indians, as well as non-Indian advocates and environmentalists. To paraphrase Carson, a question for tribes may be whether any energy tribe can wage economic sovereignty-by-extraction without losing the right to call themselves Indian. We argue that rejecting this judgment requires a paradigmatic shift away from stereotyping Indigenous peoples as colonized entities toward recognition of a people who exercise sovereignty on their own terms, not by the interpretation of Westernized land ethics or colonial mechanisms. Conflict and cognitive dissonance signify something is changing, and the values and outcomes attached to that change are determined by internal individual and cultural limits.

"Indian" is a political, cultural, and socio-tribal descriptor that protects continuity of a sovereign identity historically undermined by neoliberal ideals and colonial assimilation policies. While we do not define Indianness or determine who or what is Indian-enough,[4] the ethics of identity have historical relevance which does call us to acknowledge that, within our interviews, there were some who see pro-oil Indians as having "lost their way."

According to DeLoria (1988), the foundational social and cultural infrastructure of tribes existed even when assimilation was compelled by federal policies. Legal solutions have provided the most enduring responses to the challenges of territorial, political, and cultural subversion since First Contact, leaving open opportunities to "experiment with new social forms" (266). Casagrande and Vasquez (2009) define culture in general as "the social relationships, moral guidelines, and historical trajectories of identity and practice that provide a template for continuous experimentation in how to live correctly." Fossil fuel production is one of those experiments in process.

Sovereignty and Justice

"Indian tribes are independent, sovereign nations whose inherent right to self-determine predates contact with Euro-American peoples" (Bradford 2004: 74). Tribes are *extraconstitutional*,[5] meaning the US Constitution does not apply to "tribal exercises of inherent, retained authority" (Anderson et al. 2015: 325). Justice Sandra Day O'Connor (1997), in her call to make the "dispensation of justice… fair, efficient and principled," lauded the valuable influence of tribal customs and beliefs on its judicial processes (6). The government-to-government relationship between the United States and tribes is wholly distinct from any other group of Americans, underscoring the following facts. Energy resources have been part of the discourse of tribal sovereignty for over fifty years. The Council of Energy Resource Tribes (CERT) is a consortium of Native Nations formed in the 1970s, in part, as a response to the Organization for Petroleum Export Corporations (OPEC) oil embargo. The aim of CERT is to increase Native American control over tribal energy resources, which have an estimated total value of nearly $1.5 trillion (Anderson 2016). This wealth is greater than the combined GDPs of Sweden and Switzerland (World Bank 2020), and avers the economic power of Native Americans, if these reserves were under a united umbrella of one (tribal) nation, as equal to and greater than that of many United Nations member states. Instead, however, the functional status of the 573 federally recognized Native American nations, who administrate civil and criminal court systems, manage tribal governments and conduct unique customary practices, is part of the fractionated tribal identity which has, until relatively recently, been weakened by federal Indian policies. Throughout much of the seventeenth and eighteenth centuries, Indigenous tribes were "officially" regarded with the same primacy as international sovereigns. While the United States sought to expand its territories, legal precedence for treaty-making (even as most treaties were later broken) was customarily observed, especially with Eastern tribes. With the 1871 Indian Appropriations Act, Congress ended treaty making with Indian tribes. As instruments, treaties expressly acknowledged the inherent sovereignty of tribes; their ending marked the beginning of the Assimilation Era in federal Indian policy (Royster, Bloom, & Kronk 2013). The nineteenth-century discovery of fossil fuel resources in Indian country is one of the contributing factors that tipped the scales and emboldened "a policy officially designated as being the compulsory assimilation of American Indians into the dominant (Euroamerican) society" (Churchill 1993: 52).

Oppression of tribal identity and sovereignty is evidenced throughout federal statutory history by dishonored treaties,[6] the General Allotment Act,[7] the Indian Minerals Licensing Act,[8] Termination Era policies,[9] the Indian Relocation Act,[10] boarding schools, and countless judicial decisions limiting tribal sovereignty. The Indian Commerce Clause (1787) gives Congress the "power to regulate commerce with Foreign nations, between States, and with Indian tribes" (US Const art. I, §8, cl. 3), recognizing tribes as equal with foreign sovereigns (Ablavsky 2015). It is also considered the source for prohibiting tribal land transactions without federal authority and of Plenary Power, a judicially created doctrine granting Congress "near-full authority over Indian affairs" (Helton 2003). This doctrine limits sovereignty for tribes and, according to some scholars, is "structurally incompatible" with tribal self-determination (Wilkins & Lomawaima 2001; Bradford 2004). Paradoxically, Plenary Power grounds the special *trust relationship* between Indian tribes and the federal government, which recognizes tribal sovereignty as official US policy and charges the federal government with responsibilities in the best interest of tribes. Notwithstanding a century of inconsistent and progressively assimilative policies, in 1970, President Richard M. Nixon declared a new federal Indian policy of "self-determination without termination," launching the current Self-Determination Era. Since then, Congress has been consistently supportive of tribal governance and tribal economic development, despite modern Supreme Court decisions to the contrary (Echohawk 2003). The 2005 Indian Tribal Energy Development and Self Determination Act finally gave tribes the ability to negotiate directly with corporations to lease tribal land for resource development. However, it specifically requires tribes to first obtain a Tribal Energy Resource Agreement (TERA) with the Department of the Interior, which entails strict adherence to and demonstration of sufficient capacity to regulate the development of all contracts. Unfortunately, conditions for the TERA are so complex that tribal participation has been nearly nonexistent, as energy tribes struggle to function on a playing field supported by policies assuming Indian incompetence (Mills 2017). Bureaucratic approval and regulatory oversight of lease agreements is slow on tribal land, which systematically delays potential economic relief for tribal members reeling from decades of poverty and unemployment. These delays also reinforce corrupt market practices of oil and gas corporations who, while filling the reelection coffers of politicians, garner better profit margins by leasing Indian land at lower prices (Deloria 1985; Churchill 1993). Is this intentional or just red tape? During the Obama era, the Helping Expedite and Advance Responsible Tribal Home Ownership Act of 2012[11] addressed the difficult regulatory hurdles of leasing tribal surface land, opening the way for speedier renewable energy development, but it does not apply to leasing of energy sources like gas and oil.

Stereotypes of anti-development Indians are misguided, but not all energy tribe Indians are pro-oil (Fletcher 2017). Many energy tribes have taken up the cause of development to expand greater sovereignty (Royster 1997; Mills 2017). Some oppose fossil fuel development and have, instead, successfully developed renewables. The Campo Kumeyaay Nation operates the Kumeyaay Wind Farm, supplying 30,000 San Diego homes with renewable energy. In 2015, six tribal nations in South Dakota formed the Oceti Sakowin Power Authority[12] to jointly address developing renewable energy resources with expectations of generating up to two gigawatt of emissions-free electricity with a capacity for sixty gigawatt on tribal lands. While conflicting interests set the stage for potential competing claims of "tribal energy against tribal environments" (Fletcher 2017), cultural integrity and internally cultivated expectations for tribal sovereignty require respect and commitment to process, as well as new approaches to energy policy.

MHA Nation Case Study

Overview

Touted as the next Saudi Arabia (Cross 2011), the US Geological Survey (USGS) in 2013 estimated there are over 7.4 billion barrels (BBO) of recoverable oil in the Bakkan Formation, which stretches from Eastern Montana into Western North Dakota and across the Canadian border (Figure 2.1). At peak production, Ft. Berthold supplied one-third of North Dakota's total oil output. The present (FY2019) rate is about one-fifth. Like Williston, ND, ground zero for Bakkan oil drilling, FB has been brandished by media (Fixico & Fixico 2011; Marcus 2014; McDonald & Sontag 2014) documenting the tribe's increased costs of living, transient workers, sex trafficking, crime spikes, corruption, traffic deaths, and increased drug activity.

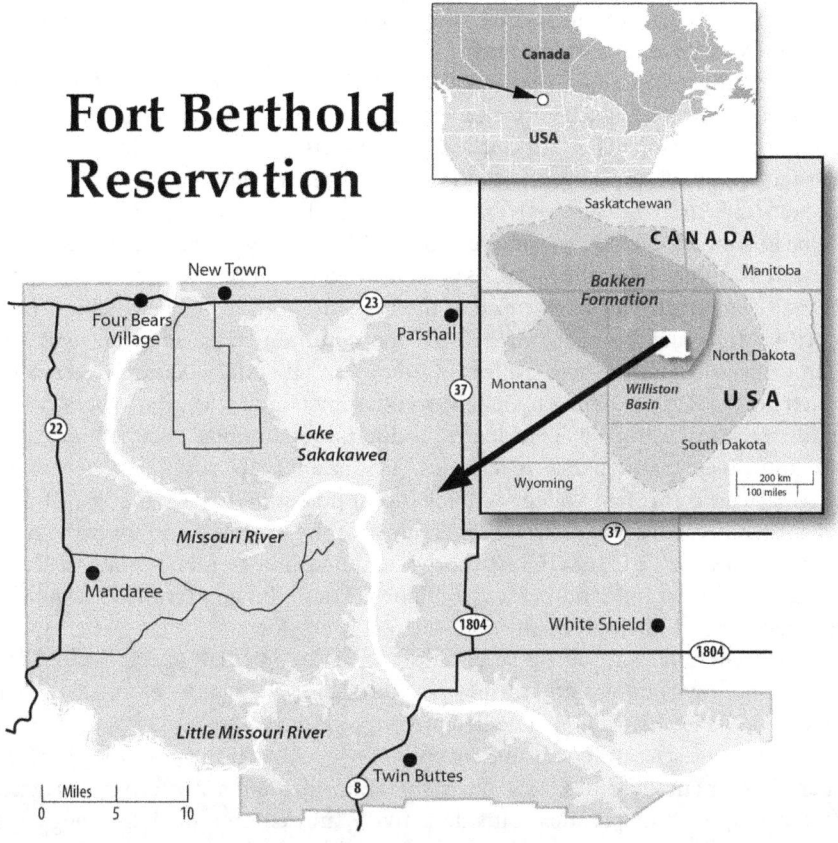

Figure 2.1 The location of Fort Berthold Reservation within the oil-rich Bakken Shale creates a paradox of using oil development to promote sovereignty without sacrificing the traditional land ethic of the Mandan, Hidatsa, and Arikara who live there. Our survey and interviews were conducted with tribal members from New Town, Mandaree, and Parshall.

The first Bakkan oil well on Fort Berthold Reservation, drilled in April 2008, produced 10,000 bbl/d by 2009. Wells are producing 300,000 bbl/day in 2019 (Ogden 2019). This increase is naturally reflected in its "before-oil" annual tribal government budgets of $5 million (Lustgarten 2013) compared to FY2019 combined General Fund, Special Projects and Investment budgets of over $300 million. Add to that the Disbursements budget of $39 million for tribal members, and the five Segment Operation and Development budget of $48 million.[13] Certainly, there is incentive and renewed intent to continue leasing land for oil and gas extraction on the reservation. A 2019 tax-sharing compact signed by North Dakota governor, Doug Burgum, guarantees the tribe 80 percent of taxes from new drilling on trust land, and 20 percent from private fee lands (Dalrymple 2019). This new arrangement increases oil tax revenue for the tribe and is an example of how the MHA exercises sovereignty.

When the extraction industry flooded the reservation, the infrastructure of FB had neither capacity for nor expectation of the demands of the revenue stream or the tsunami of socioeconomic impacts that would follow. They have learned, adapted, and applied solutions over the last decade. In June 2015, the first official MHA 100 percent tribally chartered oil production company, Missouri River Resources (MRR), began operating at FB. The royalty rate return is over 26 percent as opposed to the typical 18 percent for outsider oil production (Holdman 2016). This venture localizes more of the revenue from drilling, which translates to tribal jobs and economic benefit in the community. In addition, MRR has teamed up with the San Juan College of Energy and the MHA Nation's reservation-based Nueta Hidatsa Sahnish College to offer an associate degree program in oil industrial studies, such as petroleum production operations, occupational safety, and industrial maintenance mechanics (Holdman 2016). Building the capacity of tribal youth through college scholarship opportunities is another step toward utilizing oil resources to advance sovereignty of the tribe and empower the future of its people. In 2017, the Crestwood Mahgiddashda Center, a state-of-the-art Head Start Center in Mandaree, was built on a $1 million grant from an oil pipeline company operating at FB (Dalrymple 2016).

Researchers on and off FB reservation have documented social ills, burdens, health and environmental hazards (Vengosh 2013; Thompson et al., 2016; Wolf Tice 2016; Fletcher 2017) associated with oil development at FB. However, evidence suggests extraction and sovereignty-by-extraction is both limiting and liberating for energy tribes. As it exists, this conundrum is a Western construct. By focusing on this paradox, outside activists and environmentalists negate the potential for Indigenous constructions of paradoxes and solutions.

Current Political Climate

While the Obama administration (2008–17) attempted to expand tribal sovereignty by increasing funding and dialogue, reducing regulatory burdens, and expanding tribal jurisdiction, the Trump administration's FY2020 budget called for over $1.2 billion in overall cuts to the Bureau of Indian Affairs (U.S. Government Publishing Office 2020). According to the US Department of Commerce's Tribal Resource Guide, the "Indian Country Is Open for Business" agenda prioritizes making available Indian land for resource development. Federal regulations and wait times for drilling permits have long been an obstacle for tribes developing fossil fuels. However, the Trump administration's regulatory rollbacks for the oil and gas industries combined with its imposed and proposed reduction of federal public lands such as Bear's Ears National Monument (sacred land of the Ute, Diné, Zuni, and Hopi) endanger overall Indian sovereignty by violating the Trust Doctrine and threatening cultural properties. In the short run, privatizing resource development may supply faster economic relief to energy tribes through corporate ventures, but the longue durée suggests continued loss of sovereignty. In the words of Tom Goldtooth (Diné/Dakota) of the Indigenous Environmental Network, "Our spiritual leaders are opposed to the privatization of our lands, which means the commoditization of the nature, water, and air we hold sacred. Privatization has been the goal since colonization—to strip Native Nations of their sovereignty" (Blades 2017). Instead, tribally run enterprises such as Southern Ute Indian Tribe's Red Willow Production Company and MHA's Missouri River Resources empower tribal control of resources in Indian Country and deliver material benefit to tribal members. The Rosebud Sioux Tribe of South Dakota have recently partnered with Native Energy of Vermont on the first tribally owned large-scale 750KW wind turbine in Indian country (Indigenous Environmental Network 2018). By directly powering the tribal casino, this model establishes a replicable renewable energy venture without compromising tribal sovereignty. It may not meet the existing framework criteria of "just sustainabilities" but introduces a different way to contextualize that criteria. The significance is not that this project is environmentally sustainable but that the tribe is animating their sovereignty as a negotiation of their values. It is this dialectic of negotiation that allows the tribe to sustain cultural integrity as they adapt to shifting ecological and political contexts.

Negotiated Values

To understand how the paradox of sovereignty is situated within the lived experience of the MHA, we employed both quantitative and qualitative methods. Surveys were distributed to approximately fifty people on Ft. Berthold Indian Reservation. A thirty-question Likert scale survey was derived by combining an existing survey used to measure the effects of natural gas extraction upon Pennsylvania residents (Cooley & Casagrande 2017) with additional statements addressing cultural context developed from personal experiences and observations of traditional Indigenous knowledge and practices among the MHA Nation (Wolf Tice 2016).

Nineteen surveys were returned. We conducted in-depth interviews with eight MHA Nation member respondents. For context and analysis of survey data, we grouped related questions into categories representing indices revealing individual attitudes about environmental impacts and cultural beliefs regarding extraction practices (EIPSI), ethical considerations (LES), socioeconomic effects, and policy perceptions relating to EIP. Here, we report specific data found in the LES and EIPSI[14] with supporting qualitative data from our interviews.

The LES shows 89.5 percent of respondents ($n = 19$) experience *high or very high dissonance levels*, 10.5 percent report *moderate dissonance*, with 25 percent of responses to this scale reporting the maximum score ($max = 25$). This measure of dissonance describes the magnitude at which these respondents are challenged by EIP's impact upon MHA traditional cultural properties (Grinnell n.d.) and the cultural/ethical responsibility to respect and protect sacred places as keepers of ancestral spirits, medicines, and ceremonies. Our research also shows a significant negative correlation exists at the *.05 level* with the EIPSI, suggesting that personal approval of oil extraction conflicts with cultural values relating to land.

> You won't be able to recover the CO_2 in the atmosphere and put it back into the oil again. You've already used it. Other generations won't be able to use it and maybe we shouldn't be using it. We're compromising your generation, the future generations, your grandchildren... (interview #NT-10, male, educator)

The first question in the field interviews for this research asked each respondent to describe what is most important (valuable) in their life at FB. While most respondents gave more than one answer, this question revealed, collectively, similar answers: *environment, land, homeland, be close to the "people," children, family, Indian ways, spirituality, commitment to prayer, health, culture, work ethic, education, communication, respect.* The contrast of *functional* versus *conceptual* cultural values is apparent within this list. Functional values are bounded by their bearing on the *lived* experience—land, children, family, health, education, work, spirituality—whereas conceptual cultural values such as respect and homeland express a type of idealized *felt* experience. One historical and deeply embedded conceptual value of the MHA Nation was offered by a respondent requesting complete anonymity, who quite remarkably articulated the *spirit* of the MHA by saying simply, "We are a giving people."

Most identifiable values in this sample are of the instrumental/functional type. Subjective context and *lived experience* describe functional contexts. The existing subjective context of the MHA is *shaped* within the *common culture of community* influenced by the historical processes of assimilation and acculturation. However, it is *defined* (identified) by the socioeconomic, sociopolitical, and socio-ecological *experience of life* at Ft. Berthold. Harmon (2010) describes the "inconsistencies inherent in hegemony" (181) as dominated cultures navigate the distortion between ideology (felt experience) and practice (lived experience).

> So I don't understand how we lost who we are... you have leadership that made decisions for us and who wheel and deal in the oil and gas and who only think of the money right now and don't think of the aftermath. (interview #M-18, female, activist)

Another respondent said,

> The Tribe puffs up its chest and talks about Tribal Sovereignty—but in reality, they don't have the Codes,[15] they don't have the Law. (interview #M-31, female, elder)

As revealed in our interviews, formalized ceremonies and sacrifices are regularly made for the "spirits" of nature—animals, bodies of water, plants, earth as Mother (Byrd 2011; Fixico & Fixico 2011). The following interview excerpt illustrates the depth of a *conceptual* relationship with the Earth and the *functions* assigned to maintain that relationship. It is as if the spirit of the oil is an ancient ancestor and therefore, treated like a relative.

> I: ... everything has a spirit that is natural... water, sun, moon, stars, dirt, grass, they all have a spirit... trees, animals...
> JWT: Let me ask you a question about that oil... Do you think that oil has a spirit?
> I: Yeah.
> JWT: And... if that oil has a spirit, could we...
> I: You could talk to them.
> JWT: I would like to know somebody that maybe did that...
> I: If you really want to know, then you gotta go and pray and offer some food because everything eats. Where they're [the spirits] from, they make it a whole bunch, you know, kind of like a smorgasbord, kinda like you put chicken or meat and corn, over there on that side [spirit world], they make it just huge and all the spirits come and eat... I do all that. (interview #NT-14, male, elder)

This ties back to Grinnell's relational value of kin (human and otherwise) embodied in the MHA cultural memory and milieu. We see similar practices of respect toward spiritual relatives across the Indigenous diaspora. Relationships with kin, human or spiritual, are complicated and based on ideational and functional trade-offs.

Writer, former Green Party vice presidential nominee and Anishinaabe activist, Winona LaDuke, similarly describes this relationship:

> According to our way of looking, the world is animate... Natural things are alive; they have a spirit. Therefore, when we harvest wild rice on our reservation, we always offer tobacco to the earth because, when you take something, you must always give thanks to its spirit for giving itself to you.
>
> (LaDuke 1996)

Cultural disruption of values via some form of ethical dissonance may not be visible through expected signifiers nor explicitly appear with unequivocal context. However, our data describe functions and ideals of cultural values captured in the nuance of "local customary idiom" by which social systems are maintained and expressed (Sahlins 1999). Repeatedly it is shown we cannot assume homogeneity of identifiable attitudes. The following excerpts capture this.

> I: I really kind of believe we should hold the BIA to their responsibilities. Including health, including education, all the promises that they made... I'm all for independence and the tribe helping and taking control of some of that, but I think we let the Feds off way too easy. Taking that power back—yeah that's good, but it's not.
> JWT: The sovereignty issue seems to be a major component in how people

> interpret their relationship to the BIA and the US. But what you're saying is we have to hold their feet to the fire…
>
> I: I believe we do—I believe we should hold their feet to the fire because those were promises that were made to us.
>
> JWT: In treaties?
>
> I: Yeah… and… uh… I have mixed feelings too so I'm all for sovereignty and making our rules, and taking care of ourselves, and governing ourselves, but to what extent… Do we have to pay for it ourselves too?
>
> JWT: At what cost?
>
> I: Yea—make the policies and do all that but don't let them get off scot free you know…
>
> (interview, #NTB-12, female, self-employed)

Clearly, for this member, realization of this ideal is eclipsed by a deeper recognition that the history of genocide and the injustices of stolen land and broken treaties against Native Peoples can never really be repaid through compensatory damages. The challenge perhaps is not to redress the past so much as to ensure current Western perspectives, including environmentalism, are not recreating the injustices of the past regardless of contemporary constructions of moral patronage.

Problems in policy process and community participation, which can protect from unintended (or intended) environmental or social consequences within a population, are common in large-scale resource development ventures (Finkel, Hays, & Law 2013). Many of the respondents receive revenue from oil leases in which they own only portions of allotment land parcels,[16] resulting in fragmented revenue apportionment. While the Extraction Industry Practices Satisfaction Index (EIPSI) shows 48 percent of respondents *dissatisfied* with EIP on FB, a full 41.2 percent of respondents are *satisfied*, and less than 6 percent are *very dissatisfied*. These data suggest that over a third of the respondents' changes to their lived experience as a result of extraction, although not risk-free, are mitigated by some benefits. These favorable indicators traced to oil development cannot be eschewed.

Quantifying the dissonance, though, suggests a different level of *dispossession* or *covert culture conquest* (Teske & Nelson 1974) is threatening the MHA by undermining ethical constructs normalized within this unique group through social relationships. The following two quotes, spoken thirty minutes apart in the same interview, illustrate the dissonance between the functional and conceptual, while framing another complexity within the sovereignty paradox.

> We got ripped off just like everybody else. Why don't you get [X]'s lease and see what [X]'s lease says? It just doesn't seem right. How come he's a multi-millionaire and my mom isn't?

And, thirty minutes later:

> If I could do it all over, I wouldn't agree with the oil extraction cause it's destroying who we are. People have lost their way… (interview #M-18, female, activist)

Activist groups, such as the Protectors of Water and Earth Rights (POWER) at Ft. Berthold, are pushing back on oil's negative impacts, even as they accept its emerging value to the tribe. One of its founders, tribal member Lisa DeVille, explains, "You gotta learn how to deal with it. At first, I was upset, angry, but I thought, 'it's here no matter what'. It's not gonna go away, but we have to make sure and hold industry accountable, liable for what they're doing to us. But we also need to create laws to enforce them" (Wolf Tice 2016: 80).

Finding Our Way

Place-based cultures have a unique and distinct psychosocial identity as it relates to land, which provides a functional and conceptual grounding for religious, subsistence, cosmologic, aesthetic, ecologic, epistemological, mythic, etiologic, and critical logic frameworks. Preserving these frameworks ensures cultural continuity and is the ethical basis for just sustainabilities. The significance of multigenerational inhabitance upon a specific land base not only is intrinsic to genetic (and epigenetic) factors affecting quality of life but also impacts existential characteristics of affect, emotion, and feeling as central components of "place attachment" (Altman & Low 1992: 4). Introducing disrupting elements to that sense of place impacts homeostasis on all levels. For purveyors of the sustainability movement, and for Indigenous peoples, transcendence of the sovereignty paradox requires recognition of tribal histories, goals, systems of knowledge, and production choices as implicit and emergent Indigenous lifeways choices by sovereign nations: people with political decision-making rights "instead of vulnerable people" (Zea 2019: 4). The MHA Nation members interviewed for this research do not self-identify as victims. They persist by *co-Indigenizing*[17] the opportunity brought to the reservation by extraction industry practices and use the tools as a map to exercise sovereignty. The agency of this act is consistent with the MHA's historic characteristic of *trust*. However, political plays by self-interested individual members impact the tribe at-large and have presented structural challenges, leading some to believe there is an "occupation going on here" (interview #M-31, female, elder).

They have a point.

A "sustainable society must also be an equitable society... within and between generations" (Agyeman et al. 2003: 323). Solutions of justice for tribes are culturally relative and must be framed within the cultural constructs of that culture (Binder 1999); in this case, through the narrative of sovereignty. The promise of oil and gas development is that it expands opportunities for tribal economic sovereignty, which embraces both political and territorial spaces across generations. Values associated with the cultural identity of the MHA and standards we associate with least disruption (distributive, social, and environmental justice frameworks) may provide answers to the paradox of sovereignty; however, as long as paternalistic attitudes and directives still exist as laws and policies, tribal sovereignty via Indian land resources will be limited by politically and legally fractionated interests. The Supreme Court's *M'Intosh*[18] (1823) decision, written by Chief Justice John

Marshall, cleverly anointed Indians as "occupants," not owners of their land, and laid the groundwork for Indian policy and how dominant society perceives tribes to this day. Justice advocates must be more respectful of horizontal dialogue. We know, for example, that capitalism drives climate change (Gilio-Whitaker 2019), a leading rationale for the just sustainabilities argument. The UN Permanent Forum on Indigenous Issues recommends climate change policies incorporate Indigenous knowledge in projects and programs to reduce disaster risk in a participatory way (Zea 2019). But current corporate trends in social responsibility aim to mitigate greenhouse gas and carbon emissions still prioritize economy over ecology. It is, after all, a pervasive capitalistic-mediated relationship between tribes and governments. In this framework, an analysis of money as power, and of power as a mechanism for sovereignty, suggests a more causal reading of why tribes such as the MHA are still ensconced in economic and regulatory fights for basic autonomy in decision-making and self-governance while off-reservation leases are signed, sealed, and delivered in a fraction of the time (Regan 2014). Sovereignty, though, is not a static concept. It is a negotiation of functional relationships, internal and external, and the maintenance required to ensure its continuity (Greetham 2018).

In the case of the MHA Nation, concepts like "justice" and "sustainability" become a paradox when viewed through a lens other than sovereignty. The contradiction between landscape degradation and political liberation through oil development can only be resolved in a just manner through self-determination. Trending memes, green-shaming, and laconic lingo ("Leave it in the ground!") are shallow answers to the complex choices confronting energy tribes. What then is the appropriate role of non-Indian activists or environmentalists? Is there an appropriate or just role at all? While accessing options like renewable technologies involves nontribal members, absent express invitation or tribal consent, no historical position judging or actively impeding Indian choices about development in pursuit of sovereignty is just. Non-Indian activists who cherry-pick information like quotes from community members arguing for or against oil development not only misrepresent but preclude examination of the contradictions that are the essence of adaptation required for sustainability. Ideational-functional dialectics drive adaptation and change (Casagrande & Peters 2013). We have attempted to explain why such contradictions are inevitable for historical reasons and allow for sustainable adaptation. It is up to sovereign tribes to resolve such contradictions. Diminishment of this internal right and responsibility undermines sovereignty and reproduces discursive hegemony. No theoretical framework of just sustainabilities can be universally applied that does not explicitly include cultural relativism (Groenfeldt 2003).

The MHA have an intimate, intrinsic relationship with the land, including with the carbon elements made of their ancestors and biological relatives now being exhumed as part of the Bakkan Formation. Complex parsing of internal values and justice associated with land, sovereignty, and extraction only touches the surface of their deeply rooted *lived experience* grown from thousands of years of life along the Missouri River. By making visible the contextual nature of culture and sovereignty, a reasonable discussion of something akin to *just sustainabilities* becomes functional by enlisting tribally based solutions, on MHA terms, with the same spirit of resilience and ethical relationship toward the land which is both intrinsic to the People and an ancestral sovereign birthright. Perhaps, some energy tribes become the de facto spiritual keepers and functional allotters of subterranean fossil fuel in a just, sustainable society.

> This land has the elements of the bodies and the parts that lived before us. It's used over again and again. It's going to be part of us again… (interview #NT-10, male, elder)

Notes

1. Since 2002, one of the authors (JWT) has been invited to Fort Berthold for social and traditional practices and is a ceremonially adopted member of the tribe dedicated to the well-being and sovereignty of its people and territory.
2. The terms "Indian," "Indigenous," "Native," and "Native American" are used interchangeably throughout this chapter as a form of sovereign political recognition. Tribal affiliation is specified, such as Mandan Hidatsa Arikara (MHA) or Southern Ute or Cherokee.
3. Over 15,000 MHA tribal members (both on and off reservation) receive some benefits from the tribe's trust investment via a biannual disbursement ($1,000 per tribal member over age 21) from The People's Fund. Some oil leases net hundreds of thousands of dollars per year. Oil extraction has introduced wealth disparity on FB.
4. Author and activist Vine DeLoria, Jr. (1988) wrote in *Custer Died for Your Sins*, "Indianness has been defined by whites for many years. [It] never existed except in the mind of the beholder."
5. *Talton v. Mayes*, 163 U.S. 376 (1896), is a seminal jurisdictional case involving a Cherokee, Talton, who sought intervention from the federal government on a tribal conviction citing violation of the fourteenth amendment's Due Process Clause. The finding recognized tribes as sovereign entities whose inherent *preconstitutional* authority renders rules governing grand jury numbers inapplicable to tribal criminal proceedings.
6. Treaties are protected as "Supreme law of the land." (U.S. Const. Art. 6, Cl. 2). The 1871 Indian Appropriations Act, 25 U.S.C. § 72, abruptly ended treaty making as an arbiter of US-Indian relations.
7. General Allotment (Dawes) Act, 23 Stat. 388 (1887) imposed privatization of land, dividing reservations into individual allotments and selling "surplus" to White settlers, effectively breaking up Indian Country guaranteed by treaties. In 1890, Commissioner of Indian Affairs, Thomas J. Morgan, wrote that the "settled policy of the Government" was to "break up reservations, destroy tribal relations, settle Indians upon their own homesteads" to thereby deal not with tribes but with the individuals (Ruppel 2008: 70).
8. 25 U.S.C. ch. 9 § 331 et seq (1938) provides for leasing of minerals on tribal lands without tribal consent.
9. House Concurrent Resolution 108 (1953) removed 109 tribes from federal rolls; 2.5 M acres of tribal land taken out of trust and sold to non-Indians.

10 Public Law 959 was an assimilation strategy whereby the federal government relocated Indian individuals and families to urban cities (e.g., LA, Denver, Phoenix) for job training and housing, effectively dismantling reservation communities.
11 HEARTH Act, 25 U.S.C. § 3504(e).
12 The present consortium includes Cheyenne River, Rosebud, Oglala, Yankton, Flandreau Santee, and Standing Rock Nations. See www.ospower.org.
13 MHA Resolution No. 19-012FWF (February 14, 2019). This information is public via MHANation.com/2019-resolutions.
14 The Land Ethic Scale and Extraction Industry Practices Satisfaction Scale can be found in Wolf Tice, Jacqline, "Under the Earthlodge: Extraction of the MHA Nation" (2016). Theses and Dissertations. 2879. https://preserve.lehigh.edu/etd/2879/
15 She is referring to the regulatory codes of the TERA 25 U.S.C. § 3504(e), which states, "The Secretary shall approve an agreement if the tribe has demonstrated that it has sufficient capacity to regulate the development of the tribe's energy resources" (Royster 2006).
16 The 1887 General Allotment (Dawes) Act was one of the most destructive legislative acts ever perpetrated against Native tribes. It fractionated reservation lands into checkboards by assigning land allotments in 40, 80, or 160-acre parcels to individual tribal members, which the United States then held in trust for twenty-five years before declaring an Indian "competent."
17 Co-Indigeneity is an original term based on "Indigenize," but contextualizing imposed colonial tools of modernity. It asserts Indigenous Sovereign ideology into preestablished patterns of social organization.
18 Johnson v. M'Intosh, 21 U.S. 8 Wheat. 543 (1823). The first case in the seminal Marshal Trilogy applied the Discovery Doctrine to acquisition of tribal land. See Lindsey Robertson's *Conquest by Law: How the Discovery of America Dispossessed Indigenous Peoples of Their Lands*.

References

Ablavsky, G. (2015), "Beyond the Indian commerce clause," *Yale Law Journal*, 124(4): 882.

Agyeman, J. (2013). *Introducing Just Sustainabilities: Policy, Planning, and Practice*, London: Zed Books.

Agyeman, J., R. Bullard, & B. Evans (eds) (2003), *Just Sustainabilities: Development in an Unequal World*, Cambridge: MIT Press.

Altman I. & S.M. Low (1992), "Place attachment," in I. Altman & S.M. Low (eds), *Place Attachment, Human Behavior and Environment (Advances in Theory and Research)*, Boston: Springer.

Anderson, R.T., B. Berger, S. Krakoff, & P.P. Frickey (2015), *American Indian Law: Cases and Commentary*, 3rd edn, St. Paul: West Academic.

Anderson, T. (2016), "The wealth of Indian nations," *Hoover Institution*. Available online: https://www.hoover.org/research/wealth-indian-nations-1 (Accessed May 15, 2020).

Auty, R. & A. Gelb (2001), "Political economy of resource abundant states," in R. Auty (ed.), *Resource Abundance and Economic Development*, 126–44, Oxford: Oxford University Press.

Binder, G. (1999), "Cultural relativism and cultural imperialism in human rights law," *Buffalo Human Rights Law Review*, 5: 211–22.

Blades, M. (2017), "New drive to privatize Indian reservations has much in common with past efforts to steal Native land," *Daily Kos*, December 30. Available online: https://www.dailykos.com/stories/2017/12/30/1725310/-New-drive-to-privatize-Indian-reservations-has-much-in-common-with-past-efforts-to-steal-Native-land (Accessed May 16, 2020).

Blowers, A. (2003), "Inequality and community and challenge to modernization: Evidence from the nuclear oases," in J. Agyeman, R.D. Bullard, & B. Evans (eds), *Just Sustainabilities: Development in an Unequal World*, 64–80, Cambridge: MIT Press.

Bowers, A. (1950), *Mandan Social and Ceremonial Organization*, Chicago: University of Chicago.

Bowers, A.W. (1965), *Hidatsa Social and Ceremonial Organization*, Washington, DC: U.S. Government Printing Office.

Bradford, W. (2004), "Another such victory and we are undone: A call to an American Indian declaration of independence," *Tulsa Law Review*, 40: 71–135.

Byrd, J.A. (2011), *The Transit of Empire*, Minneapolis: University of Minnesota Press.

Callicott, J.B. (2013), *Thinking Like a Planet: The Land Ethic and the Earth Ethic*, New York: Oxford University Press.

Carson, R. (1962), *Silent Spring*, Greenwich: Fawcett Publications.

Casagrande, D.G. & C. Peters (2013), "Ecomyopia meets the longue durée: An information ecology of the increasingly arid Southwestern United States," in H. Kopnina & E. Shoreman (eds), *Environmental Anthropology: Future Directions*, 97–144, New York: Routledge.

Casagrande, D.G., & M. Vasquez (2009), "Restoring for cultural-ecological sustainability in Arizona and Connecticut," in M. Hall (ed.), *Restoration and History: The Search for a Usable Environmental Past*, 195–209, New York: Routledge.

Churchill, W. (1993), *Struggle for the Land: Indigenous Resistance to Genocide, Ecocide, and Expropriation in Contemporary North America*, Monroe: Common Courage Press.

Cohen, F.S., United States. Dept. of the Interior. Office of the Solicitor (1942), *Handbook of Federal Indian Law: With Reference Tables and Index*, Washington: U.S. G.P.O.

Cooley, R., & D.G. Casagrande (2017), "Marcellus Shale as golden goose: The discourse of development and the marginalization of resistance in Northcentral Pennsylvania," in K. Jalbert, A. Willow, D. Casagrande, & S. Paladino (eds), *Extraction: Impacts, Engagements, and Alternative Futures*, 46–60, New York: Routledge.

Cross, R. (2011), "Development's victim or it's beneficiary: The impact of oil and gas development on the Fort Berthold Indian reservation," *North Dakota Law Review*, 87: 535–69.

Dalrymple, A. (2016), "Pipeline company puts $1 million for Head Start building on reservation," *Billings Gazette*, July 20. Available online: https://billingsgazette.com/news/state-and-regional/montana/pipeline-company-puts-million-for-head-start-building-on-reservation/article_991a9573-9715-513d-bd80-2bbafce70c87.html (Accessed May 15, 2020).

Dalrymple, A. (2019), "State, tribal oil tax agreement clears final hurdle," *Bismarck Tribune*, March 20. Available online: https://bismarcktribune.com/bakken/state-tribal-oil-tax-agreement-clears-final-hurdle/article_95d9b47e-920d-5ec6-9a52-300572d04aad.html (Accessed May 15, 2020).

Deloria, V. (1985), *Behind the Trail of Broken Treaties: An Indian Declaration of Independence*, Austin: University of Texas Press.

Deloria, V. (1988), *Custer Died for Your Sins: An Indian Manifesto*, Norman: University of Oklahoma Press.

Echohawk, J. (2003), "Current issues in Native American law," *University of Kansas Law Review*, 51(2): 249–67.
Fenn, E.A. (2014), *Encounters at the Heart of the World*, New York: Hill & Wang.-7238990
Finkel, M., J. Hays, & A. Law (2013), "The shale gas boom and the need for rational policy," *American Journal of Public Health*, 103(7): 1161–3.
Fixico, D., & D.L. Fixico (2011), *The Invasion of Indian Country in the Twentieth Century: American Capitalism and Tribal Natural Resources*, 2nd edn, Boulder: University Press of Colorado.
Fletcher, M. (2017), "New divisions in Indian country over energy justice," *Turtle Talk*. Available online: https://turtletalk.blog/2017/05/02/fletcher-new-divisions-in-indian-country-over-energy-justice/ (Accessed May 15, 2020).
Gilio-Whitaker, D. (2019), "The green new deal needs to do more for indigenous populations," *Slate*, July 12. Available online: https://slate.com/technology/2019/07/green-new-deal-indigenous-native-americans-environmental-justice.html (Accessed May 15, 2020).
Gillroy, J.M. (2001), *Justice and Nature: Kantian Philosophy, Environmental Policy, and the Law*, Washington, DC: University of Georgetown Press.
Greetham, S.H. (2018), "Water planning, tribal voices, and creative approaches: Seeking new paths through tribal-state water conflict by collaboration on state water planning efforts," *Natural Resources Journal*, 58(1): 457.
Grinnell, C. (n.d.), *The Significance of the Missouri River to the Mandan Hidatsa Arikara Nation*, unpublished manuscript.
Groenfeldt, D. (2003), "The future of indigenous values: Cultural relativism in the face of economic development," *Futures*, 35(9): 917–29.
Halpert, J. (2012), "Native Americans and a changing climate," *Yale Climate Connections*. Available online: https://www.yaleclimateconnections.org/2012/06/native-americans-and-a-changing-climate/ (Accessed May 15, 2020).
Harmon, A. (2010), *Rich Indians: Native People and the Problem of Wealth in American History*, Chapel Hill: University of North Carolina Press.
Helton, T. (2003), "Current issues in Native American law," *University of Kansas Law Review*, 51(2): 249–67.
Holdman, J. (2016), "Tribal oil company partners with energy educators," *Bismarck Tribune*, April 6. Available online: https://bismarcktribune.com/bakken/tribal-oil-company-partners-with-energy-educators/article_fafd27be-e0d8-53bb-bdce-c21dd8584471.html (Accessed May 18, 2020).
Indigenous Environmental Network (2018), "Energy development in Indian Country on the upsurge with concerns from tribal groups." Available online: https://www.ienearth.org/energy-development-in-indian-country/ (Accessed May 18, 2020).
Jalbert, K., A. Willow, D. Casagrande, & S. Paladino (2017), "Introduction: Confronting extraction, taking action," in K. Jalbert, A. Willow, D. Casagrande, & S. Paladino (eds), *Extraction: Impacts, Engagements, and Alternative Futures*, 1–13, New York: Routledge.
Janicke, M. (1996), "Democracy as a condition for environmental policy success: The importance of non-institutional factors," in W.M. Lafferty & J. Meadowcroft (eds), *Democracy and the Environment: Problems and Prospects*, 71–85, Cheltenham: Edward Elgar.
LaDuke, W. (1996, September/October), "Indigenous mind," *Resurgence & Ecologist*, 178: 8.
Leopold, A. (1949), *A Sand County Almanac and Sketches Here and There*, New York: Oxford University Press.

Lustgarten, A. (2013), "Land grab cheats North Dakota tribes out of $1 billion, suits allege," *Propublica*. February 23. Available online: https://www.propublica.org/article/land-grab-cheats-north-dakota-tribes-out-of-1-billion-suits-allege (Accessed May 15, 2020).

Marcus, K. (2014), "Oil boom: See a modern-day gold rush in motion," *NPR*, January 29. Available online: http://www.npr.org/2014/01/29/266757131/welcome-to-oil-country-a-modern-day-goldrushin-north-dakota (Accessed May 15, 2020).

McDonald, B. & D. Sontag (2014), "In North Dakota, a tale of oil, corruption, and death," *New York Times*, December 28. Available online: https://www.nytimes.com/2014/12/29/us/in-north-dakota-where-oil-corruption-and-bodies-surface.html (Accessed May 15, 2020).

Mills, M. (2017), "Beyond a zero-sum federal trust responsibility: Lessons from federal Indian energy policy," *American Indian Law Journal*, 6(1), Article 2.

Murray, W.F., M. Zadeño, K. Hollenback, C. Grinnell, & E. Crows Breast (2011), "The remaking of Lake Sakakawea: Locating cultural viability in negative heritage on the Missouri River," *American Ethnologist*, 38(3): 468–83.

O'Connor, S.D. (1997), "Lessons from the third Sovereign: Indian tribal courts," *Tulsa Law Journal*, 33(1): 1–6.

Ogden, E. (2019), "ND setting new records in oil and gas production," *Minot Daily News*, August 17. Available online: https://www.minotdailynews.com/news/local-news/2019/08/nd-setting-new-records-in-oil-and-gas-production/ (Accessed May 18, 2020).

Oliver-Smith, A. (2015), "Conversations in catastrophe: Neoliberalism and the cultural construction of disaster risk," in F. Kruger, G. Bankoff, T. Cannon, B. Orlowski, & L.F. Schipper (eds), *Cultures and Disasters: Understanding Cultural Framings in Disaster Risk Reduction*, 37–52, New York: Routledge.

Parks, D. (1996), *Myths and Traditions of the Arikara Indians*, Lincoln: University of Nebraska Press.

Powell, D.E. (2018), *Landscapes of Power: Politics of Energy in the Navajo Nation*, Durham: Duke University Press.

Regan, S. (2014), *Unlocking the Wealth of Indian Nations: Overcoming Obstacles to Tribal Energy Development* (No. 1), Bozeman: PERC Policy Perspective.

Robertson, L.G. (2005), *Conquest by Law: How the Discovery of America Dispossessed Indigenous Peoples of Their Lands*, Oxford: Oxford University Press.

Rosser, E. (2010), "Ahistorical Indians and reservation resources," *Environmental Law*, 40(2): 437.

Royster, J. (1997), "Oil and water in Indian country," *Natural Resources Journal*, 37(2): 457.

Royster, J. (2006), "Indian natural resources development: Tribal energy resource agreements under the energy policy act of 2005," *Trends*, 8, (May/June).

Royster, J.V., M.C. Blumm, & E.A. Kronk (2013), *Native American Natural Resources Law*, 3rd edn, Durham: Carolina Academic Press.

Ruppel, K.T. (2008), *Unearthing Indian Land: Living with the Legacies of Allotment*, Tucson: University of Arizona Press.

Sahlins, M. (1999), "Two or three things that I know about culture," *Journal of the Royal Anthropological Institute (N.S.)*, 5(3): 399–421.

Teske, R.H.C.J., & B.H. Nelson (1974), "Acculturation and assimilation: A clarification," *American Ethnologist*, 1(2): 351–67.

Thompson, G.E.B. (2016), "The double-edged sword of sovereignty by the barrel: How native nations can wield environmental justice in the fight against the harms of fracking," *UCLA Law Review*, 63: 1818–60.

U.S. Government Publishing Office (GPO) (2020), "Department of Interior Budget," Available online: https://www.govinfo.gov/content/pkg/BUDGET-2021-APP/html/BUDGET-2021-APP-1-14.htm (Accessed May 16, 2020).

U.S. Senate (2010), "Indian energy and energy efficiency," Committee on Indian Affairs, 111th Congress. October 22, 2009.

Vengosh, A., N. Warner, R. Jackson, & T. Darraha (2013), "The effects of shale gas exploration and hydraulic fracturing on the quality of water resources in the United States," *Procedia Earth and Planetary Science*, 7(7): 863–6.

Wilkins, D.E. & K.T. Lomawaima (2001), *Uneven Ground: American Indian Sovereignty and Federal Law*, Norman: University of Oklahoma.

Wilkinson, R.G. & K. Pickett (2009), *The Spirit Level: Why More Equal Societies Almost Always Do Better*, London: Allen Lane.

Wolf Tice, J. (2016), "Under the earthlodge: Extraction of the MHA Nation," MA diss., Lehigh University, Bethlehem.

World Bank (2020), "Countries and economies." Available online: https://data.worldbank.org/country/ (Accessed May 18, 2020).

Zea, T.R. (2019), *Sustainable Development with Full Respect for the Rights of Indigenous Peoples, Women, Children and Youth*, U.N. High Level Forum on Sustainable Development, New York: ECOSOC.

3

ACTIVISM OR EXTRACTIVISM: INDIGENOUS LAND STRUGGLES IN EASTERN BOLIVIA

Evan Shenkin

Introduction

Hopes were high when Evo Morales assumed office in January 2006, becoming the first Indigenous president in the 500 years since European colonization of the Americas (Sivak 2010). This was a time of great optimism for many lowland Indigenous peoples in Bolivia whose social movements supported Morales and the *Movimiento al Socialismo* (MAS) political party that many believed would grant full recognition of Indigenous Bolivians as equals in the pluri-ethnic character of the nation. As anthropologist Nancy Postero notes, the MAS party integrated opposition to neoliberalism with Indigenous activism in dynamic ways that catalyzed the majority Indigenous population of the country. Native Bolivian peoples began receiving official communal land titles to their territories with the support of NGOs in the 1980s and 1990s under neoliberal regimes that purported to advance both conservation and social justice goals. These communal territories, called Native Community Lands (*Tierra Comunitaria de Orígen*, TCOs), were expanded when Evo Morales and the MAS government first came to power (Postero 2007).

Although highland movements received the most media attention with the Cochabamba Water War of 2000 and Gas War of 2003, significant Indigenous organizing in the lowlands was crucial for the victory of Evo Morales (Hindery 2013). In the year 2000, over one hundred Chiquitano people peacefully blockaded one of Enron's Cuiabá natural gas pipeline terminals. The action centered around community concerns that pipeline-associated road building would facilitate illegal logging, hunting, and drug trafficking in the Chiquitano dry forest, the largest intact tropical dry forest in the world (Hindery 2013). These and other actions in the natural gas-rich lowlands, along with massive urban mobilizations in El Alto, a poor suburb of La Paz, weakened the neoliberal governments of President Gonzalo Sánchez de Lozada, leading to his resignation and exile. The 2003 Gas War began a subsequent wave of protests against neoliberal restructuring and demands for greater levels of participatory democracy, publicly oriented programs, and more equitable distribution of economic rewards (Perreault 2006). Vice President Carlos Diego Mesa Gisbert assumed control until he too was forced to resign in 2005 under a second wave of gas protests that led to the election of Evo Morales in the same year (Postero 2007).

On November 10, 2019, Evo Morales, Vice President Linera, and MAS leaders of both chambers of Congress were forced to resign under threats of violence in what many are calling a coup (Davis et al. 2019). This unprecedented change in leadership, and the rapid appointment of far-right politician Jeanine Áñez as interim president under highly questionable circumstances, represents a serious political crisis in Bolivia's nascent democratic experiment. Five days later, the military and police fired into a group of Indigenous protesters, wounding 120 and killing nine. At the time of writing, state repression continues under the Áñez government who initially granted impunity for military actions against protestors, then backtracked under social movement pressures. Áñez and other interim government officials have well-documented ties to right-wing paramilitary groups, extractive interests, and openly espouse racist and anti-Indigenous rhetoric, leaving many pro-democracy advocates deeply concerned (Kovarik 2019). These recent political changes are likely to expand controversial development projects and increase threats to Native lands and peoples across the country.

Much has changed since Evo's first presidential victory when he declared, "Indigenous comrades, for the first time we are presidents… it is the epoch of the struggle against the (neoliberal) economic model" (Postero 2007: 1). Transnational capital continues to invest in deforestation and road building to facilitate vertically integrated soy agribusiness (Oliveira & Hecht 2016), palm oil and sugar cane (McKay 2017), and cattle ranching (Hinojosa et al. 2015).

Similar to the contested Bolivia-Brazil Cuiabá pipeline project in the Chiquitano dry forest two decades earlier, the original TIPNIS (*Territorio Indígena y Parque Nacional Isiboro Secure*) road proposal, officially named the Villa Tunari-San Ignacio de Moxos Highway, transects a Jamaica-sized "untouchable" reserve and Indigenous territory and was supported by transnational corporate actors. The project received funding from a Brazilian development corporation OAS, the Brazilian Development Bank (BNDES), and Bolivian state agencies (Achtenberg 2017). Foreign investment in the earlier highly contested Cuiabá pipeline included Enron and Shell (30 percent), Brazil's state oil company Petrobras (9 percent), British Gas (2 percent), El Paso (2 percent), and Total-FinaElf (2 percent) (Hindery 2013). These extractivist pressures continue to promote development that jeopardizes Indigenous forest-based communities, particularly in Santa Cruz, the principal battleground between agribusiness and rainforest conservation efforts (Zamora 2018).

In recent years, lowland Indigenous autonomy claims have resurfaced as the majority of land titles for TCOs have yet to be granted complete legal status. Processes for obtaining full legal rights for TCO lands remain embroiled in corruption, threats of violence, clientelistic networks, and competing claimants that reproduce prior elite forms of land consolidation. Although subsoil resources and land ownership are legally separated, with the state maintaining control of underground resources, both remain logistically connected for development purposes. TCOs in the lowlands are often balkanized by private cattle ranches and transected by gas pipelines that further challenge Indigenous sovereignty claims. Obtaining full legal recognition of territories would mean greater self-governance to address community development goals, regain dispossessed territories, and control hydrocarbon rents (Anthias 2018). The success of TCOs to address social and environmental needs has been mixed, and extractivist interests threaten the viability of protected lands, most notably in the ongoing TIPNIS trans-Amazonian highway conflict. Both de jure and de facto challenges to the protected status of both TCOs and national parks threaten Indigenous land sovereignty (Webber 2014).

A collective sense of institutional betrayal descended upon many Indigenous Bolivians and their nongovernmental organization (NGO) allies. Many of those most supportive of Morales during the revolutionary period of the 2000s became the government's most vocal critics later (McNelly 2017). Collective grievances centered on the state's continuation of extractive policies indicative of earlier neoliberal epochs. Foreign capital investment in land privatization continued to increase under the MAS (Webber 2017). Many lowland Indigenous criticisms centered on the Morales administration's anti-imperialist rhetoric juxtaposed with continued extractivism in Native lands. This contradiction prompted Chiquitano leader and former mayor of Concepción, Carlos Wasase, to characterize the MAS party's treatment of lowland Indigenous communities by referencing George Orwell's paradoxical words from *Animal Farm*: "all animals are equal, but some are more equal than others" (author's interview).

This chapter seeks to address the following questions: How did social and ecological conditions within lowland Indigenous communities change under the MAS government? Why did Indigenous social movements in the Bolivian lowlands continue to struggle to realize their original visions for territorial autonomy and sustainable livelihoods under the recently deposed Morales administration? To answer these questions, I integrate in-depth semi-structured interviews with central figures in lowland Indigenous social movements and NGO workers and contextualize this data with a theory-driven case study approach to understanding power relations within Bolivian Native territories (TCOs). There are thirty-six officially recognized ethnic groups of Bolivia. The majority are Quechua (49.5 percent) and Aymara (40.6 percent) peoples of the highlands, and the remaining thirty-four groups include the Chiquitano (3.6 percent) and Guarani (2.5 percent), with which the Guarayo people share a linguistic root (2.5 percent) (IWGIA 2019).

Questions about the tenuous future of TCOs remain as forms of extraction have grown worse. The mining sector expanded under Morales through the continuation of neoliberal institutional arrangements and the prioritization of transnational corporations over nationalization and community management. The state simultaneously undermined indigenous social movements while maintaining weak de facto environmental land regulations encouraging extractive industries to expand (Andreucci & Radhuber 2017).

This chapter primarily focuses on the Guarayo people's struggles for *just sustainabilities* within the Guarayos TCO, an Indigenous territory in the Department of Santa Cruz undergoing rapid deforestation and resource extraction. I also engage the controversial TIPNIS project, directly to the West, as a high-profile example of Indigenous organizing vis-à-vis the state as illustrative of larger dynamics of land and resource contestation. I explore contemporary efforts to protect TCOs from extractivist interests and link these struggles to what Geographer Derrick Hindery argues are fundamentally issues of environmental justice (2013). This chapter also explores the connections between place-based movements for *both* equality and ecology, or what Agyeman terms the "inseparability of environmental quality and human equality" (2008: 751).

Linkages Between Justice and Sustainability

The United Church of Christ's 1987 report, *Toxic Wastes and Race in the United States* (1987), first introduced the terms *environmental justice* and *environmental racism*. The environmental justice paradigm (EJP) has continued to evolve and now incorporates Native American, First Nation, Latino, and Chicano communities into struggles for substantive equity, representing "the first environmental discourse constructed by people of color" on issues of self-determination, autonomy, and human rights (Agyeman et al. 2016: 325). These are multiscalar movements that engage in place-based claims-making, in conversation with domestic and international networks that consider civil rights, race, identity, gender, and cultural issues (Urkidi & Walter 2011). For Bolivian forest-dependent communities, the concept of environmental justice is an everyday lived experience. Guarayo community members routinely discuss issues of water quality, habitat destruction, invasive species, and climate change. Guarayo leaders particularly express concern about a nearby Chinese-owned gold mine, as well as their village's downstream location relative to Santa Cruz and mysterious fish kills after heavy rains.

Bolivian Indigenous communities have in recent decades called for "autonomy" (Eaton 2007) as well as "territory and dignity" (Anthias & Radcliffe 2015). These struggles represent intergenerational efforts to build independent livelihoods after waves of colonial dispossessions of culture, economy, and territory (Alfred & Corntassel 2005), and included a 650-mile-long March for Territory and Dignity based on collective grievances against 500 years of dehumanization and for reclaiming not only Indigenous territories but unique political and cultural ways (Stephenson 2002; Dockry & Langston 2018). Coalitions of Indigenous peoples, with support from domestic and international organizations, have maintained alliances based on environmental justice claims that remain a primary bulwark against extraction in Bolivia and for an Indigenous vision of just sustainabilities; these ideas are so fundamental that the 2009 Preamble of the Bolivian constitution references, "this sacred Mother Earth… based on respect and equity for all" (Constituteproject.org 2019: 6).

For many years Indigenous peoples in Bolivia have searched for ways to enforce just sustainabilities by "achieving preventative and effective protection of their communities and their environment" (Sargent 1998: 455). These marginalized communities remain systematically excluded from meaningful legal processes and as part of an historically based racial caste system. In efforts to gain traction and overcome systemic structural violence, Indigenous groups called upon the United Nations International Labour Organization (ILO) Convention 169 on Indigenous and Tribal Peoples and successfully pressured the state to ratify and adopt the resolution into national law in 1991 (Sargent 1998). Although the de facto improvements for lowland peoples were limited, the ILO resolution's constitutional adoption at the national level constituted a successful "boomerang strategy" of movements leveraging international organizations to pressure domestic governments to respond (Keck & Sikkink 1999).

Although Indigenous peoples in Bolivia are generally treated as a homogenous group, there are distinctive differences in voting patterns and ideologies (Hirseland & Strijbis 2018). Based upon the author's interviews with representatives from COPNAG (*Central de Organizaciones de los Pueblos Nativos Guarayos*), the democratically elected Guarayo government, ideas of justice, and sustainability are closely aligned with territorial autonomy and resource rights. Additionally, state support for basic social services is seen as a means to obtain economic justice by allowing young people to resist urban pressures and remain in their forest-dependent communities, preserving traditions and being present to engage in democratic processes.

Indigenous claims-making encompasses a plurality of subaltern post-development paradigms that attempt to transcend extraction-based economies (Escobar 2018). *Vivir Bien, Suma Qamaña* in Aymara, or *Sumaq Kawsay* in Quechua, broadly translates as "living well" and is part of diverse paradigms that seek sustainable livelihoods independent from a global capitalist system responsible for environmental injustices and the crisis of climate change (Thomson 2011). Amid the national controversy over the proposed TIPNIS road in 2011, the highland Aymara and Quechua-speaking National Council of Ayllus and Markas of Qullasuyu (CONAMAQ) and the lowland Confederation of Indigenous Peoples of Bolivia (CIDOB) broke away from the Pact of Unity, the national left-Indigenous alliance that brought Morales to power. The MAS responded with a strategy to marginalize dissenting voices throughout government and civil society while consolidating loyalists (Webber 2017).

Uruguayan development theorist Eduardo Gudynas frames the concept of Vivir Bien as an ongoing synthesis of Indigenous cosmovision with contemporary post-development critiques, simultaneously rejecting classical Eurocentric development theories while promoting subaltern forms of development based on community well-being that includes nature (Gudynas 2011a). Vivir Bien forms Bolivia's national policy and is "incorporated as the backbone of the new constitution and the national development plans in the Evo Morales' era" (Lalander 2017: 6).

The concept stands in opposition to *Vivir Mejor* ("living better"), signifying the dominant global capitalist development paradigm that seeks continuous economic growth at the expense of all else. Vivir Bien contributes to Western notions of just sustainabilities by providing an Indigenous pluralistic vision that incorporates emotional and spiritual elements. Bolivian intellectual Fernando Huanacuni's 2010 book, *Buen Vivi or Vivir Bien: Filosophia, Politicas, Estrategias y Experiencias Regionales*, articulates thirteen principles for applying the concept to a range of activities: from how to work, think, and love, to how to speak, listen, and dream (Gould & Day 2017). In essence, the concept represents synergistic social and ecological insights from traditional ecological knowledge rooted in the cosmological connections between community, land, and place. There must be a spiritually rooted, emotional connection to land for Western notions of just sustainabilities to fully embody not only the Vivir Bien ideal but to achieve its larger social and ecological goals.

Lowland Indigenous communities continue to assert Vivir Bien as a critique of the state's reliance upon Western development paradigms outlined by prominent social theorist Arturo Escobar (1998) and a call for independent livelihoods that do not sacrifice long-term environmental health for short-term economic gains. Lowland social movements highlight the contradictions of the term embodied in the new constitution, pointing out the dissonance between promoting harmonious human–environmental relations while the government continues hydrocarbons and mining extraction under what former Bolivian Vice President Álvaro García Linera termed, "Andean-Amazonian capitalism" (Postero 2010: 1). Put simply, this is a paradoxical development discourse that frames extraction-based hydrocarbon rents as a necessary evil for socialist state formation (Farthing 2019). Gudynas identifies a core tension: "The paradox that development can be declared defunct and yet in the next step promoted as the only way forward is deeply embedded in modern culture" (2011b: 441).

At the nexus of these struggles are competing visions of development between the state and democratic Indigenous social movements of the lowlands concerning what development models will be implemented. Nowhere are these competing visions more intense than in the TIPNIS (*Territorio Indígena y Parque Nacional Isiboro Secure*) National Park and Indigenous territory where a state-sponsored highway is currently being constructed through the center of the territory despite massive opposition (Hirsch 2017). Although this conflict lies to the west of the Guarayo and Chiquitano territories, and is home to the Tsimané, Yuracaré, and Mojeño-Trinitario peoples, the outcome of the conflict is widely seen by Indigenous peoples and allied organizations as a bellwether for the status of other protected lands (Sanchez-Lopez 2015). Political scientist Jeffery Webber characterized the recently deposed Morales government as following a "reconstituted neoliberal model" of development where a revolutionary discourse of social movements is co-opted to legitimate an elite-dominated model based upon privatization, extraction, and inequity (2013).

The Morales administration's espoused goal of transitioning the economy away from an export-based periphery to one of communitarian production did not materialize and factored into the recent political crisis. Andreucci and Radhuber assert, "the economy is more dependent on primary exports than before" (2017: 1).

Government investment in "social spending (has increased) only modestly in absolute terms, and actually declined as an absolute percentage of GDP under Morales" (Webber 2015: 326). A prominent Bolivian economist and public intellectual criticized the MAS economic strategy by asserting, "this is the apex of consumerism... please, do not call it socialism, or anti-capitalism, have some respect for Marx, please!" (Schipani 2014). A collectively written letter to the MAS government from former public officials, activists, and intellectuals further argued:

> Today, the large majority of our people basically find themselves in the same situation of poverty, precariousness, and anguish in which they have always been. It would seem that those who have improved are those that had always been well: the bankers, transnational oil and mining companies, the smugglers, and the narco traffickers.
>
> (Almaraz et al. 2011: 3)

How are we to understand the paradox of regional and local environmental injustices based on the MAS government's transition from revolutionary social movement to replicator of prior anti-democratic neoliberal reforms? TCO Guarayo represents regional trends in respect to state vis-à-vis Indigenous community relations. Compounded with the Guarayo's limited population, resource extraction represents an existential threat for the ethnic group's long-term cultural survival. A Guarayo leader describes the internal politics in his community:

> People... are now divided because of corruption, drugs, and illegal land sales... People start thinking individualistically... there is a growing disconnect between the land and people... many leaders have to take second jobs to earn a living in addition to doing their political work.
>
> (author's interview)

This local narrative outlines a common occurrence where Indigenous leaders go unpaid for their community service. Many are teachers, farmers, or laborers who perform their leadership role at great sacrifice to their lives and those of their families. Leaders often rely on NGOs to fund their *viáticos*, basic expenses associated with travel, including daily stipends for the cost of participation in conferences. These payments are essential for leaders to organize because they often cannot afford even the bus ride to a meeting (Postero 2007).

Tierra Comunitaria de Origen (TCO) represent about 17.5 million hectares in the eastern lowlands, broken down into various classifications. The communal land ownership process has stalled for many Indigenous communities and most TCOs remain only partially titled. Forest management plans, supported by NGOs, were enacted by TCO residents to strengthen land claims and generate revenue, leaving the administration of huge land tracts to local Indigenous governments; the Guarayos TCO has a population of 31,000 spread over twelve villages and six towns (Cronkleton, Bray & Medina 2011). Municipal governments receive money from state coffers for administration; however, according to Guarayo leadership, political corruption prevents federal fund redistributions at the local level to Indigenous organizations critical of the state.

Before the creation of TCOs and *COPNAG*, the local Guarayo government, resource use was handled on the community level. Leaders are elected through general assembly of all Indigenous communities in the province—although the TCO spans three municipalities where only one has an Indigenous majority. The state's laws, under the *usos y costumbres* (traditional uses and practices) statute, give ambiguous authority for TCOs to manage resource use. COPNAG was originally conceived to act on behalf of the Guarayo peoples and to administer forest management plans within the Guarayo TCO. Land competition began increasing in the 1970s as cattle, timber, and agricultural sectors from Santa Cruz looked further east. This trend has intensified as highland peasant colonists descend from the Andean altiplano to the lowlands seeking suitable land for coca farming, and subsistence use, after the tin market collapse in the mid-1980s (Perreault 2016).

Many highland farmers have distinct cultural traditions separate from lowland Indigenous peoples, whose place-based justice struggles span generations. These Andean Indigenous colonists, or *campesinos*, have historical legacies of leftist labor organizing and place their peasant status first and Indigenous identity second (Gootenberg & Dávalos 2018). Although Santa Cruz-based agribusiness and cattle ranching have been the primary drivers of deforestation in the region, waves of campesino migration to Indigenous territories have resulted in deforestation and territorial threats (Killeen et al. 2008).

Where many lowland Native community livelihoods are based upon subsistence and agroforestry practices, highland migrants are more likely to participate in traditionally settler colonial resource use patterns in which deforestation and mercantilism predominate. Even the cocalero unions from which Morales' career originated are based upon a capitalist mode of production that stands in contrast to the predominant lowland Indigenous cultural basis to care for ancestral territories as a pragmatic and precious use-value. These inter-Indigenous land struggles further complicate the challenges for Guarayo communities' efforts for sustainable resource management and justice claims. The following section documents several specific concerns to just sustainabilities from divergent visions within and external forces.

Indigenous Responses to Territorial Threats

Despite barriers, Guarayo leaders continue to address certain forms of illegal logging in their territory. Legally, lands are indivisible. In practice, fraudulent land titles are forged by colonists working with outside interests to illegally annex Indigenous territories (IWGIA 2010). One Guarayo leader responsible for overseeing forestry and lands explained that he interferes with approximately ten cases of illegal land or logging sales per year. He explains that some Indigenous families living in the TCO attempt to sell land to colonists or trees to logging companies, to either (1) pay for a family member's medical expenses, (2) acquire a percentage of wood to build a structure, or (3) sell land to a colonist for profit. In cases where an illegal transaction has occurred, a Guarayo government representative directly confronts the individual(s) that sold land or resources. Many illegal land deals are reversed, while others continue without the knowledge of leaders because of the size of the territory and limited capacity of governance.

Indigenous communities sometimes deal directly with multinational corporations in a Faustian bargain for access to hydrocarbon rents (Anthias 2016). In the face of economic austerity, Guarayo peoples are sometimes forced to illegally sell natural resources. One seasoned development worker familiar with the internal dynamics of TCOs described the legal parameters, and challenges, to resource use within Indigenous territories:

> Families… can cut trees for 4 reasons: to build a house, a hospital, a school or… to get money for the TCO community fund. The community leaders can sign a deal with an outside company… the money is supposed to go into the account… However, some community leaders will sell trees and take part of the money directly into their pockets.
>
> (author's interview)

The sale of resources and land is well understood by Indigenous Guarayo leaders, who know the full extent of their community's economic deprivations. A Guarayo leader described the dilemma by passionately explaining, "there are no government organizations that help us, all are bought by the (MAS affiliated) municipality!" (author's interview). The structural violence of exclusion from meaningful state welfare programs often relegates desperate families to violate laws and sell their community's hard-won land and resources to private interests for a pittance. This Faustian bargain is particularly tragic because environmentalism for many Guarayo is separate from Western concerns for biodiversity or the role of the Amazon as a carbon sink; it is a matter of survival.

The treadmill functions based upon economic imperatives and weak governance structures that allow Native lands to become degraded. Community members are then less able to rely upon their lands as sources of food, medicine, and materials for basic living and are forced into greater participation in an unjust domestic labor market tied to a global capitalist system. As this treadmill self-replicates and denies alternatives, the pressures to sell out become greater and just sustainabilities become more fleeting.

State Repression of Lowland Indigenous-NGO Alliances

Far-right movements in Santa Cruz, composed of elite-owned agribusiness, ranching, and logging sectors, have autonomous, even secessionist, elements vis-à-vis the state. For the purposes of this piece, the sovereignty movements of Bolivian Indigenous peoples of the lowlands are understood solely in terms of regaining ancestral territories and increasing self-determination (Hansen & Stepputat 2006). In a 2011 report, prominent Bolivian human rights organization *Fundación Tierra* concluded the status of the approximately 20 million hectares of TCO lands in the process of titling is "paradoxical… because a government that has titled large amounts of TCOs and hectares, in turn is restricting the exercise of rights that are recognized with this ownership, such as the right to consultation, self-government, to Indigenous autonomy. So, the application to the rights… of titles is the new challenge for Native peoples and the Bolivian state itself" (PIEB 2011).

The government holds the right to exploit subsoil resources within TCOs, creating tensions between state-sponsored extraction and Indigenous autonomy, with both actors dependent on the same resource exploitation (Anthias 2016). Local territorial autonomy claims require enough revenue to allow internal governance and organizing, as well as basic healthcare, education, and infrastructure. Groups who oppose state-sponsored extraction are sometimes forced to sell resources to fund organizing efforts. For example, Fernando Vargas, a leader organizing against the TIPNIS road, allegedly illegally sold wood from the reserve. However, Vargas claimed the sale was done under a legal forest management plan and that MAS affiliates are attempting to discredit political rivals (Mealla & Condori 2013).

NGOs supportive of Indigenous rights report similar concerns over an increasingly hostile state. On August 14, 2015, the MAS publicly criticized four prominent NGOs during the TIPNIS road protests. The NGOs *Centro de Documentación e Información Bolivia* (CEDIB), *Centro de Estudios para el Desarrollo Laboral y Agrario* (CEDLA), and *Fundación Milenio;* and *Fundación Tierra* continue to be harassed (Layme 2015). Although all Bolivian, these organizations are being accused of promoting "transnational imperial policy" and threatened with expulsion (Achtenberg 2015).

The state's chilling effect looms in the minds of many development workers, particularly with the expulsion of Danish NGO Ibis in 2013. According to Unitas Director Susana Erostegui, the message from the MAS is "don't get involved in politics and definitely don't criticize the politics of the government" (Sterling 2015). Although governments are often reluctant to employ violence because of the possibility of public outcry, Birss (2017) notes that state intimidation is common throughout Latin America, as governments often criminalize activists to "hinder their work because of the time, energy, and financial resources they must dedicate to legal defense" (315).

The state's decision to crack down on those who remain loyal to lowland Indigenous communities comes under the guise of anti-foreign interventionism. Morales expelled USAID in 2013, accusing the agency of conspiring against the government (BBC 2013). In the midst of state repression, many Western NGOs also suffer from declines in funding. One long-time NGO director described the decades-long trend as an explanation for why many aid organizations are no longer able to offer the same level of resources as in prior decades:

> In the 1980s, the social democracies of Europe were pouring money into the Indigenous civil society organizations in Bolivia… But for the last 5–10 years the money has been decreasing… as the European countries move to the right (politically) and focus on… their own countries. When the Bolivian government

was neoliberal, the social democracies of Europe didn't agree and wanted to support Indigenous peoples. But when Morales was elected... Europeans did not have the same energy to help civil society.

(interview by author)

Based upon the author's interviews, the general consensus from rural Indigenous communities within TCO Guarayo is that territorial autonomy, characterized by control over land and resources, has eroded in recent years. Failing land tenure rights under Morales are also attributed to agribusiness, mining, logging, and colonist activities that are either tacitly encouraged by weak regulation or explicitly supported through subsidies. The interim Áñez government's ties to lowland elites suggest that conditions for Indigenous land security are likely to be further eroded. Vertically integrated, capital-intensive, mechanized models of agri-business also reduce the need for labor (McKay & Colque 2016) while increasing economic growth and exportation-based dependencies that exacerbate socio-environmental conflicts (Bebbington & Bebbington 2010). The state legitimizes extractivism as a long-term strategy, claiming social and environmental impacts are necessary for the greater good of the country. Former Vice President Linera summarized the paradox of TCO sovereignty vis-à-vis state interests:

> In the case of the minority Indigenous peoples in the lowlands, the state has consolidated millions of hectares as historic territoriality of many peoples with a low population density. But combined with the right of a people to the land is the right of the state, of the state led by the Indigenous-popular and campesino movement, to superimpose the greater collective interest of all the peoples.
> (Linera 2009: 1)

Linera's clean model has a paradoxical logic that imbues symbolic personhood to the state as representative of Indigeneity, over that of Indigenous communities. Critics, including sociologist Luis Tapia, former ally of Linera, argue that "the excess of commodity exports has not been used to transform production, but rather to lubricate clientele networks to increase society's political control and facilitate the rise of a new bourgeoisie" (Tapia 2014). Further, Linera's discourse frames Indigeneity as monolithic and ignores the diverse perspectives between and within Native communities. Hirseland and Strijbis point out that it would be "misleading to take the MAS government as representing all of Bolivia's ethnic diversity" (2018: 1). Fabricant and Postero argue that "the Morales government and the lowland elites have defended their positions... by obscuring this political and economic history" in an attempt to continue sacrificing lowland Indigenous people and land for the insatiable global market (2015: 452).

Peaceful Indigenous marches are sometimes met with state brutality that has only increased under the interim government. In efforts to promote the TIPNIS highway, Morales strategically deployed a machismo discourse, encouraging outside men to seduce women living in the TIPNIS in order to stop their resistance to the proposed project (Eichler 2018). To counter threats, Indigenous marchers strategically use gender as a form of what Geographer Derrick Hindery terms *dynamic pragmatism* (2013). Gambling that the military would be less likely to use violence against women within the context of a public protest, traditional gendered relations are sometimes strategically deployed by social movement actors in nonviolent marches against the highway, with mixed results.

On September 24, 2011, a confrontation began between Indigenous protesters against riot police and colonists supportive of the highway. The secretary of state arrived and spoke with the protesters. The secretary reported to the media afterward, "the women had surrounded me and there had already been problems. There had been some threats and they had forced me, they made me walk" (Cauthen 2012: 1). Female protesters nonviolently used the secretary to force a path through the police and colonists' barricade. Although the tactic averted violence in the moment, the next day the police launched a surprise raid on the camp of male and female marchers (Achtenberg 2011). The officers used tear gas and proceeded to handcuff, gag, and beat many before loading them onto buses. Resident Coordinator of the United Nations in Bolivia Yoriko Yasukawa called on the government to end the repression saying, "I remind the authorities, at all levels, that their first responsibility is to stop this violence and to respect the rights of the people, the dignity of the Indigenous marchers" (Cauthen 2012: 1).

A gender parity law was passed in 2006 that guaranteed quotas for woman's political participation, with women comprising about one-third of constitutional delegates overall and half Indigenous women in the MAS party (Htun & Ossa 2013). Despite legislative victories, more work is necessary for the struggle for substantive gender equity, particularly from an intersectional lens. Indigenous female leadership is increasingly integrated into the TIPNIS conflict, where Indigenous women play a central role in resisting the road. According to Fabricant and Postero, the La Paz-based anarchist feminist collective *Mujeres Creando* formed an alliance with Indigenous female TIPNIS organizers in efforts to bring greater public awareness. Both groups endured police teargas and firehoses together, declaring the march a victory. This successful alliance between middle class urban mestizo and rural Indigenous women challenges patriarchy within the MAS government and Indigenous communities. This also brings up larger questions of which women can speak for whom even in the context of a coalitional action rejecting patriarchy, defending the forest, and calling for justice and gender equity (Fabricant & Postero 2019).

There is a lacuna in research on women's positions on land tenure and market privatization, particularly in Latin America (Radcliffe 2014), where "women are pivotal actors in resistance to large scale extractive development" (Simpson 2017: 274). When extraction occurs, employment opportunities are often limited to a few highly skilled positions often performed by men, making women more dependent on male wages and reducing gender equality (Fabricant & Gustafson 2015). On a global scale, women of color remain the leaders of environmental justice movements and bear the greatest risks (Rainey & Johnson 2009). Further research exploring the intersectional role of gender and just sustainabilities is long overdue. These struggles continue in Bolivia where Indigenous women's voices are often undermined by state organizing.

According to Marqueza Seco, Presidenta of the Indigenous Women's Sub-Center of the TIPNIS, MAS allies actively, "recruit more and more people to change their minds and support the construction of the road" (Carrillo 2017: 1). Seco articulated her alternate vision of post-development by asserting, "we don't need a road, the river is the road" (author's interview). Seco expressed concern for the future of the TIPNIS saying, "we need to keep laws that protect Mother Earth and not eliminate the law 180" (author's interview), referring to the 2011 law that prevents the construction of roads that would transect the TIPNIS territory. Although Law 180, and the subsequent Law 222 calling for prior consent, passed under the Morales administration, the government co-opted the process, marginalized dissenting voices, and moved forward with the road (Delgado 2017). Seco admitted that "we don't have resources for the fight" and listed various basic supplies the movement needed to continue resistance, including gas and oil for boats and transport (author's interview).

Concluding Remarks: Toward Just Sustainabilities

The challenges Indigenous communities faced under the Morales administration, and the political turmoil of the current Áñez government, present novel tensions for local place-based struggles for just sustainabilities, particularly for Guarayo communities who, until recently, were seeking to challenge the notion that an Indigenous president can speak for all Indigenous peoples. Under neoliberal governance, the adversarial nature of the state to human rights and environmental claims presents a more straightforward threat. Grassroots leaders in TCO Guarayos, the TIPNIS, and across the eastern lowlands face significant barriers to the struggle for equitable and sustainable livelihoods, particularly given the massive shift toward the right under Áñez.

There have been significant efforts to articulate the problems of new form of extractivism in the modern era as well as identify alternative sustainable livelihoods. Public intellectuals including Arturo Escobar, Silvia Rivera Cusicanqui, and Naomi Klein offer post-development solutions that promote both substantive human equity and greater environmental sustainability. These visionary figures urge us to reconsider everything. Escobar, drawing upon the concept of bien vivir posit that "it is not about 'expanding the range of choices' (liberal freedom) but is intended to transform the kinds of beings we desire to be" (2018). Similar to Henry Lefebvre's notion of "the right to the city" for urban spaces (1996), bien vivir remains both a "cry and a demand" by lowland Indigenous peoples to territory and just sustainabilities. Decolonizing life-projects (Rivera 2010), improving community resiliency through local food systems (Klein 2018), and transforming relationships between nature and culture must function on multiple scales (Escobar 2018).

A territorial crisis in lowland Indigenous territories threatens to eviscerate the substantive meaning of *Native Community Lands*. If NGO-Indigenous coalitions are unable to meaningfully assert territorial autonomy in coming years, these territories will signify little more than national sacrifice zones of hyperexploitation. Challenges to Indigenous territorial autonomy will likely increase and perpetuate institutionalized forms of environmental injustice.

Sustainable livelihoods for forest-based peoples in the lowlands remain possible if The United Nations Declaration on the Rights of Indigenous Peoples (UNDRIP) and Indigenous people's rights statutes in the 2009 Bolivian Constitution are honored. Ongoing environmental degradation, deforestation, and roadbuilding are symptoms of a larger crisis of democracy for these marginalized peoples (Postero & Elinoff 2019). Unfortunately, the TIPNIS road project exemplifies the paradox between state development and lowland Indigenous people's demands. Global flows of resources, based on historically situated colonial supply chains, have placed highland and lowland Indigenous peoples at odds with each other within an economy based on extraction (Fabricant & Postero 2015). These political economic conditions have resulted in significant gains for large landholders, agribusiness, logging, and mining interests under Morales and are likely to accelerate under Áñez.

Although this chapter focused on Bolivia, the political-economic patterns of extractivism are indicative of larger trends in center left Latin American countries. An analogous crisis is taking place in Ecuador, where the government's decision to drill in the protected Yasuni National Park and Indigenous territory in October 2016 has generated widespread protest and conflict (Vasquez 2018). The extractivist resource nationalism of the Bolivian state, albeit until the 2019 political crisis, conducted as a quasi-redistributive tool of wealth transfer, remains a Faustian bargain with transnational energy corporations functioning within the banal scope of global capitalism.

If Indigenous land-based movements, supported by NGOs, continue to lose ground, a precious opportunity for marginalized peoples in the arc of history will be lost. The Guarayo TCO, and other Indigenous territories are developing answers to the central question: How do we create a just and sustainable society? Aware of climate change threats, many rural communities have adopted off-grid solar energy systems and developed small, but growing, operations for renewable production of non-timber-based medicines, artisanal crafts, ecotourism, and small-scale agroforestry. The environmental justice rhetoric of the MAS, combined with the contradictions of continued extraction, illustrates the need to radically and honestly transform the political economic system. Indigenous efforts for just sustainabilities are based on conditions within each community to find livelihoods that preserve ecosystems for everyday use and long-term survival and include a "wide range of concerns with food, energy, and climate justice" (Agyeman et al. 2016: 321). In a broader context, as Agyeman, Bullard, and Evans point out, "a truly sustainable society is one where wider questions of social needs and welfare, and economic opportunity are integrally related to environmental limits imposed by supporting ecosystems" (2002: 78). Material conditions for vulnerable communities supersede state efforts to paradoxically deploy progressive rhetoric without following through.

These meso-level struggles for autonomy and dignity, although vulnerable, constitute scalable models for alternative livelihoods. Intersectional social movements organizing across class, race, and gender remain central to revolutionary activities for sustaining the radical notion of Vivir Bien as an example of Indigenous just sustainabilities. These movements require place-based communities to maintain emotional connections to territories in order to achieve their lasting ecological goals, a key concern given strong economic pressures that continue to pull forest-based Guarayo and other lowland Indigenous peoples into ethnic enclaves within the slums of Santa Cruz.

At present, these local and regional lowland Indigenous efforts to find alternative livelihoods remain crucibles for sustainable human development apart from the growth imperative of the world system. Further, we must understand intergenerational coalitions of lowland Indigenous peoples, civil society environmental organizations, social movements for democracy, and gender equity as central levers for moving the arc of history toward just sustainabilities.

References

Achtenberg, E. (2011), "Police attack on TIPNIS marchers roils Bolivia," *NACLA*. Available online: https://nacla.org/blog/2011/9/28/police-attack-tipnis-marchers-roils-bolivia (Accessed May 27, 2020).

Achtenberg, E. (2015), "What's behind the Bolivian government's attack on NGOs?," *NACLA*. Available online: https://nacla.org/blog/2015/09/03/what%27s-behind-bolivian-government%27s-attack-ngos (Accessed May 27, 2020).

Achtenberg, E. (2017), "Why is Evo Morales reviving Bolivia's controversial TIPNIS road?" *NACLA*, Available online: https://nacla.org/blog/2017/08/22/why-evo-morales-reviving-bolivia%E2%80%99s-controversial-tipnis-road (Accessed May 27, 2020).

Agyeman, J. (2008), "Toward a 'just' sustainability?" *Continuum*, 22(6): 751–6.

Agyeman, J., R. Bullard & B. Evans (2002), "Exploring the nexus: Bringing together sustainability, environmental justice and equity," *Space & Polity*, 6(1): 70–90.

Agyeman, J., D. Schlosberg, L. Craven & C. Matthews (2016), "Trends and directions in environmental justice: From inequity to everyday life, community, and just sustainabilities," *Annual Review of Environment & Resources*, 41: 321–40.

Alfred, T. & J. Corntassel (2005), "Being indigenous: Resurgences against contemporary colonialism," *Government & Opposition*, 40(4): 597–614.

Almaraz, A., R. Fernández, O. Olivera, G. Soto & A. Hinojosa *et al.* (2011), *Manifiesto: Por la Recuperación del Proceso de Cambio para el pueblo y con el Pueblo*. Available online: http://www.papelesdesociedad.info/IMG/pdf/manifiesto-cambio-bolivia.pdf (Accessed May 20, 2020).

Andreucci, D. & I.M. Radhuber (2017), "Limits to 'counter-neoliberal' reform: Mining expansion and the marginalization of post-extractivist forces in Evo Morales's Bolivia," *Geoforum*, 84: 280–91.

Anthias, P. (2016), "Indigenous peoples and the new extraction: From territorial rights to hydrocarbon citizenship in the Bolivian Chaco," *Latin American Perspectives*, 45(5): 136–53.

Anthias, P. (2018), *Limits to Decolonization: Indigeneity, Territory, and Hydrocarbon Politics in the Bolivian Chaco*, Ithaca: Cornell University Press.

Anthias, P. & S.A. Radcliffe (2015), "The ethno-environmental fix and its limits: Indigenous land titling and the production of not-quite-neoliberal natures in Bolivia," *Geoforum*, 64: 257–69.

BBC—British Broadcasting Corporation (2013), "President Evo Morales expels USAID," May 1. Available online: https://www.bbc.com/news/world-latin-america-22371275 (Accessed May 26, 2020).

Bebbington, D.H. & A.J. Bebbington (2010), "Extraction, territory, and inequalities: Gas in the Bolivian Chaco," *Canadian Journal of Development Studies*, 30(1–2): 259–80.

Birss, M. (2017), "Criminalizing environmental activism: As threats to the environment increase across Latin America, new laws and police practices take aim against the front line activists defending their land and resources," *NACLA Report on the Americas*, 49(3): 315–22.

Carrillo, K. (3/17/2017), "Tipnis: socializan proyectos con indígenas del Conisur," *Los Tiempos*. Available online: http://www.lostiempos.com/actualidad/economia/20170317/tipnis-socializan-proyecto-indigenas-del-conisur (Accessed June 6, 2020).

Cauthin, M. (2012), "Bolivia's TIPNIS conflict: Indigenous peoples denounce legal persecution," *Upside Down World*, March 23. Available online: http://upsidedownworld.org/archives/bolivia/bolivia-tipnis-conflict-indigenous-peoples-denounce-legal-persecution/ (Accessed May 26, 2020).

Constituteproject.org (2019), *Bolivia (Plurinational State of)'s Constitution of 2009*, Oxford University Press, Available online: https://www.constituteproject.org/constitution/Bolivia_2009.pdf (Accessed January 17, 2020).

Cronkleton, P., D.B. Bray & G. Medina (2011), "Community forest management and the emergence of multi-scale governance institutions: Lessons for REDD+ development from Mexico, Brazil and Bolivia," *Forests*, 2(2): 451–73

Davis, A., N. Chomsky, M. Crabapple & J. Pilger (2019) "Repressive violence is sweeping Bolivia. The Áñez regime must be held to account," *Guardian*, November 24. Available online: https://www.theguardian.com/commentisfree/2019/nov/24/bolivia-anez-regime-violence (Accessed May 28, 2020).

Delgado, A.C. (2017), "The TIPNIS conflict in Bolivia," *Contexto Internacional*, 39(2): 373–92.

Dockry, M. & N. Langston (2018), "Indigenous protest and the roots of sustainable forestry in Bolivia," *Environmental History*, 24(1): 52–77.

Eaton, K. (2007), "Backlash in Bolivia: Regional autonomy as a reaction against indigenous mobilization," *Politics & Society*, 35(1): 71–102.

Eichler, J. (2018), "Neo-extractivist controversies in Bolivia: Indigenous perspectives on global norms," *International Journal of Law in Context*, 15(1): 88–102.

Escobar, A. (1998), *La invención del Tercer Mundo: Construcción y deconstrucción del desarrollo*, Barcelona: Grupo Editorial Norma.

Escobar, A. (2018), *Designs for the Pluriverse: Radical Interdependence, Autonomy,\and the Making of Worlds*, Durham: Duke University Press.

Fabricant, N. & B. Gustafson (2015), "Revolutionary extractivism in Bolivia? Imagining alternative world orders from the ground up," in North American Congress on Latin America (NACLA). Available online: https://nacla.org/news/2015/03/02/revolutionary-extractivism-bolivia. (Accessed January 10, 2021).

Fabricant, N. & N. Postero (2015), "Sacrificing indigenous bodies and lands: The political-economic history of lowland Bolivia in light of the recent TIPNIS debate," *Journal of Latin American & Caribbean Anthropology*, 20(3): 452–74.

Fabricant, N. & N. Postero (2019), "Performing indigeneity in Bolivia: The struggle over the TIPNIS," in C. Vindal Ødegaard & J.J. Rivera Andía (eds), *Indigenous Life Projects and Extractivism*, 245–76, Cham: Palgrave Macmillan.

Farthing, L. (2019), "An opportunity squandered? Elites, social movements, and the government of Evo Morales," *Latin American Perspectives*, 46(1): 212–29.

Gootenberg, P. & L.M. Dávalos (eds) (2018), *The Origins of Cocaine: Colonization and Failed Development in the Amazon Andes*, New York, NY: Routledge.

Gould, R. & P. Day (2017). "You are here because the land called you: Searching for vivir bien/living well," *Journal of Indigenous Wellbeing*, 2(3): 105–13.

Gudynas, E. (2011a), "Buen Vivir: Germinando alternativas al desarrollo," *América Latina en movimiento*, 462: 1–20.

Gudynas, E. (2011b), "Buen Vivir: Today's tomorrow," *Development*, 54(4): 441–7.

Hansen, T.B. & F. Stepputat (2006), "Sovereignty revisited," *Annual Review of Anthropology*, 35: 295–315.

Hindery, D. (2013), *From Enron to Evo: Pipeline Politics, Global Environmentalism, and Indigenous Rights in Bolivia*, Tuscon: University of Arizona Press.

Hinojosa, L., A. Bebbington, G. Cortez, J.P. Chumacero, D.H. Bebbington, & K. Hennermann (2015), "Gas and development: Rural territorial dynamics in Tarija, Bolivia," *World Development*, 73: 105–117.

Hirsch, C. (2017), "Between resistance and negotiation: Indigenous organizations and the Bolivian State in the case of TIPNIS," *Journal of Peasant Studies*, 46(4): 811–30.

Hirseland, A.S. & O. Strijbis (2018), "'We were forgotten': Explaining ethnic voting in Bolivia's highlands and lowlands," *Journal of Ethnic and Migration Studies*, 45(11): 2006–25.

Htun, M. & J.P. Ossa (2013), "Political inclusion of marginalized groups: Indigenous reservations and gender parity in Bolivia," *Politics, Groups, & Identities*, 1(1): 4–25.

International Work Group for Indigenous Affairs (IWGIA) (2010), "The Rights of Indigenous Peoples," *IWGIA*. Available online: https://www.iwgia.org/images/publications//0462_EB-DANIDA-BOLIVIA-ENGELSK.pdf (Accessed May 26, 2020).

International Work Group for Indigenous Affairs (IWGIA) (2019), "Indigenous peoples in Bolivia." Available online: https://www.iwgia.org/en/bolivia (Accessed May 26, 2020).

Keck, M.E. & K. Sikkink (1999), "Transnational advocacy networks in international and regional politics," *International Social Science Journal*, 51(159): 89–101.

Killeen, T.J., A. Guerra, M. Calzada, L. Correa, V. Calderon, L. Soria, B. Quezada, & M.K.Steininger (2008), "Total historical land-use change in eastern Bolivia: Who, where, when, and how much?" *Ecology & Society*, 13(1): 36.

Klein, N. (2018), *The Battle for Paradise: Puerto Rico Takes on the Disaster Capitalists*, Chicago: Haymarket Books.

Kovarik, J. (2019), "Bolivia's anti-indigenous backlash is growing," *The Nation*, November 13. Available online: https://www.thenation.com/article/bolivia-morales-whipala/(Accessed May 25, 2020).

Lalander, R. (2017), "Ethnic rights and the dilemma of extractive development in plurinational Bolivia," *International Journal of Human Rights*, 21(4): 464–81.

Layme, Beatriz, (8/11/2015). "El Gobierno acusa a 4 ONG de realizar activismo político," *Página Siete*. Available online: https://www.paginasiete.bo/nacional/2015/8/11/gobierno-acusa-realizar-activismo-politico-66197.html (Accessed June 6, 2020).

Lefebvre, H., (1996), *The Right to the City*. Available online: https://theanarchistlibrary.org/library/henri-lefebvre-right-to-the-city.lt.pdf (Accessed June 6, 2020).

Linera, Á.G. (2009), "Bolivian vice president defends MAS government's record," *Le Monde Diplomatique*. Available online: http://links.org.au/index.php?q=node/1241 (Accessed May 25, 2020).

McKay, B. & G. Colque (2016), "Bolivia's soy complex: The development of 'productive exclusion,'" *Journal of Peasant Studies*, 43(2): 583–610.

McKay, B.M. (2017), "Agrarian extractivism in Bolivia," *World Development*, 97: 199–211.

McNelly, A. (2017), "The contours of Gramscian theory in Bolivia: From government rhetoric to radical critique," *Constellations*, 24(3): 432–46.

Mealla & Condori (2013), "Gobierno cuestiona a La Paz y genera acuerdo con Santa Cruz," *El Razon*, September 18. Available online: http://eju.tv/2013/09/censo-gobierno-cuestiona-a-la-paz-y-genera-acuerdo-con-santa-cruz/(Accessed May 25, 2020).

Oliveira, G. & S. Hecht (2016), "Sacred groves, sacrifice zones and soy production: Globalization, intensification and neo-nature in South America," *Journal of Peasant Studies*, 43(2): 251–85.

Periódico Digital de Investigación de Bolivia (PIEB) (2011), "Comunidades con tierras tituladas pero sin derechos consolidados, según estudio," *PIEB*, July 18. Available online: www.pieb.com.bo/sipieb_nota.php?idn=5964 (Accessed May 25, 2020).

Perreault, T. (2006), "From the Guerra Del Agua to the Guerra Del Gas: Resource governance, neoliberalism and popular protest in Bolivia," *Antipode*, 38(1): 150–72.

Perreault, T. (2016), "Governing from the ground up? Translocal networks and the ambiguous politics of environmental justice in Bolivia," in L.S. Horowitz & M.J. Watts (eds), *Grassroots Environmental Governance*, 115–37, London: Routledge.

Postero, N. (2007), *Now We Are Citizens*, Stanford: Stanford University Press.

Postero, N. (2010), "Morales's MAS government: Building indigenous popular hegemony in Bolivia," *Latin American Perspectives*, 37(3): 18–34.

Postero, N. & E. Elinoff (2019), "Introduction: A return to politics," *Anthropological Theory*, 19(1): 3–28.

Radcliffe, S.A. (2014), "Gendered frontiers of land control: Indigenous territory, women and contests over land in Ecuador," *Gender, Place & Culture*, 21(7): 854–71.

Rainey, S.A. & G.S. Johnson (2009), "Grassroots activism: An exploration of women of color's role in the environmental justice movement," *Race, Gender & Class*, 16(3/4): 144–73.

Rivera Cusicanqui, S. (2010), *Ch'ixinakax utxiwa. Una reflexión sobre prácticas y discursos descolonizadores*, Buenos Aires, Argentina: Tinta Limon.

Sargent, L. (1998), "The indigenous peoples of Bolivia's Amazon Basin Region and ILO Convention No. 169: Real rights or rhetoric?" *University of Miami Inter-American Law Review*, 29(3): 451–524.

Sanchez-Lopez, D. (2015), "Reshaping notions of citizenship: The TIPNIS indigenous movement in Bolivia," *Development Studies Research*, 2(1): 20–32.

Schipani, Andres (2014), "Wealth redistribution and Bolivia's boom," *Financial Times*, October 10. Available online: https://www.ft.com/content/825dda59-7f3f-34e4-b949-6f6023d3f6ae (Accessed May 28, 2020).

Sivak, M. (2010), *Evo Morales: The Extraordinary Rise of the First Indigenous President of Bolivia*, New York: St. Martin's Press.

Simpson, L.B. (2017), *As We Have Always Done: Indigenous Freedom Through Radical Resistance*, Minneapolis: University of Minnesota Press.

Stephenson, M.C. (2002), "Forging an indigenous counterpublic sphere: The Taller de Historia\Oral Andina in Bolivia," *Latin American Research Review*, 37(2): 99–118.

Sterling, H.T. (2015), "Guarani people turn to the law to fight latest battle with Bolivian authorities," *Guardian*, October 6. Retrieved from: https://www.theguardian.com/global-development/2015/oct/06/guarani-people-turn-to-the-law-fight-latest-battle-bolivia-authorities (Accessed May 26, 2020).

Tapia, L. (2014), "La relación entre gobierno y movimientos indígenas en el ciclo de cambio político en Bolivia," *Movimiento indígena en América Latina: Resistencia y transformación social*, 3.

Thomson, B. (2011), "Pachakuti: Indigenous perspectives, buen vivir, sumaq kawsay and degrowth," *Development*, 54(4): 448–54.

United Church of Christ, Commission for Racial Justice (1987), *Toxic Wastes and Race in the United States: A* National Report *on the Racial and Socio-economic Characteristics of Communities with Hazardous Waste Sites*. Available online: https://www.nrc.gov/docs/ML1310/ML13109A339.pdf (Accessed May 28, 2020).

Urkidi, L. & M. Walter (2011), "Dimensions of environmental justice in anti-gold mining movements in Latin America," *Geoforum*, 42(6): 683–95.

Vasquez, P.I. (2018), *Oil Sparks in the Amazon: Local Conflicts, Indigenous Populations, and Natural Resources*, Athens: University of Georgia Press.

Webber, J.R. (2013), "From left-indigenous insurrection to reconstituted neoliberalism in Bolivia: Political economy, indigenous liberation, and class struggle, 2000–2011," in J.R. Webber & B. Carr (eds), *The New Latin American Left: Cracks in the Empire*, 149–90, Washington, DC: Rowman & Littlefield.

Webber, J.R. (2014), "Revolution against 'progress': Neo-extractivism, the compensatory state, and the TIPNIS conflict in Bolivia," in S. Spronk & J.R. Webber (eds), *Crisis and Contradiction: Marxist Perspectives on Latin America in the Global Political Economy*, 302–33, Leiden: Brill.

Webber, J.R. (2015), "The indigenous community as 'living organism': José Carlos Mariátegui, romantic marxism, and extractive capitalism in the Andes," *Theory & Society*, 44(6): 575–98.

Webber, J.R. (2017), *The Last Day of Oppression and the First Day of the Same: The Politics and Economics of the New Latin American Left*, Chicago: Haymarket Books.

Zamora, M.A.R. (2018), "Deforestation in the Bolivian Amazon: The Case of the El Choré Forest Reserve in Santa Cruz Department," in M. Ungar (ed), *The 21st Century Fight for the Amazon*, 57–70, Cham: Palgrave Macmillan.

Part II

WHOSE CITIES?

The plural nature of just sustainabilities, and the fact that there is no one-size-fits-all approach, raises a necessary question for anyone seeking to implement just and sustainable policies, plans, and practices: *who is this for*? Will attempts to meet one group's set of needs undermine the needs of others? If, as we noted in the Introduction, the goal is actionable improvement rather than perfection, who is still left in the gaps? Equally important is the question, *who is this by*? Who has the decision-making power, even in cases of ostensibly "public goods" and/or "the public good"? The case studies in this part illuminate these questions; all three cases focus on urban areas where the dense population brings an associated density of simultaneous and sometimes contesting needs.

Chapter 4 explores the "bipolar waterfront": waterfront spaces that house heightened contradictions of extreme wealth and poverty. Themes that embody city imaginaries (and futures) are explored even as these same cities enact violence and displacement of their urban poor. Chapter 5 delves into rickshaws in Dhaka, examining how infrastructure choices and government restrictions impact nonmotorized transport and the people who depend on it. Muddying the waters are differing ideas of mobility, historical and current inequalities between and within nations, and underlying assumptions about who roads are for. Chapter 6 offers an analysis of transition within the Athens urban water system, tracing a history shaped by both foreign capital and local heritage. The complex and contested relationships surrounding water access within this historic capital city raise additional questions about the respective places of infrastructure and people in planning priorities.

4

THE BIPOLAR WATERFRONT: PARADOXES OF SHORELINE PLACE-MAKING IN CONTEMPORARY ACCRA AND COLOMBO

Rapti Siriwardane-de Zoysa
Epifania A. Amoo-Adare

Introduction

Popular imaginings of the contemporary metropolitan "waterfront" embody a number of ambivalent and oppositional narratives. On the one hand, they stand to symbolize trajectories of urban rejuvenation and socio-spatial revitalization, as abandoned derelict sites such as docklands and harbors are transformed into open, vibrant communal spaces for public use. On the other, waterfront developments in the past have often encompassed mega-projects of top-down state and private investment-led planning ventures. The waterfront, therefore, also stands as an embattled leitmotif—a promised site of urban spectacle, leisured consumerism, and of neoliberal gentrification. We start with the premise that socio-environmental change often bears down disproportionately on the world's poor (Agyeman, Bullard, & Evans 2003), and that meanings of what counts as "sustainable" and socio-ecologically just are inherently cultural, as much as they are place bound and historically contingent (Agyeman 2013). At first glance waterfront development—whether marine, estuarine, or riverine—particularly across capital cities and metropolitan spaces stand as potent emblems of national development, of cultural production, and of cosmopolitan identity-making, taking for example London's Canary Wharf, Cape Town's Victoria and Alfred Waterfront, Singapore's Esplanade, or Jakarta's Jayakarta Waterfront (see Nas 2005; Ferreira & Visser 2007; Kong 2007). Arguably, contemporary waterfront developments around the world visibly mimic distinct socio-spatial orders of urban presence—not only do they replicate globalized capitalist features such as shopping malls, mesicol greenery, expansive communal squares, and artistic performance spaces but also embody distinct metropolitan identities and are themselves discursively constructed and enacted in everyday life, from tourist brochures to national media. Yet, apart from their emblematic presence—as aesthetic form and material fixity—waterfront sites also encompass inherently emotional landscapes and cultural memory, in similar ways that urban parklands and memorialized cemeteries do (see Tarlow 2000; Uggla 2014). Urban waterfront spaces have also been sites of socio-environmental struggle (Pinto & Kondolf 2020), connecting challenges such as shored litter, relative sea-level change, and land subsidence together with debates around sea walls and other forms of coastal fortification (Storbjörk & Hjerpe 2014; Boland, Bronte, & Muir 2017).

The socio-spatial diversity of urban coastal waterfronts and their built form and political contestations have been richly documented through the interrelated lenses of critical planning, urban anthropology, and geography (see Ferreira & Visser 2007; Darieva 2011, Morgia & Vicino 2013). In this chapter, while drawing on perspectives across maritime anthropology, cultural studies, coastal geography, and decolonial theory, we contemplate contemporary scholarly discourses on the urban(e) spatial production of so-called metropolitan coasts or shorelines. We explicitly focus on diverse sociocultural imaginaries of land-sea aesthetics and broader sensibilities which, as we argue, are both historically and socio-spatially contingent. Furthermore, we ask *how* this question matters and for whom, particularly in the context of rapidly transforming neoliberal cityscapes along vibrant, densely populated coastlines.

To this end, we draw inspiration from related conceptual currents spanning recent work on "just sustainabilities" and the urban condition of seeking socio-ecological modernity (Agyeman & Evans 2003; Agyeman, Bullard, & Evans 2013), with earlier theorizations on inequality, "uneven development" (Smith 2010), spatial justice (Soja 2009), and "right to the city" (Amin & Thrift 2003; Harvey 2003). As a point of departure, the practices around waterfront development are considered not only as urban planning and architectural projects but also as a grand narrative in enabling particular forms of market-led socio-ecological modernization, intended at profoundly altering the lived aesthetics and meanings of urban littoral space.

Therefore, the paradoxes we explore focus squarely on how the politics of producing and sustaining waterfronts create marginalized littorals by virtue of how shoreline spaces act as boundaries in patterning access, presence, and belonging. As an urban planning practice, the revitalization of waterfront spaces offers to be taken as examples of inclusive spatial transformation in *public* place-making. Aside from the aesthetics of urban beautification, they are often constructed as social projects that work in enriching urban livability, mobility, and wellbeing (Beatley 2014). Yet what counts as "livable," aesthetically desirable, and socioeconomically accessible remain contested, particularly when places are remade as leisured sites and when access is often singularly mediated through consumption. Thus, one of the most telling paradoxes in histories of waterfront revitalization has been the extent to which these "public" spaces remain inclusively open or closed, while embracing particular modes of leisured citizenship. While scholarly work discusses the right to the city through manifold intersectional identities spanning class, gender, ethnicity, age, and (dis)ability for example (see Dovey & Sandercock 2005; Avni & Teschner 2019), we repurpose this chapter by interrogating what the "right to the waterfront" would inherently look like across diverse urban coastlines.

We turn to the contemporary capitals of Accra and Colombo for inspiration. We call on these two cities by virtue of their postcolonial identities as "port cities" and as former Anglophone colonies. Both Ghana (known as the Gold Coast until 1957) and Sri Lanka (as Ceylon until the early 1970s) shared intermittent post-Independence histories inspired by centrally planned socialist economies before turning to market neoliberalism. More tellingly, Accra and Colombo—as "gateway" cities and maritime hubs respectively—were implicated in imperial explorative, migrant, naval, and mercantilist seaborne circuits (Grant & Nijman 2003; Noble & Panditharatne 2003; Thiranagama 2011: 29). Indeed, the evolution of numerous colonial port cities and maritime trading sites often predates their encounters with colonialism, connecting vast distances and shared sociocultural oceanic spaces. Thus Accra's and Colombo's early colonial urban identity came to be imagined through a distinctly maritime lens, and this is but one moment that did profoundly pattern their postcolonial neoliberal present. Their maritime identities have profoundly shaped everyday life in the city as these spaces have facilitated intra-regional and local migrant sojourning and the flow of ideas, goods, species, and capital. As coastal cities, they are sites of immense geoecological and intertidal flux, where land, sea, atmospheric, and tectonic dynamics shape practices in responding to socio-natural hazards such as stormwater flooding, sea-level rise, and land subsidence.

Today, Accra and Colombo suggest both similar and disparate politics of the waterfront. Gentrified urban life in coastal Accra, since Independence, ostensibly evolved away from the coastline, indicating that the reified Eurocentric fetishization of the seaside warrants deeper reflection. In the case of Colombo, where imperialist imaginaries of the sea and its discursive construction as an "island"-colony/state were reified (Sivasundaram 2013), waterfront development came to be naturalized over the past decades as an archetypal symptom of market-led neoliberal progress, also during a three-decade long civil war. To this end, Accra and Colombo are put in dialogue with each other, as distinct yet complementary case studies on how contemporary paradoxes over littoral space and place-making can be grasped through the integrative, locally focused, deep-diving lenses of "just sustainabilities" (Agyeman, Bullard, & Evans 2003).

Conceptualizing the Bipolar Waterfront

It comes as little surprise that when the marine waterfront is invoked in the context of city life, the symbol of the economic and technological entrepôt is often dominant. The very notion of what a port city entails remains wide-ranging, considering its vast heterogeneity of form, function, and sociocultural meanings (see Graf & Chua 2009). When considering postcolonial cities, how embodied sensibilities of *water* changed over time is particularly significant, given their transforming identities from port city to waterfront metropolis, taking for example spaces like Singapore, Hong Kong, and Mombasa. Scholarly discussions around water and socio-environmental justice have focused on the socioeconomic utility-derived materializations of water, bringing together themes such as surface transport and transit, and access and consumption. What is being increasingly acknowledged are the poetics and politics of water as part and parcel of everyday forms of place-making (beyond land/seascape aesthetics), particularly with regard to their multisensory affects, everyday socialities, leisured practices, and modes of dwelling. We then turn to conceptualizations of the contemporary "waterfront" with which to understand contemporary struggles over *littoral* just sustainabilities.

Conventionally, two key bodies of literature have shaped scholarly interventions on waterfront spaces, and the micro-politics of the postcolonial harbor front in general. The global diffusion of Port City Studies, particularly from a postcolonial vantage point, can be traced back to the seminal works of scholars such as Rhoades Murphey and Frank Broeze in the 1980s combining political science, history, geography, and town planning with the study of Asian and Middle Eastern port cities in particular, with an eye toward their colonial transformations (Murphey 1989; Broeze 2010). The second strand of scholarship entails what could be termed as "waterfront studies" (see Cooper 1987; Hoyle 2000; Schubert 2011), constituting a related field that is relatively more recent, interweaving disciplinary currents such as economic geography, urban anthropology, and sociology. Many of these interventions have focused explicitly on spatial transformations and the diversity of built form, together with the broader political contestations underpinning their development (see Gordon 1997; Desfor & Laidley 2011).[1]

Yet, the waterfront as a figure becomes increasingly visible when port cities themselves are futuristically envisioned against their place in a global economy that, paradoxically, makes them increasingly redundant in the face of material decline and the devaluation of old harbor spaces. Trajectories of revitalization are not all linear; in the case of diverse cities such as New Orleans and Marseille, or Lagos and Baku, stories of "ruination and decline" and of "resistance and recovery" layer over one another in deeply stratified ways (Mah 2014: 6–9). Where Indigenous pasts are virulently erased, or on the other hand, tactically invoked or remade to legitimate claims to place and meaning (see Nixon 2011), the speculative futures of a climatic apocalypse find themselves materially translated as infrastructural mega-projects and feats of geo-engineering, from giant seawalls (Colven 2017) to floating islands and "seasteads" (Steinberg, Nyman, & Caraccioli 2012). Urban climate mitigation and adaptation practices can often be seen as ad hoc, piecemeal responses that are designed and implemented over existing socio-environmental inequalities and inequities such as spatial segregation and uneven access to public services and "resilience infrastructures," leading to the further marginalization of poverty pockets (Yarina 2018). Where protective coastal infrastructures can be seen as exclusionary "planned development for some" (Malm 2012: 822), urban disaster risk reduction practices are rolled out to further serve vested interests for land acquisition, state policing, and securitization (Siriwardane-de Zoysa, Fitrinitia, & Herbeck 2018).

So what remains conceptually and empirically intriguing about the contemporary waterfront with its antipodal materialities and symbolic representations? Waterfront spaces exist as areas in which contestations around sustainability and justice play out, primarily because they carry with them the promise of common leisured access. The waterfront exists as an aesthetically unique space to be visually consumed (e.g., via skylines) and to be physically traversed (e.g., promenades). It seemingly grants its visitors a uniform sense of urban citizenship. Yet the very notion of the waterfront carries with it a hidden historicity, a spatial past that is overwritten by its remaking. For example, port-based waterfront redevelopment calls forth narratives of the "dual city," taking for example Jakarta's disjuncture between older and newer harbor spaces (Nas 2005: 32). Urban rejuvenation requires sizable public and/or private investment, and transformed spaces often assume an exclusionary identity.

Yet, the enduring presence of what we term the "bipolar waterfront" has seldom been explored against the everyday realities of postcolonial neoliberal cities such as Accra and Colombo. As our intertwined narratives reveal, coastal waterfront spaces in both these cities have occupied immensely ambivalent spaces, particularly in terms of their distinctly *urban aquatic* imaginaries. As urban coastlines materially exist as socio-natural sites in which complex land-sea interactions play out (e.g., industrial pollution, marine litter, and coastal erosion), colonial urban shores have long stood as fortified borderlands, while their waterfront harbors represent spaces of liminality in which people, species, goods, capital, and ideas have flowed, while producing cultures of immense hybridity. Meanwhile the coastlines of postcolonial cities continue to reveal striking forms of fragmentation (see Gidel 2011), and of juxtaposition, in which sites are either marked as sites of pleasure, recreation, and excess consumption, on the one hand, or as spaces of squalor, danger, mystery, and intrigue, on the other.

Moreover, megacities in Asia are often cast as risky "hotspots" prone to recurrent cataclysms such as flooding, watery inundation, vector-borne disease, and land subsidence due to excessive groundwater extraction (Siriwardane-de Zoysa, Fitrinitia, & Herbeck 2018). These two polarized worlds—of playground and informal settlement—barely crisscross in our cities. Yet, when they do, they often implicate intense events such as the razing of structures and state-propelled displacement in the name of public safety, urban beautification, and ecological modernization. Thus, the integrative notion of "just sustainabilities" enables a closer unpicking of several aspects encompassed in the re/making of bipolar waterfronts: first, the dynamics of spatial differentiation and segregation, gating and containment, and what has been referred to as "splintering urbanism" (Graham & Marvin 2001); second, a more nuanced appreciation of how formally steered practices of place-making unmake sociocultural and material identities of public spaces as "living tissue offering gathering spaces, shade and forums" (Agyeman 2013: 97); and third, how a socially inclusive and democratized politics of the waterfront can be reimagined.

While the politicalities that pattern the production of waterfront spaces remain salient, we engage with the question of bipolar socio-spatial form through a different point of entry. To echo Brian Hoyle, what does underpin the seemingly universal appeal for the urban visitors "back to the water's edge... interpreted as a tangible sign of the continuing vitality of cities." Therefore we could make the claim that urban coasts are as much in need for democratization as streetscapes, when considering questions of livability, walkability, and its role in enriching everyday practices of sociality and leisure.

Yet, as the historian Alain Corbin (1988) posits, the contemporary framing of the waterfront as a playground and leisure space is deeply rooted in the Western cultural imaginary of the picturesque waterfront, which he frames as being driven by the "inherent *magic of water*" ushering citizens and seascape, from its beaches to the romanticized harbor view, which has been evolving since the eighteenth century. In contemporary life, it is the sensory value of seascapes (akin to landscapes)—and one that is primarily *visual*—that renders consumptive significance and makes such spaces amenable to the calculus of economic valuation. To invoke Harvey (2003), the dialectics of space and place across the urban littoral constantly co-evolve, for in order to be picturesque, its antithetical Other must exist as a reference point, as evidenced in writings on poverty, "slum," and "disaster tourism" (see Shondell Miller 2008).

Moreover, the primarily Euro-American discourse on enculturing new sensibilities of "Blue Urbanism" (mirroring the terrestrial quest for "green" urbanity) brings to the fore questions around rethinking relationships between the coastal city and the ocean, and of its citizenry as *homo aqua urbanis*, purported as a paradigm that crosscuts all aspects of lived life from food culture and urban design to political activism (Beatley 2014). While we take little issue with the idealism behind this rallying call, we find the planning-oriented perspective and the flattening of transcultural differences in land-ocean imaginaries rather limiting. Furthermore, planning visions such as these barely address questions of unequal spatial access and use, fundamentally missing the question of justice. What is left to be asked is whether most urban littorals, by virtue of their proximity to the sea, interact with and privilege the marine in similar ways? Moreover, is the presence of the sea universally felt by all in the same way, through a visual sense of sublime aesthetics, spiritual being, and of embodied practices?

In subsequent sections, we explore distinct social imaginaries of the urban waterfront by putting Accra and Colombo in conversation with each other. We reflect on contemporary transformations that have flecked littoral urbanscapes in ways that produce sharper distinctions between affluence and marginality, land and sea, work and leisure. These paradoxes are framed against several subthemes that crisscross our accounts on each city: the historic narratives that Accra's and Colombo's key maritime waterfront spaces reveal, the types of visions and activities that come to be privileged, and how space comes to be shared, what constitutes as sharing if at all, and how places are reproduced as exclusionary sites.

Arguably, an inclusive politics of the waterfront concerns itself with questions of flow, connectivity, and interdependence, just as much as the mediation of access. Littoral urban place-making, particularly in coastal metropolises, constitutes an ever-evolving milieu in which localized meanings and practices on socio-environmental sustainability and justice are contested and remade. We end by exploring what a socio-ecologically inclusive politics of the waterfront would entail, when traced against the conceptual contours of "just sustainabilities" as a political project.

Waterfront Politics: Of Affluence and Marginality

Rapti (Colombo)

Colombo's urban shoreline may leave an ambiguous mark on visitors arriving from afar, beckoned by promises of pristine white coastlines yet finding a much more complicated setting. While Colombo holds the highest concentration of the country's colonial Anglophone and primarily English-speaking elite that crosscut the island's ethno-religious divisions, its urbanscape remains socioculturally, economically, and politically stratified. Colombo's contemporary securitized state, which assumed early form during its countrywide Marxist insurrections of the 1970s and 1980s, further complicated the city's urban historiography of violence, often encrusted in the social memory of its anti-Tamil pogroms, and over the course of the state's thirty-year civil war. Desolate urban beaches became semi-militarized sites, presumably spaces where extra-judiciary and other forms of clandestine violence occurred, as bodies were recurrently "discovered" washed ashore. Unmarked coastal stretches were also seen as locales of subversive activity, close to informal settlements that were implicated as reserve mobs during trajectories of state-sponsored communal violence. What remains striking about coastal Colombo, and indeed Sri Lanka, is its seeming lack of sea-related iconographies and historic-cultural references to its diversely "subaltern" littoral and maritime life worlds (Radicati 2019). While its green-clad "island" imaginary, hemmed in by a chalky coastline, appears as a well-worn tourist representation, neither Colombo nor any of the country's maritime histories were enlisted into its pre-Independence nationalist discourses. It was the precolonial and presumably rice-based hydraulic civilizations of the dryzone interior—of *Rajarata*—that were lionized, combining with the idealized imaginaries of rural village life in the interior (Nissan & Stirrat 1990). Therefore, unlike other Anglophone port cities such as Singapore or Mombasa, Colombo's littoral colonially marked identity has remained fairly muted until recent times, appearing as an ideologically absent figure or a culturally peripheral narrative, if at all.

Historically, Colombo's shoreline has sat antithetically to the island's palm-fronded coastscapes peddled in tourist guidebooks and websites. "Beaches" were produced by the interplay of economic valuation, utility, and historic patterns of consumption. They were distinctly demarcated and cordoned, effectively seen as spaces of classed cultural production, often associated with exclusive restaurants and resplendent colonial hotels. More tellingly, "the beach" was simultaneously an all-place and a non-place, often to be found *outside* Colombo's bustling city limits. Thus, the waterfront by default often presupposed the existence of a beachfront, for when Anglophone urban middle-class Lankans referred to having been "down south," the term inevitably inferred to some form of sensory engagement with the coastline or sea air. Socially, then, the marine waterfront remains far from being the "cultic" Euro-American beach site that was transformed over time from a "place of status display" to a mass "performance space for sentimental rites of family solidarity" (Gillis 2012: 152).

Arguably, to most cultural outsiders, Colombo's existing waterfront seemingly comes alive through tourist exactions, layered upon exclusionary colonial sites in which particular landmarks such as the Colombo Club and the Galle Face Hotel produced their own waterfront places and micro-politics of enclaved consumption along Galle Face Green, Colombo's only ocean-side park covering a vastly reduced space of five hectares. Open jetties, seaside walkways, and promenades are relatively uncommon for many smaller coastal towns, with the exception of larger colonial garrison-marked spaces such as Galle and Trincomalee. Thus, a site such as Galle Face stands to offer a relatively more open, capacious cosmos for public gatherings and spaces of organized resistance and protest, largely left unmediated by commercialized enclosures. For Colombo's affluent Anglophone urbanites and economic elite, the "exposed" spaces of the crowded urban waterfront are often places to be eluded.

The reconfiguration of Colombo's marine waterfronts was part and parcel of its postwar construction boom, "a development founded on an 'economy of appearances'" (Ruwanpura, Brown, & Chan 2019, citing Tsing 2011). Indeed, the blooming of public-private revitalization projects entailing luxury condominiums clearly demarcated entertainment districts festooned with sky restaurants, shopping arcades, and specialty cafes, mimicked top-down urban planning templates of priming Colombo as a "market city," and as a part of global network of investment capital, labor, and information (cf. Hutson 2016: 14–6). These development plans invariably embodied centralized mega-projects such as Colombo's "Megapolis," which began by focusing on urban livability and enhanced public mobility across the Western Province (Ministry of Megapolis & Western Development 2015).

Yet, what made these recent transformations particularly striking was the discursive militarization of its urban planning projects and policies, as the Urban Redevelopment Authority (which came under the aegis of the former secretary of defense, now president-elect) consequently deployed thousands of military personnel to revitalize a diverse patchwork of urban spaces. Narratives around urban beautification were barely associated with sustainability-driven sensibilities, however exclusionary or elitist interpretations of "sustainable" city life might be (Nagaraj 2017). Urban desires for Colombo's transformation harked back to another island metropolis—Singapore—epitomized by its self-fashioned global image as being "clean and green." Arguably these projects paid lip-service to Singapore's brand of biophilic urbanism, however contested (see Newman 2014). These narratives of change barely got past echoes of Sir Patrick Geddes' vision of planning colonial Colombo as the "Garden City of the East" (Van Horen 2002), and such discourses both politically and in local media were often peppered with nostalgia and postwar nationalism.

Derelict sites in older colonial areas such as Fort—the colonial business district—morphed into gentrified spaces within a span of a few years, while previously discrete waterfront places were marked off as high-end zones for cultural entertainment. The transformation of waterfront spaces also came to be invoked through celebratory metaphors of postwar progress, implicating narratives of "liberating" the land and of spatial purification, foregrounding the displacement of waterside tenements and squatter enclaves from economically profitable plots. This "redemptive validity to salvage the city," to borrow Beswick, Parmar, & Sil's phrase (2015: 791), from the double bind of wartime torpor and the disorderliness of informal city life stood as an urgent corrective, the discursive futuring of Colombopolitanism—as a distinct mode of seeing and being. At its blandest, it embodied a celebratory trope of and for gentrification; a popular English-language entertainment webzine Yamu.com bemoaned during one of its filmed walking tours that inner-city streets of Colombo Fort were "gentrifying, but not fast enough."

At the heart of the Megapolis Masterplan was the intensely contested 269-hectare Colombo Port City, constructed by the Chinese Harbor Engineering Corporation (CHEC) and financed by a bilateral loan. Envisioned as a 1.4-billion-dollar land reclamation project on a scale that has never been witnessed before in Sri Lanka, its economic imperative was ultimately pushed by both its main political parties as a "postwar development vision geared toward reinventing Colombo as a regional 'world class' hub for trade, tourism, and finance" and as a key node in China's One Belt, One Road initiative (Ruwanpura, Brown, & Chan 2019: 2). Meanwhile, the past decade witnessed much debate on its dubious trajectory of environmental auditing and public consultation, alongside the irreversible ecological impacts of biodiversity loss and coastal degradation, as a combined result of sand mining, dredging, and hinterland quarrying. Moreover, plans to reclaim land from sea were often questioned by critical policymakers, fisher collectives, environmental, and urban activities alike, while it was said that the CHEC had not only "corrupted" the planning process but was also said to have broken forty-seven national environmental laws (Ruwanpura, Brown, & Chan 2019: 11).

This predicament embodies a "sustainability deficit" that pits "green" and "blue" urbanism against "brown" development. Processes such as gentrification, like in cases of environmental degradation and pollution, are not only vested disproportionately on the disenfranchised (Agyeman & Evans 2004) but catalyze other forms of territorialized place-making in further impoverishing littoral poor. The figure of Colombo's "new" waterfront stands out, but not in ways that particular forms of heritage and a "politics of forgetting" are practiced in a number of other postcolonial cities (Fernandes 2004; Lee & Yeoh 2006). Instead, the conscious will to decouple and disengage almost entirely from the past remains telling.

A number of other private mega-projects such as the integrated high-rise luxury condominium and hotel development, The Waterfront (now renamed Cinnamon Life), promise residents an "iconic life capital" in which the waterfront itself is re-themed as a boundary line, accentuating a moat-like presence. Indeed, the promise of what Dear (2011: 18) terms as starchitect-designed "spectacular urbanisms" prefigures little novelty mimicking newer spaces of urbane fascination. While Bradley and Hedrén (2004: 5) argue that such processes of aesthetization often taper down to "matters of lifestyle," these waterfront developments foretell a distinct epistemological break from the island's postcolonial past, which glorified particular expressions of Orientalist indigenized architecture (see Pieris 2013). It is here that older Lefebvrean notions of the right(s) to the city can be invoked. If we are to consider the right to "produce urban life in new terms" (Attoh 2011), the waterfront as remade heritage, as gentrified space, and as a project of ecological modernization is but a sliver of a repackaged promise.

Moreover, political endeavors such as the Port City stand as symbols heralding newer visions of metropolitan living, in terms of entirely *offshoring urbanism*. Today, the docklands of the colonial port city have shrunk in both size and importance and are no longer associated with work. In moments like these, the presence of the bipolar waterfront is erased in order to achieve the project of seamless horizon-making and creeping forms of littoral enclavement. Here, the emphasis is placed on *islanding* "high-net-worth-individuals" via the creation of tax havens and its own legal systems (Ruwanpura, Brown, & Chan 2019), which are materially separated from an aging urban mainland by water. Paradoxically, the socio-materialities of water are conceived in terms of their proclivity to both socially connect and divide.

No longer does the remaking of new waterfront spaces offer to be read in terms of the novel and the innovative layering over the old and the derelict. In Colombo, emerging spaces like the "Port City" sit adjoining the old city, stitched together by markedly colonial and aging landmarks like the Galle Face Green and the Old Parliament House. Arguably, their adjacent placement recreates new dualisms and urban littorals divided along a socioeconomic boundary line: the depreciating mainland against glitzy neoliberal sites of exception. Furthermore, as opposed to the connective, (post)colonial utilitarian harborfront, the neoliberal waterfront, for the most part, exists as a pristine reflective surface, an all-present figure meditating upon the neon-lit installations of the skyscraper city foretelling not only of neoliberal progress but also of uniformity.

Epifania (Accra)

Just as in Sri Lanka, today's Ghana is moving quickly into a celebratory trope of gentrification in its capital city, Accra, as an additional consequence of growth and modernization. The country's rising urbanization trend has been mostly driven by rural-urban migration, as well as the natural increase in towns from the growth and reclassification of villages (Songsore 2003). This rapid urbanization is said to burden the nation-state with the key challenges of slum growth, urban mobility, environmental sanitation, urban security, and a housing deficit (Vanderpuye 2015). The constant and steady flow of migration to Ghana's capital is a trend with roots in the colonial era, from about 1877 to 1957, when concerted resource centralization in Accra truly began (Konadu-Agyemang 2001a). Similarly, Accra's present state of underdeveloped housing, services, and urban infrastructure also has its roots in British colonialism. More specifically, both are tied to colonial wealth accumulation derived from salt trade, the slave trade, and subsequent agricultural enterprises such as cocoa production, all of which enabled the rise of Ga merchants alongside other well-to-do in-migrants (Robertson 1990). These then-advantaged groups were able to avail themselves of the social and cultural capital imbued in a (gendered) Western education system, plus certain limited privileges inherent in the colonial policy of segregation, resulting in a significant stratification of populations living in Accra—along intersectional lines of "race," ethnicity, gender, and income.

The housing and urban infrastructural challenges in Accra, however, are not only the result of a colonial legacy rooted in urbanization policies that were discriminatory and insensitive to the local cultural context. Rather, they are also a result of the failure of successive Ghanaian governments to derive appropriate housing policies and their incorporation of the country into a rather competitive, global, and capitalist economy (Konadu-Agyemang 2001b), one which is unforgiving to the poorer segments of any society.

Accra sits within the Greater Accra Region, as the largest of Ghana's ten urban centers. In 2000, the population in Accra was already 1,657,856, of which 57.1 percent were female (Government of Ghana 2000). Today this population figure is at 2.27 million. Accra alone accounts for 30 percent of the urban population of Ghana and 10 percent of the total population of Ghana. In fact, Accra has the highest rate of urbanization in Ghana and one of the highest in West Africa (Konadu-Agyemang 2001b). Furthermore, in the city of Accra, females head 28.1 percent of households, even though there are nearly as many female migrants as male (Government of Ghana 2008), with implications for the feminization of urban dispossession and related poverty.

The continuous and increased rural-urban migration in Ghana is what has led to acute housing shortages in urban areas such as Accra, with subsequent illegal land development and the formation of several unserviced and overcrowded informal settlements (Government of Ghana 2014a). In 2001, the "slum" population for Ghana (in major cities) was estimated at a 4,993,000 with a growth rate of 1.83 percent per annum, expected to reach 5.8 million by 2010 (United Nations Centre for Human Settlements 2008b; Government of Ghana 2014b). In 2014, the population living in slums—as a percentage of the urban population—was reported as 37.9 percent.

Many of those who live within informal settlements in Ghana are subject to at least one shelter deprivation in the form of a lack of clean water and sanitation, insufficient living space, low-quality unaffordable housing structures, and/or no security of tenure (United Nations Centre for Human Settlements 2008a). Additionally, housing occupancy rates are high in Ghana's capital. As early as in 1990, when the United Nations Development Program and the Government of Ghana conducted a survey in Accra, they found that the average number of persons per room was 2.9 (greater than the United Nations standard of 2.5) and that 46.3 percent of the city's households occupied single rooms. This lack of space has had grave implications for its occupants, especially women living in Accra because they spend more time in their houses than men do (Asiama 1997) for both productive and reproductive reasons.

Uneven urban development in Accra has had an effect on residential units, lineage groupings, rules of descent, and inheritance, especially among the Ga population (Robertson 1990), who are the initial inhabitants of the city. Unfortunately, with the Government of Ghana's current wholesale embrace of neoliberal models of urban redevelopment, these historic and still existing deprivations—as experienced by low-income populations in informal settlements within Accra—are now being further compounded by forced evictions and the ensuing threat of homelessness. This is a consequence of the nation's competitive bid to modernize Accra through various urban improvements and beautification projects.

This can be seen as an acute case of what Fält (2015) describes as "urban revanchism" caused by the insistence on manifesting a "post-political visioning" of the city (3); in this case, the city of Accra being converted into an idyllic "24-hour 'live-work-play' environment" ("Accra Integrated Development" 2016; "Accra Waterfront" 2016)—replete with landmark developments, waterfront lifestyles, resort style urban nodes, and private sector leasehold and freehold sales opportunities ("Ghana Rising" 2016)—made exclusively for the well-heeled international traveler and local inhabitant.

Fält points us to one case of urban revanchism in Accra: that is, the disciplining of urban space through dispossession, in her detailed account of the demolition of Mensah Guinea, an informal settlement. In September 2014, the Government of Ghana demolished this settlement ("AMA Demolition" 2014; "Mensah Guinea Demolition" 2014) in order to make way for an exclusive waterfront enclave for tourists, which had not materialized a year and a half later (Fält 2015). In the government's bid to give substance to Accra's recently acquired Millennium City status, they saw fit to engage in a "medicalization of space": that is, the sanitization of Mensah Guinea, where they diagnosed the settlements' inhabitants as an aesthetic eyesore and health hazard in need of swift eradication (Fält 2015: 15), unjustly rendering its inhabitants as problematic to the sustainability of a rapidly modernizing city.

A similar tale of waterfront dispossession can also be told by the residents of Accra's biggest informal settlement, Old Fadama. Here too, informal settlement homes were categorized as ugly, chaotic, congested, and unruly ailments to the making of Accra into a modern city, due to the neighborhood's supposed "infestation," with loitering, criminal, and diseased inhabitants (Onuoha 2014). As a result, a section of Old Fadama, close to the Korle Lagoon, was razed to the ground in June 2015 ("Massive Demolition at Old Fadama" 2015).

Any deep analysis of the situation in Accra reveals a nuanced, complex, and contradictory story of when neoliberal urban policy meets informal settlements (Afenah 2009), especially within an age of the "globalization of gentrification" and the proliferation of leisured (waterfront) cosmopolitanism. More specifically, even though the human rights and freedoms of Ghanaian citizens are protected by the constitution, there have still been several forced evictions (Afenah 2009) in the name of public good and especially as related to alternative land use and a new urban agenda embodied by Ghana's first *National Urban Policy Framework* (Government of Ghana 2012), as well as by its *Slum Upgrading and Prevention Strategy, National Spatial Development Framework,* and *National Transportation Plan* (Vanderpuye 2015).

The case of Old Fadama—with its threatened mix of poorly serviced, residential and commercial informal developments—is symptomatic of the historic and continued inability of the Government of Ghana to deal with Accra's rapid growth, in a consistent and systematic fashion, in that much of the settlement's growth can also be attributed to official planning decisions such as the Accra Metropolitan Authority's relocation of hawkers and a yam market to Old Fadama as part of "decongestion exercises" in 1991 and 2005 (Afenah 2009). This and a string of other migration flows into the settlement—due to its low rents and central location (between the Korle Lagoon and the Odaw River)—have produced an area of high density that is also prone to flooding. Old Fadama's physical location and the associated "health risks" and the "illegal occupancy" are among the many reasons cited by the Government of Ghana for the need to "sanitize" the area and, thus, deprive its residents—alongside several other informal settlement communities located in prime urban and waterfront redevelopment sites—of their "right to (the modernizing) city" (Afenah 2009).

In such a neoliberal landscape, informal settlement communities become the social effects of dominant groups' spatial constructs, thus, "grand narratives" on what is leisure space, a business district, "modern" housing, and so on. At the same time, artisanal fisherfolk also find themselves being squeezed out of the intense modernization, that is, commercialization, of the oceanscape and its shores—be that through beach resort development, oil rigging, and/or the highly protested Chinese infiltration of the fishery industry through both legal and illegal means (Amoo-Adare 2019). In other words, the best of Accra's blue urbanism fare has not been designed for the majority of its urban population, many of whom are (and will continue to be) relied upon for servicing, guarding, cleaning, and generally maintaining these multiple "modern" offerings of lifestyle choice. And yet it is these urban regenerations (and their ideologies), alongside the historic centralization of resources in Accra, that continue to draw Ghanaian citizens from the rural and other less metropolitan hinterlands into the very imaginaries and socioeconomic spaces in which they are not necessarily welcome and indeed are often denied any real kinds of "rights to the city" (Harvey 2003) and its futuring.

Conclusion

As our intertwined narratives reveal, in the cases of both coastal Accra and Colombo, the colonial waterfront came to occupy similar utilitarian imaginaries as their bustling port cities grew into centers of maritime trade as docklands and harbor services expanded, and marginal estuarine and brackish water spaces became sites of poverty and social marginality. Today, the postcolonial waterfront transforms into a neoliberal site of leisure and consumption, as informal settlements are displaced to make way for visible expressions of modernity in their built form. In both the cases of Accra and in Colombo, which have witnessed vastly different trajectories of rural-urban migration yet share relatively similar practices of centralized spatial planning, the b/ordering of waterfront spaces forecloses a distinct micro-politics of urban revanchism (see van Eijk 2010). In particular, their metropolitan coastal spaces are not simply disciplined and reconfigured. They are reproduced in ways that create patterns of expected mimicry, over stratifications of exclusionary citizenship. Like in the case of Old Fadama, where informal housing settlements are razed to the ground to make way for developers, new forms of waterfront living in Colombo disclose futures not only of exclusionary space but of sanitized absence, as many of its luxury condominiums come to be increasingly acquired as investments. Ultimately, in the cases of both Accra and Colombo, the urban marine waterfront continues to play a significant role in trajectories of urban revanchism, and by extension socioeconomic dispossession.

As international venture capital and public-private partnerships continue to increasingly dominate the global property development landscape, the combined stories of Accra and Colombo nevertheless reveal the fact that no monolithic imaginary of the urban coastal waterfront exists. However, as these new developments overlay older micro-politics of the (post)colonial waterfront, we therefore suggest that more research is needed on exploring how distinct materialities of the coast are discursively constructed through locally embedded knowledges and perceptions, and how they are concretely experienced through embodied practices of living with (or, for that matter, without) water in an urban context.

In addition, such further research within the Global South would benefit from the growing number of decolonial approaches and processes, which seek to reconstitute diverse indigenous "world senses" and "ways of knowing." For there has always been a wealth of epistemologies, ontologies, cosmologies, and philosophies about life, which are often occluded by the universalization of Western (or more precisely Euro-North American) thought and the exportation of capitalism and its corollaries of internationalized education systems and academic knowledge regimes; neoliberal economic and governance models; "modern" lifestyles informed by global popular cultures; and other forms of "coloniality of power" (Quijano 2000, 2007).

In closing, we propose that such additional research would mean engaging in a form of social and cognitive justice that seeks an "autonomous and enabling diversity" (Santos 2014: 15) in all knowledge production for social change. Lest we seek to entangle ourselves deeper into the "colonial matrix of power," where the mobility and academic reification of certain ideas turns them into universalized and exportable "grand narratives"—be they oppositional to other globalized concepts such as "waterfront development." What is thus called for, as put forth by the tenets of "just sustainabilities," is a rejection of all types of "grand narratives," for deep, or deeper, engagement with local knowledges, sciences, imaginaries, and sensibilities (on/of urbanity), including the rescue and reconstitution of many of these oft-silenced ways of seeing, knowing, relating and/or becoming. We affirm Broto and Westman's (2017) assertion that just sustainabilities represent "a discourse of hope… its objective is to deliver discursive tools that can be appropriated by different actors to inspire visions of future sustainable and just cities and make them, or at least part of them, happen" (648), thereby, we hope, leading to many possibilities and pathways for deeply realized, locally based enactments of "the right to the waterfront."

Note

1   Formative writings on port cities, particularly those engaging with postcolonial spaces, have overwhelmingly focused on morphological evolution and the territorial organization of space (see Panditharatne 1964; McGee 1967; Grewal 1991). More recent studies on port cities, in general, have explored a host of obscured dimensions of everyday cultural life along the waterfront, paying closer attention to multiple forms of sociality, exchange, mobility (see Beaven, Bell, & James 2016).

References

"Accra Integrated Development, Ghana" (2016), Perennial Real Estate Holdings Limited. Available online: http://www.perennialrealestate.com.sg/properties/ghana/gh-accra-integrated-development.html (Accessed June 6, 2016).

"Accra Waterfront, Ghana" (2016), British Expertise International. Available online: http://www.britishexpertise.org/bx/pages/Project_view/236.php (Accessed June 6, 2016).

Afenah, A. (2009), *Conceptualizing the effects of neoliberal urban policies on housing rights: An analysis of the attempted unlawful forced eviction of and informal settlement in Accra, Ghana*, DPU Working Paper No. 139, London: UCL Development Planning Unit.

Agyeman, J. (2013), *Introducing Just Sustainabilities: Policy, Planning, and Practice*. London: Zed Books.

Agyeman, J. & B. Evans (2004), "'Just sustainability': The emerging discourse of environmental justice in Britain?" *Geographical Journal*, 170(2): 155–64.

Agyeman, J., R.D. Bullard, & B. Evans (2003), "Joined-up thinking: Bringing together sustainability, environmental justice & equity," in J. Agyeman, R.D. Bullard, & B. Evans (eds), *Just Sustainabilities: Development in an Unequal World*, Cambridge: MIT Press.

"AMA Demolition—Adom Kasee (5-9-14)" (2014), AdomTVTube, YouTube Video. Available online: https://www.youtube.com/watch?v=pUj93zN1Rlw#t=23.121208 (Accessed June 12, 2016).

Amin, A. & N. Thrift (2003), *Cities: Reimagining the Urban*, Cambridge: Polity Press.

Amoo-Adare, E. (2019), "*Who Rules the Waves? A Critical Reading of (An)Other-ed Modern Future*," Postcolonial Oceans: Contradictions and Heterogeneities in the Epistemes of Salt Water, Joint Annual Conference of GAPS and IACPL, Bremen: University of Bremen.

Asiama, S.O. (1997), "Crossing the barrier of time: The Asante woman in urban land development," *Africa LII*, 2: 212–36.

Attoh, K.A. (2011), "What kind of right is the right to the city?" *Progress in Human Geography*, 35(5): 669–85.

Avni, N. & N.A. Teschner (2019), "Urban waterfronts: Contemporary streams of planning conflicts," *Journal of Planning Literature*, 34(4): 408–20.

Beatley, T. (2014), *Blue Urbanism*, Washington, DC: Island Press.

Beaven, B., K. Bell, & R. James (2016), "Introduction," in B. Beaven, K. Bell, & R. James (eds), *Port Towns and Urban Cultures: International Histories of the Waterfront, c. 1700-2000*, 1–11, London: Palgrave MacMillan.
Beswick, K., M. Parmar, & E. Sil (2015), "Towards a spatial practice of the postcolonial city," *Interventions*, 17 (6): 789–801.
Boland, P., Bronte, J., & Muir, J. (2017), "On the waterfront: Neoliberal urbanism and the politics of public benefit," *Cities*, 61: 117–27.
Bradley, K. & J. Hedrén (2004), "Utopian thought in the making of green futures," in K. Bradley & J. Hedrén (eds), *Green Utopianism: Perspectives, Politics and Micro-Practices*, 1–7, New York & Oxford: Routledge.
Broeze, F. (2010), "Brides of the sea revisited," in F. Broeze (ed), *Gateways of Asia: Port Cities of Asia in the 13th–20th Centuries*, 1–17, London & New York: Routledge.
Broto, V.C. & L. Westman (2017), "Just sustainabilities and local action: Evidence from 400 flagship initiatives," *Local Environment*, 22(5): 635–50.
Colven, E. (2017), "Understanding the allure of big infrastructure: Jakarta's great garuda sea wall project," *Water Alternatives*, 10(2): 250–64.
Cooper, F. (1987), *On the African Waterfront: Urban Disorder and the Transformation of Work in Colonial Mombasa*, New Haven: Yale University Press.
Corbin, A. (1988/1995), *The Lure of the Sea: The discovery of the seaside 1750-1840*, trans. J. Phelps, London & New York: Penguin.
Darieva, T. (2011), "A remarkable gift in a postcolonial city: The past and present of the baku promenade," in T. Darieva, W. Kaschuba, & M. Krebs (eds), *Urban Spaces after Socialism: Ethnographies of Public Spaces in Eurasian Cities*, 153–81, Frankfurt & New York: Campus Verlag.
Dear, M. (2011), "The urban question after modernity," in H. Schmid, W. Sahr, & J. Urry (eds), *Cities and Fascination: Beyond the Surplus of Meaning*, 17–31, Surrey: Ashgate.
Desfor, G. & J. Laidley (2011), "Fixity and flow of urban waterfront change," in G. Desfor, J. Laidley, Q. Stevens, & D. Schubert (eds), *Transforming Urban Waterfronts: Fixity and Flow*, 74–101, New York & Oxford: Routledge.
Dovey, K., & L. Sandercock (2005), *Fluid City: Transforming Melbourne's Urban Waterfront*, London: Psychology Press.
Fält, L. (2015), "*From Shacks to Skyscrapers: Post-Political City Visioning in Accra*," RC21 International Conference, The Ideal City: Between Myth and Reality, Urbino: University of Urbino Carlo Bo.
Fernandes, L. (2004), "The politics of forgetting: Class politics, state power and the restructuring of urban space in India," *Urban Studies*, 41 (12): 2415–30.
Ferreira, S. & G. Visser (2007), "Creating an African Riviera: Revisiting the impact of the Victoria and Alfred waterfront development in Cape Town," *Urban Forum*, 18(3): 227–46.
"Ghana Rising: DHK's Future Plans for Accra" (2016), Available online: http://ghanarising.blogspot.de/2012/09/dhks-future-plans-for-accra.html (Accessed June 6, 2016).
Gidel, M. (2011), "Fragmentation on the waterfront: Coastal squatting settlements and urban renewal projects in the Caribbean," in G. Desfor, J. Laidley, Q. Stevens, & D. Schubert (eds), *Transforming Urban Waterfronts: Fixity and Flow*, 35–54, New York & Oxford: Routledge.
Gillis, J.R. (2012), *The Human Shore: Seacoasts in History*, Chicago: University of Chicago Press.
Gordon, D.L.A. (1997), "Managing the changing political environment in urban waterfront redevelopment," *Urban Studies*, 34(1): 61–83.

Government of Ghana (2000), *2000 Population & Housing Census: Provisional results*, Accra: Ghana Statistical Service.
Government of Ghana (2008), *Ghana Living Standards Survey: Report of the Fifth Round*, Accra: Ghana Statistical Service.
Government of Ghana (2012), *National Urban Policy Framework*, Accra: Ministry of Local Government & Rural Development.
Government of Ghana (2014a), *2010 Population & Housing Census Report: Housing in Ghana*, Accra: Ghana Statistical Service.
Government of Ghana (2014b), *2010 Population & Housing Census Report: Urbanisation*, Accra: Ghana Statistical Service.
Graf, A. & B.H. Chua (eds) (2009), *Port Cities in Asia and Europe*, Oxford: Routledge.
Graham, S. & S. Marvin (2001), *Splintering Urbanism: Networked Infrastructures, Technological Mobilities and the Urban Condition*, London & New York: Routledge.
Grant, R. & J. Nijman (2003), "Post-colonial cities in the global era: A comparative study of Mumbai and Accra," in A.K. Dutt, A.G. Noble, G. Venugopal, & S. Subbiah (eds), *Challenges to Asian Urbanization in the 21st Century*, 31–52, Dordrecht: Kluwer Academic Publishers.
Grewal, R. (1991), "Urban morphology under colonial rule," in I. Banga (ed), *The City in Indian History*, 173–90, New Delhi: Manohar.
Harvey, D. (2003), "The right to the city," *International Journal of Urban and Regional Research*, 27(4): 939–41.
Hutson, M.A. (2016), *The Urban Struggle for Economic, Environmental and Social Justice: Deepening their Roots*, London & New York: Routledge, Earthscan.
Hoyle, B. (2000), "Global and local change on the port-city waterfront," *Geographical Review*, 90(3): 359–417.
Konadu-Agyemang, K. (2001a), "A survey of housing conditions and characteristics in Accra, an African city," *Habitat International*, 25(1): 15–34.
Konadu-Agyemang, K. (2001b), *The Political Economy of Housing and Urban Development in Africa: Ghana's Experience from Colonial Times to 1998*, Westport: Praeger.
Kong, L. (2007), "Cultural icons and urban development in Asia: Economic imperative, national identity, and global city status," *Political Geography*, 26(4): 383–404.
Lee, Y. & B. Yeoh (2006), "Globalisation and the politics of forgetting," in Y. Lee & B. Yeoh (ed), *Globalisation and the Politics of Forgetting*, 1–9, Oxford & New York: Routledge.
Mah, A. (2014), *Port Cities and Global Legacies: Urban Identity, Waterfront Work, and Radicalism*, London: Palgrave MacMillan.
Malm, A. (2012), "Sea wall politics: Uneven and combined protection of the nile delta coastline in the face of sea level rise," *Critical Sociology*, 39(6): 803–32.
"Massive Demolition at Old Fadama—Accra" (2015), Joy News YouTube Video. Available online: https://www.youtube.com/watch?v=uK5IqYvRaos (Accessed June 11, 2016).
McGee, T.G. (1967), *The Southeast Asian City*, New York: Praeger.
"Mensah Guinea Demolition—AM News (8-9-15)"(2014), Joy News, YouTube Video, Available online. https://www.youtube.com/watch?v=Dfszaat0EuY (Accessed June 11, 2016).
Ministry of Megapolis & Western Development (2015), *The Megapolis: Western Region Masterplan, 2030—Sri Lanka: From Island to Continent*. Available online: http://www.slembassykorea.com/eng/download/Megapolis%20Master%20Plan.pdf (Accessed December 12, 2019)
Morgia, L. & T.J. Vicino (2013), "Waterfront politics: Revisiting the case of Camden, New Jersey's redevelopment," *Urban Research & Practice*, 6 (3): 329–45.

Murphey, R. (1989), "On the evolution of the port city," in F. Broeze (ed), *Brides of the Sea: Port Cities of Asia from the 16th to the 20th Centuries*, 223–46, Kensington: New South Wales University Press.

Nagaraj, V.K. (2017), "From smokestacks to luxury condos: The housing rights struggle of the millworkers of Mayura Place, Colombo," *Contemporary South Asia*, 24(4): 429–43.

Nas, P.J.M. (2005), "Port cities," *IIAS Newsletter*, 37: 32.

Newman, P. (2014), "Biophilic urbanism: A case study on Singapore," *Australian Planner*, 51(1): 47–65.

Nissan, E. & R.L. Stirrat (1990), "The generation of communal identities," in J. Spencer (ed), *Sri Lanka: History and the Roots of Conflict*, 19–44, London & New York: Routledge.

Nixon, R. (2011), *Slow Violence and the Environmentalism of the Poor*, Cambridge: Harvard University Press.

Noble, A.G. & B.L. Panditharatne (2003), "Colombo and the pattern of South Asian and port city models," in A.K. Dutt, A.G. Noble, G. Venugopal, & S. Subbiah (ed), *Challenges to Asian Urbanization in the 21st Century*, 53–66, Dordrecht: Kluwer Academic Publishers.

Onuoha, D. (2014), "Decongesting Accra," *The Johannesburg Salon*, 7: 123–30.

Panditharatne, B.L. (1964), "The functional zones of the Colombo City," *University of Ceylon Review*, 22 (1-2): 138–64.

Pieris, A. (2013), *Architecture and Nationalism in Sri Lanka: The Trouser Under the Cloth*, Oxford & New York: Routledge.

Pinto, P. J. & G. M. Kondolf (2020), "The Fit of urban waterfront interventions: Matters of size, money, and function," *Sustainability*, 12: 4079.

Quijano, A. (2000), "Coloniality of power, Eurocentrism, and Latin America," *Neplanta: Views from South*, 1(3): 533–80.

Quijano, A. (2007), "Coloniality and modernity/rationality," *Cultural Studies*, 21 (2): 168–78.

Radicati, A. (2019), "Island journeys: Fisher itineraries and national imaginaries in Colombo," *Contemporary South Asia*, 27(3): 330–41.

Robertson, C. (1990), *Sharing the Same Bowl: A Socioeconomic History of Women and Class in Accra, Ghana*, Bloomington: University of Michigan Press.

Ruwanpura, K.N., B. Brown, & L. Chan (2019), "(Dis)connecting Colombo: Situating the megapolis in postwar Sri Lanka," *The Professional Geographer*, 72(1): 165–79.

Santos, B.S. (2014), *Epistemologies of the South: Justice Against Epistemicide*, London: Routledge.

Schubert, D. (2011), "Waterfront revitalizations: From a local to a regional perspective in London, Barcelona, Rotterdam and Hamburg," in G. Desfor, J. Laidley, Q. Stevens, & D. Schubert (eds), *Transforming Urban Waterfronts: Fixity and Flow*, 74–101, New York & Oxford: Routledge.

Shondell Miller, D. (2008), "Disaster tourism and disaster landscape attractions after Hurricane Katrina: An auto-ethnographic journey," *International Journal of Culture, Tourism & Hospitality Research*, 2(2): 115–31.

Siriwardane-de Zoysa, R., I.S. Fitrinitia, & J. Herbeck (2018), "Watery incursions: The securitisation of everyday 'flood cultures' in metro manila and coastal Jakarta," *International Quarterly for Asian Studies*, 49(1-2): 105–26.

Sivasundaram, S. (2013), *Islanded: Britain, Sri Lanka and the Bounds of an Indian Ocean Colony*, Chicago: University of Chicago Press.

Smith, N. (2010), *Uneven Development: Nature, Capital, and the Production of Space*, Athens: University of Georgia Press.

Songsore, J. (2003), *Towards a Better Understanding of Urban Change: Urbanization, National Development and Inequality in Ghana*, Accra: Ghana Universities Press.

Soja, E. (2009), "The city and spatial justice," *Justice Spatiale/Spatial Justice*, 1(1): 1–5.

Steinberg, P.E., E. Nyman, & M.J. Caraccioli (2012), "Atlas swam: Freedom, capital, and floating sovereignties in the seasteading vision," *Antipode*, 44(4): 1532–50.

Storbjörk, S. & M. Hjerpe (2014), "'Sometimes climate adaptation is politically correct': A Case study of planners and politicians negotiating climate adaptation in waterfront spatial planning," *European Planning Studies*, 22(11): 2268–86.

Tarlow, S. (2000), "Landscapes of memory: The nineteenth-century garden cemetery," *European Journal of Archeology*, 3(2): 217–39.

Thiranagama, S. (2011), *In My Mother's House: Civil War in Sri Lanka*, Philadelphia: University of Pennsylvania Press.

Tsing, A. (2011), "Inside the economy of appearances," *Public Culture*, 12(1): 115–44.

Uggla, Y. (2014), 'The urban park as 'paradise contrived'," in K. Bradley & J. Hedrén (ed), *Green Utopianism: Perspectives, Politics and Micro-Practices*, 150–63, Oxford: Routledge.

United Nations Centre for Human Settlements (2008a), *The state of the world's cities report 2008/9*, Nairobi: UNCHS.

United Nations Centre for Human Settlements (2008b), *UN-HABITAT: Ghana—Overview of the current Housing Rights situation and related activities*, Nairobi: UNCHS.

van Eijk, G. (2010), "Exclusionary policies are not just about the 'Neoliberal City': A critique of theories of urban revanchism and the case of rotterdam," *International Journal of Urban & Regional Research*, 34(4): 820–34.

Van Horen, B. (2002), "City profile: Colombo," *Cities*, 19(3): 217–27.

Vanderpuye, E. (2015), "Statement by Hon. Edwin Nii Lantey Vanderpuye (MP), Deputy Minister for Local Government and Rural Development at the Second Preparatory Committee Meeting for United Nations Conference on Housing and Sustainable Urban Development (HABITAT III) at Nairobi, Kenya." Available online: http://habitat3.org/wp-content/uploads/GHANA.pdf (Accessed May 25, 2020).

Yarina, L. (2018), "Your sea wall won't save you," *Places Journal*, March. Available online: https://placesjournal.org/article/your-sea-wall-wont-save-you/ (Accessed January 28, 2020).

5

NEGOTIATIONS AND CONTESTATIONS OF JUST MOBILITY: RICKSHAWS IN DHAKA, BANGLADESH

Md Musleh Uddin Hasan

Introduction

In contemporary cities, a distinctive capitalist ideology of mobility (Freund & Martin 1996) makes speed and automobility synonymous with economic growth and social progress (Greene & Wegener 1997) primarily serving the interests of elites (Henderson 2004; Pendakur 2011). A renewed interest in such "mo(ta)bility" (motorized mobility) has been observed in cities within developing countries. Liu and Guan (2005) note massive road infrastructure projects in urban China that favor cars, while the city of Lahore, Pakistan, is building and expanding roads to solve traffic congestion (Imran & Low 2003). In Tehran, Iran, international consultants tried to implement "one-size-fits-all" motorization-focused solutions to urban transport problems, ignoring the local context (Farahmand-Razavi 1994). Despite international debate over the efficacy of minimum parking requirements in dense urban residential areas and prior problems in highly motorized cities in the United States, Western Europe, Japan, Hong Kong, and Singapore, enthusiasm for the same ideology is reflected in the parking policies in many Asian cities including Bangkok, Jakarta, Kuala Lumpur, Manila, Dhaka, and Ahmedabad (Asian Development Bank 2011).

This chapter argues that urban transport policy in Dhaka is no exception to this trend, and transportation interventions and outcomes in Dhaka are the result of contested and paradoxical negotiations among multiple actors across different levels and spaces. The issue may initially seem to be a physical question: allotting road space to different modes of transport. However, repeated attempts to restrict rickshaws and the promotion of costly infrastructure favoring cars indicate that policy decisions and resulting practices are value-driven and influenced by social power dynamics. Hence, an "unjust mobility" (Hasan 2013), which I define as mobility devised through unfair process and resulting in unequal distribution of benefits and burdens of decisions, exists in Dhaka and should not continue unchallenged, particularly when the previous Western model of aggressive development centering automobiles has resulted in social and ecological instability such as inequalities of transportation options, air pollution, climate change, and so on (Low & Banerjee-Guha 2003). In fact, even if pollution and climate concerns are addressed by low, or no, carbon-emitting modern transport modes, a socially just and sustainable distribution of mobility benefits and burdens may remain unachieved. Thus, finally, I will argue, like Agyeman and his colleagues (Agyeman et al. 2002; Agyeman et al. 2003; Agyeman & Evans 2003; Agyeman 2013), that a "green"-dominated sustainability agenda is not enough to address decisions that result in "unjust mobility"; adherence to a broader agenda of "just sustainabilities"—that also includes social justice along with procedural fairness— is required.

Modernization Theory and "Modern" Mobility

The fascination for motorized mobility can be explained by modernization theory espoused by Weber, Parson, and others. Decision-makers in "underdeveloped" societies seek a "progressive" transformation through "modern and developed" urban industrial developments (Mayhew 1985; Kendall 2007) by overlooking or restricting traditional non-motorized modes of transport like walking, bicycles, and rickshaws, in a pattern that has repeated itself in most developed countries and continues in developing countries. In an age of freely flowing goods and information and ever-increasing transnational mobility, expectations and global demands for "modernization" in the style of "developed" countries are increasing. Under this "modernization," the individual becomes more important than the family, community, or previously held values (Lipset 1967) and so personal mobility is portrayed as "superior." Car-oriented infrastructures are promoted at the policy level, and the car-centric lifestyle is put into practice.

Such a lifestyle, however, is not without its social and environmental costs. Since the early 1960s, scholars in urban politics have criticized decision-makers for policies that "exacerbated the disadvantages suffered" by marginalized groups (Fainstein 2010: 3). While some scholars argue that modernization follows democratization (Lipset 1960; Rostow 1971), examples from China, Latin America, and South-East Asia challenge this premise (Frank 1969; Peerenboom 2008). Therefore, we should not assume that modernization leads to equal distribution of benefits and burdens. In fact, Harvey (1982, 1996) and Logan and Molotch (1987) have argued that decisions regarding "modern" urban living and contestation of urban space are essentially contradicting outcomes of struggles over differing values and ideologies. Calls for economic growth, efficiency, and increased property values coexist and conflict with calls for conserving heritage, neighborhood characteristics, and accessibility.

Unless these value-laden struggles are acknowledged conceptually and addressed accordingly, studies have shown (Logan and Molotch 1987) that the struggle for modernization settles, among others, in favor of money and (motorized) mobility. If the "green" sustainability lens is added, it may at best result in facilitation of less polluting transport modes, including electric vehicles, and the reduced use of fossil fuels, but without attention to affordability and accessibility for the many kinds of transport users. Another lens of justice must be added, explicitly integrating the dimensions of procedural fairness, social equity, and culture in planning and managing transport-related mobility.

(R)Evolution in Transport Studies

For many years, transport and its corresponding policies were seen as a technical area handled by engineering, construction, and management (Town 1981). This assumption overlooked the on-the-ground reality of differing access to differing types of mobility among social groups. Vasconcellos (2001: 36) finds "engineers' resistance" to social and political approaches in the technical, "neutral," and "corporate" sectors of transport. However, eventually a new sociological approach was proposed (Healey 1977; Yago 1983; De Boer 1986)— not just to "complement the traditional one but replace it, without minimizing the importance of competent technical treatment in specific phases of analytical process" (Vasconcellos 2001: 33). This new approach distinguishes between social and sociological approaches (Town 1981), and argues that while social research may accept a trip as *given*, sociological transport research asks the basic questions about *why* and *how* trips are made [or not], by whom, under what conditions, and by what means, and analyzes transport data with respect to the relative economic and political assets of social groups and classes and their conflicting (or merging) interests (Vasconcellos 2001: 33). The long-held separation between engineering and sociology is no longer defensible (Healey 1977, quoted in Vasconcellos 2001). Thus an opportunity has come to question the rigid allegiance to modern machine-based mobility and to highlight the requirements and aspirations of citizens, not cars, in mobility analysis.

Unfortunately, proponents of the sustainable mobility paradigm (Banister 2008) and ideas of sustainable transport (Richardson 1999; Wiederkehr et al. 2004), which emphasize environmental sustainability of mobility services, have neglected this opportunity. Innovations for ensuring sustainable mobility are instead directed toward making motorized mobility less polluting (Janic 2006), while the role of non-motorized modes, including rickshaws, remains overlooked. A just sustainabilities paradigm could counteract this omission, including sociological and anthropological perspectives in a contemporary conceptualization of mobility, along with environmental, engineering, and economic perspectives. This chapter aims to apply such a paradigm to the transportation context of Dhaka, Bangladesh, particularly the rickshaw industry.

Transportation in Dhaka

The city of Dhaka is the capital and primate city of Bangladesh. In 2015, Dhaka was home to 17.32 million people in its metropolitan region area (1,528 sq. km.)

and produced one-third of Bangladesh's total national GDP (RAJUK 2015: 45, 24–5). Currently, it is the eleventh largest megacity in the world and is forecasted to be the sixth largest in 2030, with a projected future population of 27.37 million people (UN 2015).

Roads in Dhaka are characterized by an overwhelming amount of non-motorized transport (NMT) modes and an increasing (but much smaller) number of cars. There are a variety of modal options available (Hasan 2013; RSTP 2015); RSTP (2015: 3–18) found as many as eighteen different types of vehicles on Dhaka roads. Yet many users feel "helpless"—as stated by a road user and quoted by Hasan (2013)—on the roads. Buses are overcrowded, fare prices for other modes are unmetered and often "unreasonable," roads are blocked by illegal parking, and footpaths are encroached upon (Majumder, Haque, & Alam 2009; Hasan 2013). All these obstacles are further complicated by daily traffic variations and seasonal monsoons.

Yet, the city is vibrant and its citizens are continually moving. In 2015, 3.25 million trips were made every day in Dhaka (RAJUK 2015: 93). Of these, work and school trips accounted for 17.8 percent and 12.7 percent, respectively, while non-home-based (NHB) trips were 11.16 percent and homebound trips were 44.88 percent (RAJUK 2015). When modes are considered, foot, rickshaw, car, and public bus trips were 17.72 percent, 37.69 percent, 7.22 percent, and 36.97 percent, respectively (RAJUK 2015). According to the city's Strategic Transport Plan (STP), 54 percent of NHB trips happen by rickshaw, while for work and school trips, the figures are 27 percent and 42 percent (STP 2005a: 12). Taken altogether, rickshaws account for a significant amount of activity on Dhaka roads and play an important role in enabling mobility for Dhaka residents as they make their way through their daily lives.

Rickshaws on the Roads

Many online promotions and blogs term Dhaka as the "Rickshaw Capital of the World." Although Dhaka City Corporation (DCC) stopped providing rickshaw licenses in 1979 when the number was 79,554 (Hasan 2013), DasGupta (1981: 15) reports this had increased to 81,000 by 1979 and 100,000 by 1980. In the 1990s, the number rose to 150,000–200,000 (DITS 1994: 43), and the city's Strategic Transport Plan (STP 2005b: 17) estimated the number at between 0.4 and 0.6 million in 2004. Unofficially, the number ranges from 0.8 million in 2005 (STP 2005b) to 1.1 million, with 1 million considered illegal, in 2012 (Alam 2011). These rickshaws serve an astonishing number of passengers: 7.6 million person-trips per day in 2009 (JICA 2010: 3–15), almost double the highest number of passengers ever carried by the London Tube in a single day (4.4 million during the 2012 Olympics) (The Metro 2012).

Cervero and Kockelman (1997) have shown that in densely populated cities NMT is one of the best options for mobility. Kalabamu (1987) and Gallagher (2010) agree that Dhaka's urban structure is well-suited for rickshaw travel, with narrow roads where traditional NMTs, including cycle, rickshaw, and walking, can navigate most easily. Since "no road hierarchy [to categorize roads by functions and capacity] exists in Dhaka, designing an uninterrupted flow of motorized traffic (MT) is difficult," if not impossible (Hasan 2013). Rickshaws are also able to operate during times of crisis like transport strikes, floods, and petrol shortages (UNESCAP 1997). Fazilka, a small town in Punjab, India, has introduced the "world's first dial-a-rickshaw" (Goyal & Asija 2015), potentially a model for other regions. Rickshaws have a high utilization rate by citizens of all income categories (twenty-six trips/forty-four passengers per day) (UNESCAP 1997). A tradition of "rickshaw-sharing" in Dhaka leads *rickshaw-wallas* (rickshaw drivers) on busy routes to allow unrelated persons to become copassengers if they have the same destination, reducing the journey cost for the passengers and the prospective waiting time for the *rickshaw-walla*. In personal communications and interviews with the author, a number of senior citizens reported having benefited from this tradition since they first came to Dhaka decades before. Rahman, D'Este, & Bunker (2009) have, therefore, perfectly categorized rickshaws as Non-Motorized Public Transport (NMPT) for the city of Dhaka.

Patterns of poverty also offer important context for the abundance of rickshaws. Dhaka is the prime destination of poor people from other regions of Bangladesh looking for work. Many, having lost their harvest and land due to flooding, cyclones, or other environmental events (increasingly exacerbated by climate change), or having experienced otherwise stressful conditions, "see hope" in Dhaka, ultimately settling in the slums (Begum & Sen 2004), which accommodated 37 million people in 2005 (Islam et al. 2006). With little technical skills or social capital, many male migrants try rickshaw driving (pedaling) for their first employment in their new city (Gallagher 1992; Hasan 2013). Kurosaki et al. (2007) and Ali (2013) have reported similar stories for rickshaw-drivers in Indian cities.

The rickshaw industry is based on specific rickshaw garages (Gallagher 1992) all over Dhaka, mostly in and around the slums. The owner of the garage is the lord of the *rickshaw-wallas*. Gallagher (1992: 434) found that 20 percent of the garage owners own more than half of the city's rickshaws; Hasan (2013) found that a single garage owner could have as many as 1,200 rickshaws. Although these lords are not aristocrats, they have considerable wealth and property (Gallagher 1992; Hasan 2013) and informal control over a number of rickshaws plying on roads, amounting to a monopoly in some areas (Hasan & Davila 2018). They rent out a single rickshaw for two daily shifts—morning to 2PM and afternoon to midnight (Hasan & Davila 2018). Thus each rickshaw provides employment to two persons, and approximately 1 to 2 million persons are directly employed by the 0.5 to 1 million rickshaws in the city. Some *rickshaw-wallas* eventually buy rickshaws of their own, enjoying an increase in their income as a result.

Gallagher (1992) also identifies secondary employment opportunities created by the rickshaw industry, including mechanics, roadside eateries, and lodging houses. These external economies generated by the rickshaw industry also make Dhaka very attractive for poor, unemployed people who cannot become drivers themselves but may be able to support themselves through associated livelihoods.

Rickshaws and Climate

Globally, the transport sector is the second largest source of Carbon-dioxide (CO_2) (IEA 2007), accounting for 23 percent of global CO_2 emissions in 2005. Globally, car and light-duty vehicles were responsible for 42 percent of transport CO_2 emissions in 2005 (IEA 2007).

Rickshaws require zero fossil fuels to operate. The total annual CO_2 saved by a single rickshaw per year is 2.07 tons, whereas a single standard-sized tree would annually absorb on average 22 kg of CO_2 (Goyal & Asija 2015: 19). Thus, the annual CO_2 savings from rickshaws in Dhaka can be estimated at 1,035,000 to 2,070,000 tons. This emissions perspective alone should be enough for decision-makers to promote rickshaw use and support *rickshaw-wallas*. Instead, the opposite has happened—rickshaws are being restricted in Dhaka, little attention is given to climate change in urban transport planning, and the poor *rickshaw-wallas*, unsung climate champions, are further marginalized.

Rickshaws should also have a place in anti-pollution discussions. Citing UNEP/WHO, Schwela et al. (2006: 206) show that eight Asian cities, including Dhaka, New Delhi, Beijing, Shanghai, Jakarta, and Hanoi, have serious particulate matter (PM) air pollution. Badami (2005) identified rapid motorization as one of the causes of air pollution in Delhi, striking an ominous note for Dhaka's future if it follows suit. Dhaka's current rates of motorization are low, with approximately thirty-two vehicles per 1,000 residents (STP 2005b: 20) or one car per 190 households (Majumder, Haque, & Alam 2009). If rickshaw trips are replaced by auto trips, Dhaka's air quality may worsen further still. Adding to the risk, Schewala et al. (2006) found that capacity to monitor and control air pollution in Dhaka is much lower than that in Delhi, Beijing, Shanghai, Bangkok, and other Asian countries.

A just sustainabilities approach to climate-conscious transportation planning should emphasize the existing stocks of local options to reduce CO_2 emissions and tailor the decision-making process to fit local solutions rather than copying exogenous solutions. This has yet to happen in Dhaka—even mobility decisions made with the environment in mind are only concerned with promoting motorized modes that use less fossil fuels and emit less carbon. Promoting electric vehicles (EVs) may become one such agenda for urban transport in Dhaka, following China's recent example (Douglas 2018). This trend is an example of a conventional application of the "green" sustainability approach—reducing carbon emissions but still viewing motorization as necessary for modernity.

Drawbacks of Rickshaws

Rickshaws are not perfect. They are difficult to pedal, vulnerable when mixed with fast-moving traffic (UNESCAP 1997), un-ergonomic, and uncomfortable (Goyal & Asija 2015). There is no fixed price and often *rickshaw-wallas* demand unreasonable fares, an occurrence that has further increased after the imposition of rickshaw restrictions on various roads (Hasan 2013). Many migrant *rickshaw-*

wallas, new to the city, are not aware of traffic regulations and so create disorder on the road (Hasan 2013). Pedestrians and other non-motorized transport users are frequent victims of road crashes in Dhaka (ARI 2019), and although data is unavailable for *rickshaw-wallas* specifically, there is no doubt they constitute a good number of these crash victims.

Rickshaw-wallas also encounter many other difficulties, which often remain unheard and unaddressed. The entire rickshaw industry is run informally, with little involvement from government agencies. City Corporation in Dhaka is only concerned with registered rickshaws, which make up less than one-tenth of the unofficial estimated total, similar to the case in Delhi (Kurosaki et al. 2007). Rickshaws are very prone to theft (Hasan 2013). *Rickshaw-wallas*, in the absence of legal support and in fear of police harassment, have to seek protection against theft through monthly payments to the local mafia, money that ultimately goes to rickshaw association leaders and others who neither own nor pedal rickshaws (Gallagher 1992; Hasan 2013). Even *rickshaw-wallas* who acquire their own rickshaws are not safe. Although ownership increases their income, these *rickshaw-wallas* become more vulnerable to the effects of restrictions on rickshaws on roads (Hasan 2013). Along with the loss of livelihood like other *rickshaw-wallas*, they also find that the asset value of their rickshaws plummets; they must either relocate to new roads or sell their rickshaw at a loss. Many of the *rickshaw-wallas* already lost much of their livelihood capital once after migration to the city, so this additional blow can be devastating.

To achieve a just and sustainable urban transport and mobility system, therefore, it is not enough merely to physically accommodate rickshaws on the roads. These issues of distributive justice and procedural justice would remain unaddressed, as *rickshaw-wallas* would still lack control over the processes affecting their livelihoods. Unfortunately, there is no concern for the social equity of *rickshaw-wallas* either from conventional proponents of sustainability or from transport decision-makers in Dhaka. Metrics of air pollution and carbon emissions are necessary but not sufficient, if the goal is just sustainabilities for the *rickshaw-wallas*. An assurance of secure livelihoods by rickshaw pedaling, which is absent in the contemporary sustainable transport or mobility paradigm, should also be incorporated in sustainability analyses. Therefore, McLaren and Agyeman (2015: 14–6) envision a "sharing paradigm"—more than a sharing and green economy—for sharing economies and opportunities of cities and caring of citizens. Agyeman et al. (2002: 78) urge that "a truly sustainable society is one where wider questions of social needs and welfare, and economic opportunity are integrally related to environmental limits imposed by supporting ecosystems."

Anti-rickshaw Arguments

Despite all the positive aspects of rickshaws with respect to the urban-transport reality, climate change, and air pollution, the mode has been mostly overlooked in "scientific" transport studies for Dhaka, namely DITS (1994), DUTP (1997),

STP (2005a, 2005b, 2005c), Network Study (JICA 2010), and the Revised STP (RSTP 2015). Those studies have counted rickshaw driving, at best, as a livelihood strategy of poor migrants, and often highlight challenges and complaints. Bari and Efroymson (2008), and Gallagher (1992) have identified common complaints against rickshaws, from both urban-transport contexts and social and humanitarian concerns. Studies (Replogle 1991; Gallagher 1992; Hook & Replogle 1996; Rahman, D'Este & Bunker 2009) show that such complaints are echoed worldwide, particularly in Indonesian, Indian, Thai, Pakistani, Chinese, and other Asian cities where NMTs have been banned or restricted. Mohan and Roy (2003) argue that autorickshaw drivers in Delhi also face hostility from their elite and rich passengers, as well as a concerted attack by the government and the media.

A literature review (Gallagher 1992; Bari & Efroymson 2005, 2008; Hasan 2013) indicates that urban-transport perspectives often argue: rickshaws are (1) trouble makers for other road users, (2) unsafe and uncomfortable for rickshaw users, (3) slow-moving, (4) taking up too much road space, (5) costly, (6) responsible for increased air pollution, and (7) the main cause of traffic jams. These complaints often come from proponents of new transport interventions—including consultants and organizations, private car users, and metropolitan police in charge of Dhaka traffic. In fact, Hasan and Davila (2018) quoted an academic who asserted, "I have never seen in my professional life any individualized transport using decision-makers talking in favor of rickshaws."

The first two complaints have merit, but can also be traced to a lack of consideration to mainstream rickshaws as a vital urban transport mode (UNESCAP 1997), and a corresponding lack of policies to protect them. As long as rickshaws remain neglected in the eyes of urban transport decision-makers, problems relating to their design and operation will remain unaddressed. Complaints about rickshaws being too slow and taking up space are also dubious. Hook (2002) states that an auto-only arterial road in Taipei serves 14,000 passengers per hour, while a similar artery in Kunming, having mixed traffic and half of the total space allocated to non-motorized fuel-free transport (FFT), serves 24,000 passengers per hour. Crucially, when the flow of people rather than the movement of autos is considered, non-motorized traffic does not hamper performance of transport systems.

Anti-rickshaw discourse is also espoused by proponents of public transport in Dhaka, who argue that fares per kilometer are higher for rickshaws than for public transport. However, on average a single trip made by mini-bus, para-transit, motorized-three wheeler, and rickshaw takes 74, 43, 72, and 38 minutes respectively and costs Taka 26, 20, 194, and 39 (RSTP 2015: 3–41). Therefore, rickshaws are not the costliest mode once travel time is taken into account, and have the added bonus of door-to-door service and no waiting time, making them the best first- and last-mile accessibility provider in Dhaka. Hasan (2013) and HDRC (2004) have found that actual rickshaw users do not complain about the fare, but rather identify lower overall cost as one of the reasons for choosing rickshaws.

Surprisingly, some blame rickshaws for air pollution. A former executive director of Dhaka Transport Coordination Authority (DTCA) alleged: "Rickshaws… create traffic jams that cause vehicles to burn more fuel which in turn greatly increases the pollution levels in the city" (The Daily Star 2003). But rickshaws are not solely responsible for traffic; breaches of traffic rules by almost all types of road users, stopping and picking up passengers, illegal parking, and poor traffic management should be held equally, if not more, responsible. Even "VIP roads" in Dhaka, where rickshaws are completely banned, suffer severe congestion, suggesting that rickshaws are not the congesting factor. In fact, several interviewees shared to Hasan (2013) that in the current context of Dhaka, where overall adherence to traffic rules by all modes is very low and no functional road hierarchies exist, traffic congestion and disorder is inevitable.

These anti-rickshaw arguments from the urban-transport perspective often draw upon green sustainability reasoning, which urges limiting the use of street-space for cars and increasing the same for pedestrians and other modes, such as cycles, and public transit. Unfortunately and strikingly, proponents of these arguments in Dhaka tend not to include rickshaws in the list of other promoted modes, viewing rickshaws as outdated and unfit for a modern city—though what a "modern" city is in this case is a notably incomplete vision. No doubt the very essence of injustice prevails in such arguments and outcomes, given the lack of concern for procedural fairness, horizontal equality or formal equity, substantive equality, legitimate expectations, and so on (see Hay & Trinder 1991; Trinder et al. 1991; Hasan 2013). Adding the lens of justice is essential in such sustainability arguments.

Gallagher (1992) and Bari and Efroymson (2005) report that rickshaw "busters" in transport agencies also argue from social and humanitarian contexts, arguing that pedaling rickshaws is inhumane. However, Bari and Efroymson (2005) conclude that pedaling is better than starvation and many other tasks are equally physically demanding. A just sustainabilities lens pushes further—the goal for *rickshaw-wallas* is not just to avoid starvation but to have safe working environments, occupational safety and well-being, and sustainable livelihoods which can withstand shocks and stress in income and employment. This goal is not necessarily mutually exclusive with rickshaw pedaling. Physical labor could be reduced through rickshaw design improvements, and the welfare of the *rickshaw-wallas* could be ensured by formalizing the rickshaw industry, introducing insurance, and ensuring proper legal protection and police support instead of harassment (Gallagher 1992; UNESCAP 1997; Bari & Efroymson 2005; Goyal & Asija 2015). In other words, these same arguments can be flipped to bolster the claim for greater attention to rickshaws and *rickshaw-wallas* and policies on their behalf.

The popular press also portrays the rickshaw business to be rife with criminality (The Daily Star 2003). This is partially true, as in the absence of a formal registration system for new rickshaws, several rickshaw owner associations, in conjunction with some garage owners, city corporation staff, traffic wardens, and local "mafias," sell "illegal" number plates to new owners (Hasan 2013) that allow them to move on roads at certain times when traffic wardens will overlook them. Hasan and Davila (2018) state that at least USD 1 million is exchanged per year through this illegal industry. Here, again, government negligence in this sector has kept options open for such activities, including extortion. However, in the general crime context of Dhaka, a police officer interviewed by Hasan (2013) admitted that rickshaw-related incidents are negligible.

Decision-makers and "Modern" Pro-auto Mobility

If these common complaints against rickshaws do not stand up to analysis, why the disconnect between the arguments and the reality? *Rickshaw-wallas* have little capacity in Dhaka to influence policy decisions pertaining to them, and Goyal and Asija (2015) report the same for *rickshaw-wallas* in India. The decision-making power lies with those who favor cars. No new registrations of rickshaws have been permitted in Dhaka since 1979, while the number of registered motorized three-wheelers, motorcycles, and cars has multiplied (Hasan 2013). Hasan and Davila (2018) describe politics of mobility in Dhaka; influential decision-makers include "experts" (foreign or local, familiar with more "modern" transport models), in association with local decision-makers (either car owners or office-provided car users) and foreign donors looking for investment-intensive projects. Their pro-car policy decisions include proposals for constructing and expanding metros, flyovers, roads, and so on. Bari and Efroymson (2008) calculate that STP identified USD 5,519 million projects for Dhaka, of which 63 percent are for metro, 30 percent for car-friendly infrastructure, and 0.24 percent each for pedestrians and rickshaws. Although metro is a popular urban transport solution worldwide, urban planners in Dhaka in personal communication with the author expressed concerns that metro fares might be too high for most of the non-car trip makers to use regularly, and indicated that the introduction of the metro may be used as an excuse to be harsher on rickshaws, another example of green sustainability initiatives hampering accessible solutions due to a lack of procedural justice.

In addition to indirect anti-rickshaw decisions such as funneling infrastructure funds elsewhere, there have been direct attempts to ban rickshaws from roads. Among the first successful bans was one that occurred in 1986 on the Airport Road, in an officially stated attempt to increase "mobility" (Gallagher 1992). Two decades later in 2004, City Corporation, with financial support from the World Bank, initiated an NMT-Free Plan to increase traffic mobility on eleven major roads by allowing only motorized transport modes (Hasan & Davila 2018). The effects of these bans were felt unevenly; Bari and Efroymson (2005: 23) quote a newspaper report in which a World Bank transport specialist admitted, "Only the rich people gain benefit from bans on the rickshaws." In contrast, non-working trip makers including education trip makers, women, children, and aged people were most affected by the ban (Hasan 2013). Although the 2004 ban on eleven roads was neither officially aborted nor enforced, another two-road ban was imposed in June 2019 but failed. The Dhaka Metropolitan Police (DMP) still sometimes put sporadic restrictions on rickshaws; when they do, there is no legal recourse for the rickshaws (see Hasan & Davila 2018 for documentation).

These policies have not always been accepted easily. In the 1980s and 1990s, *rickshaw-wallas* and concerned associations along with the labor wing of several leftist political parties protested the anti-rickshaw policies and partially succeeded by forcing withdrawal of widespread bans (Gallagher 1992). The 2004 rickshaw ban plan prompted some citizens to write to newspapers and a small number of experts to directly protest to World Bank officials (Bari & Efroymson 2005; personal communication with an activist by the author in 2012). The last protest was recorded in 2011 when a lawyer filed a court case against the restriction of rickshaws in her and her schoolgoing child's regular routes (Writ 2011). Thus, the space for protest has shifted from actual road space to sporadic popular and scientific writing and the legal field—with mixed results. In the court case, the petition was heard by the court but no final ruling occurred (Hasan 2013; Hasan & Davila 2018).

Global Dynamics and Postmodern Mobilities

The "modernization" mindset is often cited as a driving force toward increasingly motorized mobility (Harvey 1989, 1992). However, in many Western societies and countries there is a growing conflict between populism and "modernism" (Giddens 1990; Rydgren 2005): nationalism versus globalism (Hutchinson 2003; James 2006), white racism versus diversity (Mann 2011; Fox 2013; Kaufmann 2019), working-class nationals versus working-class immigrants (Anderson 2005; Ryan 2011; Leitner 2012; Leddy-Owen 2014; Pratsinakis 2018), and climate change acceptance versus denial (Oreskes & Conway 2010; McCright & Dunlap 2011). This suggests a potential reversal of the "modernization" mindset and the adoption of an anti-globalism agenda, highlighted by Brexit in the UK and the election of Donald Trump in the United States with popular manifestos. This narrower approach, particularly when it comes to climate change denial, fails to meet even the standards of "green" sustainability focused on the environment. And yet, those who will face climate consequences first and worst—the poor, the disenfranchised, the politically vulnerable—may find solace in similar populist ideas. As Brexit and "America First" slogans spread hopes of reducing unemployment, rickshaw drivers and users in Dhaka and such stakeholders in other developing cities may believe these waves will raise them up too. Hasan (2013) recounted a case where a national parliament candidate promised *rickshaw-wallas* during the 2001 election that rickshaw bans in his constituency would be revoked; however, after the election, he forgot these voters and that promise.

Moreover, to postmodern theorists, mobility is a powerful discourse creating a "new mobilities" paradigm (Sheller & Urry 2006). Several studies (Urry 2000; Kaufmann et al. 2002, 2004; Kesserling 2006) have discussed a potential "hybrid" concept—*mobilities*—that is not limited to physical displacement but also integrates the mobility potential arising from intentions of the individuals, and from their strategies and negotiations in response to external factors and forces. Kaufmann et al. (2004: 749) and Kaufmann (2002: 37) identify three interdependent elements shaping mobility levels and patterns: (1) *access* to mobility-providing means, (2) *competence* to recognize and use mobility means, and (3) *appropriation* of a particular choice, including the option of nonaction. Here is an opportunity, in theory, to see mobility beyond speed and autos, essential for integrating the social dimensions of just sustainabilities into transport literature and planning.

Outside the theory, in actual streets and homes, there is a growing public awareness about the connections between human rights and sustainability, in the context of climate change (Beg et al. 2002; Bulkeley, Edwards, & Fuller 2014; Ziervogel et al. 2017; Kling 2019) and the role and importance of cities to enacting climate resilience (Carmin et al. 2013; Bulkeley, Edwards, & Fuller 2014), despite contested perceptions of climate change (Schmidt & Schäfer 2015) and setbacks, including Trump's withdrawal from the Paris Climate Agreement (Betsill 2017; Hempel 2018). Awareness does not mean agreement, and the multifaceted mobility needs of urban populations are, even in their complexity, only one piece of the puzzle. Above all there is a need "for a better understanding of conflict and collaboration as mutually reinforcing elements of an ongoing and dynamic political process" in order to "better facilitate the ability of urban populations to collectively, effectively and rapidly respond to the challenges of a changing climate" (Aylett 2010: 478). Researchers like Bulkeley, Edwards, & Fuller (2014) and Newell and Mulvaney (2013) urge for a transition in studies and policies regarding climate change with the inclusion of justice.

This tension paves the way for a fresh appreciation for humanity, modes, and mobility (mobilities)—all inseparable from issues of rights, sustainability, and climate change. It is the right time to focus on the movement of citizens rather than cars, on a mixture of modes rather than solely the modern moving machine, that is, the automobile. There is an imperative and opportunity for modernity to coexist with older, slower, non-motorized forms of transport. There is no "one-size-fits-all" solution—neither in developed cities nor in developing cities. Exploring just sustainabilities in transportation systems and urban mobility requires developing a link between the best of the modern with the best of the ancient. Lowering CO_2 emission from the transport sector is one goal, but not the only goal; the labor conditions and livelihoods of those who make the transport sector run are essential to achieving a just and sustainable urban transport system.

Conclusion

At a time when transport is already the fastest growing consumer of fossil fuels and the hardest section from which to cut emissions (Marsden & Rye 2010), developing countries are rapidly urbanizing (Mehndiratta 2012), and technological innovations including alternative fuels appear unlikely to be the "sole answer" to climate change problem (Chapman 2007), we must rediscover the importance of the rickshaw. Currently, not only are the benefits to its users overlooked but so too is justice for the *rickshaw-wallas*. Road space for rickshaws is shrinking, putting *rickshaw-wallas'* livelihoods at stake and limiting modal options for a huge number of rickshaw-dependent people in a city that lacks an alternative integrated and efficient public transport system. Decision-makers from the urban elite and middle class (Tiwari 2001; Vasconcellos 2001; Hasan & Davila 2018) with a "discriminatory mindset" (Bari & Efroymson 2005) and a false sense of modernization and mobility are (mis)using their positions, expertise, and even state policy machinery to continue opposition against rickshaws. Policy changes to encourage and facilitate a shift from auto-centric mobility to non-motorized urban mobility are essential if we are to protect the rickshaw and the *rickshaw-wallas* and reap their benefits (Chapman 2007).

Moreover, as the politics of denying scientific facts and (causes and consequences of) climate change gets louder at a global scale, the existing "systematic campaign against sustainable transport modes" (Bari & Efroymson 2008) may very well worsen, condemning NMTs to remain as "the neglected Cinderella of transport modes" (Gwilliam 2003: 212), all while local and global environments continue to pay the price. Applying a lens of justice to conceptualizing sustainability and mobility will require more attention to everyday mobility challenges—experienced differently across social and economic classes, thus necessitating diverse and integrated solutions—and the decision-making pathways that determine which challenges are addressed or ignored. Without these steps, postmodern, sustainable, and just mobility—that is, mobility beyond speed, beyond fossil fuels, balancing old and new modes, and considering the rights of all users and stakeholders—cannot be achieved.

References

Agyeman, J. (2013), *Introducing Just Sustainabilities: Policy, Planning and Practice*, London: Zed Books.
Agyeman, J. & T. Evans (2003), "Towards just sustainability in urban communities: Building equity rights with sustainable solutions," *Annals of American Academy of Political and Social Science*, 590: 35–53.
Agyeman, J., R.D. Bullard, & B. Evans (2002), "Exploring the nexus: Bringing together sustainability, environmental justice and equity," *Space and Polity*, 6(1): 77–90.
Agyeman, J., R.D. Bullard, & B. Evans (2003), *Just Sustainabilities: Development in an Unequal World*, London: Earthscan Publications Ltd.
Alam, H. (2011), "Rickshaws clog city," *The Daily Star*, March 29, Dhaka.
Ali, M. (2013), "Socio-economic analysis of rickshaw pullers in urban centres: A case study of Uttar Pradesh, India," *International Journal of Advanced Research in Management & Social Science*, 2(1): 98–109.
Anderson, K. & A. Taylor (2005), "Exclusionary politics and the question of national belonging: Australian ethnicities in 'multiscalar' focus," *Ethnicities*, 5(4): 460–85.
ARI (2019), Accident Research Institute database, Bangladesh University of Engineering & Technology (BUET), Dhaka.
Asian Development Bank (2011), *Parking Policy in Asian Cities*, Mandaluyong City: Philippines.
Aylett, A. (2010), "Conflict, collaboration and climate change: Participatory democracy and urban environmental struggles in Durban, South Africa," *International Journal of Urban and Regional Research*, 34(3): 478–95.

Badami, M.G. (2005), "Transport and urban air pollution in India," *Environmental Management*, 36(2): 195–204.
Banister, D. (2008), "The sustainable mobility paradigm," *Transport Policy*, 15: 73–80.
Bari, M.M. & D. Efroymson (2005), *Rickshaw Bans in Dhaka City: An Overview of the Arguments For and Against*, Dhaka: WBB Trust.
Bari, M.M. & D. Efroymson (2008), *Colonial Bureaucracy and Sustainable Transport Developments in Bangladesh*, Dhaka: WBB Trust.
Beg, N., J.C. Morlot, O. Davidson, Y. Afrane-Okesse, L. Tyani, F. Denton, Y. Sokona, J.P. Thomas, E.L.L. Rovere, J.K. Parikh, K. Parikh, & A.A. Rahman (2002), "Linkages between climate change and sustainable development," *Climate Policy*, 2(2–3): 129–44.
Begum, S. & B. Sen (2004), "Unsustainable livelihoods, health shocks and urban chronic poverty: Rickshaw pullers as a case study," *Chronic Poverty Research Centre Working Paper 46*, Dhaka: Bangladesh Institute of Development Studies.
Betsill, M.M. (2017), "Trump's Paris withdrawal and the reconfiguration of global climate change governance," *Chinese Journal of Population Resources and Environment*, 15(3): 189–91.
Bulkeley, H., G.A.S. Edwards, & S. Fuller (2014), "Contesting climate justice in the city: Examining politics and practice in urban climate change experiments," *Global Environmental Change*, 25: 31–40.
Carmin, J.A., V.C. Broto, G.A.S. Edwards, & S. Fuller (2013), "Climate justice and global cities: Mapping the emerging discourses," *Global Environmental Change*, 23(5): 914–25.
Cervero, R. & K. Kockleman (1997), "Travel demand and the 3Ds: Density, diversity, and design," *Transportation Research D: Transport and Environment*, 2(3): 199–219.
Chapman, L. (2007), "Transport and climate change: A review," *Journal of Transport Geography*, 15(5): 354–67.
DasGupta, T.K. (1981), "The role of the Rickshaw in the economy of Dhaka," MA thesis, Bangladesh University of Engineering and Technology, Dhaka
De Boer, E. (ed) (1986), *Transport Sociology: Social Aspects of Transport Planning*, Oxford: Pergamon Press.
DITS (1994), *Final Report: Vol 1-Database and Immediate Action Plan*, Greater Dhaka Metropolitan Area Integrated Transport Study prepared by PPK Consultants Pty Ltd, Australia, Delcan International Cooperation, Canada and Development Design Consultants, Submitted to Government of Bangladesh and UNDP.
Douglas, R. (2018), "The future of urban mobility series: China's electric horizon," *The Urban Mobility Daily*. Available online: https://urbanmobilitydaily.com/the-future-of-urban-mobility-chinas-electric-horizon/ (Accessed October 20, 2019).
DUTP (Dhaka Urban Transport Project) (1997) *Phase II, Draft Final Report*, submitted to the Government of Bangladesh.
Fainstein, S.S. (2010), *The Just City*, New York: Cornell University Press.
Farahmand-Razavi, A. (1994), "The role of international consultants in developing countries," *Transport Policy*, 1(2): 117–23.
Fox, J.E. (2013), "The uses of racism: Whitewashing new Europeans," *UK Ethnic and Racial Studies*, 36(11): 1871–89.
Frank, A.G. (1969), *Latin America: Underdevelopment or Revolution*, New York: Monthly Review Press.
Gallagher, R. (1992), *The Rickshaws of Bangladesh*, Dhaka: University Press Limited.
Gallagher, R. (2010), "Evolution of transport in Dhaka since 1947," in R. Hafiz & A.K.M.G. Rabbani (eds), *400 years of Capital Dhaka and Beyond, Vol. III: Urbanization and Urban Development*, 103–12, Dhaka: Asiatic Society of Bangladesh.

Giddens, A. (1990), *The Consequences of Modernity*, Cambridge: Polity Press.
Goyal, V. & N. Asija, (2015) "Fazilka Ecocabs: World's first dial-a-rickshaw scheme," *Case Studies in Sustainable Urban Transport No. 09*. Available online: http://www.indiaenvironmentportal.org.in/files/file/Fazilka%20Ecocabs.pdf (Accessed July 20, 2016)
Greene, D. & M. Wegener (1997), "Sustainable transport," *Journal of Transport Geography*, 5: 177–90.
Gwilliam, K. (2003), "Urban transport in developing countries," *Transport Reviews*, 23(2): 197–216.
Hasan, M.M.U. (2013), *"Unjust Mobilities—The Case of Rickshaw Bans and Restrictions in Dhaka,"* PhD diss., University College London, UK.
Hasan, M.M.U. & J.D. Davila (2018), "The politics of (im)mobility: Rickshaw bans in Dhaka, Bangladesh," *Journal of Transport Geography*, 70: 246–55.
Harvey, D. (1982), *The Limits to Capital*, Oxford, UK: Blackwell.
Harvey, D. (1989), *The Condition of Postmodernity*, Oxford: Blackwell.
Harvey, D. (1992), "Social justice, postmodernism and the city," *International Journal of Urban and Regional Research*, 16(4): 588–601.
Harvey, D. (1996), *Justice, Nature, and the Geography of Difference*, Malden, MA: Blackwell.
Hay, A. & E. Trinder (1991), "Concepts of equity, fairness, and justice expressed by local transport policymakers," *Environment and Planning C: Government and Policy*, 9(4): 453–65.
HDRC (Human Development Research Centre) (2004), *After Study on the Impact of Mirpur Demonstration Corridor Project (Gabtoli—Russel Square)*, prepared for Dhaka Transport Coordination Board (DTCB).
Healey, P. (1977), "The sociology of urban transportation planning: A socio-political perspective," in D.A. Hensher (ed), *Urban Transport Economics*, 199–227, Cambridge: Cambridge University Press.
Hempel, M. (2018), "Anthropo Trumpism: Trump and the politics of environmental disruption," *Journal of Environmental Studies & Sciences*, 8(2): 183–18.
Henderson, J. (2004), "The politics of mobility and business elites in Atlanta, Georgia," *Urban Geography*, 25(3): 193–216.
Hook, W. (2002), "Preserving and expanding the role of non-motorised transport," Module 3d of *GTZ: Sustainable Transport: A Sourcebook for Policy-makers in Developing Cities*, GTZ Transport and Mobility Group.
Hook, W. & M. Replogle (1996), "Motorization and non-motorized transport in Asia- Transport system evolution in China, Japan and Indonesia," *Land Use Policy*, 13(1): 69–84.
Hutchinson, J. (2003), "Nationalism, globalism, and the conflict of civilizations," in U. Özkırımlı (ed), *Nationalism and Its Futures*, 71–92, London: Palgrave Macmillan.
Imran, M. & N. Low (2003), "Time to change the old paradigm: Promoting sustainable urban transport in Lahore, Pakistan," *World Transport Policy & Practice*, 9(2): 32–9.
International Energy Agency (IEA) (2007), *CO2 Emissions from Fuel Combustion 2007*, Paris: OECD Publishing.
Islam, N., A. Mahbub, N.I. Nazem, G. Angeles & P. Lance (2006), *Slums of Urban Bangladesh: Mapping and Census, 2005*, Centre for Urban Studies (CUS), Dhaka; National Institute of Population Research & Training (NIPORT), Dhaka and MEASURE Evaluation, University of North Carolina at Chapel Hill.
James, P. (2006), *Globalism, Nationalism, Tribalism: Bringing Theory Back In*, London: Sage.

Janic, M. (2006), "Sustainable transport in the European Union: A review of the past research and future ideas," *Transport Reviews*, 26(1): 81–104.

JICA (2010), *Dhaka Urban Transport Network Development Study (DHUTS)—Final Report*, Submitted to Dhaka Transport Coordination Board (DTCB).

Kalabamu, F.T. (1987), "Rickshaws and the traffic problems of Dhaka," *Habitat International*, 11(2): 123–31.

Kaufmann, E. (2019), *Whiteshift: Populism, Immigration, and the Future of White Majorities*, New York: Abrams Press.

Kaufmann, V. (2002), *Re-thinking Mobility: Contemporary Sociology*, Farnham: Ashgate.

Kaufmann, V., M.M. Bergman, & D. Joye (2004), "Motility: Mobility as capital," *International Journal of Urban and Regional Research*, 28(4): 745–56.

Kendall, D. (2007), *Sociology in Our Times*, Belmont: Thomson-Wadsworth.

Kesserling, S. (2006), "Pioneering mobilities: New patterns of movement and motility in a mobile world," *Environment and Planning A*, 38(2): 269–79.

Kling, A. (2019), "Climate change and human rights—Can the courts fix it?" Available online: https://www.boell.de/en/2019/03/18/climate-change-and-human-rights-can-courts-fix-it (Accessed November 3, 2019).

Kurosaki, T., Y. Sawada, A. Banerji, & S.N. Mishra (2007), "Rural-urban migration and urban poverty: Socio-economic profiles of rickshaw pullers and owner-contractors in North-East Delhi," *CIRJE-F-485*. Available online: https://www.researchgate.net/publication/24135398 (Accessed May 28, 2018).

Leddy-Owen, C. (2014), "Reimagining Englishness: 'Race', class, progressive English identities and disrupted English communities," *Sociology*, 48(6): 1123–38.

Leitner, H. (2012), "Spaces of encounters: Immigration, race, class, and the politics of belonging in small-town America," *Annals of the Association of American Geographers*, 102(4): 828–46.

Lipset, S.M. (1960), *Political Man: The Social Bases of Politics*, New York: Doubleday & Company.

Lipset, S.M. (1967), "Values, education, and entrepreneurship," in S.M. Lipset & A. Solari (eds), *Elites in Latin America*, 3–60, New York: Oxford University Press.

Liu, R.R. and C. Guan (2005), "Mode biases of urban transportation policies in China and their implications," *Journal of Urban Planning And Development*, 131(2): 58–70.

Logan, J.R. & H. Molotch (1987), *Urban Fortunes: The Political Economy of Place*, Berkeley: University of California Press.

Low, N. & S. Banerjee-Guha (2003), "The global tyranny of roads: Observations from Mumbai & Melbourne," *World Transport Policy & Practice*, 9(2): 5–17.

Majumder, J., M.S. Haque, & M.J.B. Alam (2009), "Transport crisis in Dhaka city," in M.J.B. Alam (ed), *Transport Problems in Dhaka City: Issues, Concerns and Policy Options*, Department of Civil Engineering, 33–66, Dhaka: BUET.

Mann, R. (2011), "'It just feels English rather than multicultural': Local interpretations of Englishness and non-Englishness', *The Sociological Review*, 59(1): 109–28.

Marsden, G. & T. Rye (2010), "The governance of transport and climate change," *Journal of Transport Geography*, 15(5): 669–78.

Mayhew, L.H. (ed) (1985), *Talcott Parsons on Institutions and Social Evolutions: Selected Writings*, Chicago: University of Chicago Press.

McCright, A.M. & R.E. Dunlap (2011), "The politicization of climate change and polarization in the American public's views of global warming, 2001–2010," *The Sociological Quarterly*, 52: 155–94.

McLaren, D. & J. Agyeman (2015), *Sharing Cities—A Case for Truly Smart and Sustainable Cities*, Cambridge: The MIT Press.

Mehndiratta, S. (2012), "Introduction: Urban transport and climate change," in A. Baeumler, E. Ijjasz-Vasquez, & S. Mehndiratta (eds), *Sustainable Low-Carbon City Development in China*, 237–42, Washington, DC: The World Bank.

Metro (2012), "Record number of Tube passengers provide welcome Olympic retail boost," *The Metro*, August 6. Available online: http://metro.co.uk/2012/08/06/record-number-of-tube-passengers-provide-welcome-olympic-retail-boost-525235/ (Accessed December 20, 2012).

Mohan, D. & D. Roy (2003), "Operating on three wheels: Auto-rickshaw drivers of Delhi," *Economic and Political Weekly*, 38(3): 177–80.

Newell, P. & D. Mulvaney (2013), "The political economy of the 'just transition': the political economy of the 'just transition'," *Geographical Journal*, 179: 132–40.

Oreskes, N. & E.M. Conway (2010), *Merchant of Doubt*, London: Bloomsbury.

Peerenboom, R. (2008), *China Modernizes: Threat to the West or Model for the Rest?* Oxford: Oxford University Press.

Pendakur, V.S. (2011), "Non-motorized urban transport as neglected modes in Dimitriou," in T. Harry & R. Gakenheimer (eds), *Urban Transport in the Developing World: A Handbook of Policy and Practice*, 203–31, Cheltenham: Edward Elgar.

Pratsinakis, M. (2018), "Established and outsider nationals: Immigrant–native relations and the everyday politics of national belonging", *Ethnicities*, 18(1): 3–22.

Rahman, M.M., G. D'Este, & J.M. Bunker (2009), "Is there a future for non-motorized public transport in Asia?" in *Proceedings of the 8th International Conference of the Eastern Asia Society for Transportation Studies (EASTS)*, November 16–19, Surabaya, Indonesia.

RAJUK (Rajdhani Unnayan Kartripakha) (2015), Dhaka Structure Plan, Dhaka Metropolitan Development Planning.

Replogle, M. (1991), *Non-motorized Vehicles in Asia: Lessons for Sustainable Transport Planning and Policy*, World Bank Technical Report 162, Environmental Defense Fund, Washington DC: World Bank.

Richardson, B.C. (1999), "Towards a policy on a sustainable transportation system," *Transportation Research Record*, 1670: 27–34.

Rostow, W.W. (1971), *Politics and the Stages of Growth*, Cambridge: Cambridge University Press.

RSTP (Revised Strategic Transport Plan) (2015), *The Project on the Revision and Updating of the Strategic Transport Plan for Dhaka*, prepared by Almec Corporation, Oriental Consultants Global and Katahira & Engineers International for Dhaka Transport Coordination Authority.

Ryan, L. (2011), "Muslim women negotiating collective stigmatisation: 'We're just normal people,'" *Sociology*, 45(6): 1045–60.

Rydgren, J. (2005), "Is extreme right-wing populism contagious? Explaining the emergence of a new party family," *European Journal of Political Research*, 44: 413–37.

Schmidt, A. & M.S. Schäfer (2015), "Constructions of climate justice in German, Indian and US media," *Climate Change*, 133(3): 535–49.

Schwela, D., G. Haq, C. Huizenga, W. Han, H. Fabian, & M. Ajero (2006), *Urban Air Pollution in Asian Cities: Status, Challenges and Management*, London: Earthscan.

Sheller, M. & J. Urry (2006), "The new mobilities paradigm," *Environment and Planning A*, 38(2): 207–26.

STP (2005a), "Survey Result," Working Paper 7, *Strategic Transport Plan for Dhaka* prepared by Louis Berger Group and Bangladesh Consultant (Ltd), prepared for Dhaka Transport Coordination Board (DTCB).

STP (2005b), "The urban transport policy—Final report," *Strategic Transport Plan for Dhaka*, prepared by Louis Berger Group and Bangladesh Consultant Ltd for Dhaka Transport Coordination Board (DTCB).

STP (2005c), *Strategic Transport Plan*, prepared by Louis Berger Group and Bangladesh Consultant (Ltd), for Dhaka Transport Coordination Board (DTCB).

The Daily Star (2003), "Real beneficiaries of rickshaw trade are criminal elements, DTCB director alleges," September 8, Dhaka.

Tiwari, G. (2001), "Pedestrian infrastructure in the city transport system: Delhi case study," *World Transport Policy and Practice*, 7(4): 13–18.

Town, S. (1981), "The sociologists perspective on transport," in D. Banister & P. Hall (eds), *Transportation and Public Policy Planning*, 30–3, London: Mansel.

Trinder, E., A. Hay, J. Dignan, P. Else, & J. Skorupski (1991), "Concepts of equity, fairness, and justice in British transport legislation, 1960-88," *Environment and Planning C: Government and Policy*, 9: 31–50.

UN (United Nations) (2015), *World Urbanization Prospect: The 2014 Revision*, New York: United Nations.

UNESCAP (United Nations Economic and Social Commission for Asia and the Pacific) (1997), Background papers on Non-Motorised Transport in Dhaka, as part of the research Integration of Non-Motorised Transport in The Urban Transport System of Dhaka.

Urry, J. (2000), *Sociology Beyond Societies: Mobilities for the Twenty-first Century*, London: Psychology Press.

Vasconcellos, E. (2001), *Urban Transport, Environment and Equity: The Case for Developing Countries*, London: Earthscan.

Wiederkehr, P., R. Gilbert, P. Crist, & N. Caïd (2004), "Environmentally sustainable transport (EST): Concept, goal, and strategy—The OECD's EST project," *European Journal of Transport and Infrastructure Research*, 4(1): 11–25.

Writ (2011), Writ Petition no 7132 of 2011 in the Supreme Court of Bangladesh, High Court Division, Dhaka.

Yago, G. (1983), "The sociology of transportation," *Annual Review of Sociology*, 9(1): 171–90.

Ziervogel, G., M. Pelling, A. Cartwright, E. Chu, T. Deshpande, L. Harris, K. Hyams, J. Kaunda, B. Klaus, K. Michael, L. Pasquini, R. Pharoah, L. Rodina, D. Scott, & P. Zweig (2017), "Inserting rights and justice into urban resilience: A focus on everyday risk," *Environment and Urbanization*, 29(1): 123–38.

6

PARADOXES OF JUST SUSTAINABILITIES IN URBAN WATER SOCIOTECHNICAL SYSTEMS: LESSONS FROM ATHENS, GREECE

Marcia Rosalie Hale

Introduction

The world's most intractable conflicts intersect, characterized by the inseparability of social and environmental crises, from pollution to conflicts over water, land, timber, and mineral resources. The conceptual framework of just sustainabilities illuminates these interrelationships and offers principles for bridging "'green' or environmental strategies" with the "'brown' (agenda of) poverty reduction and human rights... human security" (Agyeman 2005: 11). The brown agenda is connected to low-income communities, and in particular to communities of color, who suffer disproportionate environmental burdens and benefits. This linkage is crucial to development and urban planning projects, which may privilege environmental or sustainability concerns of the green agenda over the human and justice issues centered in the brown agenda.

Urban water socio-technical systems are critical sites of social and environmental conflict. They are also central to development and planning projects, providing water locally to urban inhabitants while impacting regional development and sustainability through the importation of water resources and exportation of byproducts and pollutants. The principles of just sustainabilities[1] should be used to guide transitions in water socio-technical systems, as modern water systems are characterized by several paradoxes. Perhaps most obviously, while meant to provide large volumes of clean water, modern water systems are composed of massive infrastructure that often imports resources from far outside of the watershed (Kelley 2011; Pincetl, Bunje, & Holmes 2012)—a clear antithesis to the fourth just sustainabilities principle of living within ecosystem limits, and likely of the second principle of intergenerational equity. Further, many modern urban water systems violate the third principle of justice and equity in process, procedure, and outcome. This chapter focuses on the third principle and illustrates two specific ways in which it is violated within modern water system globally, through paradoxical process and design: (1) the global financing that supports many modern systems can negatively impact justice and equity in process and procedure by constraining participation in governance (Yazdanpanah et al. 2013); (2) modern water systems were constructed for buildings, not people, impacting human security and therefore justice in outcome (Hale 2019). This second paradox is thrown into stark relief by homelessness in cities; when water is supplied to and accessed from buildings, people without permanent or legal connection to building structures can find themselves without water.

This chapter explores these paradoxes through a multi-scalar analysis of transition within the urban water socio-technical system of Athens, Greece, including local, regional, global, and temporal scales. The Athens water system is especially interesting and amenable to multi-scalar analysis given its antiquity. Both historic evolution and contemporary transition in Athens' urban water system are analyzed through the principles of just sustainabilities. Justice and equity in process and procedure are then considered in regard to supranational governance, in particular the participation of Greece in the European Union (EU).

EU legislation shapes water policy and management in the Athens system and throughout Greece. However, interviewees familiar with the legislation critiqued it for focusing on ecosystems rather than people, and as serving countries of the wet north rather than the Mediterranean south. Agyeman warns that "as long as race, class, cultural, and justice concerns are marginalized because of a sole focus on environmental sustainability, then certain racial, socio-economic, and cultural groups will be excluded" (Agyeman 2013: 95). The Athens water system illustrates this point at the supranational level of governance. Encapsulated in the tension are issues of culture and identity, as well as class, given the gap in GDP between countries of the Mediterranean south and those of the north (Koukakis 2016). The environment-equity link is further illustrated; Agyeman asserts that "inequity within societies effectively excludes large proportions of citizens from a sense of citizenship and collective responsibility" (Agyeman 2013: 324). While there is high racial, ethnic, and religious homogeneity in Greece—92 percent of the population is ethnic Greek and 81–90 percent Greek Orthodox religion (CIA 2019)—marginalization occurs at the level of supranational governance. Complexity of histories and identities intermingle with unfolding inequities in regional and geopolitics, informing what one interviewee referred to as a "culture of apathy" that can act as a barrier to Greece's participation in both supranational and domestic legislation. The result is a lack of national self-determination and Greek participation in the development and implementation of water-related policy, standing in violation of the third principle of just sustainabilities.

Theory

The framework of just sustainabilities links societal and environmental health. Societal health here refers to both social justice and human security, the latter defined by scholars as conditions that meet basic needs, human development requirements, and human rights for individuals (Gasper 2005; Barnett, Matthew, & O'Brien 2010). This societal health is both reliant on and supportive of environmental sustainability, the health and vitality of ecosystems. Essentially, humanity needs a clean environment to thrive, but just sustainabilities also recognize the inverse, that is, "environmental quality is inextricably linked to that of human equality" (Agyeman, Bullard, & Evans 2002: 77). Two dimensions of the relationship between social and environmental health are especially notable in regard to just sustainabilities. First, greater income equality and civil rights are associated with higher environmental quality (Agyeman, Bullard, & Evans 2003). Second, the burden of poor environmental quality weighs heaviest on those with the least economic and political power, as environmental burdens themselves are disproportionately located in and near communities least able to politically resist noxious facilities nor pay for related healthcare costs (Agyeman, Bullard, & Evans 2003). Social sustainability, including justice and human security, is therefore an aspect of both human and environmental health.

Agyeman uses this framework to guide existing agendas, including those of sustainable development and urban governance: "What is at stake here is not less than the power to frame the broad and emerging sustainable development agenda" (Agyeman 2005: 11). Socio-technical systems are key components of both the sustainable development and urban agendas, and are therefore crucial sites to further just sustainabilities. Including infrastructures around energy, water, food, and transportation, socio-technical systems encompass material/technological components as well as social/institutional aspects (Smith, Voß, & Grin 2010; Bos & Brown 2012).

Transitions are occurring in urban sociotechnical systems around the world. Defined as fundamental changes or systemic transformation (Ferguson, Brown, & Deletic 2013), transitions are driven primarily by population growth, global environmental change, and aging infrastructure. Given the significance of socio-technical systems, it is important to frame the sustainable transition agenda (Smith, Stirling, & Berkhout 2005; Ernstson et al. 2010; Brown, Farrelly, & Loorbach 2013; Hale & Pincetl 2019) around the four principles of just sustainabilities (Agyeman, Bullard, & Evans 2003; Agyeman 2013). Human security is a notable common element underlying the first three principles, as they are related to the fulfilment of basic needs, human development, and human rights for individuals (Agyeman 2005; Gasper 2005; Barnett, Matthew, & O'Brien 2010). As the following case study will show, the human security aspect of urban water systems can easily get lost between systems designed for buildings rather than for people and current trends toward prioritizing ecosystem health. This chapter highlights the complexity of these dynamics in a racially homogenous state participating at the scale of supranational governance.

Participation in the governance of urban water systems is not only relevant to the third principle of justice and equity in process, procedure, and outcome but crucial to ensuring the others as well (Agyeman 2013). Effective participation includes representation from across affected communities and identities; therefore, intersectionality is a core tenet, illuminating the complexities of individual and group identities that need to be involved in decision-making, including race, ethnicity, gender, age, religion, and class. Case studies illustrate challenges and complexities at local and national levels (Agyeman, Bullard, & Evans 2003; Agyeman & Evans 2004; Agyeman 2005, 2013). But what considerations and challenges occur at the supranational level of governance? Supranational consideration is especially important in regard to socio-technical systems processing natural resources across political boundaries, as is the case with river and aquifer systems.

Methods

Paradoxes in regard to modern water systems generally, and the Athens case specifically, emerged from a qualitative study of transition. Historical analysis of the system's evolution contextualizes current transitions in the Athens water sociotechnical system (Brown, Keath, & Wong 2009; Smith, Voß, & Grin 2010). Analysis of the Athens water system was constructed through complementary approaches of interviews, participant observation, and text analysis (Bogdan & Biklen 2007).

I conducted interviews and participant observation in Athens, Greece, during April and May of 2017. As a researcher from the United States interested in how urban water systems are adapting to global environmental change in the Mediterranean climate zone and the justice implications of those transitions, I arrived in Athens with two key informants and then snowball sampled within the city's network of water experts (Berg 2001; Koutiva et al. 2017; Hale & Pincetl 2019). Twelve confidential, in-person interviews were conducted through a semi-structured format, which focused on the system's evolution and future trajectory. Given this study's focus on past and future transition, interviewees were all experts in the system, including scientists, municipal managers, ministry officials, and community leaders. Four of the interviewees presented as female and eight as male. Interviews averaged 2.5 hours and provided respondents with ample opportunity to explore those aspects of the system with which they are most familiar (Robson 2011).

Historic System Evolution

Like all cities, the Athens urban water system reflects temporal, human, and ecological influences. "The urban water system is a complex adaptive system composed of technical, environmental, and social components (water infrastructure, water resources, and water users, respectively) which interact dynamically and continuously with each other and whose relationships evolve in time" (Koutiva & Makropoulos 2016: 35). However, the evolution of this particular system is notable for two primary reasons. First, the city has been continuously inhabited for more than 7,000 years, ranking it among the oldest in the world (Tung 2001). The city-region is marked by a dry, Mediterranean climate, which necessitated water imports in order to grow and sustain the population. The Hadrian Aqueduct is a Roman, zero-carbon innovation built around 1,800 years ago that supplied the city until the modern system was built in the 1920s (Christaki et al. 2016); it can be considered a relic of ancient foreign capital on Athens' design and development. Second, the evolutionary path of Athens' water system has been primarily driven by actors and factors far outside of both city and country limits. Antiquity and exogenous influence are distinct traits that continue to shape the system, problematizing the benefits and challenges of exogenous forces, including foreign capital, when viewed through the lens of just sustainabilities.

Athens is the capital and largest city of Greece, with known history reaching back to the 11th millennium BC ("Ancient Athens" n.d.). It was the predominant city of ancient Greece before suffering decline under the subjugation of the Ottoman Empire. As a small, sparsely populated town with a dry, Mediterranean climate, Athens became the capital of modern Greece in 1834, following the Greek War of Independence from Ottoman rule (Economidou 1993). Early attempts to modernize the city's water system were focused on reconstructing the Roman-era Hadrian Aqueduct, which had fallen out of use during the fifteenth century, replaced by the Ottoman system of public fountains fed by wells and aqueducts (Christaki et al. 2016). From 1834 to 1889, almost all funding for Athens' urban water system went into this "archeological modernization" of the ancient Hadrian Aqueduct (Kaika 2006: 277).

The turn of the century, however, saw the return of wealthy Greeks from the diaspora, who brought with them financing, industrial knowledge, and connections to international capital, an influx that further encouraged the development of national infrastructure with Athens as the center (Kallis & Coccossis 2003). However, the city still lacked water infrastructure and funding for a modern system (Kaika 2006). The end of the Second World War and domestic economic reforms expanded linkages to foreign capital; following the new geopolitical and economic role of the United States in the postwar era, an American consortium submitted a proposal to the national government in 1918 for a dam and a reservoir to supply Athens, which would later be bid out to the New York-based multinational construction firm Ulen & Co. (Kaika 2006: 286). This began the modern era of foreign capital influencing urban design and development. The design itself was characteristic of modern water systems, including large infrastructure of pipes, dams, and aqueducts.

Regional politics and geopolitics conspired to speed up Athens' processes of modernization. A final episode of war broke out between Greece and Turkey in 1919, culminating in the Lausanne Convention, which forced the exchange of populations between the two countries (Clogg 2013). In 1923, during what has been called the "disaster of the Greek population in Asia Minor," Greeks living in what is now the Republic of Turkey were forced to flee their homes (Economidou 1993: 35), many settling in Athens and doubling the city's population to 704,247 (Kaika 2006). Water demand inflated alongside the population and in 1924 the US company Ulen was brought in to increase supply, which was first done by repairing the Hadrianic aqueduct and expanding its capacity (Christaki et al. 2016). The same company spearheaded the "Build-Operate-Transfer" scheme of the Marathon project (1928–31), an importation system from nearby Lake Marathon (Kallis & Coccossis 2003). Ulen financed, built, and operated Athens water for twenty-two years as the private company it created for the purpose, the Hellenic Water Company Inc. (EEY) (Kallis & Coccossis 2003). Previously, municipalities were responsible for supplying water. Illustrating the first paradox of modern water systems, that foreign capital often violates the third just sustainabilities principle of justice and equity in process or governance, the Marathon project represented a highly contested transfer of power from the municipality to the state, as well as from the people of the state to foreign capital (Kaika 2006). The agreement was reached in no small part due to the growing need for housing and services for refugees from Asia Minor (Kallis & Coccossis 2003), further illustrating exogenous forces that shaped the Athens water system.

Geopolitics next exerted influence on Athens water during the late 1930s and early 1940s. Starvation was the deadliest weapon of the Second World War and the end of the 1930s saw a great migration of rural populations to urban centers (Collingham 2011). Athens received much of Greece's rural population, a growth spurt which drove a construction-based economy. The state encouraged urban growth through the provision of basic infrastructure, including water and electricity. As part of this expansion, a system was built to transfer water from Lake Yliki, ninety kilometers from the city. Thus urbanization, industry expansion, and job opportunities in the 1960s earned Athens the moniker of the Greek "economic miracle" (Kallis & Coccossis 2003: 248). This massive growth resulted in consolidation of resource power into the hands of the state. It was mandated in the postwar era that all buildings in Athens and neighboring Piraeus be connected to the central water system (Kaika 2006), a response to the dearth of sewage systems and pollution that turned wells used by homes and suburbs into cesspools (Kallis & Coccossis 2003). This transition characterizes the modern water paradox of systems that deliver safe, clean drinking water and process disease-carrying sewage; yet simultaneously, modern water systems devolve resource power away from communities and ultimately ensure the delivery of water to buildings rather than to people, as public water sources, such as fountains, are replaced by indoor plumbing.

In 1980, imports expanded along with state control. Continued population growth drove the Mornos dam and aqueduct project, which transports water to Athens from 190 kilometers to the west (EYDAP n.d.). State control of water resources consolidated in 1980 with the creation of The Athens Water Supply and Sewerage Company/Εταιρεία Ύδρευσης και Αποχέτευσης Πρωτεύουσας (EYDAP Inc.) (Berg 2001; Koutiva et al. 2017; Hale & Pincetl 2019). EYDAP took over all supply and sewage debt and assets from EEY, after purchasing its Ulen shares in 1974 (Kallis & Coccossis 2003).

In 1981, Greece joined the European Union (EU), which later adopted the Water Framework Directive (WFD) in 2000, committing member states to achieving quality standards for all water bodies up to one nautical mile from shore (Water Framework Directive 2000/60/EC 2000). Resulting projects in Athens include the 2007 Psyttaleia sludge treatment facility and the still ongoing construction of additional treatment facilities to service peripheral regions (GTP Headlines 2017). Membership in the EU and the WFD continue to be central shaping mechanisms in Athens and in Greece more broadly, which will be discussed at length in the following section.

The final phase of Athens' water importation system was completed in 2001. Begun in 1992, the Evinos project consists of the Evinos Reservoir and the tunnel connecting that water to the Mornos Reservoir (EYDAP n.d.). Planned to meet Athens' water demand until 2030, the project is estimated at USD 392 million, 85 percent of which was provided by the European Union Cohesion Fund (International Water Power & Dam Construction 2002).

The Athens urban water system highlights the role that geopolitics play in system evolution, as well as in contemporary dynamics at the supranational level of governance. The region's antiquity and connection to history and culture impact current self-determination and participation in domestic and regional governance, as we will see in the next sections. Records from bygone eras also throw into stark relief the erosion of human security connected to modern urban water systems, as the city was once characterized by public fountains, now largely absent from the urban fabric. The next section explores how these characteristics are interacting with current pressures and points of change in the system.

Current System

Today, Athens' urban water system is meeting current demand by volume, in that there is enough water in the system to support the metropolitan population (Kallis 2010).

Supply is anticipated to be stable until at least 2030 (International Water Power & Dam Construction 2002). But while the system is providing Athenians with reliable water, the conditions allowing for this supply are not expected to stay stable. There is concern about aging infrastructure and inefficiency in the system (O'Riordan & Voisey 2013). Interviewees listed operational issues such as leakages and malfunction of critical system components as primary issues, which there is little funding to address. Environmental uncertainties, unstable socioeconomic conditions, and EU policy are also drivers of transition (Koutiva et al. 2017), impacting the system as outlined in the following sections.

Global Environmental Change

While the system is currently meeting demand overall, capacity could be impacted by global environmental change, including changes in hydrologic, climate, ocean, and forest systems as well as urbanization (Barnett, Matthew, & O'Brien 2010). There are also concerns with what one interviewee referred to as "non-predictable inflows." Local inflows of water supply are regionally driven, especially by imports sourced from the north. Flows are further impacted by natural disaster, the intensity of which is increased by global environmental change. Having a semi-arid, Mediterranean climate and reliance on imported water, Athens and the broader Attica peninsula are especially vulnerable to global environmental change, including more extreme floods, fires, droughts, and even desertification, such as the 2018 Attica wildfires that claimed more than 100 lives in the city-region (Becatoros 2019).

Demand is influenced by increased urbanization. Respondents voiced concern that available volume may not meet the demands of an expanded population, due to endogenous or exogenous growth. However, due to the recent financial crisis that officially began in 2009 and has lasted longer than the Great Depression in the United States (S. 2018), endogenous growth is less worrisome. In the shadow of the crisis, interviewees reported it to be common for adults well into their thirties to live with their parents. Families across generations and geographies have consolidated under one roof, hampering marriage and other family planning in the younger generation. Instability and population growth in neighboring countries could, however, drive exogenous growth. Migration increases water demand through residential use and also in the form of food and energy demand. As one respondent stated: "Refugee communities could radically change demand on cities—not demands that change gradually but a massive change—I don't think we are prepared for this." Another interviewee identified regional volatility as one of the greatest threats to the water system:

> The entire area of eastern Mediterranean security could be an issue in the near future... stable states have fallen the last 6 years: Tunisia, Egypt, Libya, Syria... Increasing population growth in northern Africa and western Asia and low growth rates in European Mediterranean, increased food demand and high energy demand... this is more risky than climate change because of big immigrant waves toward these countries. The risk is not so much invasion or terrorism but increased migration.

Such massive change in demand can stress the volume of available water resources. However, the burden of this stress, as well as human security concerns more generally, including access to shelter, food, and services, is borne most extremely by low-income and migrating people, especially those that experience homelessness. Human security, common to the first three principles of just sustainabilities, is an important frame of analysis for investigating the urbanization aspect of global environmental change. Urbanization is accelerating globally, due to both exogenous and endogenous growth (WHO 2014), with related experiences of homelessness. Inhabitants experience domestic homelessness as a result of local forces such as poverty, housing shortages, and lack of services, in addition to homelessness related to migration, both within and between national borders. The frequency of people experiencing homelessness has spiked in Athens as well as worldwide (Chamie 2017; Habitat for Humanity 2018; Homeless World Cup

Foundation 2018). Simultaneously, public water access in the form of fountains, standpipes, and wells has decreased (Phurisamban & Gleick 2017). The health implications of constrained access are dire as climate change drives increases in temperatures and aridity (Johnson & Sánchez-Lozada 2013; García-Trabanino et al. 2015; Uddin et al. 2016), especially across the Mediterranean climate region (Mackenbach 2007; McMichael 2013). And while public water was a feature of the historic city, which supplied water to people rather than to buildings, research suggests that the multiple-user public fountain was largely usurped by modern water systems (Mackenbach 2007; McMichael 2013), and the single-user fountain, which co-evolved with modernist infrastructure, has been supplanted by bottled water (Wilk 2006; Gleick 2010; Pierre-Louis 2015). Kallis paints a vivid picture of this transition in Athens:

> You are in Athens. It is the year 1830. Greece's liberation war has just ended… You are standing on top of the Acropolis watching the city below. Nothing remains but "piles of scattered ruins… stones and parts of walls."[2] You see people around water fountains waiting to fill their buckets, others pulling water from wells… Fast forward. The year is 2004. You are again standing on top of the Acropolis. Everywhere you look now there are multistorey [sic] apartments… Four million people now inhabit the city. There are no longer fountains or wells, but 4 reservoirs, far from the city, with a capacity of 1.5 billion cubic meters (cu.m). Water passes through 500 km of canals, 4 treatment plants, 7000 km of underground pipes and flows out to 1.7 million taps.
>
> (Kallis 2010: 796)

This reveals what is perhaps the greatest paradox of modern urban water systems—that they have been designed for the regulated[3] buildings that occupy city-space rather than for human inhabitants. While development data reports 100 percent access to improved water sources in most major cities of the Global North (WHO 2013), Athens included, these figures best represent access for buildings rather than for people. This paradox is evident when the city is viewed from the standpoint of inhabitants experiencing homelessness. If one is not inhabiting a building, access is constrained to public sources of water and bottled or packaged options (Hale 2019). Water is further privatized by restrooms for customers only and public restrooms for a fee. Parks remain perhaps the one reliable place for public water, but, as Agyeman details, while parks were created in the early twentieth century for the poor, these spaces themselves are increasingly privatized (Agyeman 2013: 98). The Athens case highlights the need to reintroduce public water back into urban spaces, a need which has only increased with Covid-19, where frequent hand washing is especially important; creative strategies to achieve this end include the approach of German cities which pay business owners to allow the public to use their bathrooms (Sorrel 2016), as well as by reintroducing public water fountains (Hale 2019). After all, in the words of the second-century Greek writer Pausanias, "a place is never rightfully called a 'city' without water fountains" (Phurisamban & Gleick 2017: 1).

Economic Crisis

Further exacerbating human security concerns in the Athens water system is the profound economic crisis and associated corruption that has driven economic, political, and cultural transitions across the country. Following Wall Street's crash in 2008 and waves of recession reaching across the globe, Greece announced that its economy was less stable and in more deficit than it had been reporting, which promptly resulted in the country being blocked from financial markets and, by 2010, teetering on the edge of bankruptcy ("Explaining Greece's Debt Crisis" 2016). Already in deficit before the crash, the Greek economy has suffered exponentially in the following years. While part of a global recession, its specific circumstances, notably government corruption (Kouretas & Vlamis 2010), left Greece among the most indebted countries in the world with a debt to GDP ratio of over 180 percent and the highest unemployment in the EU (Ellyatt 2016). Immediate impacts of the crisis related to the water system include a lack of funding to update aging and broken system components, as well as increased homelessness, with the attendant implications for human security outlined above.

However, compounding matters further, regional and international institutions now have a strong grasp of control over the country's policies and resources. In response to the crisis, austerity measures were imposed by foreign capital, the state, and the Troika which consists of the International Monetary Fund, the European Commission, and the European Central Bank—measures that included reducing the salaries, rights, and social benefits of workers; increasing taxes; and cutting public sector jobs and welfare benefits, even though a growing body of evidence documents severe social and environmental harms resulting from such an approach (Zeitchik 2015; Calvário, Velegrakis, & Kaikaet 2017). Economic contraction and austerity measures drove unemployment, with youth unemployment (ages 15–24) most severely impacted. Having reached up to 55 percent in Greece during 2015 (Milevska 2014), youth unemployment is directly linked to youth homelessness and increased substance abuse in what has been called a "lost generation" (Zeitchik 2015). Extreme poverty throughout Greece rose from 2.2 percent in 2009 to 15 percent in 2016, with approximately 1.6 million out of the 11 million population living in extreme poverty (Ellyatt 2016).

In addition to austerity, Greece was pressured by the Troika to privatize its infrastructure as a form of debt repayment:

> Just in the past year, 14 major regional Greek airports were privatized, as was the port of Piraeus, Greece's largest port... The port of Thessaloniki, Greece's second-largest city, was also privatized... In addition, special privatization funds have been created where the ownership of public assets such as water utilities has been transferred, leading up to their future sale.
>
> (Nevradakis 2017)

Privatization often threatens the principles of just sustainabilities, especially principle #2, increasing intergenerational equity (meeting the needs of both present and future generations), and principle #3, furthering justice and equity in process, procedure, and outcome (Agyeman, Bullard, & Evans 2003; Agyeman 2013). This perspective was echoed in Greece, where sale of the country's infrastructure can feel unjust in process and outcome, especially the loss of national resources from future generations. Interviewees report Greek sentiment across the country as mostly opposed to privatization in general. Particularly strong opposition arose in response to proposals to privatize water supply systems, especially EYDAP/ ΕΥΔΑΠ in Athens and EYATH/ΕΥΑΘ serving the northern city of Thessaloniki, the country's two largest urban systems. Public resistance took the shape of an informal referendum enacted in Thessaloniki in which 90 percent voted against privatization. In a published interview, community activist Maria Kanellopoulou offered this description: "a lot of the citizens… are obliged by outrage to take back control of the water companies… We know exactly what the consequences are, and it is shameful that cities in Europe that have long [experienced] these kinds of policies now try to impose them in a European country with economic hardship such as Greece" (Nevradakis 2017).

Harnessing terminology employed by David Harvey, Stathis Kouvelakis refers to this expropriation of national wealth as "accumulation by dispossession," going on to explain that in the case of Greece, dispossession is "not to a country of the Global South or Eastern Europe but to a member of the eurozone since its creation and of the European Economic Community since the early 1980s" (Portaliou 2016). This sale of national resources is occurring at the behest of the European Union, via the Troika, the triumvirate of the European Commission, European Central Bank, and the International Monetary Fund, which represents the EU in foreign relations. As is discussed below, the impact is to further complicate an already complex relationship, with implications for Greece's self-determination and participation in supranational or regional governance.

European Union

Since joining the European Union in 1981, Greece has been subject to EU law. EU policy and funding have been significant forces shaping the modern Greek water system. Since adoption in 2000, the Water Framework Directive 2000/60/EC (WFD) has been the guiding force for member countries. Intended to drive major legislative reform, the "WFD 2000/60/EC establishes a new institutional framework, providing guidance for a common approach, common objectives and shared principles, definitions and measures for water resources and supply management, within EU member states" (Kanakoudis, Papadopoulou, & Tsitsifli 2015).

WFD mandates require member countries to construct River Basin Management Plans, conduct economic analyses of water use to identify quality issues that could prevent fulfillment of WFD targets, and implement pricing policies that support sustainable water use (Bithas et al. 2014). Interviewees voiced frustration with these requirements, as they are seen to focus on quality and river basins rather than quantity and groundwater, and ecosystems rather than people.

These factors drive the perception that EU water policy was designed for (and by) the water-rich countries of the north, rather than those of the Mediterranean south. Regarding the marginalization of Greece at the level of supranational governance, one interviewee explained that Greece is rarely involved in drafting policy because it seldom sends representatives to participate in the prolonged EU legislative processes, a situation which has been exacerbated during budget cuts associated with the economic crisis.

Underlying these specific challenges are general issues with interpreting and applying EU policy. While the EU sets standards, member countries are responsible for interpreting and applying mandates as policies customized to national and local contexts. In Greece, the Ministry of Environment and the Agency of Water Resources were reported as responsible for applying legislation to water districts, and as one district representative explained, this can be very difficult with limited funding and manpower. Several interviewees who have participated in the legislative processes explained that most Greek secretaries approach the process as a "box ticking exercise" and translate the directives exactly.

Respondents familiar with the history of EU policy in Greece reported a culture of apathy around the legislative process and resentment of these outside mandates, resulting in EU legislation being accepted without interpretation or application, often rendering policy irrelevant and ineffectual. One respondent explained that this resistance, specifically in applying the WFD, comes in part because Greece was not involved in the process of writing the framework and therefore does not feel ownership.

Complicating this scenario is a lack of internal motivation to innovate domestic environmental standards and policy. The EU was reported as being instrumental, even necessary, to Greece's decision-making process, even though it is conversely resented for this role. One interviewee reflected that Greece needs membership in the EU and especially in NATO, as it used to be bordered by communists and now feels threatened once again from Turkey. The respondent went on to elaborate that adherence to EU policy is a price of membership; however, Greece does not share its prioritization of ecological concerns. Thus, a cultural disconnect is exacerbated by past and current issues of identity and external influence. The EU is perceived as prioritizing issues of the north; this sense of inequity is compounded by the forced privatization and sale of Greek infrastructure resulting from the economic crisis, all of which impact relationships with EU member states. These current dynamics are playing out on top of a layered history, which further informs how Greece manages its socio-technical systems and participates in supranational governance.

Culture and Identity

The third principle of just sustainabilities is further challenged by a tapestry of historic identities that respondents connect to contemporary participation in governance. Greek national identity is intertwined with the experience of occupation, the trauma of which and persistence in Greek identity is reflected in this passage written by Father George on the website of St. Andrew Greek Orthodox Church in South Bend, Indiana: "By the end of the 15th century, Greece was under Turkish Muslim rule. Over the next 400 years, the Greeks were slaves to the Turks, deprived of their human rights, considered as second-class citizens" (Konstantopoulos 2015). Yet underneath the imprint of the occupied is that of ancient Greece, the history of glory and its ongoing centrality to the culture and politics of the contemporary west. Richard Clogg opens his tome on the country by saying:

> All countries are burdened by their history, but the past weighs particularly heavily on Greece. It is still, regrettably, a common-place to talk of "modern Greece" and of "modern Greek" as though "Greece" and "Greek" must necessarily refer to the ancient world. The burden of antiquity has been both a boon and a bane.
> (Clogg 2013: 1)

Clogg notes that identification with the proud past fueled the Greek nationalist movement that separated the modern state from the Ottoman Empire and that "indeed such attitudes have persisted to the present" (Clogg 2013: 1). However, this proud identity rooted in antiquity is troubled by the memory of oppression and occupation that characterized the era of Ottoman rule, creating contradictory attitudes and apathy, as evidenced in the handling of national infrastructure. As one respondent explained, "We think it's our property but we don't have to care about it."

Both of these historical layers undergird "Greek's historical ambivalence towards the West" (Armakolas & Triantafyllou 2017: 613), and attitudes toward the EU specifically, which suggest resentment toward the legislative processes and maybe even membership itself. Membership in the EU was attractive in large part for the protection it would provide to a country still reeling from occupation and war. However, there is acute resentment held around EU involvement in national affairs, "a 'schizophrenic' situation whereby Greeks demand the protection and support of Western powers, while at the same time they constantly criticize them for their international role and the meddling in other countries' affairs" (Armakolas & Triantafyllou 2017: 613).

Self-determination is a crucial aspect of the third principle of just sustainabilities, justice in process. In the case of Greece, drive for self-determination collides with trauma of occupation. One interviewee familiar with the country's legislative interface with the EU described: "The Greek political system still follows old system of we do what we want"—a pithy statement that explains the economic mismanagement and irresponsible fiduciary actions taken by the Greek government that ultimately resulted in economic crisis (Kouretas & Vlamis 2010), which itself deepened tensions between Greece and the EU. As one interviewee exclaimed: "The whole country is up for sale—51% in private hands." Resentment is fueled by the awareness that those buying Greek infrastructure are connected to the EU countries, pushing the hardest for privatization. The intersections of these historic and current dynamics illustrate how perceptions of justice and equity can inform participation in governance and serve as barriers to meaningful participation in decision-making at regional or supranational scales.

Conclusion

The just sustainabilities lens bridges green or environmental strategies with the brown agenda of human rights and security (Agyeman 2005); included in human security is meaningful participation in decision-making and governance. This lens is especially conducive to guiding transitions within urban water systems, given their social and environmental complexity. The case of the Athens water system illustrates this complexity, as both social and environmental crisis is reflected in its evolution. Layers of history from the Classic period to Ottoman occupation, drought, foreign capital, and regional institutions have shaped both technical and social elements of the water system. Subtle social elements, including identities and attitudes, animate the institutional system of water governance, informing the extent of participation in governance and therefore the extent to which the third principle of just sustainabilities and self-determination over resources is represented within the water system, as well as within the regional structure of governance at the level of the UN. Further research is needed to expand upon this study and more fully investigate relationships between factors such as historic memory, trauma, and identity, contemporary crisis and structures of governance, and participation in governance at both local and regional scales. Such research could inform policy and processes of governance, in order to increase participation in local and regional governance and therefore Greek self-determination over water resources.

In addition, the case of the Athens system highlights a core paradox of modern urban water systems, in that they were designed to supply water to buildings rather than to people, overlooking or ignoring the ways in which these two goals can fail to overlap. This paradox also violates the third principle of just sustainabilities, in that there is no justice in outcome for people moving through cities that cannot access water. The danger of this design intensifies as global environmental change drives increases in both temperatures and human migration. Further research is needed to track and understand migration of people through cities and how water systems can be redesigned to provide access for people who are not permanently attached to buildings.

Notes

1 The four principles are as follows: (1) guiding change to improve our quality of life and well-being; (2) increasing intergenerational equity (meeting the needs of both present and future generations); (3) furthering justice and equity in process, procedure, and outcome; and (4) increasingly living within ecosystem limits (Agyeman, Bullard, & Evans 2003; Agyeman 2013).

2   French traveler Michaud cited in (Kaika 2005: 89).
3   It is important to distinguish between regulated buildings that meet municipal codes with water and electricity sources in modern cities, and temporary, unregulated settlements and structures. This chapter is focused on regulated buildings in modern city-spaces. Informal settlements globally and cities in the Global South have other distinct challenges (Bakker 2007; Mitlin et al. 2019).

References

Agyeman, J. (2005), "Alternatives for community and environment: Where justice and sustainability meet," *Environment: Science & Policy for Sustainable Development*, 47(6): 10–23.

Agyeman, J. (2013), *Introducing Just Sustainabilities: Policy, Planning, and Practice*, London: Zed Books.

Agyeman, J. & B. Evans (2004), "'Just sustainability': The emerging discourse of environmental justice in Britain?', *The Geographical Journal*, 170(2): 155–64.

Agyeman, J., R.D. Bullard, & B. Evans (2002), "Exploring the nexus: Bringing together sustainability, environmental justice and equity," *Space & Polity*, 6(1): 77–90.

Agyeman, J., R.D. Bullard, & B. Evans (2003), "Joined-up thinking: Bringing together sustainability, environmental justice and equity," in J. Agyeman, R.D. Bullard, & B. Evans (eds), *Just Sustainabilities: Development in an Unequal World*, 1–16, Cambridge: MIT Press.

"Ancient Athens: C. 1100 BCE—529" (n.d.), Oxford Reference. Available online: http://www.oxfordreference.com/view/10.1093/acref/9780191736452.timeline.0001 (Accessed January 20, 2018).

Armakolas, I. & G. Triantafyllou (2017), "Greece and EU enlargement to the Western Balkans: Understanding an ambivalent relationship," *Southeast European & Black Sea Studies*, 17(4): 611–29.

Bakker, K. (2007), "The 'commons' versus the 'commodity': Alter-globalization, anti-privatization and the human right to water in the global south," *Antipode*, 39(3): 430–55.

Barnett, J., R.A. Matthew, & K.L. O'Brien (2010), "Global environmental change and human security: An introduction," in R.A. Matthew, J. Barnett, B. McDonald, & K.L. O'Brien (eds), *Global Environmental Change and Human Security*, 3–32, Cambridge: MIT Press.

Becatoros, E. (2019), "Fire rages out of control in Greek island nature reserve," *AP NEWS*, August 13. Available online: https://apnews.com/9d0c44234a39499d813dc6fa1f5687c2 (Accessed May 31, 2020).

Berg, B.L. (2001), *Qualitative Research Methods for the Social Sciences*, 4th edn, Boston: Allyn & Bacon.

Bithas, K., A. Kollimenakis, G. Maroulis, & Z. Stylianidou (2014), "The water framework directive in Greece. Estimating the environmental and resource cost in the water districts of Western and Central Macedonia: Methods, results and proposals for water pricing," *Procedia Economics & Finance*, 8: 73–82.

Bogdan, R. & S.K. Biklen (2007), *Qualitative Research for Education: An Introduction to Theories and Methods*, 5th edn, New York: Pearson.

Bos, J.J. & R.R. Brown (2012), "Governance experimentation and factors of success in socio-technical transitions in the urban water sector," *Technological Forecasting & Social Change*, 79(7): 1340–53.

Brown, R.R., N. Keath, & T.H.F. Wong (2009), "Urban water management in cities: Historical, current and future regimes," *Water Science & Technology*, 59(5): 847.

Brown, R.R., M.A. Farrelly, & D.A. Loorbach (2013), "Actors working the institutions in sustainability transitions: The case of Melbourne's stormwater management," *Global Environmental Change*, 23(4): 701–18.

Calvário, R., G. Velegrakis, & M. Kaika (2017), "The political ecology of austerity: An analysis of socio-environmental conflict under crisis in Greece," *Capitalism Nature Socialism*, 28(3): 69–87.

Chamie, J. (2017), "As cities grow worldwide, so do the numbers of homeless," *YaleGlobal Online*, July 13. Available online: https://yaleglobal.yale.edu/content/cities-grow-worldwide-so-do-numbers-homeless (Accessed May 31, 2020).

Christaki, M., G. Stournaras, P. Nastos, & N. Mamasis (2016), "The majestic Hadrianic Aqueduct of the City of Athens," *Global Nest Journal*, 18(3), 559–68.

CIA (2019), "Europe—Greece," *The World Factbook*, Central Intelligence Agency. Available online: https://www.cia.gov/library/publications/the-world-factbook/geos/gr.html (Accessed May 31, 2020).

Clogg, R. (2013), *A Concise History of Greece*, 3rd edn, Cambridge: Cambridge University Press.

Collingham, E.M. (2011), *The Taste of War: World War Two and the Battle for Food*, London: Penguin.

Economidou, E. (1993), "The Attic landscape throughout the centuries and its human degradation," *Landscape & Urban Planning*, 24(1–4): 33–7.

Ellyatt, H. (2016), "'Nobody believes in anything anymore': Why Greece's economic crisis is not over," *CNBC*, August 22. Available online: https://www.cnbc.com/2016/08/22/nobody-believes-in-anything-anymore-why-greeces-economic-crisis-is-not-over.html (Accessed May 30, 2020).

Ernstson, H., S.E. van der Leeuw, C.L. Redman, D.J. Meffert, G. Davis, C. Alfsen, & T. Elmqvist (2010), "Urban transitions: On urban resilience and human-dominated ecosystems," *AMBIO*, 39(8): 531–45.

"Explaining Greece's debt crisis" (2016), *New York Times*, June 17. Available online: https://www.nytimes.com/interactive/2016/business/international/greece-debt-crisis-euro.html (Accessed May 30, 2020).

EYDAP (n.d.), *ΕΥΔΑΠ-Water Supply Resources*, Available online: https://www.eydap.gr/en/TheCompany/Water/WaterSources/ (Accessed January 12, 2018).

Ferguson, B.C., R.R. Brown, & A. Deletic (2013), "Diagnosing transformative change in urban water systems: Theories and frameworks," *Global Environmental Change*, 23(1): 264–80.

García-Trabanino, R., E. Jarquín, C. Wesseling, R.J. Johnson, M. González-Quiroz, I. Weiss, J. Glaser, J. José Vindell, L. Stockfelt, C. Roncal, T. Harra, & L. Barregard (2015), "Heat stress, dehydration, and kidney function in sugarcane cutters in El Salvador: A cross-shift study of workers at risk of Mesoamerican nephropathy," *Environmental Research*, 142: 746–55.

Gasper, D. (2005), "Securing humanity: Situating 'human security' as concept and discourse," *Journal of Human Development*, 6(2): 221–45.

Gleick, P.H. (2010), *Bottled and Sold: The Story Behind Our Obsession with Bottled Water*, Washington, DC: Island Press.

GTP Headlines (2017), "Greece to Receive €1.3b from EU for Infrastructure Projects," *GTP Headlines*, Mar 25. Available online: http://news.gtp.gr/2017/03/25/greece-receive-e1-3b-eu-infrastructure-projects/ (Accessed May 31, 2020).

Habitat for Humanity (2018), "The need for affordable housing," *Habitat for Humanity*. Available online: http://www.habitat.org/impact/need-for-affordable-housing (Accessed May 31, 2020).

Hale, M.R. (2019), "Fountains for environmental justice: Public water, homelessness and migration in the face of global environmental change," *Environmental Justice*, 12(2): 33–40.

Hale, M.R. & S. Pincetl (2019), "Peering through frames at conflict and change: Transition in the Los Angeles urban water system," *Journal of Transdisciplinary Peace Praxis*, 1: 39.

Homeless World Cup Foundation (2018), "Global homelessness statistics," *Homeless World Cup Foundation*. Available online: https://homelessworldcup.org/homelessness-statistics/ (Accessed May 31, 2020).

International Water Power & Dam Construction (2002), "Greek Prime Minister inaugurates Evinos scheme," *International Water Power & Dam Construction*. January 9. Available online: http://www.waterpowermagazine.com/news/newsgreek-prime-minister-inaugurates-evinos-scheme (Accessed January 12, 2018).

Johnson, R.J. & L.G. Sánchez-Lozada (2013), "Mesoamerican nephropathy—New clues to the cause: Chronic kidney disease," *Nature Reviews Nephrology*, 9(10): 560–1.

Kaika, M. (2005), *City of Flows: Modernity, Nature, and the City*, London: Psychology Press.

Kaika, M. (2006), "Dams as symbols of modernization: The urbanization of nature between geographical imagination and materiality," *Annals of the Association of American Geographers*, 96(2): 276–301.

Kallis, G. & H. Coccossis (2003), "Managing water for Athens: From the hydraulic to the rational growth paradigm," *European Planning Studies*, 11(3): 245–61.

Kallis, G. (2010), "Coevolution in water resource development: The vicious cycle of water supply and demand in Athens, Greece," *Ecological Economics*, 69(4): 796–809.

Kanakoudis, V., A. Papadopoulou, & S. Tsitsifli (2015), "Domestic water pricing in Greece: A spatial differentiation," *Desalination & Water Treatment*, 54(8): 2204–11.

Kelley, J. (2011), "China in Africa: Curing the resource curse with infrastructure and modernization," *Sustainable Development Law & Policy*, 12(3): 35–41.

Konstantopoulos, G. (2015), "400 Years Under the Ottoman Turks and War of Independence, 1821," *St. Andrew Greek Orthodox Church*. Available online: http://saintandrewgoc.org/home/2015/3/25/400-years-under-the-ottoman-turks-and-war-of-independence-1821?rq=400%20Years%20Under%20the%20Ottoman%20Turks%20and%20War%20of%20Independence%2C%201821 (Accessed May 30, 2020).

Koukakis, N. (2016), "Facing slow to no growth, EU's poor nations plot next move," *CNBC*, September 9. Available online: https://www.cnbc.com/2016/09/09/eus-struggling-economies-meet-as-north-south-divide-widens.html (Accessed May 30, 2020).

Kouretas, G. & P. Vlamis (2010), "The Greek crisis: Causes and implications," *Panoeconomicus*, 57(4): 391–404.

Koutiva, I., & C. Makropoulos (2016), "Modelling domestic water demand: An agent based approach," *Environmental Modelling & Software*, 79: 35–54.

Koutiva, I., P. Gerakopoulou, C. Makropoulos, & C. Vernardakis (2017), "Exploration of domestic water demand attitudes using qualitative and quantitative social research methods," *Urban Water Journal*, 14(3): 307–14.

Mackenbach, J.P. (2007), "Global environmental change and human health: A public health research agenda," *Journal of Epidemiology & Community Health*, 61(2): 92–4.

McMichael, A.J. (2013), "Globalization, climate change, and human health," *New England Journal of Medicine*, 368(14): 1335–43.

Milevska, T. (2014), "Study: Young people living with their parents longer," *EURACTIV*, March 25. Available online: http://www.euractiv.com/section/social-europe-jobs/news/study-young-people-living-with-their-parents-longer/ (Accessed May 31, 2020).

Mitlin, D., V.A. Beard, D. Satterthwaite, & J. Du (2019), *Unaffordable and Undrinkable: Rethinking Urban Water Access in the Global South*, World Resources Institute. Available online: https://www.wri.org/wri-citiesforall/publication/unaffordable-and-undrinkable-rethinking-urban-water-access-global-south (Accessed May 31, 2020).

Nevradakis, M. (2017), "Greece forced to sell public water utilities under EU-imposed privatization plan," *MintPress News*, June 5. Available online: http://www.mintpressnews.com/greece-forced-to-sell-public-water-utilities-under-eu-imposed-privatization-plan/228479/ (Accessed May 31, 2020).

O'Riordan, T. & H. Voisey (2013), *The Transition to Sustainability: The Politics of Agenda 21 in Europe*, Milton Park: Routledge.

Phurisamban, R. & P. Gleick (2017), *Drinking Fountains and Public Health*, Pacific Institute. Available online: http://pacinst.org/app/uploads/2017/02/Drinking_Fountains_and_Public_Health_Feb_2017-1.pdf (Accessed May 31, 2020).

Pierre-Louis, K. (2015), "We don't trust drinking fountains anymore, and that's bad for our health," *Washington Post*, July 8. Available online: https://www.washingtonpost.com/opinions/we-dont-trust-drinking-fountains-anymore-and-thats-bad-for-our-health/2015/07/02/24eca9bc-15f0-11e5-9ddc-e3353542100c_story.html (Accessed May 30, 2020).

Pincetl, S., P. Bunje, & T. Holmes (2012), "An expanded urban metabolism method: Toward a systems approach for assessing urban energy processes and causes," *Landscape & Urban Planning*, 107(3): 193–202.

Portaliou, E. (2016), "Greece: A country for sale," *Jacobin*, September 12. Available online: http://jacobinmag.com/2016/09/greece-tsipras-memorandum-privatization-public-assets/ (Accessed May, 30 2020).

Robson, C. (2011), *Real World Research: A Resource for Users of Social Research Methods in Applied Settings*, 3rd edn, Hoboken: Wiley.

S., R. (2018), "Is the Greek financial crisis over at last?" *The Economist*, August 21. Available online: https://www.economist.com/the-economist-explains/2018/08/21/is-the-greek-financial-crisis-over-at-last (Accessed May 31, 2020).

Smith, A., A. Stirling, & F. Berkhout (2005), "The governance of sustainable socio-technical transitions," *Research Policy*, 34(10): 1491–510.

Smith, A., J.P. Voß, & J. Grin (2010), "Innovation studies and sustainability transitions: The allure of the multi-level perspective and its challenges," *Research Policy*, 39(4): 435–48.

Sorrel, C. (2016), "German cities are solving the age-old public toilet problem," *Fast Company*, November 3. Available online: https://www.fastcompany.com/3065278/german-cities-are-solving-the-age-old-public-toilet-problem (Accessed May 30, 2020).

Tung, A.M. (2001), *Preserving the World's Great Cities: The Destruction and Renewal of the Historic Metropolis*, 1st paperback edn, New York: Three Rivers Press.

Uddin, S.M.N., V. Walters, J.C. Gaillard, S.M. Hridi, & A. McSherry (2016), "Water, sanitation and hygiene for homeless people," *Journal of Water & Health*, 14(1): 47–51.

Water Framework Directive 2000/60/EC, 32000L0060, EP, CONSIL, OJ L 327 (2000). Available online: http://data.europa.eu/eli/dir/2000/60/oj/eng (Accessed May 30, 2020).

WHO (2013), "Progress on sanitation and drinking-water," *World Health Organization*, Available online: https://washdata.org/data (Accessed May 31, 2020).

WHO (2014), "Urban population growth," *World Health Organization*, Available online: http://www.who.int/gho/urban_health/situation_trends/urban_population_growth/en/ (Accessed May 31, 2020).

Wilk, R. (2006), "Bottled water: The pure commodity in the age of branding," *Journal of Consumer Culture*, 6(3): 303–25.

Yazdanpanah, M., D. Hayati, G.H. Zamani, F. Karbalaee, & S. Hochrainer-Stigler (2013), "Water management from tradition to second modernity: An analysis of the water crisis in Iran," *Environment, Development & Sustainability*, 15(6): 1605–21.

Zeitchik, S. (2015), 'With jobless rate above 50%, disillusioned Greek youths becoming a 'lost generation," *Los Angeles Times*, June 2. Available online: http://www.latimes.com/world/europe/la-fg-greece-youth-economic-woes-20150602-story.html (Accessed May 31, 2020).

Part III

SCALES OF DECISION-MAKING AND ACTION

All attempts at just sustainabilities are shaped by the "where." Although this entire volume emphasizes the importance of place-based thinking, this part in particular highlights the role of spatial context and scale. The physical landscape scale sets the starting parameters for resource conflicts, including naturally uneven distribution of minerals as well as global systems of air and water (and corresponding flows of pollutants within these systems). Overlaying the landscape are human-drawn boundaries and decision-making structures, which add layered complications to enacting or derailing just sustainabilities. Mismatches among these layers form the basis of many justice and sustainability challenges, a spatial disconnect that grows ever more pressing in a world increasingly shaped by resource exploitation and global climate change.

Chapter 7 examines policy contradictions in Copenhagen, a city praised worldwide for sustainability yet facing political obstacles to battling congestion, in part due to scalar disjuncture between levels of government. Chapter 8 explores linkages across many local-scale communities in Colombia seeking to combat the national government's promotion of economic development through extractivism; transboundary entities such as multinational corporations and international non-governmental organizations also play critical roles on both sides of this "tortuous path." Chapter 9 focuses on electricity delivery in California, analyzing the potential democratizing power of "community choice" and looking critically at how rigid emphasis on "the local" might exacerbate broader regional inequities. This part explores the complex intersection of scale and decision-making as the local actors in all three cases grapple with choices that hold global relevance.

7

RESISTANCE TO RESTRICTING? THE POLITICS OF
CARS IN COPENHAGEN

Kevin T. Smiley

Introduction

Copenhagen, Denmark, is often cited as a paragon of the sustainable city because of its push to be the first carbon-neutral world capital in 2025, the city's extensive and innovative green planning, and its stake as a bicycle capital of the world where half of commuters get to work by bike (Gerdes 2013). Copenhagen is also perceived as a comparatively just city, as it is a laboratory for social welfare reforms for Denmark and beyond; left-leaning political parties have led the city for decades and installed comprehensive social democratic policies as part of a national state that emphasizes egalitarian, collective approaches to social policies from income to health to public infrastructure (Emerson & Smiley 2018). With these guiding and interlocking motifs—serious sustainability and sincere justice—as backdrops, I consider why Copenhagen, a seemingly ideal candidate city for adopting congestion charges for cars in the city center, has not adopted such a policy. This analysis asks a simple question: Why not? This deceptively simple question uncovers how complicated the successful accomplishment of just sustainabilities can be and how hard they can be to maintain (Agyeman, Bullard, & Evans 2003). It raises paradoxes in the plans and practices—but especially the policies—in cities, particularly by illuminating how scalar disjunctures in theoretically democratic processes can produce potentially undemocratic outcomes. By scalar disjunctures, I refer to how different scales—in this case, at levels of government from national to local—are disconnected from one another in ways that create tensions. Unpacking these scalar disjunctures in governance reveals how even empowered actors in a global city characterized by utopian goals of leading climate change mitigation can be stifled by business interests supported by political parties on the conservative end of the spectrum.

Using a mixed methodological analysis, I investigate why the municipal government of Copenhagen did not adopt a congestion charge for its city center

The author would like to thank the audience at the Twelfth Global Studies Conference for helpful comments.

despite a recent push to do so in 2011 to 2013. The analysis is in two parts. First, I draw on unique survey data from the Copenhagen Area Survey of more than 1,000 respondents in the city to ask: Who tends to support or oppose restricting cars in the center of Copenhagen? Does this support or opposition vary by an individual's social and demographic attributes or, notably, their political preference? To preview results, wide swaths of Copenhageners support such restrictions, but this support is deeply divided by political affiliation. Second, I relate these findings to a qualitative analysis of a political debate during 2011 to 2013, when congestion charges in Copenhagen's city center looked to be a near-lock to become policy. Crucially, policy for the potential congestion charge was decided at the national level, not the municipal level, and ultimately the measure was defeated by a coalition of business and right-leaning political interests. Pairing these findings together, the analysis of both sets of data reveals a scalar disjuncture whereby a wide swath of urban residents desire a social policy, but a misplaced governance mechanism—national-level decision-making rather than local—prevented the application of this policy of just sustainability. In this way, justice is bound by scale: the discordance between the national and the local creates different priorities and different conceptions of just policy.

Just Sustainabilities and Urban Policies

Integrating environmental justice and sustainability, the concept of *just sustainabilities* seeks to foreground the importance of justice in discussions of the environment (Agyeman, Bullard, & Evans 2003; Agyeman 2005a; McLaren & Agyeman 2015). Integrating justice and sustainability is not easily done, as sustainability tends to have more purchase in policymaking realms, while the push for environmental justice receives more support among grassroots organizations (Agyeman & Warner 2002; Agyeman 2005b; Agyeman et al. 2016). These tensions can be generative, though, because invoking justice in the context of sustainability provokes critical questions about environmental policies, and who has and should have power. One such tension of attempting to achieve a just sustainabilities relates to *scale*. In a globalizing world, the interconnectedness of people and places is not limited to immediate local environments (Sassen 1991). Interrogating the linkages between the local and the global—and everywhere in between—involves delineating the apparent boundaries around social, geographic, and environmental issues (Brenner 1999; Kurtz 2003; Sze & London 2008; Sze et al. 2009). Especially important are the contradictions between scales, such as when grassroots voices are disempowered at the benefit of larger structures such as undemocratic state policies and highly unequal flows of capital. At the same time, critiques from below, such as the "right to the city" that challenges capital and the state's role in city-making and instead foregrounds possibilities for social change by residents as co-creators of urban space (Lefebvre 1991), are at the core of just sustainabilities in an effort to achieve greater social justice. These critiques are at the core because of the focus of just sustainabilities on empowerment of marginalized groups, attention to intersectional identities, and promotion of grassroots activism. Across different scales, there are different conceptions of justices, which, in turn, lead to different articulations of just policy, and these differences between local and higher-order (e.g., national) scales animate tensions in this chapter.

Urban policy is a useful arena for considering the implications of just sustainabilities and the issue of scale, particularly in light of the dominance of exchange values over use values in most cities (Molotch & Vicari 1988; Logan, Whaley, & Crowder 1997; Logan & Molotch 2007). A focus on exchange values over use values makes central a practice of considering urban space as a commodity, which embeds class inequalities in urban space and fosters unequal remunerative development (Logan & Molotch 2007). Following this neo-Marxist perspective on exchange values and use values (Harvey 1973; Castells 1977), this support of remunerative urban development has led to what we call the market city (Emerson & Smiley 2018), which is dedicated to a neoliberal vision for society that foregrounds markets and individualized policy in a way that decentralizes and diminishes local governance and collective thinking. But alternatives for more just cities exist (Fainstein 2010), whether it is a "people city," which seeks to balance exchange values and use values (Emerson & Smiley 2018); a "sharing city," which emphasizes connectedness to oppose injustice (McLaren & Agyeman 2015); or a "rebel city," which moves outside the strictures of neoliberalism more radically (Harvey 2012). These alternatives suggest that justice is best conceptualized and empowered from the lifeways of a diverse range of residents, and is in contrast to dominant modes of early twenty-first-century neoliberal urban power. One implication for inequality between market cities and people cities is that market cities are highly unequal especially across race, ethnic, and class lines, while people cities host comparably smaller social inequalities (Emerson & Smiley 2018). History and social and economic systems of power condition a considerable amount of urban and environmental action (Abu-Lughod 1999; Molotch, Freudenberg, & Paulsen 2000), but democratic and radical critique in urban spaces can animate more just futures; concepts like people cities, sharing cities, and rebel cities seek to move toward those futures (Cole & Foster 2001; Agyeman, Bullard, & Evans 2002; Martinez-Alier et al. 2014; Caniglia, Vallée, & Frank 2016; Pellow 2018).

Many areas of urban policy are characterized by tensions wrought between market forces and their alternatives. Transportation, in particular, offers an important lens into these dynamics, as transportation is embedded within socio-spatial inequalities in cities (Agyeman & Evans 2003; Riggs 2018). Since the mid-twentieth century, the dominant mode of transportation in most cities in the West has been the car—although its uptake in Copenhagen, as will be discussed, is conspicuously lower. The impact of this shift on the physical geography of the city cannot be understated, as cities expanded into large metropolitan regions (Garreau 1991; Sudjic 1993), extending and exacerbating a highly segregated metropolis (Massey & Denton 1993; Sampson 2012). The shift to cars, especially in the United States, also directed an individualist mode of transport, which was easily wed to the neoliberal politics of development that stressed individual attainment of social goods. With these shifts came new forms of socio-spatial inequality; economically and socially disadvantaged individuals are less able to obtain a personal car, thereby reducing their spatial privilege in the city. This reduction meant less access to quality jobs, among other social goods (Glaeser, Kahn, & Rappaport 2008). It was also paired with at times ineffective public transportation, limited in scope, ambition, and access.

Alternatives to the mass deployment of cars in recent decades actually predate motor vehicles: public transportation, bicycling, and pedestrianism all have deep and continuous roots even in the car-centric city and especially in Europe. Of particular interest in this chapter are bicycling and pedestrianism. Planners, rooted in the work of Jane Jacobs (1961) and continuing with new urbanism and smart growth thinking more recently (Duany, Plater-Zyberk, & Speck 2001), champion these modes as creating a rehabilitated, more cohesive community. This is particularly the case in Copenhagen, where noted planner Jan Gehl observes that urban planning oriented away from cars creates "cities for people" (Gehl 2010). At the same time, bicycling does not guarantee just sustainabilities; critical urban studies literature documents how bicycling can intertwine with undemocratic planning and social and physical inequalities (Cupples & Ridley 2008; Hoffman & Lugo 2014; Loughran 2014; Stehlin 2014; Golub et al. 2016; Smiley, Rushing, & Scott 2016). Because of these tensions, this chapter seeks to nest the focus on pedestrianism, bicycling, and public transportation in a specific context—congestion pricing debates in Copenhagen—and consider directly how these tensions of undemocratic planning, social inequalities, and neoliberal market forces are considered by local stakeholders.

Tensions among modes of transportation have come to the fore of urban policy as congestion charges are debated in cities across the world (Li & Hensher 2012). A congestion charge, or congestion pricing, refers to a surcharge for motor vehicle users of certain urban zones, most often the central city or business district. The goals of congestion pricing include decreasing heavy traffic, improving air quality, and increasing use of alternative transportation modes (such as bicycling and pedestrianism). Congestion pricing schemes can be found in cities such as London, Milan, Singapore, and Stockholm, among others. While tolls for express lanes can be found in some US cities, no large US city to date has installed congestion pricing in the central city; New York City will become the first in 2021.

Emergent research on congestion charges points to a few intriguing conclusions (see Li & Hensher 2012). Support for congestion pricing is often linked to support for the environment (Eliasson & Jonsson 2011; Kim et al. 2013), support for active governance (Kim et al. 2013), households with young families (Gehlert et al. 2011), and positive experiences during trials for congestion pricing (Schuitema, Steg, & Forward 2010; Eliasson 2014). In Copenhagen, research has found relatively high levels of support for road pricing (Gehlert et al. 2008), and that funds raised from a congestion charge could be considerable in the growing metropolitan area (Rich & Nielsen 2007). Most of this research on congestion charges uses survey data from an urban planning perspective, and helpfully notates pathways to individual support, but leaves aside wider discussions of local politics surrounding these policies. One exception is Henderson and Gulsrud's (2019) treatment of transportation politics in Copenhagen, which includes a focus on congestion pricing that analyzes the popular support and political tensions that have long driven the issue.

Pairing this research on congestion charges and just sustainabilities together, a critical question emerges: should congestion charges in Copenhagen be considered a means of enacting just sustainability? Underlying much of this analysis is my belief that the arguments Copenhageners made in advocating for this policy were compelling. Just sustainability, according to Agyeman, is a relative notion that always necessarily connects back to its local context (Agyeman 2005a); for this reason, I leave aside the question as to whether congestion pricing in other cities is an example of just sustainability. The congestion charge plan in Copenhagen fulfills key tenets of the four essential conditions outlined by Agyeman (2005a), such as providing for higher quality of life (i.e., better air quality), and meets justice in terms of process and procedure (by recognizing the majority of Copenhageners across diverse communities). Although critics of congestion pricing argue it is regressive because it's a flat tax applied to all consumers regardless of their ability to pay, it's important to note that in Copenhagen the population of drivers tends to be economically advantaged compared to those who use other forms of transportation. In fact, only a third of Copenhageners drive, with the modal group being cyclists (now, nearly half of daily commuters). In the local context, therefore, a congestion charge in Copenhagen should not be considered a regressive tax, and indeed can be considered as a possible means to enact just sustainability.

By nesting a discussion of attitudes *and* politics of congestion pricing in a single analysis, this study melds together these literatures on just sustainabilities, urban policy, congestion pricing, and individual identities. I explore the following questions: Who tends to support restricting cars in the city center of Copenhagen? Who tends to oppose? Does support and opposition vary by income, gender, education level, and, especially important for this study, their political affiliation? And, finally, what can the opposing politics of congestion charges tell us about the (im-)possibilities for just sustainabilities? Using the case of Copenhagen, I analyze these questions in an effort to uncover why congestion pricing in Copenhagen's city center failed to become policy. The first part of this study is a quantitative analysis using survey data of the Copenhagen region to analyze local opinion about potentially restricting car usage in the city center. The second part is qualitative and investigates the recent near-push for congestion pricing by identifying key arguments made by proponents and opponents.

Research Setting

Copenhagen is at the center of urban climate change politics and of urban sustainability generally (McLaren & Agyeman 2015). As a city with a strong collective ethos, it is a "people city" characterized by a high level of interpersonal trust, low social inequality, and energetic social democratic governance (Emerson & Smiley 2018; Smiley & Emerson 2018). These themes extend directly to the environment, as a vast majority of residents acknowledge the existence of climate change (Smiley 2017) and municipal and intra-regional governments are active in pursuing sustainable urban design (McLaren & Agyeman 2015; Henderson & Gulsrud 2019). For instance, Copenhagen is seeking to become (by 2025) the first carbon-neutral capital in the world and is one of the world's cycling capitals, with nearly half of commuters in the metropolitan region using bicycles. The city is not, however, without contradictions, such as neoliberal plans for new sustainable development (Blok & Meilvang 2015), the politics of waste in the city (Emerson & Smiley 2018), or the high degree of anti-immigrant attitudes (Smiley, Emerson, & Markussen 2017; Emerson and Smiley 2018).

Quantitative Analysis

Data

Data is from the 2015 Copenhagen Area Survey (CAS), which was conducted as part of a large research project in the city, and encompassed a range of attitudes and attributes of Copenhageners (Emerson & Smiley 2018). The web survey was conducted by the Danish research firm *Epinion*, and was limited to residents aged eighteen or older who lived in Copenhagen, Frederiksberg, or fifteen suburban municipalities. The CAS utilized sample matching techniques from a large Epinion panel of more than 240,000 panelists that included matching criteria for gender, age, and the respondent's location in a central city or suburban municipality (for an extended discussion of sampling procedures of the CAS, see Emerson & Smiley 2018). There were 1,058 survey respondents.

Variables

The dependent variable in the analysis concerns the respondent's views on restricting cars in the city center of Copenhagen. The question is part of a series of policy-oriented statements that asks respondents to strongly favor, slightly favor, slightly oppose, or strongly oppose several different statements. The prompt utilized in this analysis is: "Cars and driving must be restricted in the city centre." Responses were recorded into two measures of favor or oppose, with opposition as the reference category for the binary logistic regression analyses below. Independent measures cover attitudinal, spatial, and socio-demographic measures. First, I tested to see if the respondent's political party preference is associated with the restriction on cars, as the debate has been highly politicized in Denmark. Respondents were asked which political party they planned to vote for in upcoming national elections. There were eight primary political parties in Denmark at the time of the survey.[1] Four are considered right-leaning: Denmark's Liberal Party (*Venstre*), Danish People's Party (*Dansk Folkeparti*), the Liberal Alliance, and the Conservative's People Party (*Det Konservative Folkeparti*). Four are considered left-leaning: Social Democrats (*Socialdemokartiet*), Red-Green Alliance (*Enhedlisten*), Danish Social Liberal

Party (*Radikale Venstre*), and Socialist People's Party (*Socialistisk Folkeparti*). Respondents could also choose among the following categories: undecided, vote for another party, and vote blank. The answers to this question were coded into three categories of left-leaning parties, right-leaning parties, and "other," which is the reference category. I also tested to see if the effect of air quality on health was a concern for respondents. Motor vehicles are a primary vector of unhealthful air toxins, and respondents more worried about air quality may express more support for the car restriction (Carrington 2019); additionally, those more worried about air quality may also be economically or socially disadvantaged and more likely to experience poor air quality. Respondents are coded in three categories: very worried, somewhat worried, and not worried at all, with the latter serving as the reference category.

For the spatial measures, respondents were coded into two categories of suburban dwellers and those living in the central municipalities of Copenhagen and Frederiksberg (the reference category). I also measure the modes of transportation used by the respondent with two variables: whether the respondent had ridden a bicycle in the last thirty days, and whether they take public transit at least weekly. The reference category for each is not having utilized the mode.

Finally, five sociodemographic measures add important individual attributes: educational attainment (in four categories from less than high school to advanced degree holders, with high school degree as the reference category), income (measured in four quartiles based on the overall distribution of metropolitan Copenhagen's median household income with the second quartile is the reference category), gender (measured dichotomously with male as the reference category), parenthood (with non-parents as the reference), and age (measured in years).

The analytical approach begins by examining descriptive statistics using univariate and bivariate statistics about attitudes concerning the restriction of cars. Model 1 introduces socio-demographic covariates to set a baseline model for binary logistic regression analyses. Model 2 adds the three measures as critical controls of the respondent's geographic location and transportation preferences. Model 3 is the final model that includes the attitudinal measures about political party preference and concern about air quality. Across these three models, I use multiple imputation techniques to account for missing data in the independent variables; after dropping a small number of cases ($n = 27$) that were missing on the dependent measure, the final study sample is 1,031 respondents.

Quantitative Results

Descriptive findings suggest that a large share of Copenhageners (64 percent) support the idea of restricting cars in the center of the city. This support is highly conditional on political preference, however. Specifically, 78 percent of left-leaning party adherents support the measure, as do 72 percent of "other" voters, but only 37 percent of right-leaning respondents support the measure. Majorities of both urban dwellers (70 percent) and suburban dwellers (55 percent) support the measure, as do nontransit riders (58 percent) and half of respondents who have not ridden a bicycle in the past thirty days. These descriptive statistics suggest that support is fairly widespread, but is predicated partly on political party preference. Table 7.1 portrays the results of three binary logistic regression models predicting support of the car restriction ordinance in Copenhagen. Model 1 is a baseline model that includes five socio-demographic predictors. This model indicates some support for the idea that viewpoints on the ordinance are structured by social, economic, and demographic identities of individuals, particularly that women have greater odds of supporting restriction, as do respondents with higher levels of education and who are younger. Model 2 adds important characteristics relating to geographic location within the metropolitan area as well as usage of alternatives to motor vehicles. Model 2 highlights how uses of transportation connect closely with the transportation-related measure, particularly that non-motor vehicular modes of transportation and suburban residence tend to predict more support for restricting cars. Finally, Model 3 adds the two measures about politics and air quality to the same set of covariates as Model 2. Political preference is linked to support for the ordinance: left-leaning parties have higher odds of support and right-leaning parties have much lower odds of support compared to the "other" political category. A second finding linking concern for air quality to the desire to restrict cars receives support here: compared to those not concerned about air quality, respondents who are somewhat or very concerned have greater odds of support for restricting cars in the city center.

Table 7.1 Logistic regression odds ratios (standard errors) predicting support for restricting cars in city center of copenhagen.

	Model 1		Model 2		Model 3	
Gender (male, ref.)	1.73	***	1.83	***	1.55	**
	(0.24)		(0.26)		(0.24)	
Income (lower-middle quartile, ref.)						
Lowest quartile	1.4		1.22		1.14	
	(0.31)		(0.28)		(0.27)	
Upper-middle quartile	0.73		0.7		0.77	
	(0.15)		(0.15)		(0.18)	
Upper quartile	0.67	+	0.7		0.83	
	(0.15)		(0.17)		(0.21)	
Education (high school, ref.)						
Less than high school	1.02		0.97		0.82	
	(0.23)		(0.22)		(0.19)	

Bachelor's degree	1.48	*	1.29		1.06	
	(0.26)		(0.24)		(0.21)	
Advanced degree	1.57	*	1.35		1.24	
	(0.31)		(0.28)		(0.26)	
Age	0.98	**	0.99		0.99	
	(0.01)		(0.01)		(0.01)	
Parenthood (not a parent, ref.)	1.13		1.13		0.93	
	(0.2)		(0.21)		(0.19)	
Ride transit (less than once a week, ref.)			1.61	**	1.67	**
			(0.24)		(0.27)	
Cyclist (not in last 30 days, ref.)			2.16	***	2.04	***
			(0.33)		(0.34)	
Area of city (urban, ref.)			0.69	*	0.83	
			(0.11)		(0.14)	
Political preference (other, ref.)						
Right party					0.34	***
					(0.07)	
Left party					1.56	*
					(0.33)	
Air quality concern (none, ref.)						
Somewhat concerned					1.77	**
					(0.31)	
Very concerned					2.29	**
					(0.61)	

Source: 2015 Copenhagen Area Survey; n = 1,031.

These quantitative findings can be summarized in four parts. First, respondents favoring left-leaning parties are the most likely to support car restriction in Copenhagen, and the right-wing are the least likely. This suggests that the issue is politicized along partisan lines in the city, similar to issues like immigration (Smiley, Emerson, & Markussen 2017). This partisan polarization reveals that residents who favor right-leaning parties are most strongly opposed to the measure. Second, transportation matters. Using a bicycle or public transportation is linked to greater support of car restriction. Third, concern about air quality is associated with desiring restriction of cars in the city center; this connects to the argument (see below) that improvement of air quality will be a benefit of restricting cars. Fourth, socio-demographic covariates are largely not important predictors, with the important exception of gender, which is the only statistically significant relationship in Model 3. Findings show that women tend to support the initiative more than men. In all, though there may initially seem to be a consensus around pushing bicycling and de-centering cars in the Copenhagen metropolitan area, closer attention to public opinion on restricting cars in the city center uncovers deep differences across partisan lines and across transportation types.

Qualitative Results

With this understanding of public opinion as backdrop, the analysis now moves to an investigation of the politics of car restriction in Copenhagen. Although congestion pricing in the city center has been debated on and off for more than a decade (Henderson & Gulsrud 2019), the timeline for this chapter begins with national elections in September 2011, continues through fruitless negotiations into February 2012, and ends up with the findings of a national "Congestion Commission" in August 2013. In this analysis, I highlight arguments made by proponents and opponents, and follow closely a sequence of events that prevented this once-very-likely policy from being enacted.

Highly competitive national elections set to take place in September 2011 opened debate on contrasting visions for Denmark's future. Denmark has a parliamentary system of government, and a coalition of right-wing parties had governed Denmark for a decade. Eight main parties contested this particular election, and not one won more than 27 percent of the overall vote. Therefore, coalition building proved to be very important, as is commonly the case in Danish national politics. Each coalition corresponded to the left and right, with Social Democrats leading the left (led by Helle Thorning-Schmidt) and Venstre (led by Lars Lokke Rasmussen, the prime minister at the time and again after 2015 elections) corresponding to the right.

A central point of the political platform for left-leaning parties in the 2011 elections was that the city of Copenhagen should install congestion pricing. Championed especially by the Socialist People's Party and the Red-Green Alliance, who campaigned as part of the left-leaning coalition, the coalition of left-leaning political parties emerged successful in the elections. The leadership of the coalition adopted the congestion charge as a priority. With the powerful Social Democrats formally leading the government and in support of the policy, coalition priorities aligned, and the government set to work to design the charge. Most plans had a 25 kroner (about 3.5 euros or about 4 dollars) charge for motor vehicles that entered a ring around the city during rush hour, with lower prices outside of rush hour and no charges during nights or weekends.

Proponents of the plan centered on three primary claims. First, proponents sought to decrease car traffic, as Copenhagen was rated the twenty-sixth most congested city in Europe in 2012. Analyses of the plan estimated that traffic in the city of Copenhagen could drop by as much as 23 percent because of the congestion pricing. Second, proponents sought to improve air quality, primarily to improve human health and to decrease the city's environmental impact. For human health, the plan estimates that air pollution might decrease 5 to 10 percent by decreasing toxic transportation emissions that affect respiratory systems and beyond. For the environmental impact, Copenhagen's ambitious goals to be carbon-neutral are dependent on increasing less energy-intensive modes of transportation and decreasing personal use of cars. CO_2 emissions from motor vehicles could decrease as much as 10 to 15 percent because of the plan. Third, greater financing was sought for new infrastructure and substantial improvements to public transportation. The results from our Copenhagen Area Survey indicate that public transportation users are a distant third in the total share of commuters in Greater Copenhagen, behind bicyclists and car drivers. With a new multi-billion-dollar train line under construction at that time called the City Circle Line (billed as the largest construction project in the city in 400 years), increasing access to public transportation has been a hotly debated topic. Proponents hoped that the congestion pricing would yield funds that could lower ticket prices for public transport, thereby increasing access for economically disadvantaged groups at a pivotal time of increasing infrastructure. Initial estimates stated that 2.2 billion kroner (or approximately 345 million dollars or 295 million euros) would be raised annually. One goal of one of the coalition partners, the Socialist People's Party, would be that ticket prices would be cut 40 percent using these newly raised funds.

Opponents of the plan centered on a few competing claims. First, the argument that it would have a negative impact on local business came from right-leaning parties and business groups including the car owners' association and, significantly, the Confederation of Danish Industry, a chamber of commerce-like organization for the country. They contended that business could be hurt by the inability of consumers—consumers in cars, that is—to access establishments in the city. While the science of climate change is largely accepted in Copenhagen (even as the small number of science deniers tend to be in right-leaning parties; see Smiley 2017) and support for climate action exists across the political spectrum, prospective policies on climate action are not as ambitious on the right as they are on the left. It is within this context that arguments for business interests find especially fertile ground. Second, some argued that the policy would comprise uneven taxation on suburban residents. Suburban dwellers are more likely to own a car, and more likely to use that car to commute into the city for work and play. Suburban municipalities were not altogether opposed to the potential policy, as several municipalities led by Social Democrats emerged intrigued, if still guarded, about the policy. In all, while the suburban mayors preferred improvements to public transportation before the installation of a congestion charge, they were amenable to accepting a compromise that included a toll ring. The third argument is considered the most influential: projections of the amount of funds initially forecasted to be raised by congestion charges were subject to change. While proponents relied on initial estimates of more than 2 billion kroner in revenue each year, estimates furnished postelection saw that number drop dramatically to just under half of the original figure. This provided a crucial opening. The potential congestion pricing, once considered all-but-passed, saw parties on the right, industry, and suburbs argue that the benefits were not what they seemed, and therefore the congestion charge should not be passed. These financial critiques were powerful even against other critical considerations like the environmental and social benefits. Consensus in Copenhagen around these types of environmental and social benefits was not enough to defeat the counterarguments outlined here, thereby affirming the power of right-leaning factions even in a city that has comparably egalitarian policies, plans, and practices. It perhaps mirrors what we would expect in many other, more market-oriented cities, where such counterarguments hold great sway.

This third argument proved persuasive. Infighting ensued in the left-leaning coalition, with the Social Democrats acknowledging the plan as "not perfect" and a coalition partner, the Social Liberal party, side-stepping involvement in negotiations. What was described in January 2012 as a sure thing had by February turned into a nonstarter. The congestion charge was dead—and, while some initial efforts emerged again in 2018, it was only at the municipal level, and the policy remains but a proposal (Henderson & Gulsrud 2019).

In the place of the congestion pricing plan, a new framework was adopted. One billion kroner (about USD 150 million) was set aside to improve public transportation, including lower ticket fares. But lower ticket fares would not come close to matching the 40 percent drop desired by one of the congestion charge's primary proponents, the Socialist People's Party. The new fund for public transportation would be paid for partly by a higher tax on leased vehicles.

In addition to the 1 billion kroner outlay, a Congestion Commission was established bringing in stakeholders from across the political spectrum and from community groups. The Congestion Commission released its final report in August 2013. The goal of the commission was to decrease car usage, although this cautious wording was again a major difference from 2011 election claims that favored dramatic drops. Bicycling stakeholders in the city were particularly displeased with the commission's work because it did not meaningfully discuss how bicycling could be better accommodated other than bicycling "super-highways," which were deemed by these advocates to be little more than refurbishing existing routes. In all, the Congestion Commission's findings formalized what was already known in February 2012: that systematic policies seeking to limit cars through congestion pricing would not be influential in the city of Copenhagen, and that the bicycle capital of the world had significant pushback from car drivers.

Discussion and Conclusion

Congestion pricing is an emergent urban policy aimed at de-centering car usage in high impact areas of cities. Copenhagen appeared to be an ideal candidate: imbued with a collective spirit, a world leader in sustainability policy, and eager about bicycling infrastructure in particular. But congestion pricing did not come to pass in Copenhagen. Why?

To answer this question, I explored two sources of data, each providing different answers. Using quantitative data, I discussed that restricting car use in the city center had a high degree of support among the public: 64 percent of Greater Copenhagen residents supported the measure. There were critical differences in support by political party preference, with right-leaning respondents weighted heavily against restriction of cars in the city center. There were also differences in the mode of transportation, with those who bike or take public transportation being more in support than those who do not. Residents worried about air quality also tended to support the measure more than Copenhageners who were not worried. Women supported the measure in greater numbers than men, indicating a key axis of difference, aligning with broader understandings that women tend to favor environment-related initiatives more than men (Kennedy & Dzialo 2015).

Using qualitative data, I reconstructed the timeline and politics of the most recent and important contestation surrounding congestion charges between 2011 and 2013. The timeline shows that national elections and coalition building provided a firm foundation for congestion pricing proposals, but this unraveled in the face of changing data on tax outputs, distaste among business, and stiff opposition from right-leaning parties.

In synthesizing the quantitative and qualitative data, two reasons can be highlighted for the congestion charge policy failure in Copenhagen. The first is the most specific: the steep drop of the anticipated toll funds provided a political opportunity for those challenging the congestion charge. There was widespread consensus that public transportation needed an influx of funds to increase access and improve infrastructure, and originally widespread expectation that the amount raised by the congestion pricing could provide such an influx. But uneasy coalition partners yoked to one party's campaign platform gave up on congestion pricing amid changing expectations about the actual amount projected and bitter critique from industry and political foes. The governing coalition instead found funds from taxing leased cars and setting more modest goals.

The second reason for why congestion pricing did not succeed concerns the governance structure around this transportation issue. The responsibility for the issue lay with the national government, not the municipal government of Copenhagen or the local region, Hovedstaden. This is due to the strong national structure of government in Denmark. A reorganization of the country's political jurisdictions in 2007 dropped the number of municipalities from 298 to 97, and the number of regions (akin to states or provinces) from 13 to 5. As a result, the power of the national government increased, and that of municipalities and regions decreased. Under this governance structure, much of the metropolitan or regional planning for a toll system did not occur on the municipal or regional level, but rather on the national level. With a quarter of the country's residents living in Greater Copenhagen, local interests are well-represented in the national legislature, but are just a fraction of the overall total. This means that fully three quarters of the decision-makers for this decision do not represent constituencies in or around Copenhagen. While the drop in expected tax base helps to explain why the governing coalition fractured around this issue, the division of labor for different scales of government helps to explain why public opinion could be circumvented, and why the failure could even occur in the first place. Put another way, the coalition infighting might not have been relevant if the debate had taken place on the municipal or regional level.

This second reason is of particular interest for just sustainabilities, and for urban policy in cities more generally. Some urbanists call for a "metropolitan revolution" where cities are laboratories for social change (Katz & Bradley 2013) or, more radically, for a new set of "rebel cities" to contest late capitalism (Harvey 2012). But the application of just sustainabilities in such contexts may encounter limits to their power in the form of scalar disjunctures. In the case of congestion charges in Copenhagen, the scalar disjuncture was simple: municipal or regional governing bodies did not have the jurisdiction to decide their own fate. Instead, the national government was in charge of this ostensibly urban policy.

The implications, theoretical advances, and political challenges for just sustainabilities are clear: scalar disjunctures can create undemocratic processes that prevent the realization of a just sustainability. Had these more local governments been empowered in this particular area of decision-making, the outcome may well have been different; public support, for instance, might be easily marshaled to enact such an agenda. The idea of cities as hotspots for social change connects readily to just sustainabilities' focus on bottom-up action, as these local areas may be able to be more nimble in their policy process, more just in the overall political orientation, and more well-positioned to make inroads on local environmental improvements. These trends could produce a more inclusive set of stakeholders that seek out more progressive action. In Copenhagen (but not necessarily elsewhere), I argue that congestion pricing is a form of just sustainability, and therefore fits this model of more progressive action to improve social justice and the environment. Finally, it might also be noted that this local empowerment model could also be used for initiatives *opposing* just sustainabilities, as sometimes local or regional citizenries and governments may be less progressive than the larger states in which they are a part. Still, as it relates to the specific case of Copenhagen and the specific issue of congestion pricing, downscaling democratic responsibility to the local level would have increased the likelihood of the popular congestion pricing in Copenhagen.

This locally empowered action can be slowed and stopped in many ways. In the case of congestion charges in Copenhagen, it was slowed and stopped through a scalar disjuncture in political power. Copenhagen's goal of reaching carbon neutrality—and to do so sustainably and justly—relies on local empowerment that this case reveals is not always present. In other cities, this may also be the case, as national governments typically have more power in a federal-style political structure such as that found in Denmark and other places (like the United States), and this power may undercut local initiatives. One policy implication is that the enactment of just sustainabilities should closely consider the governance structure at hand, and work to match the possibility for change to that structure. This could mean seeking a smaller scale like a municipality as the convener for social changes instead of a larger scale like a federal government. More than this, uncovering the political configurations at the heart of urban policy can reveal paradoxes that stymie such policies to begin with. Future possibilities for just sustainabilities for Copenhagen and elsewhere can uncover these paradoxes and provoke a more just and sustainable future.

Note

1   A new political party, the Alternative (*Alternativet*), also fielded candidates for the 2015 parliamentary elections, receiving approximately 4.8 percent of the overall vote throughout Denmark. Unfortunately, the CAS did not feature this party as an option, as the survey was in the field shortly after the signatures to put the party on the 2015 ballot were submitted.

References

Abu-Lughod, J.L. (1999), *New York, Chicago, Los Angeles: America's Global Cities*, Minneapolis: University of Minnesota Press.

Agyeman, J. (2005a), *Sustainable Communities and the Challenge of Environmental Justice*, New York: NYU Press.

Agyeman, J. (2005b), "Alternatives for community and environment: Where justice and sustainability meet," *Environment: Science & Policy for Sustainable Development*, 47(6): 10–23.

Agyeman, J. & B. Evans (2003), "Toward just sustainability in urban communities: Building equity rights with sustainable solutions," *Annals of the American Academy of Political & Social Science*, 590: 35–53.

Agyeman, J. & K. Warner (2002), "Putting 'just sustainability' into place: From paradigm to practice," *Policy & Management Review*, 2(1): 8–40.

Agyeman, J., R.D. Bullard, & B. Evans (2002), "Exploring the nexus: Bringing together sustainability, environmental justice, and equity," *Space & Polity*, 6(1): 77–90.

Agyeman, J., R.D. Bullard, & B. Evans (2003), *Just Sustainabilities: Development in an Unequal World*, Cambridge: MIT Press.

Agyeman, J., D. Schlosberg, L. Craven, & C. Matthews (2016), "Trends and directions in environmental justice: From inequity to everyday life, community, and just sustainabilities," *Annual Review of Environmental Resources*, 41: 321–40.

Blok, A. & M.L. Meilvang (2015), "Picturing urban green attachments: Civic activists moving between familiar and public engagements in the city," *Sociology*, 49(1): 19–37.

Brenner, N. (1999), "Globalisation as reterritorialisation: The re-scaling of urban governance in the European Union," *Urban Studies*, 36(3): 431–51.

Caniglia, B.S., M. Vallée, & B. Frank (eds) (2016), *Resilience, Environmental Justice and the City*, New York: Routledge.

Carrington, D. (2019), 'Revealed: Air pollution may be damaging 'every organ in your body,' *Guardian*, May 17. Available online: https://www.theguardian.com/environment/ng-interactive/2019/may/17/air-pollution-may-be-damaging-every-organ-and-cell-in-the-body-finds-global-review (Accessed May 25, 2020).

Castells, M. (1977), *The Urban Question: A Marxist Approach*, Cambridge: MIT Press.
Cole, L.W. & S.R. Foster (2001), *From the Ground Up: Environmental Racism and the Rise of the Environmental Justice Movement*, New York: NYU Press.
Cupples, J. & E. Ridley (2008), "Towards a heterogeneous environmental responsibility: sustainability and cycling fundamentalism," *Area*, 40(2): 254–64.
Duany, A., E. Plater-Zyberk, & J. Speck (2001), *Suburban Nation: The Rise of Sprawl and the Decline of the American Dream*, New York: Farrar, Straus & Giroux.
Eliasson, J. (2014), "The role of attitude structures, direct experience and reframing for the success of congestion pricing," *Transportation Research Part A*, 67: 81–95.
Eliasson, J. & L. Jonsson (2011), "The unexpected 'yes': Explanatory factors behind the positive attitudes to congestion charges in Stockholm," *Transport Policy*, 18: 636–47.
Emerson, M.O. & K.T. Smiley (2018), *Market Cities, People Cities: The Shape of Our Urban Future*, New York: NYU Press.
Fainstein, S.S. (2010), *The Just City*, Ithaca: Cornell University Press.
Garreau, J. (1991), *Edge City: Life on the New Frontier*, New York: Anchor Books.
Gehl, J. (2010), *Cities for People*, Washington: Island Press.
Gehlert, T., O.A. Nielsen, J. Rich, & B. Schlag (2008), "Public acceptability change of urban road pricing schemes," *Proceedings of the Institutions of Civil Engineers—Transport*, 161(3): 111–21.
Gehlert, T., C. Kramer, O.A. Nielsen, & B. Schlag (2011), "Socioeconomic differences in public acceptability and car use adaptation towards urban road pricing," *Transport Policy*, 18: 685–94.
Gerdes, J. (2013), "Copenhagen's ambitious push to be carbon neutral by 2025," *Yale Environment 360*, April 11. Available online: https://e360.yale.edu/features/copenhagens_ambitious_push_to_be_carbon_neutral_by_2025 (Accessed May 30, 2019).
Glaeser, E.L., M.E. Kahn, & J. Rappaport (2008), "Why do the poor live in cities? The role of public transportation," *Journal of Urban Economics*, 63: 1–24.
Golub, A., M.L. Hoffman, A.E. Lugo, & G.F. Sandoval (eds) (2016), *Bicycling and Urban Transformation: Biking for All?* New York: Routledge.
Harvey, D. (1973), *Social Justice and the City*, Athens: University of Georgia Press.
Harvey, D. (2012), *Rebel Cities: From the Right to the City to the Urban Revolution*, New York: Verso.
Henderson, J. & N.M. Gulsrud (2019), *Street Fits In Copenhagen: Bicycle and Car Politics in A Green Mobility City*, New York: Routledge.
Hoffman, M.L. & A. Lugo (2014), "Who is 'world class'? Transportation justice and bicycle policy," *Urbanities*, 4(1): 45–61.
Jacobs, J. (1961), *The Death and Life of Great American Cities*, New York: Random House.
Katz, B. & J. Bradley (2013), *The Metropolitan Revolution: How Cities and Metros are Fixing our Broken Politics and Fragile Economy*, Washington, DC: Brookings Institution Press.
Kennedy, E.H. & L. Dzialo (2015), "Locating gender in environmental sociology," *Sociology Compass*, 9/10: 920–9.
Kim, J., J. Schmöcker, S. Fujii, & R.B. Noland (2013), "Attitudes towards road pricing and environmental taxation among US and UK students," *Transportation Research Part A*, 48: 50–62.
Kurtz, H.E. (2003), "Scale frames and counter-scale frames: Constructing the problem of environmental justice," *Political Geography*, 22: 887–916.
Lefebvre, H. (1991), *The Production of Space*, Cambridge: Blackwell Publishing.

Li, Z. & D.A. Hensher (2012) "Congestion charging and car use: A review of state preference and opinion studies and market monitoring evidence," *Transport Policy*, 20: 47–61.

Logan, J.R. & H.L. Molotch (2007), *Urban Fortunes: The Political Economy of Place*, Berkeley: University of California Press.

Logan, J.R., R.B. Whaley, & K. Crowder (1997), "The character and consequences of growth regimes: An assessment of twenty years of research," *Urban Affairs Review*, 32: 603–30.

Loughran, K. (2014), "Parks for profit: The High Line, growth machines, and the uneven development of urban public spaces," *City & Community*, 13(1): 49–68.

Martinez-Alier, J., I. Anguelovski, P. Bond, D.D. Bene, F. Demaria, J. Gerber, L. Greyl, W. Haas, H. Healy, V. Marín-Burgos, G. Ojo, M. Porto, L. Rijnhout, B. Rodíguez-Labajos, J. Spangenberg, L. Temper, R. Warlenius, & I. Yánez (2014), "Between activism and science: Grassroots concepts for sustainability coined by Environmental Justice Organizations," *Journal of Political Ecology*, 21: 19–60.

Massey, D.S. & N.A. Denton (1993), *American Apartheid: Segregation and the Making of the Underclass*, Cambridge: Harvard University Press.

McLaren, D. & J. Agyeman (2015), *Sharing Cities: A Case for Truly Smart and Sustainable Cities*, Cambridge: MIT Press.

Molotch, H. & S. Vicari (1988), "Three ways to build: The development process in the United States, Japan and Italy," *Urban Affairs Quarterly*, 24: 188–214.

Molotch, H., W. Freudenberg, & K.E. Paulsen (2000), "History repeats itself, but how? City character, urban tradition, and the accomplishment of place," *American Sociological Review*, 65(6): 791–823.

Pellow, D. (2018), *What Is Critical Environmental Justice?* Medford: Polity Press.

Rich, J. & O.A. Nielsen (2007), "A socio-economic assessment of proposed road user charging schemes in Copenhagen," *Transport Policy*, 14: 330–45.

Riggs, W. (ed) (2018), *Disruptive Transport: Driverless Cars, Transport Innovation and the Sustainable City of Tomorrow*, New York: Routledge.

Sampson, R.J. (2012), *Great American City: Chicago and the Enduring Neighborhood Effect*, Chicago: University of Chicago Press.

Sassen, S. (1991), *The Global City: New York, London, Tokyo*, Princeton: Princeton University Press.

Schuitema, G., L. Steg, & S. Forward (2010), "Explaining differences in acceptability before and acceptance after the implementation of a congestion charge in Stockholm," *Transportation Research Part A*, 44: 99–109.

Smiley, K.T. (2017), "Climate change denial, political beliefs, and cities: Evidence from Copenhagen and Houston," *Environmental Sociology*, 3(1): 76–86.

Smiley, K.T. & M.O. Emerson (2018), "A spirit of urban capitalism: Market cities, people cities, and cultural justifications," *Urban Research & Practice*. DOI: 10.1080/17535069.2018.1559351

Smiley, K.T., W. Rushing, & M. Scott (2016), "Behind a bicycling boom: Governance, cultural change and place character in Memphis, Tennessee," *Urban Studies*, 53(1): 193–209.

Smiley, K.T., M.O. Emerson, & J.W. Markussen (2017), "Immigration attitudes before and after tragedy in Copenhagen: The importance of political affiliation and safety concerns," *Sociological Forum*, 32(2): 321–38.

Stehlin, J. (2014), "Regulating inclusion: Spatial form, social process, and the normalization of cyclic practice in the USA," *Mobilities*, 9(1): 21–41.

Sudjic, D. (1993), *The 100-Mile City*, Boston: Harcourt.
Sze, J. & J.K. London (2008), "Environmental justice at the crossroads," *Sociology Compass*, 2(4): 1331–54.
Sze, J., J. London, F. Shilling, G. Gambirazzio, T. Filan, & M. Cadenasso (2009), "Defining and contesting environmental justice: Socio-natures and the politics of scale in the Delta," *Antipode*, 41(4): 807–43.

8

POPULAR CONSULTATIONS AND EXTRACTIVISM IN COLOMBIA: FROM LOCAL TO GLOBAL ACTIONS AGAINST MINING AND CLIMATE CHANGE

Aracely Burgos-Ayala
Emerson Harvey Cepeda-Rodríguez

Introduction

On July 28th, 2013, in the village of Piedras in Colombia, 2,971 people rejected mining activities in their territory through Popular Consultation (PC), a public referendum on a yes-or-no question. This community vote—in a rural village of approximately 5,662 inhabitants with a poverty rate of over 50 percent (Gobernación del Tolima 2015)—had enough impact to influence the world's third biggest transnational mining corporation, Anglo Gold Ashanti, to halt their operations in the area and inspired public consultations by other villages in Colombia facing similar cases. In response to this wave of local resistance, the national government and Anglo Gold Ashanti and other corporations—like Mansoravar Energy, Minesa, Gran Colombia Gold, and Eco Oro—have created impediments against local collective action by developing new laws, administrative actions, judicial procedures, and public policies at the expense of communities and the environment. These political efforts have hampered popular participation, leading to a difficult state of affairs that Pardo (2016) calls "the tortuous path towards popular consultation."

Colombia produces coal, gold, and traditional fossil fuels and has been focusing its economy around these resources for the past twenty years, leading to "mining-energy locomotives"[1] (PND 2002–2006; PND 2006–2010; PND 2010–2014; PND 2014–2018). Over the same period, anti-mining activism has emerged in response to large-scale mining projects operated mainly by multinational companies. As a result, Colombia has the third largest number of environmental conflicts—128—after India (317) and Brazil (136) (Rincón-Pérez 2016; Environmental Justice Atlas 2018).

We would like to express our sincere gratitude and admiration to Julián Viña, Jully Méndez Clavijo, Luis Jaime Ortíz, Mónica Florez, Jhon Jairo Villa, and all Popular Consultation leaders in Colombia.

The inhabitants of Piedras, though voting locally, were thinking bigger; one voter explained that they voted in order "to save Piedras, to save Cajamarca, to save Tolima and to save the Nation" ("Piedras en el Zapato" 2013). A wave of similar popular votes, inspired by Piedras, took place in 2017. Out of nine referendums, seven rejected economic activities harmful to the community and the environment. Fifty-four initiatives to forbid energy mining projects, advanced by many city departments as well as fourteen municipalities and a large city's Municipal Council, are currently in progress. Never in Colombia's history has participatory democracy been more evident than now.

On the other hand, in spite of Colombia's officially democratic system, social participation often faces obstacles, including police violence and stigmatization, delays in administrative approval, legal challenges, and claims that locally based PCMs were against national development. National and international economic interests promote an agenda based on large-scale exploitation of Colombia's natural resources, often in direct contrast to local government priorities for protecting ecosystems and enhancing tourism (Piedras Development Plan 2011–2013). This threat is faced on multiple fronts, not just in Piedras. AngloGold Ashanti's project "La Colosa" included a gold deposit in Cajamarca and fifteen towns to hold the treatment and storage of gold and hazardous wastes (BM Colombia Solidarity Campaign 2013). Among the perceived consequences of the proposed project was pollution of the Opia River, the main hydrographical basin providing drinking water to Piedras, Coello, and Ibagué (Hernández 2017).

Popular consultation movements (PCM) provide a useful case study to consider Agyeman's (2013) just sustainabilities framework. First, PCM expose an economic model focused on the exploitation of natural resources generating high poverty levels, threatening environmental and human well-being and highlighting the connection between multiple types of injustices. Second, PCM defend nature as the shared heritage of humanity, making the intergenerational connection that animates the temporal goal of just sustainabilities. Third, PCM claim the right to drinking water and the landscape, autonomy of the peoples, and the reconfiguration of power through participatory mechanisms that constitute real practice and process, an emerging theme in just sustainabilities scholarship (Agyeman et al. 2016). Fourth, PCM promote the rights of nature; one of the transversal claims of the PC's leaders is to include nature as a subject of rights in national law. Referencing Escobar (2000), we affirm that the quest for any future that can be called just *and* sustainable must take into account the cultural, ecological, and economic practices and rationales of the people involved and the ways in which they negotiate their specific processes for the enrichment of the world.

This chapter reflects on Colombia's PCM within the context of just sustainabilities, while exploring the following tensions within the movements that challenge its success and yet simultaneously prompt its enactment: (1) A national domestic development policy that relies on extractive industries with steep environmental and social costs despite opposition at the community level; (2) The obstacles to popular participation in democratic states, and the concurrent emergence of social movements seeking to defend their identities and relationships with nature;

(3) The connection of injustices locally and globally that build regional, national, and transnational alliances, such as climate change as a challenge of collective action.

Through this research, we found that the inception and reproduction of the PC experience in Piedras established a multifaceted model to address other environmental conflicts. Notably, community leaders found common ground amid the feelings and concerns of an urban area (Ibagué) and a rural area (Piedras) to stop gold-mining projects. The public resistance in Piedras was strengthened by knowledge of environmental referendums in other countries (Tambogrande, Huancabamba, Ayabaca, Michiquillay, and Islay in Peru; Esquel in Argentina; Balcombe in the United Kingdom) and how foreign social organizations could support those who oppose extraction projects. This knowledge flows both ways, as the administration and the results of the first PC then opened the doors to use this participatory mechanism in other places. The trend ultimately grew into the "Movimiento Nacional Ambiental"[2] in Colombia (Heinrich-Böll-Stiftung 2019), composed of more than 200 environmental organizations and communities from all corners of Colombia who assert the right to protect the environment and call for public policy against climate change and deforestation, prohibition of extractivist activities, and protection of the right to participation.

The social mobilization in Piedras also demonstrated the utility of specific strategies to resist extractive industries, such as: (1) the assembly of multiple social groups recognizing a common concern, facilitated through house-to-house outreach by PCM leaders explaining the effects of mining on people's health and livelihoods, and on the environment; (2) the use of institutional tools such as lobbying, the *tutela* (an action of protection in the 1991 Colombian Constitution), petitioning information from regional environmental institutions, and litigation; and (3) the implementation of popular education to understand consequences of extractivism. Altogether, the outreach to spread knowledge of extractivism impacts the reciprocal recognition of shared concerns during communal assemblies, and protests and symbolic diffusion tools like "La Marcha Carnaval" (The Carnival March) allowed people who shared the same worries to unite. The social mobilization process established alliances with external organizations and social movements with common purposes. These tools are useful for enacting Agyeman's (2008) call to make visible the ecosystems' limits, to defend the local farmers' economies, and to protect dignified life conditions for future generations, in the quest for just sustainabilities.

These strategies entwine legal tools with constitutional mechanisms of participation (like Popular Consultations) and the emotional resonance of the public's values and perceptions, in order to address the need to both protect natural resources and guarantee a decent life. This model assesses the regulatory capacity of the law to help grow a participatory sense and to build a public political scenario (Santos & Rodríguez Garavito 2007), and can be valuable to generate normative changes (e.g., Rights of Nature). These strategies also connect injustice experiences from different locations in Colombia and abroad, supporting Agyeman & Evans' (2003) observation that common environmental and social injustices generate links between affected communities, allowing them to collectively attract attention to reinvent the notion of progress. We believe that this case study can give people hope and show that "La Lucha" against greater powers is possible. Hope does not mean we win each battle, but that we are able to continue fighting.

This chapter is divided into three parts. First, we analyze what the growth of PCs has meant to just sustainabilities in Colombia, considering that the nation's economy is based on natural resource exploitation, as well as the government and corporate barriers to this participation mechanism. Second, we discuss the objectives of this mobilization and how they connect to global efforts to combat climate change through just sustainabilities. Third, we describe how local stories were spread through other villages, revealing that the sum of joined solidarities among different movements is an essential element to achieve just sustainabilities.

Methodology

Our research process had two stages. First, we conducted a literature review using the key term "Popular Consultations" in scientific and gray literature, including state briefings and reports from the two main newspapers in Colombia: "El Tiempo" and "El Espectador." Second, we interviewed five leaders of PCs developed in Colombia: Julián Viña (Piedras, Tolima), Jully Katherine Méndez Clavijo (Tauramena, Casanare), Luis Jaime Ortíz Vásquez (Arbeláez, Cundinamarca), and Mónica Florez and Jhon Jairo Villa Monsalve (Pijao, Quindío). These leaders talked eagerly about their hopes, experiences, and fears, demonstrating that they do not hoard their knowledge, but want to share it so their struggles can be known and replicated. Monica Flórez, our first contact, linked us with the other leaders. The interviews were conducted through online correspondence from October to December 2017. All interviewees consented to being recorded and having their names published. Our guiding questions asked them to discuss (1) the obstacles they encountered before, during, and after the PC; (2) their personal motivations; (3) any previous support from national and foreign organizations; (4) any national and international PC precedents from which they drew inspiration; and (5) any local, national and transnational activism established after the consultation.

Environmental Popular Consultations and the Barriers to Its Growth in Colombia

Social participation[3] as a core element in environmental decision-making is not new. The Rio Conference in 1992 recognized social participation as crucial to addressing ecological resolutions, although obstacles remain to implementation in Latin America (CEPAL 2013). In Colombia, social participation has been given legal strength[4] through various mechanisms such as the Colombian Political Constitution of 1991[5] and Laws 134 and 1757. Popular consultation exerted by nonethnic communities[6] has been the favored defense mechanism against the projects that threaten the environment in the last few years. Since PC results are compulsory (Roa 2016; Hincapié 2017), this mechanism allows collective actions to generate social transformation. Although the strategies used by anti-extraction social movements have been numerous and varied, the PC has created a possibility of success (Rincón-Pérez 2016). Perhaps one of the greatest accomplishments of the PC process is to publicize injustices generated by extractivism and demonstrate a path toward fighting these injustices at an institutional level, opposing the forces that would remove the decision-making choices of local communities noted by Carmin & Agyeman (2011).

In Colombia, various local and national courts have determined, through their jurisprudence, the value of rural communities' participation in the economic projects that affect them, as well as the implementation of plans to protect and reestablish social-ecological systems.[7] In all PC, more than 90 percent of the electors voted against mining projects (Registraduría Nacional del Estado Civil 2019a). Additionally, each place where a PC was realized had similar representation of women and men as potential electors (Registraduría Nacional del Estado Civil 2019b), adding a critical element of gender equity in decision-making.

Nevertheless, PCs have faced serious obstacles, and in some cases the mechanism is portrayed as being opposed to Colombia's national development model. The obstacles represent the inconsistencies of democracy in Colombia. Although the Colombia Constitution formally recognizes participation mechanisms and rights, in praxis, Colombian people do not have access to their rights and their participation is limited to topics exclusive to social elites. In our interviews, the movement leaders, three women and three men, named some initial barriers to their work: "pressure of the Government by means of the Ministry of Mining, Environment and State, the Attorney-General's Office and Ecopetrol (National Oil Company)" (Jully, Tauramena); "the authorities lack compromise, public official co-optation, police attack and abuse of power, and the indifference and denial of the situations on behalf of the general population" (Julián, Piedras). On voting day there were complaints about "lack of public transportation for the inhabitants in rural zones" (Jully, Tauramena, and Julián, Piedras) and "reduction of polling stations and the low participation of the younger generations" (Mónica, Pijao). Even after a vote, the decisions made by communities can be declared illegitimate by the national government, under claims of being "illegal and unconstitutional, as well as the use of many other legal strategies, not just from the Government but also corporations" (Jully, Tauramena) or by means of "judicial resolutions being delayed on behalf of the institutions in charge of the verification of the prior and posterior processes of the PC" (Mónica and Jhon, Pijao).

The government's scant recognition and support of democratic participation in Colombia (Hincapié 2017) discredits the legitimacy of the PCs (i.e., Decree 934 of 2013, later suspended). The state has often undermined the decisions of local authorities inside national political arenas, and sometimes imposes restrictions at an individual or community level (e.g., elimination of mayors' powers and giving them to legislative bodies) (Hincapié 2017). The result of this structural violence—violation of survival, well-being, identity, and liberty needs—(Galtung

1985) is tension between local communities who want to employ this participatory mechanism and the larger bodies who oppose them, primarily the national government and the international corporations (Roa 2016).

Popular Consultations and the Climate Change Agenda in Colombia

Each popular consultation is based on its own local context, community, and their explicit claims. For our interviewees, these communities consist mainly of poor farmers, with a similar number of women and men. Their motivations for resisting the mining industries, in their own words, include "the love I have for the land where I live and to keep the autonomy of the communities" (Mónica, Pijao), a desire to "continue to save the agricultural vocation and the respect to a [specific] form of living by preserving the culture and the natural landscape" (Jhon, Piedras), "[t]he absence of participation in the decision making affects the land" (Luis, Arbelaez), "[the] detrimental effects on the local economic development, the environment, economic and social influences; and the violation of the statutory prohibitions of the industrial development in protected areas" (Jully, Tauramena), and "the protection of community unions, the exaltation of the human dignity and public heritage" (Julián, Piedras).

Common themes that generate public mobilizations in Colombia include the defense of water, ecosystems, and biodiversity, which support all forms of life. People do not battle against large-scale exploitations only for the sake of the land but for the sake of their own future, and the sacred connection between the two. This connection is a spiritual one, with a voice and governance ascribed to environmental elements such as rivers and other natural elements (Roa 2016; "Piedras en el Zapato" 2013; Hernández 2017). The leading threads of environmental democratization also emerge as common concerns: the right to participate as equal partners at every level of decision-making through autonomy and participation in local scopes—all of which resonate with the framework of just sustainabilities.

This finding aligns with Leff's (1998) assertion that

> civic movements appear as a response to the destruction of the environment and the dispositioning of its life forms and its means of production... they are mobilizations of social reappropriation of nature linked to democratic processes, territory protection, and their ethnic identities... with which new patterns of environmental rationale were incorporated to provide environmental significance into their culture and create new social values.
> (Leff 1998)

The recognition of alternative social values is essential—these represent a way to reconsider the environmental needs to best allow for the existence of life itself (e.g., water, space, soil, etc.), outside of the economic sphere of marketing and cost-benefit assessment (Martínez Alier 2009). As such, the notions of justice and sustainability can be reassessed for the present and the future: (1) justice goes far beyond the satisfaction of humans' basic needs and includes recognition of the intrinsic value of nature and its corresponding rights, and (2) sustainability must involve radical transformation to consumption practices and immediate measures to protect the existence of life.

Furthermore, these PCs are occurring in a broader context of global climate change. Locally, people are motivated by their contextual concerns about resource extraction, including their economy, their culture, and the integrity of their natural assets; global climate change is not their focus. The results of these referendums obstruct transnational corporations' extraction practices, generating tensions either directly with the communities or at the different government levels, where climate change is not an explicit part of the conflict either. However, through collective actions against extractivism such as the PC, these local communities of resistance are preventing high levels of greenhouse gas emissions that affect the entire planet (Phillips 2016).

Climate change is one of the biggest challenges of the Anthropocene (Gosling & Arnell 2016; Madumere 2017) and biggest problem (or possibility) of a collective action that humankind has had to face. Ostrom (1990) argues that climate change should be incorporated as a potential agent of social territory organization in every level of political agendas. In Colombia, a country with a minimal contribution of GHG (0.4 percent), emissions are generated mainly by deforestation and livestock (60 percent), alongside energy-mining activities (15 percent) (International Energy Agency 2010; PNCC 2017). Although industrialized and developed countries like China or the USA have greater carbon emissions, climate change consequences (e.g., droughts, floods, wildfires and other natural disasters) are more intense in the poorest places of the world (Anguelovski & Roberts 2011). Within Colombia, climate change is one of the main drivers of forest transformation, damage to ecosystem services, and Colombian species extinction (Gómez et al. 2016), although some of these impacts might be mitigated through comprehensive management (Rinaudo 2017).

Many mitigation and vulnerability communications have been spread since 2001 (Rinaudo 2017) but it was not until 2017 that Colombia implemented climate change national policies (PNCC 2017) and a Climate Change Adjustment Plan (PNACC 2017). At the same time, the Colombian government facilitates mining by multinational corporations and suppresses environmental movements like the PCM. Both the PNCC and the PNACC include mining and hydrocarbon exploitation as a potential cause of GHG, but the PNACC offers only a single course of action to seek the management of ecosystems and their benefits; as a result, the Colombian people think that their government does little to combat climate change (IDEAM, PNUD, MADS, DNP, & CANCILLERÍA 2016; Pardo Martinez & Alfonso 2018).

Similar to the global scale, the risks and impacts of climate change within Colombia are not distributed evenly. *The Instituto de Hidrología, Meteorología y Estudios Ambientales* led the construction of an index to analyze climate vulnerability and risks in the country (IDEAM, PNUD, MADS, DNP, & CANCILLERÍA 2017). Of the municipalities that used PCs to vote against large-scale oil and mining projects, the risks of climate change impacting water resources

Table 8.1 CC contributions to vulnerability in the dimensions of food security, water resources, biodiversity, and health, in the municipalities where popular consultations have been held.

Municipal (department)	Dangers of CC against food security	Dangers of CC against water resources	Dangers of CC against biodiversity	Dangers of CC against health
Piedras (Tolima)	M	H	H	M
Tauramena (Casanare)	M	M	L	VL
Cabrera (Cundinamarca)	L	H	M	M
Cajamarca (Tolima)	L	M	H	VL
Cumaral (Casanare)	M	H	H	L
Arbeláez (Cundinamarca)	M	H	H	L
Pijao (Quindío)	M	H	H	L
Jesús María (Santander)	M	VH	H	L
Sucre (Santander)	VH	M	L	L

Source: IDEAM, PNUD, MADS, DNP, & CANCILLERÍA 2017. Scale of contribution: Very High (VH); High (H); Medium (M); Low (L); Very Low (VL).

were "very high" and "high" in one and five municipalities, respectively, while six other municipalities have a "high" danger level in their biodiversity (Table 8.1). Although the PCs were not explicitly motivated by climate change, according to the leaders, the connection to their towns, their local food security, water, biodiversity, and human well-being is inescapable.

Local Stories and Impacts of Popular Consultations

The PC in Piedras and the germination of its results reveal how social demands can begin to create new realities beyond a single territory, highlighting social mobilizations, coalitions from different geographical scales, and the opportunities to transform local knowledge into power, particularly in struggles regarding natural resources. This solidarities creation—accomplished through sharing experiences, creating alliances, and implementing joint actions—is part of just sustainabilities.

In response to the need for stronger mechanisms to terminate a transnational company extraction project, the rural village of Piedras made use of the bidding participatory PC outlined in the Constitution, an effort that was combined with the "Carnival March in Defense of Water, Life and Territory" that brings together more than 12,000[8] people since 2011 in the city of Ibague. This coordination, starting in 2011, brought life to the PC, allowing unity between a rural territory (Piedras) and an urban space (Ibagué). The idea of the "Marcha Carnaval" arose from students and teachers through the *Comité Ambiental en Defensa de la Vida*, (Environmental Committee for the Defense of Life) at the Universidad del Tolima in Ibagué, and combined with the work of the rural leaders. In the words of Julián Viñas (Piedras), "We had understood only through union, we may combat life destruction." After a request for support and articulations of Piedras' community to the committee to strengthen the movement in the town (Comité Ambiental en Defensa de la Vida nd), the "Marcha Carnaval" in 2012 proceeded from Piedras' rural territory to the urban area as a symbolic tool of manifestation and education.

This social mobilization marked a crucial moment for the typical agrarian society: the first steps toward a new relationship that goes beyond the traditional provision of goods and services from the rural to the urban context. The role of the countryside environment becomes broader, moving beyond just the use of natural resources to the role of keepers of the ecosystems (Méndez 2005; Ramírez 2005), changing urban perceptions of the value of the services it provides. The interviewed leaders mentioned that they were invited to other towns and cities (e.g., Bogotá) to participate in popular education programs and support other mobilization processes. These new farmers and rural life roles, as mentioned by Jully Katherine Mendez Clavio (Tauramena's social leader), permitted the synergy of more than seventy organizations in Colombia through social mobilizations, PCs, education programs, and support for other PCs in the country.

The struggles faced by Piedras were shared by other communities elsewhere in the world. The inhabitants of Piedras researched similar environmental referendums of Tambogrande, Huancabamba, Islay, and Cajamarca in Peru, and Esquel in Argentina (Martinez Alier 2009; Segura 2017). At the same time, support networks began cropping up with similar cases in Balcombe in the United Kingdom, as well as in Peru, Ghana, South Africa, Alaska, and France (Gómez 2016). One such network is the web platform "Yes to Life, No to Mining," which brings together more than sixty-four organizations from Africa, Europe, and the Americas to support communities affected by mining.

Paradoxes, Contradictions, and Tensions

Following the arguments of Martínez Alier (2009), the strategies that are used to defend people's homes/cultures/identities as part of the environment come from local resistances and knowledge. The following paradoxes, contradictions, and tensions must be addressed, step by step, in order to build a comprehensive socio-environmental approach stemming from the history of the PC in Piedras:

1. The national government's alignment with global economic interests and the local cooperative resistance against these economic interests, through alternate ecological and economic practices and rationalities (e.g., Piedras).

Escobar (2000) explains globalization as international capital dominating impoverished countries, making invisible people's power to make decisions over their own territories. However, capitalist actions are not inevitable. Agyeman et al. (2016) note that people mobilize against power asymmetries in the areas where they live, and these local identities are thus linked to the larger-scale damages caused by the neoliberal globalization; the Piedras case study is a clear example.

2. The tendency to frame environmental problems as either "global" or "local," making invisible the institutional responsibilities at different levels (Cash et al. 2006) and their inseparability (e.g., water, air, species, people, trade, etc. are all both local and global).
3. The differences between the general principles expressed during international summits and the measures through which that environment language is translated and reappropriated in distinct orders (Merry 2006; Goodale 2007; Eslava 2016).
4. The evolution and adoption of coalitions that surpass national, regional, and local states (Bringel 2014; Pérez 2016). This involves the creation of collective identities, by means of local, national, and global social movement networks built through common concerns (e.g., "Vía Campesina" links forty-eight organizations in sixty-nine countries through the fight for food sovereignty, as well as the aforementioned "Yes to Life, No to Mining").

When considering the enactment of just sustainabilities, we should not overlook the snowball effect: the establishment of relationships between movements in different places, the creation of social mobilization networks, surpassing differences within networks, and the completion of joint actions (Ezbawi 2011). The example of Piedras incited other villages into taking action themselves. One of the main formulas of propagation, according to Mónica Flórez, leader of the popular consultation in Pijao, was previous relationships with the people and entities involved with the PC in Piedras. The PC leaders we interviewed also indicated that after the successful outcome of the PCs in their locales, they were contacted to explain the experience in other areas.

Other tools can be important to spreading movements, including third parties close to successful social mobilizations, the media (Bringel 2014), and social networks. The PC leaders interviewed explained that national and international nongovernmental organizations that supported their popular consultations would also serve as mediators in other places facing similar challenges. One such example is the "Center for the Study of Law, Justice and Society"—DEJUSTICIA—a national think tank with an international reputation. Other organizations that facilitated the dissemination of PCs included Marcha Carnaval, Corporation Podion, Conciencia Campesina, Movimiento Nueva Cultura, Escuela de Pensamiento Circulo de Fuego, el Colectivo Socio-ambiental Juvenil de Cajamarca, and Censat "Agua Viva," among others. At the international level, the Heinrich Boll Stiftung Foundation and PAX-Holland stand out as key supporters. In contrast, the media was not mentioned by the interviewees as a means to broadcast the PCs. Finally, online cyberspace allowed us to establish dialogue channels with the leaders of the popular consultations, indicating that social networks such as Facebook and WhatsApp can assist with knowledge sharing across physical distances. This suggests possibilities of a deep, decentralized, and plural-based interactive scenario through digital technologies, which facilitates the creation of a reality that crosses great areas (Escobar 2000, 2009).

The wave of municipalities reproducing PC efforts shows how effective such knowledge sharing can be. The echo of the PC in Piedras first reached the municipalities of Tauramena in 2013 (Arauca) and then expanded in 2019 to Cabrera and Arbeláez (Cundinamarca), Cajamarca (Tolima), Cumaral (Meta), Pijao (Quindío), Jesús María and Sucre (Santander), Fusagasuga (Cundinamarca), and Mercaderes (Cauca). In total fifty-four PCs were enacted by 2018, as well as additional pressure exercised by the citizens in fifteen town councils to ban these economic activities (Figure 8.1; Table 8.2).

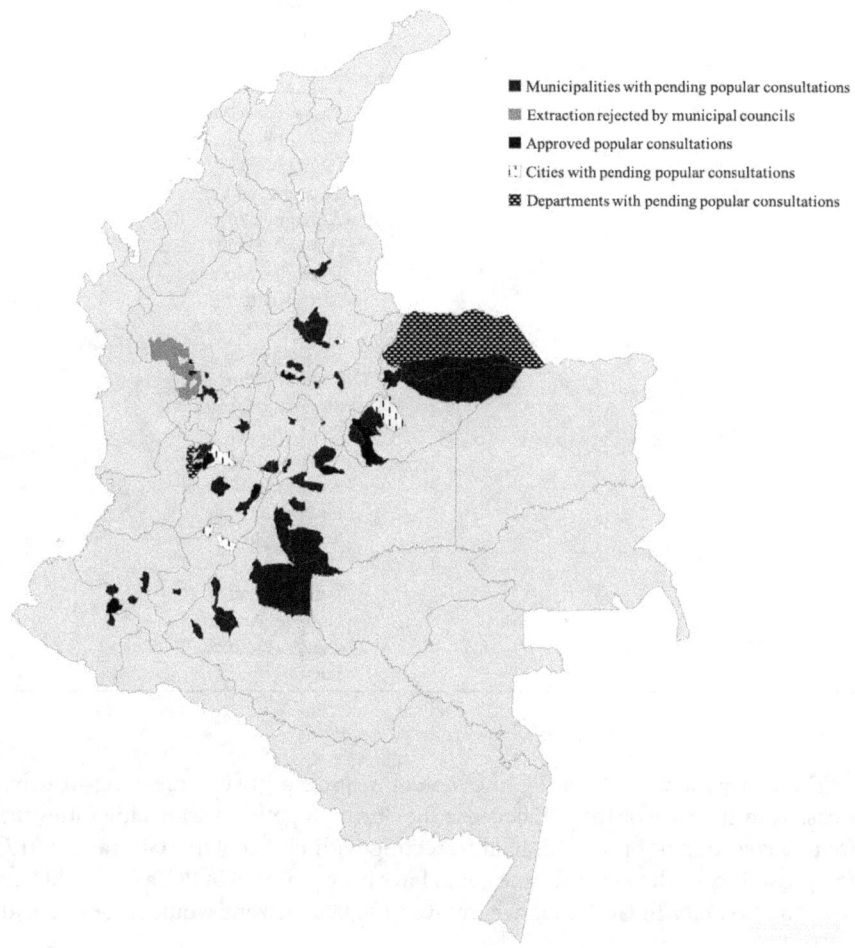

Figure 8.1 Municipalities, cities, and departments in Colombia where popular consultations and institutional actions were made against extractivism from 2013 to 2018.

Table 8.2 Municipalities, cities, and departments with popular consultations and institutional actions against extractivism in Colombia (2013–2018).

Approved popular consultations	Extraction rejected by municipal councils	Cities with pending popular consultations	Municipalities with pending popular consultations	Departments with pending popular consultations
Piedras, Cabrera, Cajamarca, Cumaral, Arbeláez, Pijao, Tauramena, Jesús María, Sucre, Fusagasuga, Mercaderes	Betulia, Caicedo, Concordia, Fredonia, Jericó, Jardín, Pueblorrico, Salgar, Támesis, Tarso, Titiribí, Urrao, Neiva	Ibagué, San Gil, Yopal y Neiva	Acacías, Granada, Cubarral, El Castillo, Vista Hermosa, Mesetas, Uribe, Calarcá, La Macarena, Córdoba (Quindío), Salento, Támara, Aguazul, Monterrey, Paz de Aríporo, Paipa, Tenza, Gachantivá, Cogua, Medina, Pasca, Fusagasugá, Une, El Peñón (Santander), Oparapa, La Vega, Almaguer, Sucre (Cauca), Paujil, Doncello, Morelia, San Vicente de Chucurí, El Carmén de Chucurí, Pinchote, Simacota, Líbano, San Lorenzo, Marmato, Puerto Asís, San Martín, La Pintada, Montebello, Valparaíso, Venecia, Hato Corozal, Armero, Ortega, Dolores, Líbano	Arauca, Quindío

The consequences of the PC movement acquire a greater meaning in urban areas, as in the case of Ibagué, because they bring together various identities that are reflected in rural populations intersecting with city centers (Giarracca 2017). The possibility of the PC in Ibagué could have been a model of PC, as it would have been the first city in Colombia where over 400,000 citizens would vote to decide whether to allow economic activities that would endanger the environment. Unfortunately, this PC did not occur.

Multiple obstacles stood in the way of the PC in Ibagué, the capital city of the Region of Tolima. A lack of financial resources hindered its implementation by the government, a common obstacle that has blocked at least eleven PCs. The treasury department, in charge of financing the PCs, did not assign the resources in the National Budget; in response, some social movements have decided to fund their own consultations (e.g., Mercaderes). The PC's referendum was also judged unconstitutional by the Administrative Tribunal of Tolima (the regional court), arguing that the referendum question was not neutral or objective (Administrative Court of Tolima 2016), which has necessitated the creation of a new question (El Tiempo 2017). The act adopted by Ibague's Town Council to prohibit mining exploitation was declared unconstitutional by the Administrative Court of Tolima, which argued that only the national government is authorized to decide such a question. Despite this discouraging result, the path to enact PCs has not been abandoned by the cities. Larger locations, like the city of Yopal, and larger regions, such as the states of Quindío and Arauca, are currently working to ban mining in their territories (La Voz de Yopal 2017; Bonilla 2018).

As PC popularity increased, the obstacles created by the State prompted other organizations and individuals to become involved.[9] In November 2017, more than 200 organizations from all corners of Colombia met in Ibagué to create the Movimiento Nacional Ambiental[10] (El Espectador 2017). Two fundamental goals were articulated by the gathering: (1) to strengthen the defense of water, life, and territories and (2) to participate, promote, and oblige, in all areas, legitimate spaces for the construction of life projects (Heinrich-Böll-Stiftung 2019). The first objective increases the possibility of establishing new environmental identities, which are exemplified in the interest of maintaining relationships between human practices, communities, and nature, echoing Agyeman et al.'s (2016) call to include the nonhuman world in relational attachments and communities. The second purpose recognizes that there is not just one place on which to focus attention and effort but rather many ways to meet the overarching goal of confronting environmental crises. As mentioned by Rootes, Zito, and Barry (2012), practices to combat climate change must be articulated at local, national, and international levels. International human rights networks increasingly recognize and include organizations involved in the promotion of popular consultations against mining, as in the case of the Committee on Economic, Social, and Cultural Rights of the United Nations (CESCR). In September of 2017, twenty-five local social organizations[11] of Colombia presented to the CESCR the "Parallel Report on the mechanisms of citizen participation in Colombia (Popular Consultation and Prior Consultation, Free and Informed) and the human rights state" (Red Internacional de Derechos Humanos 2017), seeking support from the CESCR to insist that the national state of Colombia respect and promote popular consultations. All of these arenas for action highlight the plural nature of solutions, and indeed the need for just sustainabilities.

Furthermore, social movements extend beyond the extraction sites, supporting Rootes' (2013) argument that the increase of local power allows activists to fight for their claims to international organizations modeled by formal international government officials (UN, World Bank, etc.). Complaints are also generated in informal scenarios by nongovernmental organizations, struggling communities, entrepreneurs' summits, and so on. The "Colectivo Socio-Ambiental Juvenil de Cajamarca," Cosajuca (Socio-environmental Youth Collective of Cajamarca), leaders of the PC in Cajamarca, along with leaders from the Philippines (Kalikasan People's Network for the Environment), and Uganda (Buliisa in Albertine Graben), and several London organizations (London Mining Network, War on Want, and the Gaia Foundation) took their opposition straight to the Mines and Money Conference in December 2017, the global power center of mining and finances (Garavito, Ordóñez, & Rhoades 2017). In this meeting, social organizations described the threats and impacts of mining. The communities' and social organizations' goals were to oppose and protest commercial agreements for natural resources exploitation. This protest in the business sphere could constitute a framework different from the institutional sphere, facilitating a possible direct conciliation for the resolution of common problems.

We believe that the National Environmental Movement in Colombia, the Civil Society Panel at the Climate Change Summit in Paris in 2017, the initiative "Yes to Life, No to Mining," and the repeated protests against the Mines and Money Conference will continue to strengthen local battles against extractions and connect practitioners to similar efforts across the globe. This battle requires recognizing a fundamental tension—many developing countries depend on extractivism for supporting their budgets and development, as is the case in Colombia—and identifying alternatives to support livelihoods and economic security (one such example is the agro-ecological systems proposed by "Yes to Life, No to Mining").

Conclusion

The PCM in Colombia has arisen through more than sixty socio-environmental conflicts which incited the mechanism of environmental participation through popular consultations. This situation has (1) activated a new social transformation and empowerment through the environmental participation mechanisms with the intention of blocking large-scale projects and (2) led to conflict between the communities who vote on these referendums and the Government and development companies that seek to dispute their results.

Furthermore, the individual and collective petitions of the PCs are occurring within the multifaceted and complex context of a considerable environmental and social turning point: climate change's impact on the integrity of life's systems and humankind's potential response. PCs combat a root cause and impacts of climate change, joining with collective policies and practices around the world. The demands of social equity, economic security, and environmental protection, interacting together, make possible a fair and equitable sustainability.

On the other hand, the fight for these principles has been affected by elitism, intellectualization, and depoliticization. Policies against climate change often continue to be formulated without consulting communities. As noted earlier, civic movements based on specific localities, like the PCs in Colombia, show the power present in supposedly unterritorialized spaces from capitalism, the very same places where its impacts are felt most. It is necessary to sustain the power in the villages and cities that oppose and resist the globalized hegemony of extractive capitalism. Likewise, the PCs in Colombia revitalize traces of territory that surpass the borders. Through the PC, the Piedras community revitalized the horizontal relationship between society and nature, recognizing the existence of a socio-ecological system with human well-being as the result of healthy ecosystems (Berkes & Folke 1998). Plural and horizontal relationships among local fights against the extractive economy are bringing more pressure to the government to fulfill people's participation and conservation demands.

The PCs in Colombia demonstrate the practice of the principles of environmental justice stated by Agyeman & Evans (2003) in several ways: (1) The demand to the right to participate in the planning, implementation, and evaluation of public policies—PCs strategically use institutional participation mechanisms to influence decisions that affect the environment and human well-being, and generate alternative participation spaces as community assemblies; (2) the rejection of transnational corporations that destroy the environment, such as the municipality of Piedras expelling from their territory the Anglogold Ashanti company; and (3) the achievement of popular environmental education, based on dialogue among academics, social leaders, public officials, farmers, and participants from other towns and cities, who from their own experiences, needs, and concern, reached an agreement to implement actions such as popular consultations, demonstrations, and roadblock protests, among others.

Furthermore, the PCs represent the praxis of just sustainabilities in several ways: (1) to question the current model for economic development in order to defend a local sustainable production model for the well-being of the communities; (2) to defend nature as a heritage of humanity; (3) to demand the right to access to drinking water; (4) to promote the rights of nature; (5) to link traditional values (quality of life and human well-being) to other petitions (e.g., intergenerational justice, rights of nature); and (6) to diversify the resistance actions involving institutional activism and art (e.g., Carnival March) to increase popular awareness.

Within the national environmental movement in Colombia, challenges still remain: (1) to reach broader sectors of society, with the purpose of generating a collective environmental awareness; (2) to connect to other social movements that do not have the environment as their main objective but which also identify with principles of equality and environmental justice; and (3) to create a just sustainabilities by and for the populations that made the decision to disallow mining projects through popular consultations.

Further research is needed on life in these communities after the PCs, on multiple fronts: (1) to understand if PCs increased the active participation of people in other public affairs, (2) to better understand and articulate connections between

PCs and climate change, (3) to analyze possible mechanisms for greater outreach to communities, (4) to characterize the internal debates within the *Movimiento Nacional Ambiental*, (5) to continue to build connections between people and organizations at local and international levels with the PCM, and (6) to understand the experiences and resistance of social leaders and environmentalists who suffer violence because of their role (702 were leaders murdered in Colombia between January 2016 and May 2019). Finally, the future of just sustainabilities must be a matter of debate in the practice, a blend of research and activism to comprehend how injustices are created and challenged and how to build alternatives at multiple scales and in multiple spheres, to enact the broad visions of just sustainabilities for all Colombians.

Interviews

October–December, 2017.

Interviewees: Julián Viña (Piedras, Tolima), Jully Katherine Méndez Clavijo (Tauramena, Casanare), Luis Jaime Ortíz Vásquez (Arbeláez, Cundinamarca), and Mónica Florez and Jhon Jairo Villa Monsalve (Pijao, Quindío).

Notes

1   Name given by the national government to investments in mining-energy projects as the main objective in the National Development Plan aimed to strengthen Colombian economy.
2   National Environmental Movement.
3   See Agarwal (2010) ("Participation in decision making is a complex concept. (…) At its narrowest, participation in a group can be defined in terms of nominal membership and at its broadest in terms of a dynamic interactive process in which the disadvantaged have voice and influence in decision making").
4   Colombian Political Constitution 1991, article 40; act 136 of 1994; Statutory act 134 of 1994 y 1757 of 2015; Parques con la gente, 2001; Decree T-445, 2016, among others.
5   Environmental hearings, prior consultations, public hearings, and popular consultation.
6   Colombian law establishes a Prior Consultation among ethnic minorities. This mechanism is compulsory in projects that affect Indigenous communities.
7   Constitutional Court of Colombia: Judgment SU-039 of 1997, Judgment T-129 of 2011; Judgment T-135 of 2013; Judgment T-154 of 2013. "Páramo de Pisba, en Boyacá, el primero del país en ser declarado sujeto de derechos" (Pisba's Moorland, the first in the country declared subject of law) El Espectador, August 13, 2018.
8   In recent years the march has been replicated in other regions of Colombia and worldwide as well.
9   E.g., Asociación Curibano, Censat Agua Viva, Cinturón Occidental Ambiental, Colectivo Socio Ambiental Juvenil de Cajamarca, Comité Ambiental en Defensa de la Vida, Comité Ambiental en Defensa de la Vida de Anaime y Cajamarca, Comité

Ambiental en Defensa de la vida de Ibagué, Comité Ambiental en Defensa de la Vida de Saldaña, Comité Consulta Popular San Vicente de Chucuri Santander, Comité Ecológico de Pijao Quindío, Comité Estudiantil Unidos Contra el Fracking—CEUCF, Comisiones por la vida del agua del Sur de Caquetá, Corporación Defensora del Agua, Territorio y Ecosistemas—CORDATEC, Corporación SOS Ambiental, Escuela de Pensamiento Círculo de Fuego y Unidad, Mesa departamental para la defensa del agua y el territorio del Caquetá, Mesa municipal por la defensa del agua y la vida de Puerto Rico, Movimiento social por la vida y la defensa del territorio del oriente antioqueño. MOVETE, Organizacion Juvenil Semillas Nativas de la Amazonia (SENAM) de Curillo, Tierra Libre.

10 National Environmental Movement. https://twitter.com/mambientalcol?lang=es
11 1. Comité Pro Consulta Popular Cumaral, Meta—Colombia. Carolina Orduz Romero. 2. COSAJUCA (Colectivo Socioambiental Juvenil de Cajamarca), Tolima. Robinson Mejía Alonso. 3. Comité Ambiental y Campesino de Cajamarca y Anaime, Tolima. José Domingo Rodríguez. 4. Fundación Pijao Cittaslow. Mónica Liliana Flórez Arcila. 5. Comité ambiental del municipio de Arbeláez, Cundinamarca—Colombia. Diego rojas. 6. GUACANA Comité ambiental de Arbeláez—Cundinamarca. Javier Linares. 7. Comité de impulso a la Zona de Reserva Campesina del municipio de Cabrera, Cundinamarca—Colombia. Edisson Villalobos. 8. Comité Ambiental en Defensa de la Vida del Tolima—Colombia. Renzo García. 9. Mesa departamental por la defensa del agua y el territorio del departamento del Caquetá. Mercedes Mejía—Leudo. 10. Mesa municipal por la defensa del agua, el territorio y la vida del municipio del Paujil, Caquetá Colombia. Martín Trujillo. 11. Mesa municipal en defensa del territorio. Agua y de la vida del municipio de Puerto Rico, Caquetá—Colombia. Joselito Sánchez. 12. Veeduría ambiental del municipio de Piedras, Tolima. Julián Viña Vizcaíno. 13. Observatorio de Derechos Humanos, Facultad de Derecho Universidad la Gran Colombia. 14. Comité por la defensa del agua del municipio de Tauramena-Casanare. July Katherine Méndez. 15. Congreso de los pueblos Congreso de los Pueblos, movimiento político de masas social y popular del centro oriente de Colombia. Ricardo Apolinar. 16. Movimiento de Masas Político Social y Popular del Centro Oriente de Colombia. Tauramena—Casanare. 17. Asociación Nacional Campesina. José Antonio Galán Zorro-ASONALCA. Casanare. 18. Veeduría ambiental municipio de Piedras—Tolima, integrante Comité Ambiental en Defensa de la Vida Tolima. Julián Viña Vizcaíno. 19. Veeduría ecológica del municipio de Arbeláez—Cundinamarca. Cesar Danilo Umaña. 20. Asociación de Juntas de Acción Comunal-ASOJUNTAS-del municipio de Arbeláez—Cundinamarca. Luis Ortiz. 21. Fundación GUCHIPAZ. 22. Corporación PODION. 23. Proceso Tejido Territorial. 24. Corporación SOS Ambiental. Alejandro García Pedraza. 25. Red de Comités Ambientales del departamento del Tolima. Jaime Andrés Tocora Lozano.

References

Administrative Court of Tolima (2016), "RADICACION No. 73001-23-33-006-2016-00207-00." Available online: https://justiciaambientalcolombia.org/wp-content/uploads/2016/09/sentencia-consulta-popular-ibaguecc81.pdf (Accessed May 14, 2020).

Agarwal B. (2010), "Does women's proportional strength affect their participation? Governing local forests in South Asia," *World Development*, 38: 98–112.

Agyeman, J. (2008), "Toward a 'just' sustainability?" *Continuum: Journal of Media & Cultural Studies*, 22(6): 751–6.

Agyeman, J. (2013), *Introducing Just Sustainabilities: Policy, Planning and Practice*, London: Zed Books.

Agyeman, J. & T. Evans (2003), "Toward just sustainability in urban communities: Building equity rights with sustainable solutions," *The Annals of the American Academy of Political and Social Science*, 590: 35–53.

Agyeman, J., D. Schlosberg, L. Craven, & C. Matthews (2016), "Trends and directions in environmental justice: From inequity to everyday life, community, and just sustainabilities," *Annual Review of Environment & Resources*, 41: 321–40.

Anguelovski, I. & D. Roberts (2011), "Spatial justice and climate change : Multiscale impacts and local development in Durban, South Africa," in J. Carmin & J. Agyeman (eds), *Environmental Inequalities Beyond Borders. Local Perspectives on Global Injustices*, 19–44, Cambridge: MIT Press.

Berkes F. & C. Folke (1998), *Linking Social and Ecological Systems: Management Practices and Social Mechanisms for Building Resilience*, Cambridge: Cambridge University Press.

BM Colombia Solidarity Campaign (2013), *La Colosa: A Death Foretold*, London: Colombia Solidarity Campaing. https://www.colombiasolidarity.org.uk/2013/12/report-la-colosa-a-death-foretold

Bonilla, R.F.A. (2018), "En Quindío alcaldes realizarán consultas mineras simbólicas," *RCN Radio*, November 30. Available online: https://www.rcnradio.com/colombia/eje-cafetero/en-quindio-alcaldes-realizaran-consultas-mineras-simbolicas (Accessed May 20, 2020).

Bringel, B. (2014), "Ativismo transnacional, o estudo dos movimentos sociais e as novas geografias pós-coloniais," *Estudos de Sociologia, Rev. do Progr. de Pós-Graduação em Sociologia da UFPE*,16(2): 185–215.

Carmin, J. & J. Agyeman (eds) (2011), *Environmental Inequalities Beyond Borders. Local Perspectives on Global Injustices*, Cambridge: MIT Press.

Cash, D.W., W. Adger, F. Berkes, P. Garden, L. Lebel, P. Olsson, L. Pritchard, & O. Young (2006), "Scale and cross-scale dynamics: governance and information in a multilevel world," *Ecology and Society*, 11(2): 8.

CEPAL (2013). *Medio Ambiente y Desarrollo. Acceso a la Información, Participación y Justicia en Temas Ambientales en América Latina y el Caribe*, Santiago de Chile: Naciones Unidas.

Corte Constitucional de Colombia [Constitucional Court] Sentencia SU-039 de 1997.

Corte Constitucional de Colombia [Constitucional Court] Sentencia T-129 de 2011.

Corte Constitucional de Colombia [Constitucional Court] Sentencia T-135 de 2013.

Corte Constitucional de Colombia [Constitucional Court] Sentencia T-154 de 2013.

Decree T-445, 2016.

El Espectador (2018), "Páramo de Pisba, en Boyacá, el primero del país en ser declarado sujeto de derechos," *El Espectador*, August 13. Available online: https://www.elespectador.com/noticias/medio-ambiente/paramo-de-pisba-en-boyaca-el-primero-del-pais-en-ser-declarado-sujeto-de-derechos-articulo-805839 (Accessed May 14, 2020).

El Espectador (2017), "Organizaciones ambientales se dieron cita en Ibagué para defender a Santurbán," *El Espectador*, November 20. Available online: https://www.elespectador.com/noticias/medio-ambiente/organizaciones-ambientales-se-dieron-cita-en-ibague-para-defender-santurban-articulo-724145 (Accessed May 14, 2020).

El Tiempo (2017), "La Consulta Popular sería revivida en Ibagué para prohibir la minería," *El Tiempo*, December 5. Available online: http://www.eltiempo.com/colombia/otras-ciudades/consulta-popular-seria-revivida-en-ibague-para-prohibir-la-mineria-158920 (Accessed May 14, 2020).

Environmental Justice Atlas (2018), Available online: https://ejatlas.org/ (Accessed May 14, 2020).

Escobar, A. (2000), "El lugar de la naturaleza y la naturaleza del lugar: ¿Globalización o postdesarrollo?" in E. Lander (ed.), *La colonialidad del saber: Eurocentrismo y Ciencias Sociales. Perspectivas Latinoamericana*, 113–43, Buenos Aires: CLACSO.

Escobar, A. (2009), "Other worlds are (already) possible: Self-organization, complexity, and post-capitalist cultures," in J. Sen & P. Waterman (eds), *World Social Forum Challenging Empires*, 393–404, Montreal: Black Rose Books.

Eslava, L. (2016), *Local Space, Global Life: The Everyday Operation of International Law & Development*, Cambridge: Cambridge University Press.

Ezbawi, Y. (2011), "The role of the youth's new protest movements in the January 25th Revolution," *IDS Bulletin*, 43: 26.

Galtung, J. (1985), *Sobre la Paz*, Barcelona: Fontamara.

Garavito, T., S. Ordoñez, & H. Rhoades (2017), "Meet the frontline activists facing down the global mining industry," *Red Pepper*, December 11. Available online: https://www.redpepper.org.uk/meet-the-frontline-activists-facing-down-the-global-mining-industry/ (Accessed May 16, 2020).

Giarracca, N. (2017), "América Latina: nuevas ruralidades, viejas y nuevas acciones colectivas," in M. Teubal (ed.), *Estudios rurales y movimientos sociales: miradas desde el Sur*, 187–96, Buenos Aires: Clacso.

Gobernación Del Tolima (2015), *Estadísticas 2011–2014 Piedras*, Secretaría de Planeación y TIC.

Gómez, M. (2016), "Piedras dijo NO a la Minería," *A la Orilla del Río*, January 27. Available online: http://alaorilladelrio.com/2016/01/27/piedras-dijo-no-a-la-gran-mineria-experiencias-para-compartir-con-las-comunidades-del-caqueta/ (Accessed May 20, 2020).

Gómez, M.F., L.A. Moreno, G.I. Andrade, & C. Rueda (2016), *Biodiversidad 2015*, Bogotá, DC: Instituto Alexander von Humboldt.

Gosling, S.N. & N.W. Arnell (2016), "A global assessment of the impact of climate change on water scarcity," *Climate Change*, 134: 371–85.

Goodale, M. (2007), "Locating rights, envisioning law between the global and the local," in M. Goodale & S. Merry (eds), *The Practice of Human Rights. Tracking Law between the Global and the Local*, 1–35, Cambridge: Cambridge University Press.

Heinrich-Böll-Stiftung, (2019), *Movimiento Nacional Ambiental*. Available online: https://co.boell.org/es/2019/01/25/movimiento-nacional-ambiental (Accessed May 20, 2020).

Hernández, L. (2017), "David contra Goliat. Procesos socioculturales de resistencia extractiva en Piedras, Colombia," MA diss., Facultad Latinoamericana de Ciencias Sociales-Ecuador, Quito.

Hincapié, S. (2017), "Extractivismo, consultas populares y derechos políticos ¿El renacimiento de la democracia local en Colombia?" *Reflexión Política*, 19(37): 86–99.

IDEAM, PNUD, MADS, DNP, & CANCILLERÍA (2016), *¿Qué piensan los colombianos sobre el cambio climático?* Bogotá D.C.: Colombia.

IDEAM, PNUD, MADS, DNP, & CANCILLERÍA (2017), *Análisis de vulnerabilidad y riesgo por cambio climático en Colombia*, Bogotá D.C.: Colombia.

International Energy Agency (2010). Available online: https://www.iea.org/

La Voz de Yopal (2017), "Explotación de petróleo no ha traído desarrollo económico a la región: Promotor de consulta popular en Yopal," *La Voz de Yopal*, February 22. Available online: https://www.lavozdeyopal.co/explotacion-petroleo-no-ha-traido-desarrollo-economico-la-region-promotor-consulta-popular-yopal/ (Accessed May 20, 2020).

Leff, E. (1998), *Saber Ambiental, Sustentabilidad, Racionalidad, Complejidad, Poder*, Mexico: Siglo Veintiuno Editores.

Madumere, N. (2017), "Public enlightenment and participation—A major contribution in mitigating climate change," *International Journal of Sustainable Built Environment*, 6: 9–15.

Martínez Alier, J. (2009), "El ecologismo de los pobres, veinte años después: India, México y Perú," *Nomadas*. Available online: https://nomadas.ourproject.org/el-ecologismo-de-los-pobres-india-mexico-y-peru/ (Accessed May 20, 2020).

Méndez, M. (2005), "Contradicción, complementariedad e hibridación en las relaciones entre lo rural y lo urbano," in H. Ávila (ed.), *Lo Urbano-Rural, ¿Nuevas Expresiones Territoriales?* 87–122, México: Clacso.

Merry, S. (2006), *Human Rights & Gender Violence, Translating International Law into Local Justice*, Chicago: University of Chicago Press.

Ostrom, E. (1990), *Governing the Commons: The Evolution of Institutions for Collective Action*, Cambridge: Cambridge University Press.

Pardo Martinez, C.I. & W.H. Alfonso P WH (2018), "Climate change in Colombia: A study to evaluate trends and perspectives for achieving sustainable development from society," *International Journal of Climate Change Strategies & Management*, 10(4): 632–52.

Pardo, T. (2016), "El tortuoso camino de la consulta popular minera en Ibagué," *El Espectador*, December 16. Available online: https://www.elespectador.com/noticias/medio-ambiente/el-tortuoso-camino-de-consulta-popular-minera-ibague-articulo-670729 (Accessed May 20, 2020).

Pérez, M. (2016), "Las territorialidades urbano rurales contemporáneas: Un debate epistémico y metodológico para su abordaje," *Bitácora Urbano Territorial*, 26(2): 103–12.

Phillips, J. (2016), "Climate change and surface mining: A review of environment-human interactions & their spatial dynamics," *Applied Geography*, 74: 95–108.

Piedras Development Plan, 2011-2013.

"Piedras en el Zapato" (2013). Available online: https://www.youtube.com/watch?v=V1rGv3y8YUg (Accessed May 20, 2020).

PNACC (Plan Nacional de Adaptación al Cambio Climático) (2017), Departamento Nacional de Planeación.

PNCC (Política Nacional de Cambio Climático) (2017), *Documento Para Tomadores de Decisiones*, Ministerio de Ambiente y Desarrollo Sostenible, Colombia: Bogotá, D.C. Colombia.

PND (Plan Nacional de Desarrollo) (2002–6), *Hacia un estado comunitario*, Departamento Nacional de Planeación.

PND (Plan Nacional de Desarrollo) (2002–6), *Todos por un nuevo país*, Departamento Nacional de Planeación.

PND (Plan Nacional de Desarrollo) (2006–10), *Hacia un estado comunitario: desarrollo para todos*, Departamento Nacional de Planeación.

PND (Plan Nacional de Desarrollo) (2010–14), *Prosperidad para todos*, Departamento Nacional de Planeación.

Ramírez, B. (2005), "Miradas y posturas frente a la ciudad y el campo," in H. Ávila (ed.), *Lo Urbano-Rural, ¿Nuevas Expresiones Territoriales?* 61–86, México: Clacso.

Red Internacional de Derechos Humanos (2017), Informe paralelo sobre los mecanismos de participación ciudadana en Colombia (Consultas Populares y Consulta Previa, Libre e Informada) y la situación de derechos humanos para el Comité de Derechos Económicos, Sociales y Culturales.

Registraduría Nacional del Estado Civil (2019a), "Histórico Consultas Populares," Available online: https://www.registraduria.gov.co/-Historico-Consultas-populares-.html (Accessed May 20, 2020).

Registraduría Nacional del Estado Civil (2019b), Censo Electoral de Colombia, Available online: https://www.registraduria.gov.co/-Censo-Electoral,3661-.html (Accessed May 20, 2020).

Rinaudo, M. (2017), "Biodiversidad: innovación frente al cambio climático," in L. Moreno, G. Andrade & L. Ruíz Contreras (eds), *Biodiversidad 2016*, 28, Bogotá D.C.: Instituto Alexander von Humboldt.

Rincón-Pérez, M. (2016), *Caracterizando las injusticias ambientales en Colombia. Estudio para 115 casos de conflictos socio-ambientales*, Cali: Editorial Universidad del Valle.

Roa, C. (2016), "Agua, democratización ambiental y fronteras extractivas en Colombia" *GIGA Working Paper*, 291.

Rootes, C. (2013), "From local conflict to national issue: When and how environmental campaigns succeed in transcending the local," *Environmental Politics*, 22(1): 95–114.

Rootes, C., A. Zito & J. Barry (2012), "Climate change, national politics and grassroots action: An introduction," *Environmental Politics*, 21(5): 677–90.

Santos, B.S. & C. Rodriguez Garavito (2007), "El derecho, la política y lo subalterno en la globalización contrahegemónica," in B.S. Santos & C. Rodriguez Garavito (eds), *El Derecho y la Globalización desde Abajo*, 7–28, Mexico: Antrophos.

Segura, J. (2017), "La organización comunal y la justicia ambiental: defensa de la autonomía territorial ante el modelo extractivo nacional. El caso del municipio de Piedras, Tolima," MA diss. Universidad Nacional de Colombia, Bogotá.

9

RESCALING ENERGY GOVERNANCE AND THE DEMOCRATIZING POTENTIAL OF "COMMUNITY CHOICE"

Sean Kennedy

Introduction: Community Choice, Energy Democracy, and "Just Sustainabilities"

The transition from fossil fuels to renewable energy sources such as wind and solar has long served as the cornerstone of state, national, and global efforts to limit future impacts of climate change. In the United States, the state of California has been a leader in this transition. Since 2001, the number of large-scale solar facilities in the state has grown from one to over 700, generating enough electricity to power over 400,000 homes (CEC 2018a). In 2018, renewable energy sources—excluding nuclear and large hydro—accounted for over 30 percent of all electricity generation consumed within the state (CEC 2018b).

In addition to sustained political support for climate action at the state level, the rapid expansion of renewable energy generation and consumption in California owes much of its success to the state's regulated electricity sector. Since the state's energy crisis in the early 2000s, investor-owned electric and natural gas utilities operating in California have been regulated by the state in terms of consumer rates, infrastructure development, and energy procurement (CPUC 2020). Through the Renewable Portfolio Standard (RPS),[1] the state has leveraged its authority to require utilities to purchase an increasing share of electricity generated from renewable energy sources, including specific requirements for a share of electricity generated within the state (CEC 2019). By combining requirements regarding the type and location of generation sources, the RPS has proven successful in increasing renewable energy consumption, while also promoting the development of renewable energy resources, such as solar and wind, across the state (CARB 2019).

While California has relied heavily on its regulated utilities to implement the state's ambitious renewable energy targets, a growing coalition of climate advocacy groups and local governments view these utilities—particularly those that are privately owned—as barriers to an even more ambitious and more democratic energy transition (Hess 2019). In recent years, local governments dissatisfied with the utility model have sought to rescale state-electricity governance through the establishment of community choice aggregation, or CCA (CPUC 2017). CCA is a model of energy supply whereby local governments combine the energy loads of their constituents to purchase energy directly from electricity generators instead of from a utility. Control over energy procurement allows CCAs to pursue their own renewable energy targets, and to administer programs focused on energy efficiency, electric vehicle infrastructure, and incentives to encourage household and community-scale energy generation (Welton 2017). By emphasizing democratic governance and community participation as key elements of program design, the CCA movement seeks to give voice to those diverse community interests that have long been ignored in the context of the shareholder-oriented utility model (CalCCA 2018). As of September 2018, there are seventeen CCAs operating in California, with at least nine more anticipated to launch by 2020 (Figure 9.1). With CCAs projected to account for 60 percent of Californian customers currently served by independently owned utilities by 2020 (CCP 2016), the CCA movement

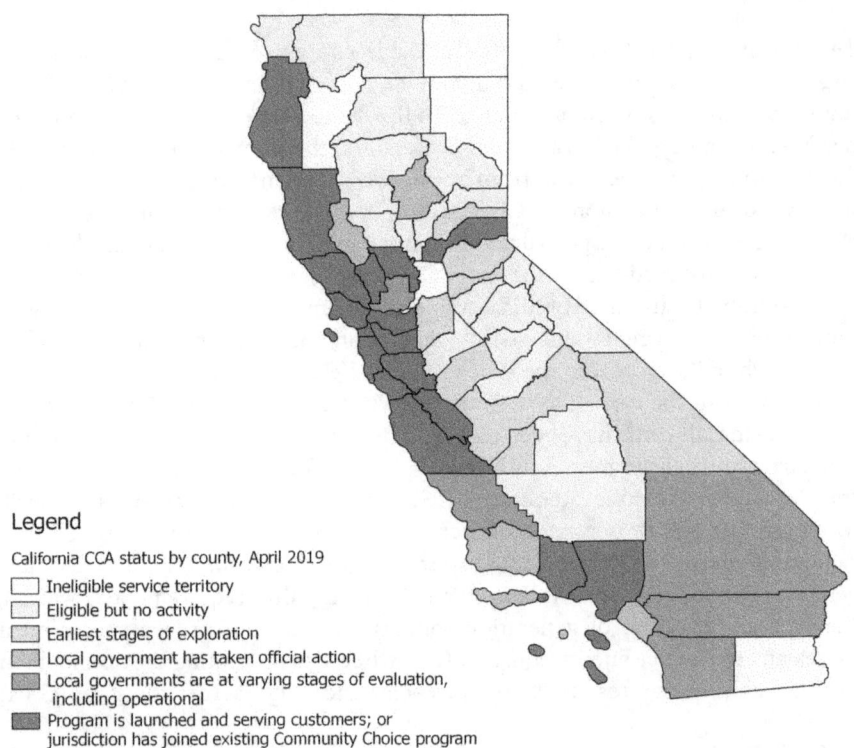

Figure 9.1 California CCAs.
Source: Kennedy & Rosen 2020.

poses significant disruption to the utility-based model of electricity governance that has dominated for over a century (Boyd & Carlson 2016).

Since its inception in the early 2000s, the CCA movement in California has been closely aligned with the concept of energy democracy (Hess 2019). Energy democracy discourse is grounded in a distributed energy politics that posits that distributed energy sources and technologies enable and organize distributed political power and vice versa (Burke & Stephens 2018). The term "distributed" in this sense refers not only to the scale and location of energy generation facilities but also to their ownership, the related decision-making, and the responsibility for their use (Moroni, Antoniucci, & Biselleo 2016). Echoing the notion of "just sustainabilities" (Agyeman 2002, 2013), energy democracy infuses ideas of equity and justice into concerns around environmental sustainability, while representing an intersectional environmental politics attuned to the ways that the production, distribution, and consumption of energy shapes and is shaped by individual and community experiences of class, race, and gender (McCauley & Heffron 2018; van Veelen & van der Horst 2018; Allen, Lyons, & Stephens 2019). Viewing decentralized energy-related decision-making and distributed renewable energy generation such as rooftop and community solar as key steps in facilitating a more democratic model of energy governance (Farrell 2016; Becker & Naumann 2017; Szulecki 2018), energy democracy entails not just a shift to alternative energy sources but a shift to an alternative energy system predicated on notions of community ownership and control, participatory governance, and decentralized distributed renewable energy resources (Farrell 2014; Burke & Stephens 2017).

While the CCA movement first emerged in California's central valley—an area that consistently ranks among the lowest in per capita income, median household income, and median family income in California—the state's first operational CCA was launched in Marin County, an affluent and predominantly white community located in the San Francisco Bay Area with a long history of progressive environmentalism (CalCCA 2018; Dillon 2018). Since the launch of Marin Clean Energy in 2010, support for CCAs has expanded to include climate justice advocates, trade unions, academics, local governments, and nonprofits focused on environmental and social justice (Hess 2019). This diverse support base has had a direct influence on CCA objectives, many of which now go beyond providing affordable renewable energy to include workforce development in the areas of solar installation and energy efficiency, and efforts to address existing forms of environmental injustice, such as facilitating access to renewable energy resources in communities that have borne a disproportionate share of the pollution burden associated with fossil fuel-based electricity generation (CalCCA 2018).

While reflecting a seemingly disparate range of viewpoints and political agendas, these groups are united in the assumption that "local control" over the energy system will deliver a more democratic alternative to the prevailing utility-based model of electricity governance. The assumed relationship between localization with more just and sustainable outcomes reflects a more pervasive phenomenon among planners and community activists, known as the "local trap" (Born & Purcell 2006). The local trap thesis builds on a long history of theoretical work in political and economic geography arguing that scales (e.g., national, regional, and local) are not independent entities with inherent qualities but, rather, strategies pursued by social actors with a particular agenda (Born & Purcell 2006). In the context of the local food movement, for example, overemphasizing the "local" confuses ends (e.g., a more ecologically sustainable food system) with means (locally grown food), while obscuring other scalar options that might be more effective in achieving a desired outcome (Born & Purcell 2006). Given that energy systems also embody multiple socially constructed scalar dimensions (Bridge et al. 2013; Calvert 2016), the uncritical acceptance that localized energy systems are inherently more democratic and just than the prevailing centralized model holds the potential to produce seemingly paradoxical outcomes.

While the just sustainabilities narrative has increasingly been incorporated into critical energy scholarship in recent years, particularly through work on energy justice and "just transitions" (McCauley et al. 2019), to date the notion of "local control" as it pertains to energy governance and the potential paradoxes such framing might produce has received limited critical attention. This chapter addresses this gap through a critical analysis of CCA energy procurement strategies and their intersection with the technical and financial dimensions of the prevailing energy system. Despite gaining a degree of autonomy from their incumbent utilities in terms of their ability to exercise control over energy procurement, I argue that the apparent success of the CCA movement in promoting just sustainabilities has more to do with the way in which the discourse around "local control" has been leveraged to serve a particular political agenda than it has to do with the physical rescaling of the technical and financial dimensions of the energy system. This apparent paradox simultaneously highlights specific limitations of the CCA movement in achieving a more just and sustainable energy system, while pointing to opportunities to refine specific CCA strategies that may better align with the movement's overarching goals.

The Promise of Community Choice

For over a century, decisions regarding the source, location, and price of electricity procurement in the United States have rested in the hands of monopoly utilities (Boyd & Carlson 2016). Electric utilities are granted a specific service territory by the state government in which they are the exclusive provider or distributor of electricity service. While utilities in most states are subject to regulation by state public utilities commissions—independent commissions tasked with ensuring rates are just, reasonable, and nondiscriminatory (Boyd & Carlson 2016)—the regulated monopoly structure provides no option for the majority of electricity customers to procure electricity from alternative sources. As a result, monopoly utilities have long faced limited market-based pressure to meet customer demands in terms of electricity rates and energy sources. In addition, California's investor-owned utilities have long been subject to public criticism for placing shareholder interests before broader social and environmental concerns. Fierce critique of Pacific Gas & Electric's role in the 2000–2001 California energy crisis (Holson 2001), the 2015 Camp Fire in northern California (Penn, Eavis, & Glanz 2019), and the highly uneven socioeconomic impacts resulting from intentional rolling blackouts in October 2019 (Karlis 2019) are just three examples.

CCA currently exists by law in eight states—Illinois, Massachusetts, New York, New Jersey, Ohio, Rhode Island, Virginia, and California—and is under consideration in several others. CCAs are established either by a single municipality or through a joint commitment between multiple jurisdictions. CCAs are governed by a board or council of local elected officials who oversee power purchasing, programs, and rate setting, and are directly accountable to the people who elected them (O'Shaughnessy et al. 2019). Many CCAs also have a community advisory committee, which often comprises volunteers who represent the participating agencies and labor and commercial, agricultural, industrial, or other stakeholders (CalCCA 2018). In most states electricity customers within a municipality are automatically enrolled in a CCA following its formation, with the option to opt out if they wish to do so (O'Shaughnessy et al. 2019). While CCA in most states exists alongside other measures allowing retail choice in the electricity sector, California is the only state in which CCAs operate in direct competition for customers with existing utilities (Hess 2019).

While subject to many of the renewable energy-purchasing and reporting requirements that apply to electricity retailers across California (O'Shaughnessy et al. 2019), CCAs differ from investor- and publicly owned utilities in several ways with implications for the pursuit of just sustainabilities. Unlike utilities, for which maximizing returns to shareholders is a primary concern, CCAs are not-for-profit public agencies that operate under a much wider range of objectives. While ownership of energy infrastructure under the CCA model is restricted to energy generation and storage, under the current Californian regulatory framework, CCAs have considerable freedom to pursue a range of policies and programs that may work to facilitate public and cooperative ownership of energy infrastructures. These include community-based energy initiatives such as household-level energy generation, energy cooperatives, virtual net metering, and microgrids (Weinrub 2017). Virtual net metering is a payment system that allows renters and those lacking access to a suitable generating site to share the output from a single renewable energy facility (Burke & Stephens 2017). In contrast to most grid infrastructure that balances energy generation and consumption across multiple states, microgrids improve access to locally generated renewable energy by distributing electricity at the community scale (Burke & Stephens 2018); microgrids can also operate as closed circuits during periods in which the larger grid is not operating (Chen et al. 2016), such as the recent California blackouts (Fuller 2019).

Community-based organizations focused on clean energy, such as the Bay Area's Local Clean Energy Alliance, view CCAs as an important vehicle through which to pursue energy democracy objectives, such as increased energy access and affordability, community control over purchasing of electricity, and increasing democratic oversight and involvement in the energy planning process (Weinrub 2017). By absolving investor requirements for stable returns on investment, which are often reflected in utility preferences for procuring electricity from large-scale generation facilities, CCAs are free to procure electricity in a way that allows for a much broader variety and distribution of socioeconomic and ecological benefits, particularly at the municipal scale (Burke & Stephens 2017; Weinrub 2017).

Finally, there exists considerable variation in the extent to which utilities and CCAs have made stated commitments to social equity and environmental justice—two core pillars of just sustainabilities. Of the three Californian investor-owned utilities, none have made explicit commitments to social equity or environmental justice. In terms of publicly owned utilities, in 2016 LADWP established the Equity Metrics Data Initiative (EMDI) to understand how its programs are provided to all residents of Los Angeles, while SMUD's Building Sustainable Communities Program aims to bring environmental equity and economic vitality to all communities within its service area, with special attention given to historically underserved neighborhoods.

In contrast, issues of social justice and environmental justice serve as core elements of the broader CCA discourse. In a report prepared for the California Public Utilities Commission, for example, the official CCA trade association in California states that "CCAs share a commitment to inclusion and representation of our diverse communities through democratic governance and intensive community engagement" (CalCCA 2018: 2). The report details CCA efforts to promote diversity and inclusion through a combination of workforce development in low-income communities, rate structures designed to benefit low-income households, and agreements with private sector partners to provide community benefits in the form of financial contributions, volunteer hours, and in-kind contributions (CalCCA 2018). While the report is not a comprehensive analysis, since many CCAs are relatively new and not all CCAs participated in the data collection process, it nevertheless provides evidence of greater attention to issues of justice and inequity than has historically been demonstrated by IOUs, at least when viewed in the aggregate. Appendix A provides an overview of the types of programs and initiatives adopted by each CCA, including a list of those CCAs who did not participate in the report.

In sum, the CCA model presents an alternative to the prevailing utility-based model and positions local control as an essential element of a more just and democratic energy system. As other localization experiments have demonstrated, whether "local control" is viewed as a strategy or as an end in itself holds great potential to shape the potential for achieving just and sustainable change (Brown & Purcell 2005; Purcell 2006; Sonnino 2010). The following analysis interrogates the assumed relationship between local control, energy democracy, and just sustainabilities through an examination of the energy procurement practices of California's three longest-established CCAs: MCE Clean Energy (MCE), Sonoma Clean Power (SCP), and Lancaster Clean Energy (LCE) (Figure 9.2).

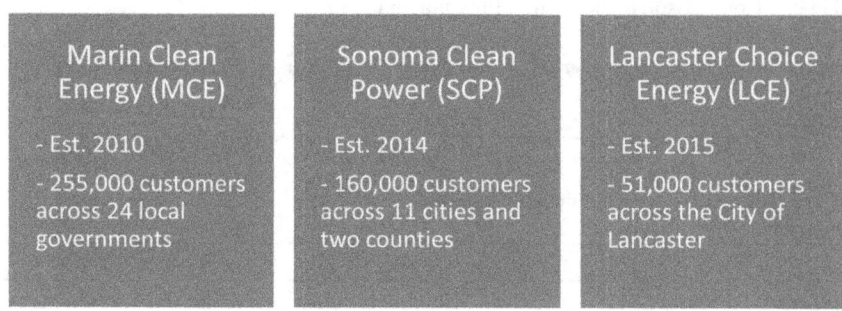

Figure 9.2 CCA case studies.

Delivering Energy Democracy

CCAs can offer a wide range of energy-related products and services to their customers, including energy efficiency (MCE Clean Energy 2015) and electric vehicle incentive programs (SCP 2018). It is through energy procurement, however, that CCAs can meet broader objectives such as providing a greater share of renewable energy, decreasing greenhouse gas emissions, lowering energy costs, and promoting local economic development. Energy procurement—particularly the ability of a CCA to procure electricity from local distributed renewable energy resources—thus serves as an integral means through which CCAs may fulfill their democratizing potential.

CCA procurement strategies are influenced by a range of factors, many of which closely relate to the broader objectives a CCA is intended to pursue. CCAs are operated by locally elected officials, and thus, the decisions these officials make are often—at least in theory—reflective of the political will of the community they have been elected to represent. CCAs established in more affluent areas may prioritize local renewable energy and electric vehicle charging stations, whereas CCAs established in traditionally disadvantaged communities may prioritize energy access and affordability (see Appendix A). While CCA advocacy groups such as CalCCA promote CCAs on the grounds that they can deliver affordable, local, and renewable energy (CalCCA 2019), these objectives—while not mutually exclusive—do present trade-offs for local governments that manifest as particular approaches to energy procurement, and the democratic outcomes such procurement may produce.

An analysis of CCA procurement strategies, based on data obtained from the California power content disclosure program,[2] reveals stark differences and similarities when compared to their incumbent utilities. MCE, SCP, and LCE each offer their consumers at least two energy portfolio options: a default option that offers a higher renewable energy mix at a rate competitive with that of the utility, and one with significantly higher renewable energy content mix (anywhere from 50 percent to 100 percent) at a slightly more expensive rate than the default option.

Table 9.1 Comparison of CCA and utility portfolio mixes CEC 2017.

Community choice aggregators	Marin clean energy		Sonoma clean power		Lancaster choice energy	
Retail package	Light green	Deep green	Clean start	Ever-green	Clear choice	Smart choice
RPS eligible renewable	52%	100%	37%	100%	35%	100%
Utilities & California average	LADWP		SCE	PG&E	SDG&E	CA
Retail package	Default	Green power	Default	Default	Default	State-wide power mix
RPS eligible renewable	21%	100%	25%	30%	35%	22%

As shown in Table 9.1, each of the three CCAs outperform their incumbent utilities in the share of the overall energy mix procured from renewable resources eligible under California's renewable portfolio standard.

Assessing procurement in this way, however, fails to account for the specific location, age, and size of the generating facilities or the nature of the agreements between energy providers and generators, which may have direct implications for meeting energy democracy objectives. Analysis of these attributes, also from the power source disclosure data, provides additional insight. Since its launch in 2010, MCE has exceeded the share of renewable electricity offered to its customers relative to the incumbent utility PG&E. In its early years of operation, however, MCE relied heavily on the purchase of out-of-state renewable energy certificates (RECs) to support these claims. As depicted in Figure 9.3, RECs can be either "bundled" with the electrical power produced by a generation facility or "unbundled" and sold separately from the power that is produced (Holt, Sumner, & Bird 2011). While permitted under the California RPS,[3] the use of unbundled RECs alleviates the need for the development of new renewable energy resources and may thus result in lower costs for carbon-free electricity. However, as many benefits associated with CCA such as local economic development are largely contingent upon the construction of local energy resources (Mormann 2015), a reliance on RECs in favor of local generation will have direct implications for energy democracy outcomes.

In 2013, RECs accounted for more than half of MCE's renewable energy procurement, the majority of which were derived from small hydro and wind projects in Oregon, Washington, Wyoming, and Idaho. Procurement from within California was limited to small hydro (2.4 percent), biomass and biowaste (4.2 percent), and large hydro (7.1 percent), the latter of which is ineligible under the California RPS. Thirty-nine percent of MCE's total retail sales—derived from an unspecified mix of renewable and nonrenewable energy sources—were provided

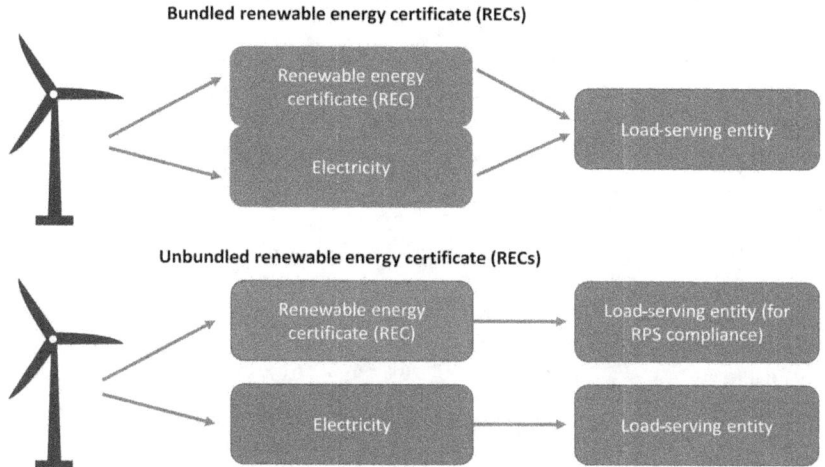

Figure 9.3 Bundled versus unbundled renewable energy certificates (RECs).

by Shell Energy North America, a third-party energy provider and subsidiary of Shell Oil Company.

CCAs are typically established in a way that creates a degree of separation between the future liabilities of the CCA and the assets of its member cities and towns (O'Shaughnessy et al. 2019). While this governance structure protects municipal finances in the wake of potential CCA bankruptcy, it means CCAs typically commence operations with limited resources and no credit rating, which can serve as a barrier to meeting energy procurement objectives (Gattaciecca, DeShazo, & Trumbull 2017; Kennedy 2017). In the case of MCE, a lack of credit rating initially prevented it from entering long-term contracts with energy generators, while also limiting its ability to access funds to pursue energy generation projects of their own. Absent access to credit, MCE was reliant on the services of a third-party power provider who could use their own credit to enter power purchase agreements directly and then pass this electricity on to the CCA (Kennedy 2017).

While presenting significant barriers to procurement of local energy resources in the early years of operations, over time, growing acceptance of the viability of the CCA model among lenders and developers has allowed CCAs to increase the number of longer-term local generation contracts in their procurement portfolio while reducing their reliance on unbundled RECs (Table 9.2). MCE's 2017 Integrated Resource Plan points to a continuing shift away from the use of third-party providers and unbundled RECs toward a greater share of local generation. As of February 2017, MCE had entered twenty-six medium-to-long-term contracts with developers of new and existing RPS eligible renewable energy projects in California (MCE 2017a).

Table 9.2 Location of renewable energy generation facilities delivering to IOUs & CCAs (2018).

	PG&E	MCE	SCP	SCE	LCE
Renewable	36%	62%	49%	34%	37%
Biomass & biowaste (CA)	4.0%	4.2%	0.6%	0.9%	1.7%
Out of state	0.0%	0.0%	0.0%	0.0%	9.4%
Geothermal (CA)	3.5%	2.9%	18.2%	7.7%	0.0%
Out of state	0.0%	0.0%	0.0%	0.0%	0.0%
Eligible hydroelectric (CA)	2.5%	2.4%	0.0%	0.6%	0.8%
Out of state	0.0%	0.0%	0.0%	0.0%	1.9%
Solar (CA)	13.9%	11.3%	7.6%	12.2%	11.2%
Out of state	3.1%	1.6%	0.0%	0.0%	2.4%
Wind (CA)	5.0%	15.4%	22.6%	6.7%	4.7%
Out of state	4.3%	24.3%	0.0%	5.9%	5.0%
Coal	0.0%	0.0%	0.0%	0.0%	0.0%
Large hydroelectric (CA)	13.2%	7.1%	0.0%	4.0%	0.0%
Out of state	13.2%	12.7%	41.7%	4.2%	12.9%
Natural gas (CA)	26.6%	0.0%	0.0%	17.5%	0.0%
Nuclear (CA)	34.9%	0.0%	0.0%	0.0%	0.0%
Out of state	0.0%	0.0%	0.0%	6.3%	0.0%
Unspecific power	0.0%	25.2%	9.4%	38.1%	50.0%
Net GWh procured	52,293	4,437	2,410	77,918	580

Source: Data from California Energy Commission Power Source Disclosure Program, 2018.

In addition to the default "Light Green" option of 50 percent renewables and "Deep Green" 100 percent California-based renewable plan, MCE now offers a "Local Sol" option consisting of electricity derived entirely from solar projects within MCE's service territory. MCE also offers a feed-in tariff for up to fifteen megawatt of small-scale renewables, and now has 9,600 net metering patrons—about 4 percent of its customers—who collectively own seventy-seven megawatt of solar capacity and get paid full retail rate plus 1¢/kWh for surplus energy.

MCE's emphasis on local distributed generation demonstrates significant overlap between CCA operations and energy democracy objectives, yet is by no means shared by all CCAs. Like MCE and SCP, LCE offers a default product comprised of 37 percent RPS eligible renewable sources, as well as a 100 percent renewable option. Despite providing a similar share of renewable sources, however, LCE's energy mix is by far the least diverse of the three CCAs examined in this analysis. While attributable in part to LCE's relative infancy, the lack of diversity and reliance on out-of-state RECs reflects the primary motivations behind the establishment of LCE, which themselves reflect the demographic and socioeconomic composition of the community. In 2016, the City of Lancaster had a median household income of $47,684, compared to $66,833 in Sonoma County and $100,310 in Marin County (U.S. Census Bureau 2016). As such, LCE has emphasized low-cost energy over issues such as GHG reductions or promotion of local generation that have served as core elements of both MCE and SCP.

Over time, the ability of CCAs to access capital appears to improve. In 2017, MCE's board of directors approved a USD 25-million line of credit with River City Bank (MCE 2017b), a commercial bank for successful mid-sized businesses and affluent individuals in California (RCB 2018), to be used as credit support for MCE's forward purchases of energy. As CCAs mature, however, the nature of procurement appears to more closely resemble that of financialized investor-owned utilities than the energy democracy ideals of local ownership and control of decentralized renewable energy generation. In 2016, MCE began construction on a ten- megawatt solar project on a sixty-acre brownfield site owned by the Chevron oil refinery in Richmond, CA—the largest such project in the Bay Area. While pre-development costs were covered in part by customers participating in MCE's Deep Green 100 percent renewable energy service, in May 2017 the project was sold to Utah-based developer sPower (MCE Clean Energy 2017), the largest private owner of operating solar assets in the United States (PR Newswire 2017).

Lancaster and the surrounding Antelope Valley is now home to over 800 megawatt of utility-scale either operational or approved and in various stages of construction, yet to date, LCE has only signed one 10 megawatt power purchase agreement with a local developer. MCE, however, sources a significant share of solar supply from the Antelope Valley, with the largest contract in excess of 100 megawatt (sPower 2019). Again, credit ratings play a key role, enabling MCE—the only CCA as of 2018 to obtain an investment-grade credit rating—to enter longer-term contracts for new renewable energy generation. LCE, without a credit rating, remains largely reliant on third-party providers and out-of-state RECs.

The Paradox of "Local Control" and Implications for Just Sustainabilities

Although still in the initial stages of development, the three CCAs discussed in this analysis raise significant questions over whether the emphasis on decentralization and "local control" in the CCA model can deliver on the socially and environmentally just distributed renewable energy system envisaged by energy democracy advocates.

Decentralization is often viewed by energy democracy advocates as lower cost, more efficient, more resilient, and more climate-friendly alternatives to the centralized systems that have dominated the US energy landscape for almost a century (Farrell 2014; Burke & Stephens 2018). What is often overlooked, however, is the extent to which such benefits depend on the specific context in which decentralization is deployed (Bauknecht, Funcke, & Vogel 2020). For example, while decentralization may reduce transmission infrastructure requirements and overall energy costs by allowing for generation facilities to be sited in close proximity to sites of consumption, this only holds in locations that are suitable for renewable energy development. Generation facilities installed in areas with lower resource potential will have lower capacity factors, meaning larger installations will be required to generate the same volume of electricity as in more resource-rich locations (Bauknecht, Funcke, & Vogel 2020). Pursuing local generation in sites with limited resource potential may meet local control objectives but do so at the cost of increased energy costs and a reduction in energy access (Bauknecht, Funcke, & Vogel 2020).

While decentralization, public and cooperative ownership, and participatory governance are widely accepted as core aspects of the community choice movement (Hess 2019; O'Shaughnessy et al. 2019), and thus link closely to notions of energy democracy (Burke & Stephens 2017), the three CCAs exhibit considerable variation in the extent to which they translated the energy democracy's goals into procurement strategies and specific policy instruments. While all CCAs have demonstrated the exercise of control over their energy procurement, much of their energy needs continue to be sourced from distant locations. MCE's initial reliance on RECs, while allowing MCE to provide low-carbon electricity to its customers at lowest possible cost, negates the need for the development of local distributed energy resources and thus does little to promote local employment opportunities and decentralized ownership of energy infrastructure, both of which are commonly associated with energy democracy (Burke & Stephens 2017). While the increase in the procurement of California solar photovoltaic as a share of total MCE from around 0.16 percent in 2013 to 11.3 percent in 2018 suggests CCAs may shift from unbundled RECs to local generation sources as they mature, the increase in out-of-state wind procurement also suggests CCAs may substitute RECs for other forms of low-cost energy that do little to promote the development of additional renewable energy resources.

While proving successful in procuring energy from a range of renewable energy resources, the mix of renewable resources provided by CCAs—consisting of out-of-state wind and small hydro renewable energy certificates—remains considerably less diverse than that of the IOUs. While this discrepancy may reflect minimum volume requirements for competitively priced power purchase agreements that CCAs struggle to meet, this analysis suggests IOUs, which procure between 14 percent and 19 percent of their electricity from relatively recently constructed California solar and wind projects, are making a much greater contribution to the development of in-state—and thus more localized—renewable energy resources than CCAs, despite having a lower overall share of renewables.

MCE's geographic expansion points to another potential failure from the perspective of energy democracy and just sustainabilities. Since its inception, MCE has now expanded its coverage from six cities within a single country, Marin, to include eight additional cities in neighboring Napa and Contra Costa counties (MCE 2019). The cities and counties that now comprise MCE's service area vary considerably in their levels of wealth, demographic composition, and exposure to environmental injustices (OEHHA 2018). The city of San Rafael, for example, a predominantly white community in Marin County, ranks as one of the lowest in the state in terms of impacts and vulnerability to pollution. The city of Richmond in Contra Costa County, a community on the opposite side of the San Francisco Bay in which Latinx and African Americans comprise 42 percent and 20.2 percent of the population, respectively, ranks as one of highest in terms of impacts and vulnerability to pollution. At $816,000, the median property value in San Rafael is almost triple that of Richmond (DataUSA 2018).

From a conventional business perspective, MCE's expansion can be viewed as a success, reflecting a growing customer base and an overall increase in revenues. On the other hand, this expansion serves to complicate the very notion of "local" on which MCE and the CCA movement in general is based. While the Local Sol program defines local as "within MCE's service territory," this definition fails to account for the racial and socioeconomic diversity that exists within that expanding territory, and the implications of that diversity in terms of the types and locations of infrastructure projects deployed. Whereas San Rafael, with its relatively higher property values, has seen the development of electric vehicle charging infrastructure and solar development on existing structures, MCE's activity in Richmond has been dominated by the sixty-acre MCE Solar One project. Paradoxically, improved access to capital as CCAs mature may also result in a reversion to the centralized, corporate-based model of energy procurement that energy democracy advocates have long resisted, and at worst, may reinscribe existing patterns of industrial development in which energy is generated in lower-socioeconomic Richmond for the benefit of the more affluent communities across the Bay.

On the surface, the procurement practices of each of the three CCAs discussed in the previous section could be viewed as a failure to deliver on the promises of energy democracy, and by extension, a failure to promote just sustainabilities. Somewhat paradoxically, the three CCAs demonstrate that the pursuit of just sustainabilities is not contingent upon the full and complete exercise of local control over the political, technical, and financial aspects of an energy system. What has proven successful in the case of CCAs is the way in which the discourse around "local control" has been leveraged to reshape the conditions of possibility for a more equitable and just system. The use of RECs and third-party providers limits the potential for community control and ownership over specific renewable energy resources, yet this approach has allowed CCAs to meet immediate energy requirements and renewable energy targets in the short-term while improving access to renewable energy for low-income energy consumers. Given that public and cooperative ownership of energy infrastructures is viewed as an important means of facilitating a more equitable distribution of energy system benefits (Becker & Naumann 2017), the promotion of local small-scale renewable energy and support of rooftop solar through favorable feed-in tariffs suggest that MCE is making some tangible progress toward their energy democracy objectives.

These examples illustrate specific ways in which various elements of a decentralized energy system—be it in terms of control, infrastructure, or financial arrangements—are layered on top of existing patterns of social inequity and environmental justice. Social, political, and economic variation across CCA contexts may result in the pursuit of divergent objectives, each with differing consequences for the promotion of energy democracy and just sustainabilities, illustrating the challenges of bounding something as diffuse and complex as an energy system by the socially constructed notion of "local." In fact, blind adherence to "local control" may have created new injustices by opting for high-cost local generation in favor of extra lower-cost alternatives that may do more to improve access to renewable energy resources for low-income households.

Conclusion

This study highlights potential limits of the energy democracy concept when put into practice through CCA, and thus provides some clarification on the extent to which localized renewable energy initiatives can meaningfully contribute to the pursuit of just sustainabilities. The variety of CCA approaches represents a significant degree of contention over who defines energy democracy, on what terms, and to what end. Given the growing variation in constituencies CCAs represent—from affluent coastal communities to less wealthy inland areas—policymakers should attend to the ways in which these dynamics may either alleviate or exacerbate existing inequalities.

While energy transitions may on the surface appear intended to promote energy justice—for instance, by alleviating the need for emissions- and pollution-intensive forms of electricity generation in favor of "cleaner" alternatives—the uneven power dynamics driving such transitions and the broad and variegated constituencies such transitions affect may also give rise to new injustices (Newell & Mulvaney 2013; Jenkins et al. 2016). Critical attention to the assumed complementarity of different energy transition objectives is needed to better understand this relationship, and the potentially adverse consequences that can result from an unquestioning commitment to "local control." Finally, while there is mounting theoretical support for a relationship between energy infrastructure and the distribution of political power (Burke & Stephens 2018), attention to the underlying logics and political economic processes that inform particular infrastructure investment decisions will provide a more meaningful approach to understanding the conditions under which a more radical, systemic, and democratic energy transition may arise.

While decentralization produces more opportunities for cost reductions, greenhouse gas reductions, and public participation (Bauknecht, Funcke, & Vogel 2020), there is also the possibility that the distribution of new opportunities may serve to reinscribe existing patterns of inequity and injustice across multiple scales. While promoted as workforce development, MCE's strategy of developing large-scale energy infrastructure in lower socioeconomic areas such as Richmond and Lancaster points to ways existing patterns of uneven development may be reproduced through CCA. While technological decentralization provides greater options for participation, the extent and quality of that participation remains closely tied to existing distribution of resources and political power. As noted in the introduction, the CCA movement first emerged in California's central valley—an area that consistently ranks among the lowest in per capita income, median household income, and median family income in California. To date, however, the CCA movement remains concentrated in California's more affluent coastal communities, with no representation in the central valley. This points to the role of political power as a necessary precondition in order to push for the types of rescaling and redistribution of benefits advocated by many of the Bay Area CCAs. Managing these trade-offs and processes of redistribution in a way that continues to work toward a transformative agenda requires thoughtful consideration of the ways in which local control can and should be asserted over the political, technical, and financial dimensions of the broader energy system.

Together, the examples complicate core assumptions embedded in the pro-CCA discourse by demonstrating the CCA movement's use of "local" to pursue other scalar options that might be more effective in achieving a just and democratic energy system. However, it is still early days for the CCA model in California, and there are significant dangers in making comparisons between relatively recent innovations in energy governance and utilities that evolved over a century or more. With these limitations in mind, this study, linking just sustainabilities with energy democracy, is intended as a preliminary assessment, providing a theoretical and case-specific baseline analysis which can be built upon in future years as both movements and the presence of mature CCAs expand across the state and potentially beyond.

References

Agyeman, J. (2002), "Putting 'just sustainability' into place: From paradigm to practice," *Policy Management Review*, 2: 8–40.

Agyeman, J. (2013), *Introducing Just Sustainabilities: Policy, Planning, and Practice*, London: Zed Books.

Allen, E., H. Lyons, & J.C. Stephens (2019), "Women's leadership in renewable transformation, energy justice and energy democracy: Redistributing power," *Energy Research & Social Science*, 57: 101233.

Bauknecht, D., S. Funcke, & M. Vogel (2020), "Is small beautiful? A framework for assessing decentralised electricity systems," *Renewable & Sustainable Energy Reviews*, 118: 109543.

Becker, S. & M. Naumann (2017), "Energy democracy: Mapping the debate on energy alternatives," *Geography Compass*, 11(8): e12321.

Born, B. & M. Purcell (2006), "Avoiding the local trap: Scale and food systems in planning research," *Journal of Planning Education & Research*, 26: 195–207.

Boyd, W. & A.E. Carlson (2016), "Accidents of federalism: Ratemaking and policy innovation in public utility law," *UCLA Law Review*, 63: 810–93.

Bridge, G., S. Bouzarovski, M. Bradshaw, & N. Eyre (2013), "Geographies of energy transition: Space, place and the low-carbon economy," *Energy Policy*, 53: 331–40.
Brown, J.C. & M. Purcell (2005), "There's nothing inherent about scale: Political ecology, the local trap, and the politics of development in the Brazilian Amazon," *Geoforum*, 36: 607–24.
Burke, M.J. & J.C. Stephens (2017), "Energy democracy: Goals and policy instruments for sociotechnical transitions," *Energy Research & Social Science*, 33: 35–48.
Burke, M.J. & J.C. Stephens (2018), "Political power and renewable energy futures: A critical review," *Energy Research & Social Science*, 35: 78–93.
CalCCA (2018), *Beyond Supplier Diversity Report*, Concord: California Community Choice Association.
CalCCA (2019), "California Community Choice Association," Available online: https://cal-cca.org/ (Accessed September 6, 2019).
Calvert, K. (2016), "From 'energy geography' to 'energy geographies': Perspectives on a fertile academic borderland," *Progress in Human Geography*, 40(1): 105–25.
CARB (2019), *California Greenhouse Gas Emissions for 2000 to 2017: Trends of Emissions and Other Indicators*, Sacramento: California Air Resources Board.
CCP (2016), *Community Choice Energy: What Is the Local Economic Impact? San José, California, Case Study*, Santa Rosa: Center for Climate Protection.
CEC (2018a), "California Solar Energy Statistics and Data," *California Energy Commission*. Available online: https://ww2.energy.ca.gov/almanac/renewables_data/solar/index_cms.php (Accessed January 25, 2020).
CEC (2018b), "Total System Electric Generation," *California Energy Commission*. Available online: https://ww2.energy.ca.gov/almanac/electricity_data/total_system_power.html (Accessed January 25, 2020).
CEC (2019), "Renewables Portfolio Standard—RPS," *California Energy Commission*. Available online: https://www.energy.ca.gov/programs-and-topics/programs/renewables-portfolio-standard (Accessed September 3, 2019).
Chen, C., J. Wang, F. Qiu & D. Zhao (2016), "Resilient distribution system by microgrids formation after natural disasters," *IEEE Transactions on Smart Grid*, 7(2): 958–66.
CPUC (2017), *Community Choice Aggregation En Banc Background Paper*, Sacramento: California Public Utilities Commission.
CPUC (2020), "Energy—Electric and natural gas," *California Public Utilities Commission*. Available online: https://www.cpuc.ca.gov/energy/ (Accessed February 5, 2020).
DataUSA (2018), "San Rafael, CA & Richmond, CA," *DataUSA*. Available online: https://datausa.io/profile/geo/san-rafael-ca?compare=richmond-ca (Accessed February 4, 2020).
Dillon, L. (2018), "Marin County has long resisted growth in the name of environmentalism. But high housing costs and segregation persist," *Los Angeles Times*, January 7. Available online: https://www.latimes.com/politics/la-pol-ca-marin-county-affordable-housing-20170107-story.html (Accessed February 6, 2020).
Farrell, J. (2014), *Beyond Utility 2.0 to Energy Democracy: Why a Technological Transformation in the Electricity Business Should Unlock an Economic Transformation That Grants Power to the People*, Minneapolis: Democratic Energy Initiative, Institute for Local Self-Reliance.
Farrell, J. (2016), "A new logo, and a definition of energy democracy," *Institute for Local Self-Reliance*. Available online: https://ilsr.org/a-new-logo-and-a-definition-of-energy-democracy/ (Accessed February 27, 2018).
Fuller, T. (2019), "For the most vulnerable, California blackouts 'can be life or death,'" *New York Times*, October 10. Available online: https://www.nytimes.com/2019/10/10/us/california-power-outage.html (Accessed June 4, 2020).

Gattaciecca, J., J.R. DeShazo, & K. Trumbull (2017), *The Promises and Challenges of Community Choice Aggregation in California*, Los Angeles: UCLA Luskin Center for Innovation.

Hess, D.J. (2019), "Coalitions, framing, and the politics of energy transitions: Local democracy and community choice in California," *Energy Research & Social Science*, 50: 38–50.

Holson, L.M. (2001), "Power, politics and glory dimmed; Pacific Gas and Electric finds no sympathy among customers or once-docile state legislature," *New York Times*. February 22. Available online: https://www.nytimes.com/2001/02/22/business/power-politics-glory-dimmed-pacific-gas-electric-finds-no-sympathy-among.html (Accessed June 4, 2020).

Holt, E., J. Sumner, & L. Bird (2011), "The role of renewable energy certificates in developing new renewable energy projects," *Contract*, 303: 275–300.

Jenkins, K., D. McCauley, R. Heffron, H. Stephan, & R. Rehner (2016), "Energy justice: A conceptual review," *Energy Research & Social Science*, 11: 174–82.

Karlis, N. (2019), "After choosing profits over maintenance, California utility giant forces blackouts on customers," *Salon*, October 9. Available online: https://www.salon.com/2019/10/09/after-choosing-profits-over-maintenance-california-utility-giant-forces-blackouts-on-customers/(Accessed January 25, 2020).

Kennedy, S.F. (2017), *"Greening" the Mix Through Community Choice*, Los Angeles: UCLA Institute of the Environment & Sustainability.

Kennedy, S.F. & B. Rosen (2020), "The rise of community choice aggregation and its implications for California's energy transition: A preliminary assessment," *Energy & Environment* https://doi.org/10.1177/0958305X20927381.

McCauley, D. & R. Heffron (2018), "Just transition: Integrating climate, energy and environmental justice," *Energy Policy*, 119: 1–7.

McCauley, D., V. Ramasar, R.J. Heffron, B.K. Sovacool, D. Mebratu, & L. Mundaca (2019), "Energy justice in the transition to low carbon energy systems: Exploring key themes in interdisciplinary research," *Applied Energy*, 233–234: 916–21.

MCE (2017a), *2017 Integrated Resource Plan*, San Rafael: Marin Clean Energy.

MCE (2017b), *Resolution No.2017-08 Marin Clean Energy—A Resolution of the Board of Directors of Marin Clean Energy Approving Third Amendment to Credit Agreement with River City Bank in the Principal Amount of $25,000,000*. Available online: https://www.mcecleanenergy.org/wp-content/uploads/2017/07/7.20.17-Board-Packet-1.pdf (Accessed June 4, 2020).

MCE (2019), "About us," *MCE Community Choice Energy*. Available online: https://www.mcecleanenergy.org/about-us/ (Accessed September 6, 2019).

MCE Clean Energy (2015), *2015 MCE Energy Efficiency Annual Report*, San Rafael: MCE Clean Energy.

MCE Clean Energy (2017), *Financial Statement: Years Ended March 31, 2017 & 2016 with Report of Independent Auditors*. Available online: https://www.mcecleanenergy.org/wp-content/uploads/2017/08/MCE-Audited-Financial-Statements-2016-2017.pdf (Accessed June 4, 2020).

Mormann, F. (2015), "Clean energy federalism," *Florida Law Review*, 67: 1621–82.

Moroni, S., V. Antoniucci, & A. Bisello (2016), "Energy sprawl, land taking and distributed generation: Towards a multi-layered density," *Energy Policy*, 98: 266–73.

Newell, P. & D. Mulvaney (2013), "The political economy of the 'just transition'," *Geographical Journal*, 179: 132–40.

OEHHA (2018), "CalEnviroScreen 3.0," *California Office of Environmental Health Hazard Assessment*. Available online: https://oehha.ca.gov/calenviroscreen/report/calenviroscreen-30 (Accessed February 8, 2020).

O'Shaughnessy, E., J. Heeter, J. Gattaciecca, J. Sauer, K. Trumbull, & E. Chen (2019), *Community Choice Aggregation: Challenges, Opportunities, and Impacts on Renewable Energy Markets (No. NREL/TP-6A20-72195)*, Golden: National Renewable Energy Lab.

Penn, I., P. Eavis, & J. Glanz (2019), "California wildfires: How PG&E ignored risks in favor of profits," *New York Times*, March 18. Available online: https://www.nytimes.com/interactive/2019/03/18/business/pge-california-wildfires.html (Accessed June 4, 2020).

PR Newswire (2017), "Fir Tree Partners completes sale of sPower, the largest US independent solar developer, to AES and AIMCo for $1.6 Billion." *PR Newswire*, Jul 31. Available online: https://www.prnewswire.com/news-releases/fir-tree-partners-completes-sale-of-spower-the-largest-us-independent-solar-developer-to-aes-and-aimco-for-16-billion-300496781.html (Accessed January 14, 2020).

Purcell, M. (2006), "Urban democracy and the local trap," *Urban Studies*, 43(11): 1921–41.

RCB (2018), "Vision & values," *River City Bank*. Available online: https://rivercitybank.com/values/(Accessed May 3, 2018).

SCP (2018), "Drive EverGreen," *Sonoma Clean Power*. Available online: https://sonomacleanpower.org/drive-evergreen/(Accessed April 30, 2018).

Sonnino, R. (2010), "Escaping the local trap: Insights on re-localization from school food reform," *Journal of Environmental Policy & Planning*, 12: 23–40.

sPower (2019), "sPower and MCE complete largest operational CCA solar project in California," *SPower—News*. Available online: https://www.spower.com/news_2019/news-2019-04-29.php (Accessed September 6, 2019).

Szulecki, K. (2018), "Conceptualizing energy democracy," *Environmental Politics*, 27(1): 21–41.

U.S Census Bureau (2016), "Quick Facts, U.S. Census Bureau." Available online: https://www.census.gov/quickfacts/fact/table/US/PST045219 (Accessed June 4, 2020).

van Veelen, B. & D. van der Horst (2018), "What is energy democracy? Connecting social science energy research and political theory," *Energy Research & Social Science*, 46: 19–28.

Weinrub, A. (2017), "Democratizing municipal-scale power," in D. Fairchild & A. Weinrub (eds), *Energy Democracy*, 139–71, Washington, DC: Island Press.

Welton, S. (2017), "Public energy," *New York University Law Review*, 92: 267–349.

Appendix A

1   The California RPS requires electricity retailers to derive 60 percent of their retail sales from eligible renewable energy resources, such as wind, solar, and geothermal by 2030, and all the state's electricity to come from carbon-free resources by 2045 (CEC 2019).

2   The California power source disclosure program requires electricity retailers to submit an annual summary of all electricity purchases to the California Energy Commission. This information is then summarized and made public in the form of power content labels—a Californian regulatory requirement and the primary means through which electricity providers communicate details of their energy mix to consumers.

3   The California RPS allows electricity retailers to meet 25 percent of their RPS requirements through the purchase of renewable energy certificates (RECs).

CCA	Service areas	Procurement & contracting	Rate design	Net energy metering	Community engagement	Workforce development	Electric vehicle programs	Energy efficiency	Wildfire rebuild support	Total program areas
MCE	Marin, Napa, Contra Costa, Solano Counties	X		X	X	X	X	X	X	7
Redwood Coast Energy Authority (RCEA)	Humboldt County	X	X	X	X	X	X	X		7
Sonoma Clean Power (SCP)	Sonoma, Mendocino Counties	X		X	X		X	X	X	6
Peninsula Clean Energy (PCE)	San Mateo Counties	X	X	X		X	X			5
CleanPowerSF (CPSF)	City of San Francisco	X			X		X			3
Monterey Bay Community Power (MBCP)	Monterey, Santa Cruz, San Benito Counties		X		X		X			3
East Bay Community Energy (EBCE)	Alameda County	X			X	X				3
Lancaster Choice Energy (LCE)	City of Lancaster		X				X	X		3
Clean Power Alliance (CPA)	Los Angeles, Ventura Counties		X		X					2
Pioneer Community Energy (Pioneer)	Placer County		X					X		2
San Jose Clean Energy (SJCE)	City of San Jose			X	X					2

CCA	Service areas	Procurement & contracting	Rate design	Net energy metering	Community engagement	Workforce development	Electric vehicle programs	Energy efficiency	Wildfire rebuild support	Total program areas
Silicon Valley Clean Energy (SVCE)	Santa Clara County	X								1
Pico Rivera Innovative Municipal Energy (PRIME)	City of Pico Rivera									0
Rancho Mirage Energy Authority	City of Rancho Mirage									0
San Jacinto Power (SJP)	City of San Jacinto									0
Did not report										
Apple Valley Choice Energy (AVCE)	Town of Apple Valley									0
Desert Community Energy	Cities of Palm Springs, Palm Desert, Cathedral City									0
King City Community Power	King City									0
Solana Energy Alliance (SEA)	City of Solana Beach									0
Valley Clean Energy	Yolo County									0

Part IV

REIMAGINING THE POSSIBLE

Through the prior case studies, we have explored the many intersecting threads both enabling and inhibiting policies, plans, and practices for just sustainabilities. So what next? Amid the current political and social uncertainty, a growing number of people are working to collectively create alternative futures. This final part offers three chapters and some hope, moving from questions of *when* and *where*, *who for* and *who by*, onto questions of *how?* A common thread is the tendency to build from the ground up—sometimes literally. Advocates for alternative policies, plans, and practices must grapple with ideological questions to avoid re-perpetuating past injustice, as well as institutional barriers and limited resources. Chapter 10 traces the practices of a grassroots community development project, deeply grounded in its locale north of Melbourne. Chapter 11 examines the potential of the Holistic Grazing Method for reconceptualizing the roles of grasslands and livestock within food-based ecosystems, and how much of its success is built upon a paradoxical anticipation of failure. Chapter 12 examines collective organizing around food sovereignty, anti-racism, and anti-poverty in Baltimore at the reclaimed Tubman House. These place-based examples offer encouragement for transitioning to just and sustainable societies, but are marked by contradictions and shortcomings of their own.

10

ORGANIC (DIS)ORGANIZATION AND TRANSFORMATION: STORIES OF RESISTANCE AND RETURN AT CERES COMMUNITY ENVIRONMENT PARK

Natalie Osborne
Deanna Grant-Smith

Introduction

If it is true, as Nobel Prize–winning economist Joseph Stiglitz has suggested, that neoliberalism is dying, it does not necessarily hold that we are in the process of transitioning to a more just, let alone sustainable, future. In Western democracies, high-profile instances of the increasing influence of the hard-right mean that the left must concern itself not only with questions of sustainability, climate change, redistribution, and social justice but also how to guard against the political, economic, social, and environmental impacts of neofascism (or ecofascism), corporate greed, and hyperindividualism. Further, a reversal of environmental priorities—exemplified by Trump's policy rejection of the Paris Climate Agreement and the recent approval of Australia's largest coal mine—with increasingly devastating impacts on the World Heritage listed Great Barrier Reef and catastrophic implications for climate change—elicits despair and adds to the hopelessness and ontological insecurity already experienced by many green/left activists (Osborne 2019).

In this complex, contested, and at times paradoxical context, where the scale of transformation demanded seems overwhelming, those of us organizing for social and environmental justice may benefit from thinking about our actions in terms of prefigurative politics. Prefigurative politics seeks to enact theories, philosophies, hopes, visions, and plans for futures in everyday practices; desired futures are embodied, modelled, played with, and enacted in the present, compromised, partial, and ephemeral as such attempts might be (Curnow 2016). Prefigurative politics is a politics of contradiction, complicity, and paradox, rather than purity or perfection. The research drawn on in this chapter was conducted during the early stages of the Global Financial Crisis of 2008. As such, participants do not speak directly to the troubling recent developments in global and national politics. However, by considering the case through the lens of prefigurative politics, the work described in this chapter may offer hope and guidance to those concerned with just sustainabilities (see Agyeman, Bullard, & Evans 2003) and just transitions in their communities in the context of increasing instability.

Where there is limited political will for—or indeed, open hostility to—the active pursuit of a more just and sustainable national and global economy, more locally based, cooperative, diverse, ecologically and socially conscious economic practices that attempt to prefigure just transitions may be an important strategy. This chapter examines the role of resilience, independence, and collective identities at the Centre for Education and Research in Environmental Strategies Community Environment Park (CERES), an inner city, nonresidential, intentional community working toward this goal.

Established in 1982, CERES is a not-for-profit organization comprising a community garden, demonstration projects, and social enterprises. It is situated on four and a half hectares of rehabilitated landfill on the banks of the Merri Creek in Brunswick East, a few kilometers north of Melbourne's central business district in Australia. It is a "place filled with trees, flowers and food intermingling with people and thoughtfully constructed buildings, with the arm of a river wrapping around it" (Bailey 2016: 53). Operating for more than three decades CERES is a pioneer of community arts, experiential education, sustainable urban agriculture, and the demonstration of innovative solutions to pressing environmental, urban, and social issues. Employing tactical urbanism in the advancement of sustainability, resilience, and just transitions, CERES showcases alternative approaches for more environmentally and socially conscious living, and has been held up as a model for grassroots community development focused on the implementation of social, economic, and environmental transition programs at the local scale and the nurturing of diverse local economies.

CERES deliberately seeks and receives little government or corporate support to ensure its continued independence. It is largely self-supported or, perhaps more accurately, is supported by the community who participate in its various enterprises and programs. This chapter explores the tensions of operating a successful community and locally based organization, features of CERES that have arguably contributed to its success and longevity, against pressures for more bureaucratic forms of organizing and increasing external oversight. Paradoxically, projects that attend to local contexts and entanglements and ecosystems are often only seen as provisionally successful on their own "turf"; it is common in green/left organizing for any successful project to become expansionist, even where that would contradict the foundational values of the project. Place-based, small-scale, and/or prefigurative projects may be seen as insufficiently effective or insufficiently revolutionary—they may be constructed as (and, to be fair, may in some cases actually be) parochial or pacifying (see Srnicek & Williams 2015 and Danowski & Viveiros de Castro 2017 for a rebuttal). And in the emerging catastrophe of the sixth great extinction, climate change, and rising precarity, it is easy to see why green/left organizing often emphasizes the rhizomatic—what can spread, what can grow. This chapter offers an account of an anti-expansionist project: one that remains rooted in place and indeed finds its strength and longevity there.

Acting Locally

CERES is located in the inner-city, ethnically diverse suburb of Brunswick East. Brunswick East was formerly an industrial area, but is now mixed-use residential and commercial, with a higher-than-average proportion of multi-unit dwellings. CERES is more than a suburban park or community garden; it is an intentional community actively engaged in developing strategies and models for more environmentally conscious communities. Its mission is to create "a place for community-based learning and action to create environmentally beneficial, socially just, economically satisfying, culturally enriching and spiritually nurturing ways of living together" (CERES 2016). It is a site of experimental and subversive interventions and demonstrations, with the goal of informing and inspiring radical, community-based actions on and from the margins elsewhere, in the tradition of DIY and tactical urbanism (Lydon & Garcia 2015). In pursuing these goals and ways of organizing, CERES is attempting to create the kind of community, relationships, and spaces required for a more just and sustainable world.

CERES is both a community of place and a community of interest (Nasar & Julian 1995) and shares characteristics of both traditional communities and postmodern communities; similar to ecovillages, it includes applied research in food-growing technology, energy efficiency, and energy generation (Dawson 2006), but is not residential. As such, defining the CERES community is complex. CERES has a paid membership base of approximately 300+ employees and volunteers with a formal tie to the community. The CERES community also consists of those who support the onsite enterprises, shop at the markets, attend events, or use the open spaces on either a regular or ad hoc basis. Close to half a million people actively engage with the CERES community annually through its suite of programs, events, and activities. This constitutes a broad reach of people exposed to the ideas and ideals of CERES and its demonstrated possibilities.

CERES enterprises and programs have included education programs for school groups; an organic café, organic market, and shop; a permaculture and bushfood nursery; plant propagation; event and function planning; and social enterprises. CERES is also host to a number of site groups which operate somewhat independently of the official CERES management structure but are part of the CERES community. One of the most vibrant and innovative site groups is the Bike Shed Group, which helps people repair and restore their own or donated bicycles using recycled parts, and through which people share knowledge and tips about travelling by bicycle. CERES also includes a community garden which, similar to other community garden projects, is used to promote ecological sustainability through local food growing (Stocker & Barnett 1998) as a site of training, research, skills development (Firth, Maye, & Pearson 2011), and "political performance" (Nettle 2014).

CERES is also a hub for innovation and information that are *brought into CERES* through employees and volunteers with previous experience or knowledge, *generated within CERES* through research and experimentation, and *shared through CERES* to the wider community through visitation and education programs and bridging social capital. The influx and efflux of ideas and information facilitate change within the CERES community, and in building social capital, community, and organizational capacity reflects one of the main characteristics of tactical urbanism (Lydon et al. 2012). This role as a hub of exchange sits alongside an understanding of the importance of acting within a local context when building community agency, capacity, resilience, and sustainable transitions (Kretzmann & McKnight 1996; Dietz, Ostrom, & Stern 2003). This "hub" model also suggests a theory of change centered on translation; that is, ideas, examples, and techniques developed and/or demonstrated at CERES are widely shared, but those seeking to implement them elsewhere will need to translate, adapt, and transform them, rather than merely reproduce them, for their own local context. The model is "learn with us," not "copy us." This is as close as CERES comes to expansionist politics—the goal is not to make more versions of CERES. Rather, it is to demonstrate a set of practices and approaches, tools and techniques that may be adapted and applied, advanced and added to, elsewhere. CERES' commitment to place-based modes of environmental and social care makes place foundational; it is antithetical, even nonsensical, to assume that a practice or technology that *emerged from and works at* CERES, in inner-city Melbourne, on the banks of the Merri Creek, could be directly transposed to any other context. CERES educators invite others to engage with the places they want to work with, care with, and adapt rather than adopt, learn rather than copy.

The understanding of sustainable and just transitions at CERES is one that is deeply contextual and situated. Unlike some other locally based just transition projects, they are not explicitly focused on "upward harmonization" (Stevis & Felli 2016: 40), or otherwise broader, vertical uptake of their practices at a governmental/institutional level. Research participants were emphatic about the dangers inherent in assuming that a successful solution in one local area will be successful in another; indeed, this assumption can undermine the ability of communities to discover innovative and improved solutions, and inhibit resilience by not encouraging autonomy and particularity. While there are instances of individuals or groups from other communities visiting CERES for inspiration to develop their own, locally contextual community initiatives (e.g., see Cameron & Gibson 2005), participants warned of the temptation to become "missionaries" for local solutions. Despite this, they remained excited when someone from another country or community expressed an interest in coming to learn from the CERES experience; not because they believed CERES provided a template but rather because it had the potential to inspire and empower others to adapt ideas to their local context. This feeling was expressed by a volunteer who noted:

> I go away with all these ideas, and then I can transform these ideas… translate them into my life, and express them to people around me through my filter…

And that's what I think is brilliant about this place is that all of these people come here and get filled up and they go off and filter it through themselves to the world… it's such a beautiful thing to see other people coming up with their own ideas.

At CERES, livelihoods are understood as comprising multiple forms of exchange, enterprise, and labor beyond what is typically included in mainstream capitalist models (Gibson-Graham 2008; Gibson-Graham, Cameron, & Healey 2013). Localizing and diversifying livelihood activities is characteristic of a resilient city (Newman, Beatley, & Boyer 2009) and important to alternative economies (Gibson-Graham 2008; Eisenstein 2011). CERES encourages the proliferation of livelihood activities that are more equitable and sustainable, and experiments with new ways of sustaining urban life. The diverse economies paradigm applied at CERES does not rely on overthrowing capitalism for change to occur. Rather, it advocates everyday, accessible changes to production, reproduction, and exchange, labelling alternatives that already exist and facilitating the imagining and generation of others in the cracks of existing economic models. Some of the diverse economic activities observed at CERES include in-kind work, gift-giving, local trading systems, cooperatives, fair trade systems, volunteer work, care work, self-provisioning, and nonprofit enterprises. Further, localized energy and food production are already occurring, as is the encouragement of local and neighborhood-level social and economic (and social-economic) activity. The people engaged in these activities also remain entangled with and complicit in capitalist economies—they also do the work of reproducing capitalism. These paradoxes and contradictions can be uncomfortable, but there is no space of purity from which to prefigure diverse economies.

The idea that a diverse community, as well as economy, is more resilient than a homogenous community is well supported by the literature (Adger 2000; Wilson 2005; Norris et al. 2008) and this is acknowledged by the CERES community. The complexity and diversity within the CERES membership base, enterprises, and activities is an asset which contributes to individual and collective resilience. Indeed, this diversity ensures that there is usually someone who has the skills, knowledge, expertise, and availability "to step in and help out" (CERES employee). Part of the diversity that is central to CERES' sustainable and just transitions ethic is cultural and linguistic diversity. The CERES site includes a "Cultural Village," where cultural education and celebrations occur. There are also programs aimed at helping migrants gain qualifications and/or establish social enterprises. The area in which CERES is located used to be a manufacturing district. Interview participants recalled that when this manufacturing base collapsed, it hit the migrant population particularly hard, and that CERES stepped in to provide employment, training, and networking opportunities for marginalized and disadvantaged people and people from different cultures.

CERES sits on land belonging to the Wurundjeri People and has a commitment to providing space for local Indigenous peoples and cultures. There are a number of educational and engagement programs run by Aboriginal and Torres Strait

Islander educators on topics including Indigenous peoples, cultures, histories, country and protocols, and skills including using native plants and bushfoods. Some of the history of the Wurundjeri People and their experiences of invasion is made visible on the CERES grounds—a level of visibility that is somewhat unusual in urban Australian landscapes. Building relationships between the Wurundjeri People and the current occupants of the (stolen) land is an ongoing project. The existence of CERES, and the city of so-called Melbourne itself, is entangled in histories and present practices of colonialism—as with all cities and towns in settler-colonial contexts, they have been brought into being through, and are sustained by, practices of displacement, dispossession, and exclusion. The presence of Indigenous educators and education programs at CERES is a practice of respect and recognition and provides a space through which to build and negotiate new ways of coexistence (Flynn 2013; Bailey 2016). But CERES' commitment to more just futures is sustained by their occupation of stolen land; crucially, this is not a tension that can be "fixed" or settled, but it will require ongoing engagement and (re)negotiation. The State of Victoria is currently engaged in treaty negotiations with (some of) the Aboriginal Peoples of the State, which may influence the shape of those engagements in the future. This understanding and acceptance of ongoing obligations—rather than imagining some fixed state of the ideal future—is critical to enacting just sustainabilities, an insight that applies well beyond the case of CERES.

CERES and Collective Identity

CERES develops, promotes, and provides alternatives to global capitalism and understandings of the economy and society dominated by neoliberalism. It provides a sharp contrast to the way things are done outside CERES, proving that other kinds of communities, economies, and relationships to the Earth are possible, even if only in "wastelands" like the abandoned rubbish tip on which CERES was founded. Similarly, CERES highlights that those who may drive transitions and the creation of alternatives may also be those who have been marginalized, rejected, or subjugated by that system—indeed, perhaps Othered people and Othered places have particular capacities to demonstrate that other worlds are possible (Osborne 2019).

Managed by a collectivity that "resembles neither the state nor the market" (Ostrom 1990: 1), CERES can be perceived as something of a commons. Access is not regulated or controlled except during events, where a small fee may be charged (though labor may be substituted for a fee), and in order to shape what occurs on the space, one need only be a participating member of the community. CERES strives to be an inclusive and equitable space, but in practice being included relies on at least some shared set of values and interests (e.g., justice, sustainability, community economies) and some form of participation, though the nature and degree of that participation may vary considerably. Although CERES has some paid employees, volunteers are critical to its success. Identity is one of the most important components of urban communities (Ferman & Kaylor 2001), and it is an important motivator behind involvement and volunteerism at CERES. Collective identity at CERES is developed in part through a sense of belonging to an alternative group, in opposition to the status quo (Burgmann 2003). This is similar to activist spaces, with their shared position of contestation or subversion, and the formation of coalitions and shared identities around radical/alternative imaginaries of city life (Soja 2010).

Collective identity is also built through the development of a community mythos—stories and traditions with a spiritual edge that tie the community to each other and to the Earth. These traditions include the Return of the Sacred Kingfisher Festival and the Harvest Festival, which celebrates the seasonal cycles and productivity of the Earth. These community celebrations attract newcomers and form traditions and rituals that bond the community, reinforce their collective identity, and link the community to place (Measham 2006). Indeed, CERES itself declares "spiritually nurturing ways of living together" (CERES 2016) one of its core aims. The importance of this spiritual component to the constitution of the community and its activities can be understood through Eisenstein's work on the sacred economy—that which is local, and emerges from a collective recognition of the "spiritual dimension to the planetary crisis" (Eisenstein 2011: 10).

CERES' longevity, self-sufficiency, and profile are testament to its success. However, although the growth of CERES—in part triggered by growth in, and mainstreaming of, the environmental movement—may be considered a measure of its success as a community, and an indicator of change at a wider community level, this increased profile has caused some concern about the future of CERES. These concerns are in part based on what Davison (2006) refers to as the routinization of environmentalism. Part of the attraction of CERES for its volunteers and employees is that it represents an *alternative* lifestyle. Activities at CERES occur on the margins and are in many ways radical and subversive—particularly in their stance toward the mainstream economy and consumption cultures.

Some expressed concern that the increasing popularity of CERES, combined with the decreasing uniqueness of the alternative "green" movement, will affect the sense of community at CERES and encourage the transformation of CERES into a mainstream entity rather than a community for the demonstration of alternatives to the mainstream. This concern is grounded in a fear that the community will lose some of the values that attracted people to CERES in the first place, and that as the community grows, the focus may shift to managing money and finances, rather than achieving the stated strategic goals of the community. Thus, while feelings of belonging to an alternative community are important for collective identity and the resilience of the group (Burgmann 2003), it is possible that the loss of alternativism and the sense of prevailing against dominant norms may cause a loss of identity and decrease resilience—a difficult, paradoxical tension.

That said, this fear now seems a bit unlikely; the environmental movement hit its mainstream "high" in Australia at the time this research was conducted, but there was a swing back against environmental regulation and emission reduction measures. The fossil fuel industry remains powerful, and pro-growth rhetoric has proved resilient. Rather than environmentalism becoming structurally transformative, it has been mainstreamed to center on "green" consumption (e.g., reusable coffee cups and bags); significant transformations in production, consumption, and the ordering of our lives remain "alternative" or fringe. Further, some local residents for whom CERES could provide much-needed greenspace and community space believe it is not for them, feeling instead that it has been appropriated by people from outside Brunswick East—"hippies... who come to bang their drums" (Woodcock, Willan, & Dovey 2011: 7), perhaps indicating that CERES remains somewhat of an "alternative" space.

CERES is a kind of heterotopia: a space in and through which people practice counterhegemonic ways of being and relating and attempt to prefigure more just and sustainable modes of living. Its goal is not self-proliferation; it is not expanding its borders or duplicating itself elsewhere. And although some participants were afraid of what sustainability achieving hegemony would do to the identity derived from being "outsiders" and counterhegemonic, this has not eventuated. Spaces of struggle are generally working to undo the structures and relations that necessitate their existence—struggling for their own obsolescence. As a result, sometimes we lose something in winning. But the practices of community, commons, and collaboration we learn in these spaces may move with us, even if the organizations or places themselves fall away.

Self-sufficient and Sustainable, Independent and Interdependent

Many of the activities at CERES are undertaken to prove that measures to conserve resources, reduce waste and consumption, and improve community well-being can be done at a community level, without government or corporate sponsorship and/or leadership. This is essential for a community whose ethics and values are radically opposed to those that dominate the corporate and government sectors. If their projects and strategies are to be transformative and support just sustainabilities and transitions, they cannot exist solely at the whim of the system they are resisting. CERES has conducted research into: green technology, intensive food production, renewable energy, electric car conversion (converting standard cars into electric vehicles), water efficiency and storage, flood remediation, and local biogas and/or gasification plants. Research at CERES is funded at least in part by the other CERES enterprises, such as the markets and the café. The development of economic resources is important for the development of resilience by enabling research and self-sufficiency. Although designed around a largely noneconomic agenda, CERES' activities produce economic benefits with what Gibson and Cameron (2001: 13) refer to as "the potential to percolate up." Indeed, the collective reimagining of the place of the economy, and the importance of diverse, local, and sustainable economic activities, is perhaps an emergent example of an economics embodying "the human identity of the connected self living in cocreative partnership with Earth" (Eisenstein 2011: 115). As Frankel (1987: 13) observed, "moral exhortation is just not enough, if radicals cannot answer the serious questions as to feasibility, organisation and finance."

This commitment to economic self-sufficiency has not been without problems and failures. CERES has had to make some difficult financial decisions, particularly around the operation of the on-site café (which has now been leased to a third party) and the financial catastrophe of attempting to run a restaurant. Both initiatives were aligned with CERES' mission but could not compete in Melbourne's highly competitive hospitality scene.

Despite some missteps, CERES remains committed to independence. Tan and Neo (2009) have highlighted problems that emerge when similar projects have close links with government apparatus; in Singapore, community gardens are viewed by some as exclusionary spaces because of such links, which constrains civic activism. This not only affects the extent to which these gardens can forge communal bonds but also challenges their integral spirit. CERES, on the other hand, receives (and seeks) little government or corporate support. CERES is largely self-sufficient; 95 percent of CERES' income is derived from its social enterprises and educational services (CERES 2016). Revenue from enterprises, programs, and, to a lesser extent, membership fees support the research programs and other community initiatives that don't generate a profit but contribute to other parts of CERES' mission. The remainder of funding comes from government and philanthropic grants, which are primarily used to fund new initiatives rather than day-to-day operations. The significant exception to this commitment to self-sufficiency is that they are only charged a nominal rent for the land they occupy. The paradox here is that they are arguably more vulnerable to rent increases or eviction; the more they rehabilitate the former rubbish dump they are sited on.

CERES is not alone in their ambitions for financial independence; indeed, many groups committed to just sustainabilities and transitions prefer untied, grassroots fundraising over corporate or state-proctored funding models, due to the precarious nature of such funding and the strong potential for political interference. An overreliance on these external forms of funding has the potential to limit opportunities for transformative change and experimentation, as activities can be constrained by the need to shape programs in a way that meets the requirements of granting bodies, and promotes competition and noncollaboration between those seeking funding (Smith 2017). At the time of the interviews, some CERES members were concerned that growth in CERES' profile, combined with increasing societal desire to become (or be seen as) "greener," could lead to more funding from corporate or government sources. It was feared that an increased reliance on external funding may result in an increasing focus on managing the money, rather than the achievement of CERES' mission, and have the potential to undermine resilience by making community initiatives dependent on the will of external entities. Indeed, Abel Cumming and Anderies (2006) warn that too much external management can undermine resilience and the capacity of the community to self-organize. Reliance on external funding was thus seen by participants as something to be resisted as an existential threat to the community.

The relative fiscal self-sufficiency of CERES and wariness of external influence and financial support is important on a psychological level for the community and contributes to the resilience of the community. To date, the fears outlined above have not been realized and CERES remains largely self-supporting, demonstrating that government or corporate leadership is not vital to the creation of solutions that enable us to live more lightly on the Earth. Rather, the example of CERES suggests that solutions lie in building community capacity, and developing and proliferating local, community-sustained and sustaining, diverse economic activities.

Organic (Dis)organization

Rydin and Holman (2004) hypothesize a lack of coordination and cooperation as significant barriers to sustainability. Community-level responses are often "organic in nature" (Newman & Dale 2005: 478), which may, in fact, be what makes them more inclusive and accessible than more structured approaches. Yet this may also be coupled with a lack of coordination and organization that can threaten the longevity of groups and activities.

At the time of the research, CERES lacked a rigid hierarchical structure and had adopted a somewhat laissez-faire management style. CERES is an incorporated not-for-profit organization governed by a Committee of Management—a Board—including a representative from Moreland City Council. All members of CERES are eligible to attend and vote at general meetings, and inspect the minutes of board meetings and financial statements. There are grievance processes in place that allow the use of mediators to address disputes between members or with the Board.

Bureaucratic details aside, CERES' management structure was understood by members as a circular organization of linked teams rather than a more typical hierarchical pyramid power structure or matrix model of management. At the time of research, there were few formalized, whole-of-community planning systems, which created some inefficiencies and communication problems. Unclear expectations and difficulties experienced in communicating and coordinating had led to frustration and confusion for some employees and for volunteers. These difficulties are exacerbated by CERES' large volunteer and part-time workforce. At the time of the interviews, there were approximately 60 full-time positions at CERES, filled by more than 100 individuals. Although this contributes to the diversity of skills and knowledge within the community, the lack of centralized, uniform communication channels for planning, policy, and operational matters, combined with unpredictable staff availability, can lead to inefficiencies, mistakes, and other difficulties.

Despite acknowledging the frustrations and inefficiencies of their organizational structure, the community remains committed to it. This more organic, dispersed model of organization and decision-making is seen as necessary for maintaining themselves as a grassroots, egalitarian organization. Indeed, they actively oppose a more corporate style of management, and despite complaints, this appeared essential to the collective identity of CERES, and to maintaining their commitment to justice and inclusion in the pursuit of sustainable alternatives. Many CERES members felt alienated and disempowered by corporate or bureaucratic management structures, yet, as indicated by the following quote, felt safe, welcome and empowered at CERES due to its apparent rejection of hierarchy: "that's par for the course of working in a community organisation, no one dictates if it could affect somebody else… I value the idea that individuals can have that level of input rather than being told" (CERES employee). Power in this context is understood in terms of *power with* one another, through the collective, through grassroots organizing and capacity building—power as "energy and competence" (Hartsock 1983: 224). This is essential to the model of experimentation and demonstration embodied at CERES. The absence of onerous, centralized decision-making processes creates spaces for experimentation, and for failing fast: "CERES is a place of experimentation or learning for everyone. So give it a go, and if it works you learn from it, if it doesn't, well, then you find something else" (CERES employee).

Some expressed concern that greater rigidity in management and decision-making structures could undermine the ability of the community to continue to "thrive on shift and change" (CERES volunteer)—a crucial component of resilience (Folke, Colding, & Berkes 2003; Folke 2006) and essential to the ongoing engagement and re-adjustments necessary for potentially and ideally enacting just sustainabilities. Despite the frustrations and inefficiencies caused by differing systems and a lack of uniformity across different areas at CERES, this was considered necessary in order to facilitate a grassroots structure and ability to innovate, create, and experiment. As such, disorganization and inefficiencies were more or less accepted and tolerated.

Return of the Sacred Kingfisher

The park that is now CERES was once a rubbish tip, which the CERES community transformed into fertile and productive land. The success of these efforts to restore the local environment saw the Sacred Kingfisher (*Todiramphus sanctus*) return to the site after a twenty-year absence. CERES has since celebrated this event with an annual festival, which celebrates "that people's efforts in improving the environment has had this result" (CERES employee). To the CERES community, the site itself with its fertility, productivity, and the presence of native wildlife demonstrates the capacity of its members "to act in concert" (Arendt 1972: 151) to "heal the Earth" (CERES volunteer) and the impacts of their tactical interventions and experiments. CERES' story of the kingfisher is built on narratives that reference the experiences of the Wurundjeri people, particularly of banishment and of returning to country (Nettle 2014). The Wurundjeri people actively work with CERES in the design and performance of the festival (Nettle 2014), and the kingfisher itself has come to symbolize the collective identity of CERES (Measham 2006).

The success of CERES relies on the passion of the community, fueled in part by their collective identity and shared values. When asked why employees and volunteers persist despite struggles and failures, one respondent replied that it was due to "commitment to the principle" (CERES employee). Many employees are responsible for initiating new projects almost single-handedly, while only working part-time. CERES employees and volunteers appear to be people who are passionate enough about the one or more of the principles or missions represented by the CERES community that they persist despite frustrations and failures. Yet this reliance on passion risks "campaign burnout" (CERES employee). It was noted that the risk of burnout was partially due to the sort of personality that was attracted to CERES: "people are passionate about things, are keen on wanting to help, so that we set ourselves up for that" (CERES employee). Burnout is not only demoralizing but can affect the achievement of outcomes, highlighting the regenerative importance of festivals, the arts, cultural celebrations, general conviviality, and the spiritual undertone of much of CERES' community life. These help protect community members from fear and despair that can otherwise affect the longevity of movements for just sustainabilities and transitions.

Building a New World in the Dump of the Old

Among its many definitions, community can be understood as a group of people with a "shared fate" (Norris et al. 2008: 128). CERES has demonstrated strong commitments to and achievements in adopting environmentally conscious and resilient behaviors, as well as the ability to deliver many key goods and services on a local scale. It balances internal community-building with externally oriented education and engagement, the human and the nonhuman, and financial independence with social interdependence. This is not to suggest that there are not some residual tensions between insider and outsider participants and the extent to which CERES is truly embracing of others. However, CERES has been successful in using its various activities to establish and maintain a strong community based on the principles of internal movement building and revitalization (Nettle 2014). Perhaps CERES' example to others is best described by Deborah Bird Rose (2013), who recognizes the work of this community as "engag[ing] with the lives and stories of nonhuman city folk with the aim of pulling back the human to make space for others... [and] where new forms of conviviality could arise" (219). The Sacred Kingfisher, CERES' most visible ambassador, through its return and its namesake festival, is evidence of this.

Communities like CERES are acting out the change they want to see in the world (Garden 2006) though ongoing daily practices—even as these practices may be partial, imperfect, and supported in part by complicity in systems they are otherwise working to undo. CERES has been particularly successful in its programs for schoolchildren, which support participants to become more "ecoliterate as they grapple with what it means to live sustainably" (Smith 2007: 35). However, although green living and sustainability are common goals for intentional communities, transferrable models for sustainability do not exist. Communities like CERES are, instead, engaging in tactical and DIY urbanism, experimentation, and hands-on learning and seeking currently unimagined solutions through community engagement and capacity building. CERES is not, nor does it purport to be, a scalable model for an entire metropolitan area; its impact and importance are more subtle. Bailey (2016) argues that CERES enacts the "think globally, act locally" ethos, and provides a sense of place and connection between people and between people and the environment, and nonhuman beings. This, Bailey contends, will help people recognize broader environmental issues, and appreciate the scale of transformation required for just, sustainable worlds, while reminding us that we are connected to each other, and our daily practices matter.

The value of CERES, as a learning case, lies in its prefigurative politics and in how it demonstrates the possibilities of *space*. Environmentally degraded wasteland can be rehabilitated, and species may return to areas they fled. Diverse, more sustainable economies can proliferate. More inclusive and just social relationships can be built and experienced with ongoing efforts. Alternative forms of organization, management, and collaboration may be trialed and implemented at a local level, even as people are increasingly alienated from mainstream politics. CERES reminds us there are possibilities in the present, and in overlooked spaces, and that partial and peripheral actions can enable us to imagine new and previously unthought worlds, and expand what is possible. As Curnow (2016: 42–3) argues:

> Prefigurative praxis operationalizes the idea of legitimate peripheral participation in that it demonstrates how participants in radical communities of practice become more radical, and in their process of becoming radical, create a world in which further radical action is possible, and indeed necessary, to realize an increasingly radical vision of transformed social relations.

It is impossible to overestimate the importance of space in the CERES project, and in prefigurative politics. Space for the community, space to experiment and practice with different modes of social and spatial organization and decision-making, space to experiment, and space to be together is essential, especially given the erosion and commodification of the public realm in many cities. The prefigurative and transformative capacities of CERES originate in its community and in its physical occupation of a large inner-suburban site—indeed, people and place co-constitute one another in this example. Prefigurative politics suggests that we can build a new world in the shell of the old. The building process will not have a fixed end; instead, it will rely on us to continually engage with each other and adjust accordingly. CERES demonstrates that we can prefigure more just and sustainable social and economic practices in the literal rubbish tips of the old world.

References

Abel N., D.H.M. Cumming, & J.M. Anderies (2006), "Collapse and reorganization in social-ecological systems: Questions, some ideas, and policy implications," *Ecology and Society*, 11(1): 17. http://www.ecologyandsociety.org/vol11/iss1/art17/.

Adger W.N. (2000), "Social and ecological resilience: Are they related?" *Progress in Human Geography*, 24(3): 347–64.

Agyeman, J., R.D. Bullard, & B. Evans (2003), *Just Sustainabilities: Development in an Unequal World*, London: Earthscan Publications Ltd.

Arendt H. (1972), *Crises of the Republic*, San Diego, CA: Harcourt Brace & Company.

Bailey, A. (2016), "Wellbeing at CERES," *PAN: Philosophy Activism Nature*, 12: 51–9.

Burgmann, V. (2003), *Power, Profit and Protest: Australian Social Movements and Globalisation*, Crows Nest, NSW: Allen & Unwin.

Cameron, J. & K. Gibson (2005), "Alternative pathways to community and economic development: The Latrobe Valley Community Partnering Project," *Geographical Research*, 43(3): 274–85.

CERES Community Environmental Park (CERES) (2016). Available online http://ceres.org.au/ (Accessed June 5, 2016).

Curnow, J. (2016), "Towards a radical theory of learning: Prefiguration as legitimate peripheral participation," in S. Springer, M.L. de Souza, & R.J. White (eds), *The Radicalization of Pedagogy: Anarchism, Geography, and the Spirit of Revolt*, 27–49, London: Rowman and Littlefield.

Danowski, D. & E. Viveiros de Castro (2017), *The Ends of the World*, trans. R. G. Nunes, Cambridge: Polity Press.

Davison, A. (2006), "New environmental movements, city gardens and the not-for-profit business, Sustaining Settlements Inc.: An obituary," in S. Paulin (ed.), *Community Voices: Creating Sustainable Spaces*, 205–18, Perth WA: University of Western Australia.

Dawson, J. (2006). "Peak oil as 'opportunity'? Overestimating the preparedness of the ecovillage and permaculture movement," *Communities*, 130: 48–50.

Dietz, T., E. Ostrom, & P.C. Stern (2003), "The struggle to govern the commons," *Science*, 302: 1907–12.

Eisenstein, C. (2011), *Sacred Economics: Money, Gift and Society in the Age of Transition*, Berkeley, CA: North Atlantic Books.

Ferman, B. & P. Kaylor (2001), "Building the spatial community: A case study of neighborhood institutions," *Policy Studies Review*, 18(4): 53–70.

Firth, C., D. Maye, & D. Pearson (2011), "Developing 'community' in community gardens," *Local Environment*, 16(6): 555–68.

Flynn, A. (2013), "Off to school we go: Inspiring Indigenous initiatives," *EarthSong Journal: Perspectives in Ecology, Spirituality and Education*, 2(5): 27–8.

Folke, C. (2006), "Resilience: The emergence of a perspective for social-ecological systems analyses," *Global Environmental Change*, 16(3): 253–67.

Folke, C., J. Colding, & F. Berkes (2003), "Synthesis: Building resilience and adaptive capacity in social-ecological systems," in F. Berkes, J. Colding, & C. Folke (eds), *Navigating Social-ecological Systems: Building Resilience for Complexity and Change*, 352–87, Cambridge: Cambridge University Press.

Frankel, B. (1987), *The Post-Industrial Utopians*, Cambridge: Polity Press.

Garden, M. (2006), "The eco-village movement: Divorced from reality," *The International Journal of Inclusive Democracy*, 2(3).

Gibson, K. & J. Cameron (2001), "Transforming communities: Towards a research agenda," *Urban Policy and Research*, 19(1): 7–24.

Gibson-Graham, J.K. (2008), "Diverse economies: Performative practices for 'other worlds,'" *Progress in Human Geography*, 32(5): 613–32.

Gibson-Graham, J.K., J. Cameron, & S. Healey (2013), *Take Back the Economy: An Ethical Guide for Transforming Our Communities*, Minneapolis: University of Minnesota Press.

Hartsock, N. (1983), *Money, Sex, and Power: Toward a Feminist Historical Materialism*, Boston: Northeastern University Press.
Kretzmann, J & J. McKnight (1996), "Assets-based community development," *National Civic Review*, 85(4): 23–9.
Lydon, M. & A. Garcia (2015), *Tactical Urbanism: Short-term Action for Long-term Change*, Washington, DC: Island Press.
Lydon, M., D. Bartman, T. Garcia, R. Preston, & R. Woudstra (2012), *Tactical Urbanism 2*, New York: The Street Plans Collaborative.
Measham, T.G. (2006), "Learning about environments: The significance of primal landscapes," *Environmental Management*, 38(3): 426–34.
Nasar, J.L. & D.A. Julian (1995), "The psychological sense of community in the neighborhood," *Journal of the American Planning Association*, 61(2): 178–84.
Nettle, C. (2014), *City Gardening as Social Action*, Surrey: Ashgate.
Newman, L. & A. Dale (2005), "The role of agency in sustainable local community development," *Local Environment*, 10(5): 477–86.
Newman, P., T. Beatley, & H. Boyer (2009), *Resilient Cities: Responding to Peak Oil and Climate Change*, Washington, DC: Island Press.
Norris, F.H., S.P. Stevens, B. Pfefferbaum, K.F. Wyche, & R.L. Pfefferbaum (2008), "Community resilience as a metaphor, theory, set of capacities, and strategy for disaster readiness," *American Journal of Community Psychology*, 41(1–2): 127–50.
Osborne, N. (2019), "For still possible cities: A politics of failure for the politically depressed," *Australian Geographer*, 50(2): 145–54.
Ostrom, E. (1990), *Governing the Commons: The Evolution of Institutions for Collective Action*, Cambridge: Cambridge University Press.
Rose, D.B. (2013), "Anthropocene noir," *Arena Journal*, 41/42: 206–19.
Rydin, Y. & N. Holman (2004), "Re-evaluating the contribution of social capital in achieving sustainable development," *Local Environment*, 9(2): 117–33.
Smith, A. (2017), "Introduction," in Incite! Women of Colour Against Violence (eds) *The Revolution Will Not Be Funded: Beyond The Non-profit Industrial Complex*, 1–18, Durham: Duke University Press.
Smith, C. (2007), "Education and society: The case for ecoliteracy," *Education and Society*, 25(1): 25–37.
Soja, E.W. (2010), *Seeking Spatial Justice*, Minneapolis: University of Minnesota Press.
Srnicek, N. & A. Williams (2015), *Inventing the Future: Postcapitalism and a World Without Work*, London: Verso Books.
Stevis, D. & R. Felli (2016), "Green transitions, just transitions? Broadening and deepening justice," *Kurswechsel*, 3: 35–45.
Stocker, L. & K. Barnett (1998), "The significance and praxis of community-based sustainability projects: Community gardens in Western Australia," *Local Environment*, 3(2): 179–189.
Tan, L.H.H. & H. Neo (2009), "'Community in Bloom': Local participation of community gardens in urban Singapore," *Local Environment*, 14(6): 529–39.
Wilson, V. (2005), "Ecological and social systems: Essential system conditions," in A. Dale & J. Onyx (eds), *A Dynamic Balance: Social Capital and Sustainable Community Development*, 33–47, Vancouver: UBC Press.
Woodcock, I., S. Wollan, & K. Dovey (2011), "Mapping neighbourhood fields of care," *State of Australian Cities National Conference*, 29 November–2 December, Melbourne, Australia. http://soac.fbe.unsw.edu.au/2011/papers/SOAC2011_0210_final.pdf

11

JUST SUSTAINABILITIES ON THE RANGE: EMPOWERING DECISIONS AT THE SOIL SURFACE

Andrea Malmberg
Tony Malmberg

Introduction

The foundation of life begins at the thickness of a dime beneath our feet. Erosion of that dime, according to the National Association of Conservation Districts (2014), generally is thought to equal five tons of soil per acre. The foundation extends downward with soil organic matter, roots, mycorrhizal fungi, and complex life that we barely understand. The stability of this foundation dictates our food quantity, its nutrient density, income to the producers, wealth of the community, level of biodiversity, and stability of our climate. Managed respectfully and equitably, soil can help us slow the release of carbon into the atmosphere, teach us to recognize and respond to the complexity within which we reside, and bridge the gap between our present reality and a just and sustainable future.

Grasslands go by many names and exist on every continent except Antarctica. In Eurasia, grasslands are referred to as steppes; in South America, they are pampas; and African grasslands are savannas. In the middle part of the United States, they are prairies, and in the west, where we live, they are rangelands. Depending on how they are defined, grasslands compose 31 to 43 percent of the earth's surface (Whittaker & Likens 1975; Atjay, Ketner, & Duvigneaud 1979; Olson, Watts, & Allison 1983). Seasonally dry is a common denominator of these landscapes, and all of this grass has to break down biologically before the next seasonal onslaught of precipitation and growth for the life cycle to continue as it has over billions of years.

For many centuries grasslands have been degrading primarily through cropland conversion of permanent grasslands and improperly managed livestock (Millennium Ecosystem Assessment 2005). Farmers have plowed and mined the most productive grasslands of the world until the remaining soil has become dirt that only has the purpose of holding plants upright, releasing an enormous amount of carbon into the atmosphere in the process. Half of all temperate grasslands and 16 percent of tropical grasslands have been converted to agricultural or industrial uses, and only 1 percent of the original tallgrass prairie exists today (Wolters

2019). In the Great Plains of the United States, homesteader plows ripped diverse grasslands, converting them to corn, wheat, and other simple monocultures. It is said the first plow sounded like rifle shots breaking deep roots, separating the soil surface from its regenerative diversity underground (Schuyler 1978).

Now, these lands are predominately home to growing annual plants that are genetically modified (GMO), fed fertilizer, sprayed with herbicides such as glyphosates, and other pesticides poisoning our food supply (Gilles-Eric Séralini et al. 2014). Most of these crops do not feed people directly but instead feed livestock in confined animal operations (CAFOs). Without the rich regenerative process of diverse root systems drawing deep minerals, decomposition from massive herds of herbivores, and a covered soil surface binding and holding water and soil from erosion, the soil is depleted, blanched, washed, and baked. For the farmers and CAFO managers, escalating inputs require a cash crop and government subsidies to secure mortgages and operating loans. This becomes a negative feedback loop tied to dependence on seed and chemical companies and Wall Street speculation on commodity crops as machinery depreciates, and many families require jobs in towns, or in energy extraction, just to make ends meet. Many of those who grow our food and fiber commiserate with each other about escalating interest rates, federal reserve policy, John Deere tractors, government corruption, minimum wages, regulations, land taking, herbicide and fertilizer costs, as dime after dime of our foundation blow away, wash away, and become dead to life. The result is a tangled social and environmental crisis that exacerbates poverty, hunger, rural migrations, droughts, and floods, and leads to the loss of place-based traditions and knowledge.

Over a billion people call grasslands home, all with their own pastoral traditions. From the Masai to the gaucho to the cowboy to the herder, pastoralists derive their livelihoods from grasslands, mostly through livestock production for food and fiber (Ragab & Prudhomme 2002; Neely, Bunning, & Wiles 2009). These varied place-based traditions affect the management of grasslands, and more broadly, their management of this ecological complexity affects all of humanity.

Due to the current climate crisis, healthy grasslands are critically important to humanity's survival, and the states of these environments are dependent upon how pastoralists steward these lands (Notenbaert et al. 2012). While forests store more tons of carbon per hectare, they only comprise 28 percent of the landmass (White, Murray, & Rohweder 2000). Moreover, pastoralists can restore grasslands' ecological function much more quickly than forests (Xu et al. 2019). Grasslands' inherent ability to store more carbon in their soils than any other environment deserves special attention, as does the evolutionary symbiotic relationship between healthy grasslands and ruminants. Despite their global importance, pastoralists are often ignored or viewed as artifacts of the past at best and vilified and forcefully removed from their ancestral lands at worst (Thomson & Homewood 2002; Nori 2007). Pastoral communities are increasingly becoming marginalized and generally not given due consideration in wider sociopolitical analyses (International Fund for Agricultural Development 2010). However, it would serve humanity well at this critical time to honor the importance of pastoralists and to build their capacity to thrive because of the ecological wealth that functional grasslands can provide.

In a time of crisis, we may find false comfort in denial or react with extremes. This tendency results in treating symptoms without recognizing and reaching the complexity of the underlying systems and the ways in which they reinforce or counteract existing sustainability and justice concerns. How do we get past the hyperbole, confirmation bias, paralysis of paradox, outright lies, and the tweet of the minute? We must define what is at risk, look past the symptoms to identify the root causes of the problems, and find the most significant points of leverage to remedy the situations.

Although many attempts have been made to adopt technical solutions to reverse grassland degradation, most involve large amounts of capital and expensive technology, including energy inputs from unsustainable sources, can be culturally inappropriate, and have not been successful in creating large-scale, sustained improvements to the landscape (Dregne & Chou 1994). Fortunately, a convergent evolution of thought, much of it building on lessons from indigenous practice, occurred a few generations ago. Masanobu Fukuoka from Japan, Bill Mollison from Australia, J.I. Rodale and Rachel Carson from the United States, and Allan Savory from Zimbabwe inspired the growth of many different disciplines that have improved land management, grown healthier food, and increased biodiversity (Rodale 1961; Carson 1962; Fukuoka 1978; Hombre 1979; Savory & Parsons 1980). We argue that Allan Savory's holistic management decision-making framework that guides pastoralists around the globe in livestock management practice has great potential to help restore degraded grasslands across many geographies, economies, and cultures within their cultural and spatial context. (Holling & Meffe 1996; Tainton, Aucamp, & Danckwerts 1999).

To achieve restoration and sustain it worldwide requires little to no technology, but it does require sociocultural shifts that embrace decision-making and management procedures readily adapted to the local context. The soil surface, that dime-sized layer on which we stand, is the place where justice and sustainability efforts must start. Many progressive farmers and ranchers, from the Great Plains of the United States, to Patagonia, to the Savannahs of Botswana, to the Outback of Australia, collectively referred to here as pastoralists, have changed their decision-making to drive ecological restoration and quality of life, which does not have to come at the expense of production and profit. They focus on creating healthy soils and enhancing ecological function—water and mineral cycles, solar energy flow to maximize photosynthesis, and biodiversity—in turn renewing the foundation upon which we and future generations will depend. With place-based and collective decision-making starting at the soil surface, regenerating grasslands has the potential to create sustainability rooted in social and soil justice.

Empowerment of Pastoralists at the Soil Surface

Empowering decisions at the soil surface takes root within a given local context—every soil surface is located in a specific place—yet simultaneously requires a global view. First, land managers need access to knowledge and skills that reject the reductionist thinking that produces monocultures and instead embraces biodiversity. Industrial agriculture education that predominates our institutions misses how we manage complexity. Being self-organizing, nature's complexity cannot be controlled but only influenced by a humble land steward.

Who are these land stewards? Pastoralism is an ancient form of agriculture that is still in extensive use today throughout the world (Weber & Horst 2011). Through animal husbandry, pastoralists care, tend to, and use animals such as camels, goats, cattle, yaks, llamas, and sheep to support their livelihoods. Pastoralism generally has a mobile aspect, moving herds to fresh pasture and water. Pastoralists live in places where the potential for crop cultivation is limited due to low and highly variable precipitation, steep terrain, or extreme temperatures, and have developed adaptive mechanisms for their unpredictable, vulnerable, and dynamic environments (International Fund for Agricultural Development 2010).

Pastoralism exists in many variations throughout the world. Horses are the preferred species for most pastoralists in Mongolia and elsewhere in Central Asia, while in East Africa, the preference is cattle. In the mountainous regions of Southwest Asia, pastoralists mainly keep sheep and goats, wherein the lowland areas of the region camels are preferred, as is the case in North and East Africa. Among the Saami people or Lapps of northern Scandinavia, it is reindeer. Composition of herds, management practices, social organization, and all other aspects of pastoralism vary between areas and between social groups. Many traditional practices have also had to adapt to the changing circumstances of the modern world, including climatic conditions affecting the availability of forages and sociopolitical realities. Ranches of the United States and Canada, estancias in Patagonia, and sheep and cattle stations of Australia are modern variations of traditional practices that embody traditional skills (Malmberg 2013).

Many of these changes are negatively impacting agricultural communities throughout the world, resulting in increasing levels of depression and suicide (Rosmann 2010), although we do not have data on pastoralists in particular. Statistics show the suicide rate is higher among farmers than other occupations in the United States, India, Japan, the United Kingdom, and Australia (Sanne et al. 2004). In the past, studies have shown that farmers, in general, had better mental health than the average working population; some research shows that this advantage may be decreasing (Thelin 1995). What has changed? Why is it that many food and fiber producers are no longer enjoying the well-being they deserve? Proposed explanations for this trend include removing people from traditional livelihoods through mechanization, financial strain, and social isolation (Sanne et al. 2004).

Although many grasslands have been badly degraded (much of it through improperly managed livestock), it is possible to properly manage livestock to reverse this trend—but we must recognize our dependence upon pastoralists to make this happen. Grasslands evolved with herbivores (Frank, McNaughton, & Tracy 1998), and pastoralists can use their herds to mimic this ancient relationship, ensure the biodiversity of grasslands, and prevent them from deteriorating into scrubland and deserts (Krätli et al. 2013). How can we support pastoralists and land under their control to provide the ecosystem services that humanity needs?

In addition to the knowledge access mentioned earlier, we need funding from an equity community that does not rely on government-funded programs and cash crops, as well as consumer support appreciating the added value of nutrient-dense foods to keep our dollars circulating in the community.

At the core of the idea of empowering decisions at the soil surface is a set of goals focused not only on producing commodities but on envisioning an improved quality of life—for both producers and consumers—by restoring biodiversity and complexity to the land. There is no way to live on the land and not change it— any planning for future justice or sustainability must acknowledge this upfront. However, change need not continue the degradation of resources and habitat. A change in mindset, including sociocultural practices, can recognize and value the interconnectedness of our social structures with the hidden soil. The driver of change comes from understanding this new framework, how we build soil rather than growing the assets of global industrial, agricultural monopolies. Well-managed grasslands have a crucial role to play globally as providers of livelihoods, water catchments, in-soil water reservoirs, and diverse habitats for a multitude of plants and animals (Milchunas & Lauenroth 1993); with sound planning and action, pastoralists and supporters can restore grasslands to a healthy biota by substituting past ideals of maximum efficiency and commodity production with ideals that allow for a complex diversity of habitat. This understanding, turned into practice, can reverse harmful trends; under restorative management, degraded grasslands can enhance soil carbon sequestration (Allard et al. 2007; Soussana, Tallec, & Blanfort 2010; Teague et al. 2011). Many of the socially linked issues that torment us—soil erosion, poor food quality, high operating costs, climate change, fractured families—are symptoms of the same cheap, destructive, and discriminatory food policies that are always driving higher production. To get out of this rut, we must choose to create healthy soil, healthy animals, nutrient-dense foods, and scalable markets for locally based food. The key to managing for just sustainabilities (Agyeman 2013), which includes society, food, ecosystems, and a just climate, begins by empowering decisions at the soil surface.

From the Paralysis of Paradox to Empowering Decisions at the Soil Surface

Unfortunately, most climate change advocates fiercely resist the idea of using grazing animals, particularly livestock, to sequester carbon in soils. There are several reasons for this, all of which create barriers to empowering decisions at the soil surface:

1. Misunderstanding of the capacity of grassland soils to sequester carbon;
2. Ignorance of the extent of carbon emissions from soil loss through human activity;
3. The degradation caused by improperly managed livestock; and
4. The obsession with emissions reductions.

Obstacles to reestablishing the evolutionary grassland–grazer relationship for long-term sequestration of carbon in soils include assumptions based on conventional livestock mismanagement, such as:

1. Grazing animals chronically overgraze rangelands and destroy soils, which must be rested to be restored;
2. Soils are a limited carbon sink, and new biologically generated soils are not part of the equation; and
3. Soil sequestration of carbon is only significant in the first thirty centimeters, and soil carbon cycles through the atmosphere in twenty-five years or less.

A better understanding of how grassland soils function and the role grazing animals can play, if managed properly, in rebuilding them to enhance their carbon-storing capacity may begin to turn this troubling situation around.

The modern industrial approach to animal husbandry, including grain-feeding cattle in gigantic feedlots, has distorted the broad conception of what it means to raise cattle and other grazing animals. The broad paradigm commonly and erroneously believes that any grazing by livestock degrades grasslands and causes desertification (Savory & Butterfield 1999; Janzen 2011). However, in the past, herds of grazers remain bunched in response to predators and kept on the move to avoid feeding on ground fouled by their wastes, thereby aerating, fertilizing, and restoring the soils (Frank, McNaughton, & Tracy 1998) and deepening plant roots (Baskin 2005); furthermore, in a complex grass, forb, and shrub community, microbes in the soil eat what little methane livestock produce (Hristov 2012). Under natural conditions, these herds tended not to return to an area until it had recovered. Unfortunately, over time, the wild herds have been replaced by small numbers of domestic, sedentary livestock, interrupting the cycle of biological decay in grasslands and turning once-rich soils into dry, exposed desert land, dramatically decreasing the effectiveness of rainfall (Savory & Butterfield 1999). The knee-jerk assumption that "cows are bad" must therefore be overcome in order to achieve regenerative landscapes. Indeed, prioritizing crops over livestock to "feed our hungry world" ignores the fact that arable land is not distributed evenly; in the vast region extending across North Africa, through China and India, 5 percent of the land at best can grow crops. The remaining 95 percent can only feed people from livestock (Savory 2013).

Realizing Just Sustainabilities Through Holistic Management

Often people in livestock production are demonized as destroyers of the environment. However, depending on how they manage livestock, grasslands, and soils, pastoralists can be champions in mitigating climate change. Alkon and Agyeman (2011) note the importance of including multiple perspectives in sustainability efforts, saying:

Our goal in highlighting these additional stories is not to chastise the food movement, but to work toward building a stronger and deeper critique of industrialized agriculture, which includes injustice along with environmental and social degradation. If activists in the food movement are to go beyond providing alternatives and truly challenge agribusiness's destructive power, they will need a broad coalition of supporters. (3)

The injustice along with the environmental and social degradation that Agyeman, Bullard, & Evans (2002) refer to can be addressed when land managers have the power to build healthy soils, thereby sequestering carbon, increasing production, producing nutritiously dense food, supporting social justice through food justice, and addressing climate justice through ecological justice.

The good news is that numerous instances from around the world attest to the fact that degraded grasslands can be restored by properly managing livestock to benefit biodiversity and ecosystem health (Hodgson & Illius 1996; Tainton, Aucamp, & Danckwerts 1999). Holistic management (Savory & Butterfield 1999) is one such tool to bridge this gap; this approach embraces and honors the complexity of nature, using nature's models to bring practical approaches to land management and restoration. Most land management policies today address symptoms of biological diversity loss and land degradation, rather than root causes, rendering the policies ineffective and unsuccessful. Holistic management emphasizes the interconnectedness of all life, recognizing that human actions have myriad unintended consequences that ripple well beyond our area of influence. By acknowledging the complexity of the natural world and using the holistic framework, decisions can be made that are simultaneously environmentally regenerative, socially sound, and financially viable in the short and long term. Critically, pastoralists' decisions also must enhance their own well-being. These decisions will need to be born from the specific grassland and social context and will not always look the same, in line with the plural natures of just sustainabilities.

How can we navigate from degradation to a future of just sustainability? To achieve restoration and sustainable use of resources worldwide requires low-input technology, as well as management procedures that are adaptable and use a suitable flexible framework to restore ecosystem function (Savory & Butterfield 1999; Chiavegato et al. 2015). Inspired by Allan Savory, holistic management practitioners throughout the world have been learning how to restore grasslands by emphasizing the synergistic nature of eco-restoration and reestablishing evolutionary relationships between grazing animals and grasslands. This simultaneously provides ecosystem services through building soil, water, and plant resources (Barnes et al. 2008; Lovell 2011). Holistic management's unique decision-making process brings contextual relevance to diverse situations, enabling just sustainability. The holistic management decision-making process defines the Whole Under Management and checks potential outcomes ensuring resilience within one's holistic context. The remainder of Holistic Management Framework can be seen as a set of prompts helping us execute getting from here to there, asking the right questions to identify skills we will need to mimic nature and its self-organizing scheme of life and death.

Managing the Unmanageable

Every tool can be misused, hence terms like "overgrazing" and "overrest." Grazing and rest can be good or bad, depending on the context of the situation, and the how, when, where, and what of livestock management can be adjusted to improve rangeland health. First, the manager must consider the local environment, the topography, infrastructure, production, season, plant diversity, ecological condition, skills, knowledge, labor, and money. This myriad of complexity changes every year, if not every season. The success of influencing complexity toward a regenerative outcome rests with the cowboy, the gaucho, the herder, and the pastoralist closest to the soil surface.

Ecosystems are shaped by tools of rest, living organisms including grazing/animal impact, fire, and technology. In the past, these tools were influenced by natural predator–prey relationships which kept animals moving; technology use by indigenous populations was also governed by movement, as the use of horses, arrows, and spears followed animal movement, unlike modern use of technology which interrupts natural processes (Savory & Butterfield 1999). Holistic Planned Grazing manages the movement of animals to mimic the nature that developed our ecosystems. Execution of the grazing plan routinely monitors grazing and trampling, adjusting timings as needed. This feedback loop is an essential element of holistic management: managers plan, monitor the plan, control, adjust, replan, and repeat (Savory & Bufferfield 1999).

The paradox of assuming our plan will be wrong (or incomplete, or short-lived, or misconceived) remains critical to designing a relevant monitoring plan, given the complexity of natural systems. By assuming we are wrong, we can identify the earliest warning indicator to signal that we are going off track—indicators like percent of bare ground, species diversity, residual cover, plant litter, livestock performance, and more. Indeed, even criticism of, and controversy over, holistic management itself (Holechek et al. 2000; Joseph et al. 2002) ensures continuing questioning and investigation of grazing practices. This lends support to the need for ongoing iterative engagement with questions of sustainability and justice in practice.

Planning and Execution

Holistic management practitioners must plan for the onset of the growing season and the onset of the nongrowing season. In the growing season, once a plant has been bitten, its roots and leaves need a recovery period to regrow. If bitten again before recovery, the plant will be overgrazed. In the dormant season, grassland plants are not growing or only growing very slowly; the plants will not be overgrazed and so recovery periods are not as necessary to plan in the nongrowing season. Insuring an adequate amount of forage for livestock and wildlife is the primary goal of the nongrowing season plan. Animals perform much better if they continue to move off the ground they have fouled with their own dung and urine and do not return to the same piece of ground more than a few times before the new growing season starts.

By using the tools of grazing and animal impact and monitoring plant recovery, measurable regeneration of the land begins within the first year, and, in as few as three years, many long-disabled processes come back to life. Dung beetles return, retrieving ruminant dung and storing it beneath the surface, creating new soil and storing carbon in the process (Richardson & Richardson 2000). Worms and small mammals such as moles and prairie dogs churn the soil, while deep-rooted perennial grasses regrow and create channels for water and nutrient absorption. Mycorrhizal fungi transport nutrients they obtain from soil minerals and exchange them for carbohydrates from photosynthesizing plants. The fungi synthesize a stable glycoprotein—glomalin—which holds four to twenty times its weight in water. Microorganisms join the elaborate fray and, in the process, create complex carbon molecules that store carbon deep in the soils for an extended period (Ragab & Prudhomme 2002). These are the healthy soils that holistic managers throughout the world strive to recreate, capturing carbon, providing food, reestablishing effective water and mineral cycles, and imparting beauty to the land.

Overcoming Paradox

Despite the common illusion that we can manage natural resources and control multiple variables, complexity self-organizes. Nature functions in wholes, and a holistic perspective is essential; the path to ecological justice requires flexibility to follow and mimic the self-organizing processes toward greater diversity and complexity, and ultimately regeneration. The paradox? We cannot manage complexity, like ecosystems, social systems, and economies; we can only influence their self-organization. If we assume changing one variable will result in our desired outcome, we are likely to be disappointed. Humility is key for reaching a continually developing and evolving functional ecosystem.

Holistic management begins by defining our holistic context, which includes our "Whole Under Management," describing the present state of our land and the people and money involved. Then, we describe our desired quality of life, grounded on a fully functional ecosystem, including plant diversity, fertile soil, and abundant wildlife. Finally comes the essential question of holistic management: "How must I behave to bridge the present reality to our desired Quality of Life and Future Resource Base" (Savory & Butterfield 2016).

As another facet of complexity, different environments respond differently to the same tool. The brittleness scale describes how decomposition happens from primarily biological in a tropical rainforest to primarily chemical (fire and oxidation) in a desert. Biological decomposition will build soil without grazing in a rainforest, but in a setting without constant humidity at the soil surface, like most grasslands throughout the world, biological decomposition must come through the gut of a grazing animal. Even two environments equal on the brittleness scale, but different in terms of plant production, respond differently to the same tool. Lower production environments require more extended recovery periods to build enough plant material to cover the soil surface. Higher production environments require more frequent grazing to keep the plant base open to sunlight energy.

Many of our industrial technologies and cultural ideologies want to control nature's attempt to express diversity by sustaining monocultures rather than build on evolutionary forces, but if we fail to mimic nature, our grasslands will never perform as they evolved, shaped by the predatory-prey connection. Paradoxically, despite the misleading term "overgrazing," the governing factor is time, not numbers. Overgrazing results primarily from land ownership and fencing that stops the natural movement of grazing animals. Holistic managers rethink the use of a fence to mimic nature and manage plant recovery periods, including when and for how long plants are grazed.

Just Sustainabilities on the Range

Since the 1970s, holistic management's effectiveness has been well documented on millions of hectares on four continents (Stinner, Stinner, & Marsolf 1997; McCosker 2000; Muñoz-Erickson, Aguilar-González, & Sisk 2007; McLachlan & Yestrau 2009; Alfaro-Arguello et al. 2010; Sherren, Fischer, & Fazey 2012; Ferguson et al. 2013; Teague et al. 2013). The sequestration potential of restored grasslands, when applied to up to 5 billion hectares of degraded soils, could return 10 billion tons or more of excess atmospheric carbon to the terrestrial sink annually (Conant 2010). Moreover, we can do this while restoring agricultural productivity, increasing retention of soil water to rebuild "in-soil reservoirs," improving the living conditions of livestock, and enhancing wildlife habitat—while also supplying high-quality protein for millions and providing jobs for thousands of people in rural communities. All these goals are simultaneous and interconnected, and the previous success of holistic management suggests a paradox in itself: that although ongoing radical humility and skepticism are key to the practice of just sustainabilities, we might still have reason for hope, which, like the soil, only needs to be the thickness of a dime.

References

Agyeman, J. (2013), *Introducing Just Sustainabilities: Policy, Planning and Practice*, London: Zed Books.
Agyeman, J, R.D. Bullard, & B. Evans (2002), "Exploring the nexus: Bringing together sustainability, environmental justice and equity," *Space & Polity*, 6(1): 77–90.

Alfaro-Arguello, R., S.A.W. Diemont, B.G. Ferguson, J.F. Martin, J. Nahed-Toral, J.D. Álvarez-Solís, & R. Pinto Ruíz (2010), "Steps toward sustainable ranching: An emergy evaluation of conventional and holistic management in Chiapas, Mexico," *Agricultural Systems*, 103(9): 639-46.

Alkon, A.H. & J. Agyeman (2011), "Introduction: The food movement as polyculture," in A.H. Alkon & J. Agyeman (eds), *Cultivating Food Justice: Race, Class and Sustainability*, 1-20, Cambridge: MIT Press.

Allard, V., J.F. Soussana, R. Falcimagne, P. Berbigier, J.M. Bonnefond, E. Ceschia, P. D'hour, C.Hénault, P.Laville, C. Martin, & C. Pinarès-Patino (2007), "The role of grazing management for the net biome productivity and greenhouse gas budget of semi-natural grassland," *Agriculture, Ecosystems & Environment*, 121(1): 47-58.

Atjay, G.L., P. Ketner, & P. Duvigneaud (1979), "Terrestrial primary production and phytomass," in B. Bolin, E.T. Degens, S. Kempe, & P. Ketner (eds), *The Global Carbon Cycle*, 129-81, Chichester: John Wiley & Sons.

Barnes, K., B.E. Norton, M. Maeno, & J.C. Malechek (2008), "Paddock size and stocking density affect spatial heterogeneity of grazing," *Rangeland Ecology & Management*, 61(4): 380-8.

Baskin, Y. (2005), *Under Ground: How Creatures of Mud and Dirt Shape Our World*, Washington, DC: Island Press.

Carson, R. (1962), *Silent Spring*, Boston: Houghton Mifflin.

Chiavegato, M.B., J.E. Rowntree, D. Carmichael, & W.J. Powers (2015), "Enteric methane from lactating beef cows managed with high- and low-input grazing systems," *Journal of Animal Science*, 93(3): 1365-75.

Conant, R.T. (2010), *Challenges and Opportunities for Carbon Sequestration in Grassland Systems: A Technical Report on Grassland Management and Climate Change Mitigation, Plant Production & Protection Division*, Food & Agriculture Organization of the United Nations (FAO).

Dregne, H.E. & N. Chou (1994), "Global desertification dimensions and costs," in H.E. Dregne (ed), *Degradation and Restoration of Arid Lands*, 249-82, Lubbock: Texas Technical University.

Ferguson, B. G., S.A. Diemont, R. Alfaro-Arguello, J.F. Martin, J. Nahed-Toral, D. Álvarez-Solís, & R. Pinto-Ruíz (2013), "Sustainability of holistic and conventional cattle ranching in the seasonally dry tropics of Chiapas, Mexico," *Agricultural Systems*, 120: 38-48.

Frank, D. A., S.J. McNaughton, & B.F. Tracy (1998), "The ecology of the Earth's grazing ecosystems," *Bioscience*, 48: 513-21.

Fukuoka, M. (1978), *The One-straw Revolution: An Introduction to Natural Farming*, Emmaus: Rodale Press.

Gilles-Eric, S., E.C.R Mesnage, S. Gress, N. Defarge, M. Malatesta, D. Hennequin, & J. Spiroux de Vendômois (2014), "Long-term toxicity of a Roundup herbicide and a Roundup-tolerant genetically modified maize," *Environmental Sciences Europe*, 26: 14.

Hodgson, J. & A.W. Illius (eds) (1996), *The Ecology and Management of Grazing Systems*, London: CAB.

Holechek, J L, H. Gomes, F. Molinar, D. Galt, & R. Valdez (2000), "Short-duration grazing: The facts in 1999," *Rangelands*, 22(1): 18-22.

Holling, C.S. & G.K. Meffe (1996), "Command and control and the pathology of natural resource management," *Conservation Biology*, 10(2): 328-37.

Hombre, D. (1979), *Permaculture One: A Perennial Agriculture for Human Settlements*, Sisters Creek: Tagari Publications.

Hristov, A.N. (2012), "Historic, pre-European settlement, and present-day contribution of wild ruminants to enteric methane emissions in the United States," *Journal of Animal Science*, 90: 1371–5.

International Fund for Agricultural Development (2010), *Livestock and Pastoralists*, Rome: International Fund for Agricultural Development.

Janzen, H.H. (2011) "What place for livestock on a re-greening earth," *Animal Feed Science & Technology*, 166(167): 783–96.

Joseph, J., F. Molinar, D. Galt, R. Valdez, & J. Holechek (2002), "Short duration grazing research in Africa: An extensive review of the Charter Grazing Trials and other short duration grazing studies on African rangelands," *Rangelands* 24(4): 9–12.

Krätli, S., C. Huelsebusch, B. Brooks, & B. Kaufmann (2013), "Pastoralism: A critical asset for food security under global climate change," *Animal Frontiers*, 3(1): 42–50.

Lovell, T. (2011), "Soil Carbon: Putting Carbon Back Where It Belongs," *TEDx Talk*. Available online: http://www.youtube.com/watch?v=wgmssrVInP0 (Accessed June 17, 2020).

Malmberg, A.M. (2013), "Flourishing pastoralists: Managing for well-being while restoring the grasslands of the world," MAPP capstone, College of Liberal & Professional Studies, University of Pennsylvania, Philadelphia.

McCosker, T. (2000), "Cell grazing—The first 10 years in Australia," *Tropical Grasslands*, 34(3): 207–218.

McLachlan, S.M. & M. Yestrau (2009), "From the ground up: Holistic management and grassroots rural adaptation to bovine spongiform encephalopathy across western Canada," *Mitigating Strategies Global Change*, 14: 299–316.

Milchunas, D.G. & W.K. Lauenroth (1993), "Quantitative effects of grazing on vegetation and soils over a global range of environments," *Ecological Monographs*, 63(4): 327–66.

Millennium Ecosystem Assessment (2005), *Ecosystems & Human Well-Being*. Available online: http://www.bioquest.org/wp-content/blogs.dir/files/2009/06/ecosystems-and-health.pdf (Accessed June 17, 2020).

Muñoz-Erickson, T.A., B. Aguilar-González, & T.D. Sisk (2007), "Linking ecosystem health indicators and collaborative management: A systematic framework to evaluate ecological and social outcomes," *Ecology & Society*, 12(2): 6.

National Association of Conservation Districts (2014), *New Landowner's Manual*. Available online: https://www.nacdnet.org/wp-content/uploads/2016/06/New_Landowners_Manual_4.2014.pdf (Accessed June 17, 2020).

Neely, C., S. Bunning, & A. Wiles (2009), *Review of Evidence on Drylands Pastoral Systems and Climate Change: Implication and Opportunities for Mitigation and Adaptation*, Rome: Food & Agriculture Organization of the United Nations.

Nori, M. (2007), *Mobile Livelihoods, Patchy Resources and Shifting Rights: Approaching Pastoral Territories*, Rome: International Land Coalition.

Notenbaert, A. M., J. Davies, J. De Leeuw, M. Said, M. Herrero, P. Manzano, & S. Omondi (2012), "Policies in support of pastoralism and biodiversity in the heterogeneous drylands of East Africa," *Pastoralism*, 2(1): 1–17.

Olson, J.S., J.A. Watts, & L.J. Allison (1983), "Carbon in live vegetation of major world ecosystems," *Report ORNL-5862*, Oak Ridge National Laboratory.

Ragab, R. & C. Prudhomme (2002), "Soil and water: Climate change and water resources management in arid and semi-arid regions: Prospective and challenges for the 21st Century," *Biosystems Engineering*, 81(1): 3–34

Richardson, P.Q. & R.H. Richardson (2000), "Dung beetles and their effects on soil," *Ecological Restoration*, 18: 116–7.

Rodale, J.I. (1961), *How to Grow Vegetables and Fruits by the Organic Method*, Emmaus: Rodale Books.

Rosmann, M.R. (2010), "The agrarian imperative," *Journal of Agromedicine*, 15(2): 71–5.

Sanne B., A. Mykletun, B.E. Moen, A.A. Dahl, & G.S. Tell (2004), "Farmers are at risk for anxiety and depression: The Hordaland health study," *Occupational Medicine*, 54: 92–100.

Savory, A. (2013), *The Grazing Revolution: A Radical Plan to Save the Earth*, New York: TED Books, 39.

Savory, A. & J. Butterfield (1999), *Holistic Management: A New Framework for Decision Making*, Washington, DC: Island Press.

Savory, A. & J. Butterfield (2016), *Holistic Management: A Commonsense Revolution to Restore Our Environment*, Washington, DC: Island Press.

Savory, A. & S. Parsons (1980), "The Savory Grazing Method," *Rangelands*, 2: 234–7.

Schuyler, M.W. (1978), "The plow the broke the plains," Buffalo County Historical Society, 1(4). Available online: http://www.bchs.us/BTales_197804.htm (Accessed June 17, 2020).

Sherren, K., J. Fischer, & I. Fazey (2012), "Managing the grazing landscape: Insights foragricultural adaptation from a mid-drought photo-elicitation study in the Australian sheep-wheat belt," *Agricultural Systems*, 106(1): 72–83.

Soussana, J.F., T. Tallec, & V. Blanfort (2010), "Mitigating the greenhouse gas balance of ruminant production systems through carbon sequestration in grasslands," *Animal*, 4(3): 334–50.

Stinner, D.H., B.R. Stinner, & E. Marsolf (1997), "Biodiversity as an organizing principle in agroecosystem management: Case studies of holistic resource management practitioners in the USA," *Agriculture, Ecosystems & Environment*, 62: 199–213.

Tainton, N.M., A.J. Aucamp, & J.E. Danckwerts (1999), "Principles of managing veld," in N.M. Tainton (ed.), *Veld Management in South Africa*, 169–93, Pietermaritzburg: University of Natal Press.

Teague, W.R., S.L. Dowhower, S.A. Baker, N. Haile, P.B. DeLaune, & D.M. Conover (2011), "Grazing management impacts on vegetation, soil biota and soil chemical, physical and hydrological properties in tall grass prairie," *Agriculture, Ecosystems & Environment*, 141(3): 310–22.

Teague, W.R., F. Provenza, U. Kreuter, T. Steffens, & M. Barnes (2013), "Multi-paddock grazing on rangelands: Why the perceptual dichotomy between research results and rancher experience?" *Journal of Environmental Management*, 128: 699–717.

Thelin, A. (1995). "Psychosocial factors in farming," *Annals of Agricultural and Environmental Medicine*, 2(2): 1–26.

Thomson, M. & K. Homewood (2002), "Entrepreneurs, elites and exclusion in Maasailand: Trends in wildlife conservation and pastoralist development," *Human Ecology*, 30: 107–38.

Weber, K.T. & S. Horst (2011), "Desertification and livestock grazing: The roles of sedentarization, mobility and rest," *Pastoralism: Research, Policy & Practice*, 1(1): 1–19.

White, R., S. Murray, & M. Rohweder (2000), *Pilot Analysis of Global Ecosystems: Grassland Ecosystems*, Washington, DC: World Resources Institute.

Whittaker, R.H. & E. Likens (1975), "The biosphere and man," in H. Lieth & R.H. Whittaker (eds), *Primary Productivity of the Biosphere, Ecological Studies*, Table 15-1, 305–28, Berlin: Springer-Verlag.

Wolters, C. (2019), "Grassland threats explained," *National Geographic*, August 22. Available online: https://www.nationalgeographic.com/environment/habitats/grassland-threats/ (Accessed June 17, 2020).

Xu, S., J. Rowntree, P. Borrelli, J. Hodbod, & M.R. Raven (2019), "Ecological health index: A short term monitoring method for land managers to assess grazing lands ecological health," *Environments*, 6: 67.

12

WELCOME TO TUBMAN HOUSE

Anthony Bayani Rodriguez

At a corner lot on Presbury Street, where a vacant rowhouse once stood, are several raised garden beds made of plywood where apples, corn, radishes, dinosaur kale, watermelons, squash, peppers, herbs, strawberries, yams, garlic, and sunflowers grow. In this neighborhood there are more liquor stores than health clinics or playgrounds combined, and the nearest affordable grocery store with fresh produce is a half-hour trip by bus. But, five years ago a group of local organizers came up with a plan. They claimed that place on behalf of the neighborhood and began building a "safe zone" for their community. Besides the food, local residents come for free educational programs, teach-ins, movies, and discussions of local, national, and international issues. At the Juneteenth block party there will be barbecue, music, games, free haircuts, presentations on Black history, and meditation classes. Meanwhile, the children have work to do. Tomorrow, "Mr. Farmer" will meet them at the new passively heated greenhouse and solar-powered aquaponics system for more lessons on photosynthesis, composting, and renewable energy.

The geographies of social inequality in the early twenty-first century are as palpable as the planet's climbing temperatures, rising sea levels, and continually growing list of endangered species. Significant weather events over the past two decades reiterate that the toll of environmental hazards is not experienced uniformly. It is well understood that poverty and political disenfranchisement are among the strongest determinants of individual and collective risk of injury, sickness, or death as a result of ecological disturbances (Shepard et al. 2013). This applies to the destructive force wrought by tsunamis and hurricanes, as well as to the spread of infectious diseases. Structurally marginalized people are far more vulnerable to such phenomenon, but neither because they simply *happen* to live in areas where nature wreaks havoc nor because of any biologically predetermined susceptibilities. In the wake of the mass death and displacement suffered by residents of the city of New Orleans' poorest and Blackest neighborhoods after Hurricane Katrina, in 2005, geographer Neil Smith put it plainly enough: "There is no such thing as a natural disaster, and the supposed naturalness of the market is the last place to look for a solution to this disastrous havoc" (Smith 2006).

A group of local organizers in Baltimore, Maryland, known as "The 1619 Coalition," decided in 2016 that the only viable solutions for the challenges faced by the residents of the 72-block neighborhood of Sandtown-Winchester would have to be determined by the community itself. "Neighborhood improvement" schemes of city officials and developers have persistently failed to address underlying forms of disenfranchisement, disinvestment, and structural inequality that impact nearly every facet of people's lives in Sandtown-Winchester. This chapter examines the conditions that led to the formation of the 1619 Coalition and the political ambitions behind their distinctive approach to transformative justice. Their efforts represent a model of what "just sustainabilities" (Agyeman, Bullard, & Evans 2003) ought to mean in theory and in practice.

A Legacy of Inequality

The City of Baltimore's waste output persistently exceeds the collection and disposal capacities of its Department of Public Works, and recent studies show that basic city services and public amenities are far less consistent in areas of Baltimore with a Black majority of residents (Brown 2016; Dance 2017). In 2019 residents issued complaints about garbage trucks passing through Sandtown-Winchester, leaving trash bins unemptied or knocked over (Ortiz 2019). Residents also reported illegal garbage dumping in alleys (Ortiz 2019). Stretches of unkempt streets are among the visible reminders of overlapping regimes of economic disinvestment and political disenfranchisement that have devastated neighborhoods in East and West Baltimore. At a 2017 rally organized by the 1619 Coalition, one community activist held a sign commemorating the once "vibrant Black community" of the neighborhood that had been "destroyed by capitalism, drained of all wealth by the rich, murdered by the government, mis-educated by crooks, [and] butchered by the cops," noting that "the people still fight on" (Tubman House Baltimore 2017). This transformation brings into focus economic and political forces that continue to shape the city's geographies of inequality, highlighting a pattern in twentieth- and early twenty-first-century American urban policy and planning in which structurally marginalized people and communities pay the immediate and long-term, intended and unintended costs of urban development, renewal, and *re*development.

In 2016, Dr. Lawrence Brown, a professor of community health and policy at Morgan State University, plotted the location of White majority and Black majority neighborhoods in Baltimore on a city map. White majority neighborhoods were concentrated within the borders of the most expensive neighborhoods of Downtown and the Inner Harbor, in the shape of a capital letter "L." Black majority neighborhoods were concentrated throughout the lower-income areas on either side of the "L," resembling the wings of a butterfly. Further investigations revealed spatialized patterns of "structured advantage" and "structured disadvantage" that corresponded with the "White L" and the "Black Butterfly" (Brown 2016). Examples of "structured advantage" that were mapped in this study included the historical application of city policies and practices that provide free public transit services, highways that provide easy access to Downtown, proximity to traditional banks that offer home and small business bank loans, policing that leads to community engagement versus high rates of arrest (i.e., Stop-and-Frisk), well-resourced public schools, and food security (Brown 2016). In all cases, these kinds of amenities, entitlements, welfare programs, and resources were concentrated within the White L. Subsequent studies by other researchers found further correspondences with the White L and Black Butterfly and other metrics of "capital flow"—such as public and private investment in building construction, rehabilitation, or demolition (Marton & Harris 2015; Hoffberger 2019; Theodos, Hangen, & Meixell 2019).

These spatialized patterns of inequality are part of Sandtown-Winchester's history. In the 1950s and 1960s, the neighborhood was known as "Baltimore's Harlem." Black families lived on steady paychecks, Frederick Douglass High School offered a model of academic excellence, and historic landmarks like the Royal Theatre hosted performances by renowned African American entertainers like Diana Ross, Billie Holiday, and Cab Calloway (Bock 1993: 1A). Yet even this period of relative stability for Black people in Sandtown-Winchester was marked by social inequalities set into motion several decades before. Racially restrictive housing covenants were introduced in Baltimore in 1911 by developers and homeowners associations who wanted to block families of color from White neighborhoods (Shoenfeld & Cherkasky 2017), and proved so effective at reinforcing racial segregation that by 1920 they became a model for cities throughout the United States (Shoenfeld & Cherkasky 2017). The racialized contours of inequality were further propelled by the popularization of mortgage "redlining" policies beginning in the 1930s. Redlining discouraged banks from giving low-interest home mortgages and loans based on the racial or ethnic composition of applicants' places of residence, rather than on creditworthiness (Rothstein 2017: 97). In the early 1950s the Citizens Planning & Housing Association (CPHA), an independent organization, convinced city government that supporting "free enterprise" would transform Baltimore's "blighted areas" and "slums" and lead to far better results than funding public housing programs (Leclair-Paquet 2017). Their rehabilitation project in a 27-block "Pilot Area" in East Baltimore was promoted as such a groundbreaking success that it received an outpouring of public praise from realtors, bankers, and politicians across the country, who saw the Baltimore Plan as a blueprint for "urban renewal" (Leclair-Paquet 2017: 532–3). These celebratory narratives obscured various faults in the Baltimore Plan, which residents of the Pilot Area experienced firsthand. By the 1970s Downtown and the Inner Harbor were being transformed into focal points of economic growth. Meanwhile, rising costs of living continued to outpace growth in average income, educational accessibility, and employment opportunities for working-class people (Yiep 2015). This exacerbated already existing structural obstacles faced by Baltimore's Black working-class and middle-class families.

By the late 1980s, more than 40 percent of families in Sandtown-Winchester lived below the poverty line and almost 20 percent were chronically unemployed (DeLuca & Rosenblatt 2013). It was seen as a prime location for a new multimillion-dollar

"Neighborhood Transformation" initiative unveiled by the Enterprise Foundation, with the goal of "creating and implementing comprehensive community change" (Brown, Butler, & Hamilton 2001: 3). Enterprise Foundation founder James Rouse was pivotal in the CPHA's success during the 1950s because of his criticisms of public housing and defense of private development strategies. Rouse believed his Neighbor Transformation Initiative (NTI) would "help low-income people move up and out of poverty" by addressing "conditions that distress our cities—crime, drugs, joblessness, homelessness, unfit housing, and poverty" (Brown, Butler, & Hamilton 2001). The NTI's vision of "community accountability" presented an alternative to neighborhood rehabilitation plans that became paradigmatic after the 1950s. Rouse chose Sandtown-Winchester as the primary target of the NTI in 1990. DeLuca and Rosenblatt (2013: 9–10) note that between 1990 and 2009, rates of poverty in Sandtown-Winchester dropped from 41 percent to 33 percent, homeownership rates increased from 24 percent to 35 percent, overall rates of crime declined, and a greater proportion of residents had high school and college degrees. These changes nonetheless paralleled similar changes that occurred throughout the city during the same twenty-year period, and so cannot simply be attributed to the "revitalization" initiatives of the 1990s (2013).

Today, Sandtown-Winchester's residents continue to face many of the same challenges as in the early 1990s, some of which have worsened. While the neighborhood benefited from a booming housing market during the mid-2000s, the subprime mortgage crisis between 2007 and 2010 revealed its heightened vulnerabilities to economic instability in comparison to wealthier (and Whiter) neighborhoods. By 2010, the nationwide financial crisis left Sandtown-Winchester with over 16,800 vacant buildings (Duncan 2018). Rates of unemployment in Sandtown-Winchester have remained consistently high over the past three decades, higher than in other neighborhoods in the city (DeLuca & Rosenblatt 2013: 10). Average life expectancy in Sandtown-Winchester is about seven years shorter than the citywide average, and its residents see far higher rates of lead poisoning, pollutant-related lung disorders, heart disease, diabetes, opiate addiction, HIV infection, and other illnesses, in comparison to wealthier and White majority areas of the city only a few miles away (DeLuca & Rosenblatt 2013; Akerlof et al. 2016; Baltimore City Health Department 2017). One study in 2015 found that 7 percent of children in Sandtown-Winchester had elevated blood-lead levels (a symptom of substandard housing conditions), whereas forty-seven of Baltimore's fifty-five communities did not have a single child with elevated blood-lead levels (Prison Policy Initiative 2015: 4). The political and economic factors that bring increased health risks to Sandtown-Winchester residents were only reiterated during the Covid-19 pandemic. Within a month, epidemiologists noticed that rates of Covid-19 infection in the United States were disproportionately higher among low-income and working-class African Americans and Latinos (COVID Tracking Project 2020). The toll of this global health crisis on Sandtown-Winchester and other historically Black neighborhoods in Baltimore fit this larger pattern. According to census data, the state of Maryland's total population was approximately 30 percent Black, but Black people accounted for an estimated 49.4

percent of the state's Covid-19 infections and 53 percent of deaths by April 2020 (Maryland Department of Health 2020).

Black Butterflies

The city of Baltimore was built in an area of the Chesapeake Bay where four major watersheds converge. At 3.4 millimeter per year, the rate of sea-level rise around the Chesapeake Bay is currently double the rate worldwide and faster than nearly any other place along the east coast of North America (DeJong et al. 2015). In 2004, as part of a stormwater management strategy to curb the city's rising water table, the Department of Public Works began an urban "greening" experiment at the 930-acre area of Baltimore known as "Watershed 263" as a way to meet the requirements of the National Pollutant Discharge Elimination System (NPDES), a program that aims to regulate the discharge of pollutants into US waters ("Revitalization of Watershed 263" 2019). Watershed 263 is where an underground drainage system cuts southward through West Baltimore just a few blocks from the western boundaries of Downtown. Sandtown-Winchester sits on top of the furthest point of Watershed 263's forty-three-mile-long corridor of underground concrete pipes, which pump water polluted with garbage, oil, heavy metals, nitrogen, and phosphorous into the Patapsco River. Two thousand vacant lots in West Baltimore were replaced with "green spaces" ("Revitalization of Watershed 263" 2019). Millions of dollars went toward planting trees and installing parks to beautify the area, encourage outdoor recreation among local residents, reduce surges of stormwater into the system, and improve water quality ("Revitalization of Watershed 263" 2019).

After five years, water quality in the southern section of Watershed 263 had improved, with a 50 percent drop in nitrogen and phosphorous levels (Hager et al. 2013). However, researchers could not conclude whether it was the greening project that caused the change (Hager et al. 2013). During the same period revamped public street-sweeping operations and repaired sewer lines (both initiated in response to persistent complaints by local residents) may have played a factor (Hager et al. 2013). Surveys furthermore showed that while people living within Watershed 263 appreciated the social and mental health benefits they derived from the new green spaces, they expressed concerns about the campaign in relation to other urgent issues (Hager et al. 2013). The upkeep of these green spaces would require continued funding, and many suggested that all the money that would go toward these greening projects could have been directed toward job creation, neighborhood safety, improvements to local schools, amenities and afterschool programs for children, drug rehabilitation programs, high rates of food insecurity, and better access to healthcare facilities (Hager et al. 2013).

The ecological benefits promised by the "greening" of Watershed 263 are unquestionable, but the short- and long-term outcomes of such projects shore up the oversights and blindspots that limit the social impact of dominant, top-down approaches to environmental responsibility. Large-scale, macroeconomic, delocalized schemes of social engineering are a fundamental feature of modern nation-building and evident in contemporary "official" public discourse on "sustainability" in the United States. In its 2017 National Security Strategy report the White House characterized the pursuit of "sustainability" as a matter that hinges on "an economic strategy that rejuvenates the domestic economy, benefits the American worker, revitalizes the US manufacturing base, creates middle-class jobs, encourages innovation, preserves technological advantage, safeguards the environment, and achieves energy dominance" (*National Security Strategy* 2017: 18). The conceit of progressive change conveyed by this rendition of "sustainability" rests on the assumption that the regulatory changes adopted by the US government in collaboration with private industries will yield the most expedient and universally beneficial solutions to the imminent ecological catastrophes of the twenty-first century. The means by which this more sustainable future is achieved for "America" erase the relationships and group-differentiated inequalities among the country's multitudes, rendering them inessential features of an otherwise exemplary social order. In turn, it renders those communities with the least influence in matters of national and international policymaking nothing more than passengers in the nation's unequal forward advance into the twenty-first century.

One example of such top-down, market-oriented approaches to sustainability is presently enacted through "cap-and-trade" (CAT) programs of "emissions trading." CAT programs motivate companies to reduce carbon emissions in such a way that is not simply "cost-efficient" but also potentially highly profitable. Companies that participate in CAT programs are taxed by states if they exceed the annual emissions allocated to them by special permits. They are also free to sell any unused "credits" to other companies, for the highest bid, while other credits are reallocated to companies backed by the government. A recent study of CAT programs in the European Union Emissions Trading System (EU ETS)—the biggest of twenty-five CAT systems currently in effect worldwide—found that the EU ETS program "induced carbon emissions reductions in the order of −10% between 2005 and 2012, but had no negative impact on the economic performance of regulated firms" (Dechezleprêtre, Nachtigall, & Venmans 2018: 3). Among this study's conclusions was that "concerns that the EU ETS would come at a cost in terms of competitiveness have been vastly overplayed... In fact, we even find that the EU ETS led to an increase in regulated firms' revenues and fixed assets" (Dechezleprêtre, Nachtigall, & Venmans 2018). With data that shows CAT programs can reduce emissions and in fact *increase* corporate profits, "emissions trading" will likely continue to be an international model by which states and private firms participate in the global pursuit of "environmental justice." Climate activists describe profit-based, corporate environmentalism as the "greenwashing" of early-twenty-first-century capitalism, where the science of climate change serves as a basis for establishing new markets in which capital flows and profits are reaped (Marquis, Toffel, & Zhou 2016). One of the outcomes of greenwashing is the prevalence of environmentalist language in corporate "social responsibility" statements, commercial advertising campaigns, and government-funded "greening" initiatives (Alkon & Mares 2012). Yet, as carbon credits are scrupulously claimed by agribusinesses that plant trees at factory farms, and energy companies install wind turbines to meet the "sustainability" benchmarks of their government contracts, there are no guarantees how exactly any of these practices will benefit structurally disenfranchised communities, if at all.

So where, then, should we look? Agyeman and Warner (2002) propose a research framework for bringing the lens of just sustainabilities to place-building that emphasizes building community capacity and guiding development with "equity at the forefront" (21). The 1619 Coalition and Tubman House illustrate such a framework in action.

1618 Presbury Street

I met Eddie Conway for the first time in 2003, about fifteen miles south of Sandtown-Winchester, in the visiting room of the Maryland House of Corrections. By then, he had been locked up for thirty-three years after being wrongfully convicted for the killing of a Baltimore police officer in 1971 (Conway & Stevenson 2011). He was arrested in 1970 two years after a wave of protests took hold of Baltimore, along with 125 other cities across the United States, following the assassination of Reverend Martin Luther King, Jr. (Rodriguez 2017). These urban rebellions inspired Eddie to join the Black Panther Party and found a chapter in Baltimore (Rodriguez 2017). The Baltimore chapter of the Black Panthers went on to organize free community medical clinics, breakfast programs for children, and other community-based initiatives that brought vital resources to the poorest neighborhoods of the city (Rodriguez 2017). The excitement surrounding this work was short-lived. After only a year and a half of operation, the Baltimore chapter was among twenty-five out of thirty-seven chapters of the BPP that were destroyed under the auspices of the Counter Intelligence Program (known as COINTELPRO) of the Federal Bureau of Investigation. COINTELPRO was a covert domestic counterinsurgency initiative created in 1956 to surveil, infiltrate, discredit, and neutralize political organizations considered "subversive" by the FBI (Rodriguez 2017). By the late 1960s, the Black Panther Party and militant factions of the Civil Rights movement, the Black Power movement, the American Indian Movement, the "New Left," along with high-profile feminists, anti-war activists, and anti-imperialists, were among COINTELPRO's primary targets (Rodriguez 2017). COINTELPRO was publicly exposed to the American public two months after Eddie's imprisonment. Twelve years later it was determined that the state of Maryland had illegally tried and wrongfully convicted Eddie, but he remained in prison for another thirty-two years fighting a legal battle for his freedom, until he was finally released in 2014 (Rodriguez 2017).

Eddie's forty-four years in prison made the changes wrought by Baltimore's urban development discussed earlier in this chapter seem strikingly apparent. He commented in an interview a year and a half after his release that places like the Inner Harbor "looked completely different" from what he remembered (qtd in

Rodriguez 2017: 141–2). By the 1970s, the city had just completed the first phase of a long-term redevelopment plan to replace vacant warehouses and industrial sites along the Inner Harbor's waterfront with parks, a public promenade, commercial businesses, and cultural attractions to attract city residents and tourists (del Rio 2018). In subsequent decades the city transformed the Inner Harbor into a hub of economic growth under a banner of "social responsibility," and the success of their redevelopment strategy became a model for urban waterfront revitalization worldwide (del Rio 2018: 66). Eddie noted that the neighborhoods which were once home to many working-class and middle-class Black families had been utterly devastated by decades of disinvestment and disenfranchisement.

With the support of family, friends, and local activists, Eddie transitioned back to life "outside" and was soon involved with several community organizations. During his imprisonment, he worked with Dominque Stevenson to start the "Friend of a Friend" (FoF) program at the Maryland House of Corrections. Through the Friend of a Friend program they helped newly incarcerated people maintain connections with the outside world, pursue educations, and prepare for the challenges they will face after prison. After his release, Eddie and Dominque extended the work they began with Friend of a Friend by creating the "Coalition of Friends," a mentoring program for the young people of Gilmor Homes, the largest public housing complex in Sandtown-Winchester. This particular form of grassroots organizing is especially relevant to the neighborhood because it has become a "ground zero" for a nationwide regime of intensified domestic policing, prison-building, and mass incarceration that has made the United States home to the largest population of incarcerated people of any country since the late 1970s (Gilmore 2007). Between 1979 and 2013, total state and local corrections expenditures throughout the United States increased three times more than expenditures on public PK–12 education (Stullich, Morgan, & Schak 2016: 5). In 2010, the State of Maryland spent nearly $17 million to incarcerate people from the Sandtown-Winchester and Harlem Park neighborhoods alone (Prison Policy Initiative 2015: 4), more than any other community in Baltimore County. Meanwhile, numerous recent studies (including those by the US Department of Education) suggest that investing in educational attainment, drug treatment programs, and support services for at-risk families not only reduce criminal activity, along with rates of incarceration and recidivism, but are also less costly than expanded "crime control" measures (Stullich, Morgan, & Schak 2016: 3). High rates of arrest, incarceration, and recidivism in Sandtown-Winchester are inextricably linked to extraordinary challenges the neighborhood's residents face with regard to educational attainment, safe housing, drug addiction rehabilitation programs, and a range of health issues (Stullich, Morgan, & Schak 2016).

In Spring 2016, Eddie, Dominque, the Coalition of Friends, and other local activists and community organizations (such as United for Change and Leaders of a Beautiful Struggle) formed "the 1619 Coalition," in reference to the year in which the first Africans were first brought to the New World as slaves for the English colony of Virginia. News that the city planned to demolish an entire block of row houses in Sandtown-Winchester as part of a new "redevelopment" campaign signaled that it was time for the coalition to take action. One of the lots to be destroyed, 1618 Presbury Street, had recently become a major landmark for the people of Sandtown-Winchester and the city of Baltimore. A year before, on April 12th, 2015, twenty-five-year-old Freddie Gray Jr. was arrested for possession of an illegal knife on the sidewalk outside of 1618 Presbury, two blocks from his home at the Gilmor Homes public housing complex (Cox, Bui, & Brown 2015). He was taken to a van and sustained catastrophic injuries under the custody of six police officers on the way to the nearby station. Doctors found him completely unresponsive and determined that his spinal cord had been severed. His subsequent death, a week later, and decades of frustration with several forms of systemic injustice triggered six days of protests and public disobedience subsequently known as the "Baltimore uprisings." The city had not seen a mass protest of such a scale since the 1960s, and they were an important precedent for marches against structural racism and police violence that were organized throughout the world in 2020, when George Floyd, a forty-six-year-old resident of Minneapolis, Minnesota, was killed by an officer while being arrested for using a counterfeit twenty-dollar bill.

After the Baltimore uprisings, the coalition tried for several months to purchase 1618 Presbury from the city in order to build a multipurpose community center for local residents. Their requests were repeatedly denied, and it came as no surprise when they learned about the city's plans to level the entire block. The coalition decided they would have to resort to other means. By widely publicizing their intention to occupy the lot in defiance of the city, the coalition garnered enough local and national support to compel city officials to delay the demolition project. On April 12, 2016, members of the coalition along with more than fifty local activists and residents of Gilmore Homes gathered in front of 1618 Presbury Street. With reporters and police officers watching, they claimed that corner of the 1600 block of Presbury Street as the site of a new community safe zone and meeting place. They named it "Tubman House," in honor of Black abolitionist, Harriet Tubman, and to mark the beginning of an abolitionist struggle that the future of their neighborhood depended upon.

Toward a Radical Praxis of Just Sustainabilities

When Baltimore's public schools were shut down for one week following the 2015 uprisings, low-income parents from East and West Baltimore raised concerns over the already high rates of child food insecurity in their neighborhoods, which would only worsen without the support of publicly subsidized school lunch programs (Mayhugh 2015). As one among several interlocking forms of structural inequality that drew particularly stringent public scrutiny in the wake of the uprisings, the 1619 Coalition made "food justice" a cornerstone of their organizing efforts (Woods 2016). In the summer of 2016 several volunteers built the first set of raised garden beds for a community initiative they named "Hamer-Acoli Farm," after civil rights activist Fannie Lou Hamer and former Black Panther Party member Sundiata Acoli. Ausar-Mesh Amen took on the responsibility of managing the farms day-to-day operations from its early stages and has since become referred to fondly in the neighborhood as "Mr. Farmer" (Adedoyin 2019). Besides earning degrees in oceanography and geology, he grew up in a family of herbalists and environmentalists, and credits his father—a sharecropper, blacksmith, and self-taught engineer—as a major inspiration for his commitment to Tubman House (Adedoyin 2019). In the fall of 2016, just a few months after the first seeds were planted at the farm, Ausar-Mesh told a journalist about everything they had accomplished that summer:

> We grow food here, we do youth education around food, health and wellness. We help them with conflict resolution and we just go through the whole gambit here… That's one thing we learn here at the garden is that things grow inch by inch. Millimeter by millimeter. They grow very slowly but they do grow. Steady work does make progress. So when we give out things like book bags or we do food drives, it's not enough food to feed the whole hood here. But it's enough food that it's a model that can be imitated. We're making a change because we're not overlooking those small things and those small things are what is practical. It's what's practical and it's a small win… [W]e've been beat down. So we need small wins because it lets us know that we can triumph over this very big problem. It lets us know that we can take it brick by brick and build a house of liberation or make things different around here. (qtd by Granadino & Noor 2016)

Although the rowhouse at 1618 Presbury Street was eventually razed along with others on that block, "Tubman House" was never just a physical structure. Above all, it stands for a refusal to leave the future of Sandtown-Winchester's people up to a system that continually marginalizes them in the name of "progress," "improvement," and, of late, "sustainability." The organizers of Tubman House have not wavered from their core principle that "all residents should have access to education, food, healthcare and land," and "all residents [should] have a role and voice in the policies and practices that affect them" (Amen 2018). Those who are committed to the pursuit of "just sustainabilities" would be remiss to diminish what is being accomplished at that corner of Presbury Street. Tubman House is one among many places in the early twenty-first century that seem perpetually "marked for demolition," but are where new ways of life are being discovered, which may very well prove relevant to us all.

References

Adedoyin, O. (2019), "At Tubman House, a free garden grows in Sandtown-Winchester," *The Baltimore Sun*, July 31. Available online: https://www.baltimoresun.com/features/bs-fe-tubman-house-garden-20190731-ysdewdmxkbfvniqazelipqkdhy-story.html (Accessed May 12, 2020).

Agyeman, J. & K. Warner (2002), "Putting 'just sustainability' into place: From paradigm to practice," *Policy and Management Review*, 2(1): 8–40.

Agyeman, J.R.D., Bullard, & B. Evans (2003), *Just Sustainabilities: Development in an Unequal World*, Cambridge: MIT Press.

Akerlof, K., F. Moser, J. Dindinger, & K. Rowan (2016), *Perceptions of Community Resilience: A Maryland Community Pilot Study, 2016*, Fairfax, VA: Center for ClimateChange Communication, George Mason University.

Alkon, A. & T.M. Mares, (2012), "Food sovereignty in US food movements: Radical visions and neoliberal constraints," *Agriculture and Human Values*, 29: 1–13.

Amen, A. (2018), "Interviewed by Laura Flanders for *The Laura Flanders Show*," May 29. Available online at https://www.youtube.com/watch?v=ADzJ4iJnQqg (Accessed May 10, 2020)

Baltimore City Health Department (2017), *Baltimore City: 2017 Neighborhood Health Profile*.

Bock, J. (1993), "Hard part still ahead for 'urban lab' Sandtown: Hope on the horizon," *Baltimore Sun*, November 23: 1A.

Brown, L. (2016), "Two Baltimores: The White L vs. the Black butterfly," *Baltimore Sun*, June 28. Available online: https://www.baltimoresun.com/citypaper/bcpnews-two-baltimores-the-white-l-vs-the-black-butterfly-20160628-htmlstory.html (Accessed May 10, 2020).

Brown, P., B. Butler, & R. Hamilton (2001), *The Sandtown-Winchester Neighborhood Transformation Initiative: Lessons Learned about Community Building & Implementation*, Columbia, MD: The Enterprise Foundation.

Conway, M. "Eddie" & D. Stevenson (2011), *Marshall Law: The Life & Times of a Baltimore Black Panther*, Chico: AK Press.

COVID Tracking Project (2020), "Assessment of New CDC COVID-19 Data Reporting," May 18. Available online: https://covidtracking.com/cdc-paper (Accessed June 12, 2020)

Cox, J.W., L. Bui, & D.L. Brown (2015), "Who was Freddie Gray? How did he die? And what led to the mistrial in Baltimore?" *Washington Post*, December 16. Available online: https://www.washingtonpost.com/local/who-was-freddie-gray-and-how-did-his-death-lead-to-a-mistrial-in-baltimore/2015/12/16/b08df7ce-a433-11e5-9c4e-be37f66848bb_story.html (Accessed May 10, 2020).

Dance, S. (2017), "How a trash incinerator—Baltimore's biggest polluter— became 'green' energy," *Baltimore Sun*, December 15. Available online: https://www.baltimoresun.com/news/environment/bs-md-trash-incineration-20171107-story.html (Accessed May 12, 2020).

Dechezleprêtre, A., D. Nachtigall, & F. Venmans (2018), "The joint impact of the European Union emissions trading system on carbon emissions and economic performance," *OECD Economics Department Working Papers*, No. 1515, Paris: OECD Publishing.

DeJong, B., P.R. Bierman, W.L. Newell, T.M. Rittenour, S.A. Mahan, G. Balco, D.H. Rood (2015), "Pleistocene relative sea levels in the Chesapeake Bay region and their implications for the next century," *The Geological Society of America Today*, 25(8): 4–10.

Del Rio, V. (2018), "From downtown to the Inner Harbor: Baltimore's sustainable revitalization—Part 2: The Inner Harbor plan (1967 to 2005)," *Focus*, 14 (1): 62–76.

DeLuca, S. & P. Rosenblatt (2013), "Sandtown-Winchester Baltimore's daring experiment in urban renewal | The Abell Foundation—Working to enhance the quality of life in Baltimore and in Maryland," *The Abell Report*, 26 (8): 1–12.

Duncan, I. (2018), "In 2010, Baltimore had 16,800 vacants. Eight years and millions of dollars later, the number Is down to 16,500," *Baltimore Sun*, April 26. Available online: https://www.baltimoresun.com/maryland/baltimore-city/bs-md-ci-vacant-demolition-blocks-20180227-story.html (Accessed May 8, 2020).

Gilmore, R.W. (2007), *Golden Gulag: Prisons, Surplus, Crisis, and Opposition in Globalizing California*, Berkeley: University of California Press.

Granadino, C. & D. Noor (2016), "Back to the basics: Backpack giveaway at Tubman House," *The Real News Network*, September 5. Available online: https://therealnews.com/stories/econway0831backtoschool (Accessed May 12, 2020).

Hager, G.W., K.T. Belt, W. Stack, K. Burgess, J.M. Grove, B. Caplan, M. Hardcastle, D. Shelley, S.T.A. Pickett, & P.M. Groffman (2013), "Socioecological revitalization of an urban watershed," *Frontiers in Ecology and the Environment*, 11(1): 28–36.

Hoffberger, C. (2019), "In Baltimore, money still follows the segregation map," *Baltimore Brew*, February 5. Available online: https://www.baltimorebrew.com/2019/02/05/in-baltimore-money-still-follows-the-segregation-map/ (Accessed May 14, 2020).

Leclair-Paquet, B. (2017), "The 'Baltimore Plan': Case-study from the prehistory of urban rehabilitation," *Urban History*, 44(3): 516–43.

Marquis, C., M.L. Toffel, & Y. Zhou (2016), "Scrutiny, norms, and selective disclosure: A global study of greenwashing," *Organization Science*, 27(2): 483–504

Marton, A. & E.P. Harris (2015), "Sandtown-Winchester neighborhood ranks well below city average in most health factors," *The Baltimore Sun*, April 30. Available online: http://www.baltimoresun.com/news/data/bal-sandtownwinchester-neighborhood-health-well-below-city-average-in-most-factors-20150430-htmlstory.html (Accessed May 13, 2020).

Maryland Department of Health (2020), "COVID-19 data dashboard." Available online: https://coronavirus.maryland.gov/ (Accessed June 18, 2020).

Mayhugh, J. (2015), "Cleanups, free lunches, and meetings after the riots," *Baltimore Magazine*, April 28. Available online: https://www.baltimoremagazine.com/2015/4/28/clean-ups-free-lunches-and-meetings-after-the-riots (Accessed May 14, 2020).

National Security Strategy of the United States of America (2017), "The white house," Available online: https://www.whitehouse.gov/wp-content/uploads/2017/12/NSS-Final-12-18-2017-0905.pdf. (Accessed May 14, 2020).

Ortiz, L. (2019), "Resident frustrated after trash truck fails to pick up trash in West Baltimore," *Fox Baltimore*, September 6. Available online: https://foxbaltimore.com/news/local/resident-frustrated-after-trash-truck-fails-to-pick-up-trash-in-west-baltimore (Accessed May 14, 2020).

Prison Policy Initiative (2015), *The Right Investment?: Correction Spending in Baltimore City*. Justice Policy Institute. Available online: http://www.justicepolicy.org/research/8764?utm_source=%2ftherightinvestment&utm_medium=web&utm_campaign=redirect (Accessed May 4, 2020).

"Revitalization of Watershed 263" (2019), Baltimore Field Station, United States Department of Agriculture. Available online: https://www.nrs.fs.fed.us/baltimore/focus/governance-engagement/watershed263/ (Accessed May 12, 2020).

Rodriguez, A.B. (2017), "Former Black Panther Marshall Eddie Conway on revolutionary political education in the twenty-first century," *Journal of African American Studies*, 21(1): 138–49.

Rothstein, R. (2017), *The Color of Law: A Forgotten History of How Our Government Segregated America*, New York: Liveright.

Shepard, A., T. Mitchell, K. Lewis, A. Lendhardt, L. Jones, L. Scott, & R. Muir-Wood (2013), *The Geography of Poverty, Disasters and Climate Extremes in 2030*, London: Overseas Development Institute.

Shoenfeld, S.J. & M. Cherkasky (2017), "'A strictly white residential section': The rise and demise of racially restrictive covenants in Bloomingdale," *Washington History*, 29 (1): 24–41.

Smith, N. (2006), "There's no such thing as a natural disaster," *Items: Insights From the Social Sciences*, Social Science Research Council. Available online: https://items.ssrc.org/understanding-katrina/theres-no-such-thing-as-a-natural-disaster/ (Accessed May 14, 2020).

Stullich, S., I. Morgan, & O. Schak (2016), *State and Local Expenditures on Corrections and Education: A Brief from the U.S. Department of Education Policy & Program Studies Service*, Washington, DC: United States Department of Education Policy & Program Studies Service.

Theodos, B., E. Hangen, & B. Meixell (2019), "The Black Butterfly: Racial segregation and investment patterns in Baltimore," *Urban Institute*. Available online: https://urbn.is/baltimore (Accessed May 10, 2020).

Tubman House Baltimore (2017), *Once stood here a vibrant black community*, May 9. Available online: https://www.instagram.com/p/BT5TYHxlnkB/(Accessed May 10, 2020)

Yiep, R (2015), "Baltimore's demographic divide," *Wall Street Journal*, May 1. Available online: graphics.wsj.com/baltimore-demographics (Accessed May 10, 2020)

Woods, B. (2016), "Battle for Tubman House: Baltimore Residents Rally for Community Center," *The Guardian*, April 23. Available online: https://www.theguardian.com/us-news/2016/apr/23/freddie-gray-baltimore-harriet-tubman-house-community (Accessed May 10, 2020).

Conclusion: Global [Im]-Possibilities for Just Sustainabilities?

Phoebe Godfrey
Mary Buchanan

In a volume that places so much emphasis on paradoxes, pluralities, and Faustian bargains, we cannot hope to wrap things up with a neat bow. We end with a question mark, or perhaps an ellipsis, as evaluations of policies, plans, and practices must be a process of ongoing engagement, from multiple vantage points, some of which may contradict each other even while they exist simultaneously. Indeed, even our final section, which offers a few models for achieving aspects of just sustainabilities, is tempered by the realization that these success stories, existing as they do in "alternatives" spaces and discourses, further illustrate broader state and global failures.

At our present moment, with the Covid-19 pandemic still upon us and the ongoing exposures of systemic racism and continuing dread of worsening climate change before us, it has never been more important to face the challenges inherent in working for just sustainabilities, both now and into the future. The global scale of the pandemic response has forced a reckoning about how much change is possible when the stakes are high enough—a realization born of tragedy but critical for a better future. By acknowledging head-on the paradoxes of increasingly catastrophic social and ecological conditions, by wrestling intentionally with pluralities—*both/and*—found through deep dives into the local, and by centering and re-centering peoples in planning rather than cars, oil, buildings, or dollars, we find our hope. This hope is not the hope of the optimist expecting the wind to change but of the realist adjusting the sails, based on actual nascent struggles embodying both "the spring of hope, and the winter of despair," that could—with continual courage and commitment—eventually emerge locally and globally into just sustainabilities.

INDEX

Accra 71, 73–4, 78–82
Amen, Ausar-Mesh 229–30
Andean-Amazonian capitalism 52
Áñez, Jeanine 48, 57, 59–60
anti-rickshaw 95–9
assimilation 30–1, 36, 42
Athens, Greece 107–8, 110–17, 120
Atlanta 7–18, 21
Atlanta BeltLine 13
Atlanta Falcons 12, 15
Atlanta Olympics 9–11
Atlanta Vine City 12, 15
Australia 191–2, 196–7

Bakkan Formation 25, 32, 40
Baltimore 222–5, 227–9
Baltimore Plan 223
Baltimore uprisings 229
Bangladesh 89, 91–3
bicycling 90, 129, 132, 134–41
biodiversity 55, 77, 152–4, 207, 209–11, 213
Black Panther Party 227, 229
Bolivia 47–53, 55–8, 60
Brazilian Development Bank (BNDES) 48

California 169–83
campesinos 54, 57
cap-and-trade 226
Centre for Education and Research in Environmental Strategies Community Environment Park (CERES) 192–203
Centro de Documentación e Información Bolivia (CEDIB) 56
Centro de Estudios para el Desarrollo Laboral y Agrario (CEDLA) 56
Chiquitano 47, 49, 52
Chiquitano dry forest 47–8
citizenship 70, 73, 82, 108
climate change
   denial 99–101
   response 40, 60, 94–5, 133–43, 149, 159–62, 169, 211–12, 226
   threat 50–1, 93, 115, 153
Colombia 147–55, 157–62
Colombo 71, 73–8, 81–2
community choice 169–70, 172–80
community wellbeing 51, 148, 161, 198, 213
Confederation of Indigenous Peoples of Bolivia (CIDOB) 51
congestion charge/pricing 129–30, 132–3, 138–42
context 36–7, 194, 213–15
Conway, Marshall "Eddie" 227–8
Copenhagen Area Study 130, 134, 137, 139
Copenhagen, Denmark 129–43
Central de Pueblos Nativos Guarayos (COPNAG) 51, 54
Counter Intelligence Program (COINTELPRO) 227
COVID-19 115, 224–5
Cuiabá pipeline 47–8

Dakota 35
Dhaka 89, 91–9
displacement 10, 19, 73–7, 99, 196, 221
dissonance 26–7, 30, 35, 37–8, 52
diverse economies 195
dynamic pragmatism 58

ecological function 208–9
ecological modernization 70, 73, 78
economic development 8–13, 18–19, 27–31, 152, 161, 175–6
ecosystem services 153, 210, 213
emotional landscapes 70
energy democracy 169, 171, 173–6, 178–83
energy transition 170, 182
energy tribes 26–7, 30, 32, 34–5, 40–1

environmental movements 160–1, 197
European Union 108, 112–13, 116–19, 226
extraction
    extraction paradox 29
    gold 50, 147–9
    groundwater 73
    mining 49–60, 77, 147–9, 151–61
    oil and gas 25–42
extractivism 49, 57, 59–60, 149, 151–8, 160

Faustian bargain 55, 60
food justice 213, 229
food security 7, 154, 223, 225, 229
foreign capital 48–9, 98, 111–12, 116, 120
Fort Berthold 25–7, 32–3, 35–6, 39
fountains 111–13, 115
Fundación Milenio 56
Fundación Tierra 55–6

gardens 192–3, 221, 229–30
Gas War (Guerra del Gas) 47
gentrification 10, 13, 19, 69, 71, 76–8, 80
governance 120, 129–33, 141–2, 170–7, 180
    energy governance 169–72, 183
    self-governance 31, 40, 49, 56
    supranational governance 108–10, 113, 117–18
grasslands 207–14, 216
Gray Jr., Freddie 229
Guarayos 49–55, 57, 59–61

holistic management 209, 212–16
homelessness 11, 80, 108, 114–16, 224
human security 11, 107–9, 113–14, 116, 120

identities 69–73, 108–10, 118–20, 148, 152–9
    collective identity 196–7, 201
ILO Convention 51
Indian Country 34–5, 41
indigenous social movements 47, 49, 51–2, 58–61
informal settlements 73, 75, 79–83, 121
interdependence 74, 202

just sustainabilities
    connection to Vivir Bien 50–2, 58–61
    potential for 8–10, 18–19, 173–4, 179–83, 201–2
    praxis of 94–8, 129–33, 142–3, 154, 156–62, 196, 199, 211–12, 216, 222, 229–30
    principles of 107–9, 111–12, 114, 116, 118–20
    related scholarship 15, 70–4, 82, 172, 212–13
    theory of 1–3, 26–9, 39–40, 90–1, 148, 213, 222
    threats to 54–5
justice
    energy justice 171–2, 181–2
    environmental justice 8, 15–19, 50, 58, 60, 71, 100–1, 130, 161, 174, 191, 226
    procedural justice 8, 10, 18–19, 90–1, 95–8, 107–9, 112, 117, 120, 133
    racial justice 7–9, 15, 108, 223, 229
    in relation to just sustainabilities 1, 13, 107–10, 222
    in relation to nature 152–3
    in relation to sovereignty 26–8, 30–2, 39–40, 51
    soil justice 209–15
    spatial justice 70–4, 129–31

land ethic 27, 33
land reclamation 77
Latin America 56–8, 90, 150
life cycle assessment 15
local control 171–4, 179–83

Mandan Hidatsa Arikara (MHA) 25–9, 32–41
March for Territory and Dignity 50
market cities 76, 131
market neoliberalism 71
memory 28, 37, 70, 75, 119–20
migration 54, 78–81, 93–6, 112–14, 120, 208
mobility 10, 70–8, 82, 89–92, 94–5, 98–101
modern 81–2, 90–1, 97–9, 107–8, 115, 119–20

modernity 42, 70, 81, 94, 100
modernization 70–3, 78, 81, 90, 99–101, 111
Morales, Evo 47–9, 51–4, 56–7, 59–60
Movimiento al Socialismo (MAS) 47–9, 51, 53, 55–60

National Council of Ayllus and Markas of Qullasuyu (CONAMAQ) 51
non-governmental organization (NGO) 49, 55–9, 149–60, 192, 200, 228
Non Motorized Transport (NMT) 90–3, 95–6, 98, 100–1

pastoralist 208–14
people cities 131, 133
place attachment 39
place-based 27–9, 39, 50–61, 192–4, 208–9
policy
  EU policy 108, 113, 117–18
  federal Indian policy 31–2, 40–1
  sustainability policy 15, 18
  "transnational imperial policy" 56
  transportation policy 7, 10, 16, 89–90, 94, 98–101, 129–33, 136–43
  urban policy 7, 19, 80, 129–33, 136–43, 222
pollution 9, 94–7, 112, 139, 148, 181–2
popular consultations 147–50, 152–62
port cities 71–2, 75, 77–8, 81–3
post-development 59
postmodern mobility 99
prefigurative politics 191–2, 203
public transportation 97, 132–41, 151, 223

redlining 7, 9, 233
regeneration 81, 215
renewable energy 15, 32, 35, 40, 169–71, 173–82
resilience 41, 72, 100, 192, 194–201, 213
retail choice 173
rickshaw 89–101

Sacred 27, 34–5, 50, 152, 197, 201–2
Sandtown-Winchester 222–30
scalar disjuncture 129–31, 142–3
Scale 108–9, 153–4, 170–4, 181–3, 192, 202

self-determination 31, 40, 50, 55, 108, 113–20
sharing 74, 93, 95, 131, 154, 157
shorelines 70, 75
1619 Coalition 222, 227–9
Social Democrats 134, 138–40
social welfare 55, 116, 129, 223
Socialist People's Party 135, 138–40
soil carbon 211–12
soil organic matter 207
sovereignty 25–41
Stevenson, Dominque 228
suburbs 8–9, 14, 112, 134–6, 139–40, 193
sustainability planning 8, 15
systemic racism 15, 18, 50–1, 229

tactical urbanism 192–4, 202
Territorio Indígena y Parque Nacional Isiboro Secure (TIPNIS) 48–52, 56–60
Tierra Comunitaria de Orígen (TCO) 48–60
transition 52–3, 100, 107–16, 169–72, 182, 191–9
transnational activism 149–50
trauma 18, 118–20
tribal 26–41
Trump administration 34, 99–100, 191
Tubman House 221–30

United Nations Declaration on the Rights of Indigenous Peoples (UNDRIP) 60
United States Agency for International Development (USAID) 56
urban planning 10, 14–19, 70, 76, 107, 132
urban renewal 7, 10–11, 222–4
urban revanchism 80–2
urban sustainability 18, 133
urban water systems 107–15, 120

Vivir Bien 51–2, 59–61
Vivir Mejor 51

waste disposal 222
waterfront revitalization 69–76
World Commission on Environment and Development 1
Wurundjeri People 195–6, 201

www.ingramcontent.com/pod-product-compliance
Lightning Source LLC
Chambersburg PA
CBHW062138300426
44115CB00012BA/1974